Microsoft®

Access 2002

Volume II

Microsoft®

Access 2002

Volume II

Robert T. Grauer   Maryann Barber

University of Miami   *University of Miami*

PRENTICE HALL   *Upper Saddle River, New Jersey 07458*

Senior Acquisitions Editor: David Alexander
VP/Publisher: Natalie Anderson
Managing Editor: Melissa Whitaker
Assistant Editor: Kerri Limpert
Editorial Assistant: Maryann Broadnax
Technical Editor: Cecil Yarbrough
Media Project Manager: Cathleen Profitko
Marketing Assistant: Jason Smith
Production Manager: Gail Steier de Acevedo
Project Manager: Lynne Breitfeller
Production Editor: Greg Hubit
Associate Director, Manufacturing: Vincent Scelta
Manufacturing Buyer: Lynne Breitfeller
Design Manager: Pat Smythe
Interior Design: Jill Yutkowitz
Cover Design: Blair Brown
Cover Illustration: Marjorie Dressler
Composition: GTS
Printer/Binder: Banta Menasha

10 9 8 7 6 5 4 3 2 1
ISBN 0-13-067485-0

To Marion —
my wife, my lover, and my best friend

Robert Grauer

To Frank —
for giving me the encouragement, love, and the space

Maryann Barber

CONTENTS

6

MANY-TO-MANY RELATIONSHIPS: A MORE COMPLEX SYSTEM

7

BUILDING APPLICATIONS: MACROS AND A MULTILEVEL SWITCHBOARD 313

8

CREATING MORE POWERFUL APPLICATIONS: INTRODUCTION TO VBA 367

A VBA Primer: Extending Microsoft® Office XP

PREFACE

ABOUT THIS SERIES........

Continuing a tradition of excellence, Prentice Hall is proud to announce the latest update in Microsoft Office texts: the new Exploring Microsoft Office XP series by Robert T. Grauer and Maryann Barber.

The hands-on approach and conceptual framework of this comprehensive series helps students master all aspects of the Microsoft Office XP software, while providing the background necessary to transfer and use these skills in their personal and professional lives.

WHAT'S NEW IN THE EXPLORING OFFICE SERIES FOR XP

The entire Exploring Office series has been revised to include the new features found in the Office XP Suite, which contains Word 2002, Excel 2002, Access 2002, PowerPoint 2002, Publisher 2000, FrontPage 2002, and Outlook 2002.

In addition, this revision includes fully revised end-of-chapter material that provides an extensive review of concepts and techniques discussed in the chapter. Many of these exercises feature the World Wide Web and application integration.

Building on the success of the Web site provided for previous editions of this series, Exploring Office XP will introduce the MyPHLIP Companion Web site, a site customized for each instructor that includes on-line, interactive study guides, data file downloads, current news feeds, additional case studies and exercises, and other helpful information. Start out at www.prenhall.com/grauer to explore these resources!

Organization of the Exploring Office Series for XP

The new Exploring Microsoft Office XP series includes four combined Office XP texts from which to choose:

- **Volume I** is MOUS certified in each of the major applications in the Office suite (Word, Excel, Access, and PowerPoint). Three additional modules (Essential Computer Concepts, Essentials of Windows, and Essentials of the Internet) are also included.

- **Volume II** picks up where Volume I left off, covering the advanced topics for the individual applications. A VBA primer has been added.

- The **Brief Microsoft Office XP** edition provides less coverage of the individual applications than Volume I (a total of 8 chapters as opposed to 14). The supplementary modules (Windows, Internet, and Concepts) are not included.

- A new volume, **Getting Started with Office XP**, contains the first chapter from each application (Word, Excel, Access, and PowerPoint), plus three additional modules: Essentials of Windows, Essentials of the Internet, and Essential Computer Concepts.

Individual texts for Word 2002, Excel 2002, Access 2002, and PowerPoint 2002 provide complete coverage of the application and are MOUS certified. For shorter courses, we have created brief versions of the Exploring texts that give students a four-chapter introduction to each application. Each of these volumes is MOUS certified at the Core level.

To complete the full coverage of this series, custom modules on Microsoft Outlook 2002, Microsoft FrontPage 2002, Microsoft Publisher 2002, and a generic introduction to Microsoft Windows are also available.

APPROVED COURSEWARE

This series has been approved by Microsoft to be used in preparation for Microsoft Office User Specialist exams.

The Microsoft Office User Specialist (MOUS) program is globally recognized as the standard for demonstrating desktop skills with the Microsoft Office suite of business productivity applications (Microsoft Word, Microsoft Excel, Microsoft PowerPoint, Microsoft Access, and Microsoft Outlook). With a MOUS certification, thousands of people have demonstrated increased productivity and have proved their ability to utilize the advanced functionality of these Microsoft applications.

By encouraging individuals to develop advanced skills with Microsoft's leading business desktop software, the MOUS program helps fill the demand for qualified, knowledgeable people in the modern workplace. At the same time, MOUS helps satisfy an organization's need for a qualitative assessment of employee skills.

Customize the Exploring Office Series with Prentice Hall's Right PHit Binding Program

The Exploring Office XP series is part of the Right PHit Custom Binding Program, enabling instructors to create their own texts by selecting modules from Office XP Volume I, Volume II, Outlook, FrontPage, and Publisher to suit the needs of a specific course. An instructor could, for example, create a custom text consisting of the core modules in Word and Excel, coupled with the brief modules for Access and PowerPoint, and a brief introduction to computer concepts.

Instructors can also take advantage of Prentice Hall's Value Pack program to shrinkwrap multiple texts together at substantial savings to the student. A value pack is ideal in courses that require complete coverage of multiple applications.

The **Instructor's CD** that accompanies the Exploring Office series contains:

- Student data disks
- Solutions to all exercises and problems
- PowerPoint lectures
- Instructor's manuals in Word format enable the instructor to annotate portions of the instructor manual for distribution to the class
- A Windows-based test manager and the associated test bank in Word format

Prentice Hall's New MyPHLIP Companion Web site at www.prenhall.com/grauer offers current events, exercises, and downloadable supplements. This site also includes an on-line study guide containing true/false, multiple-choice, and essay questions.

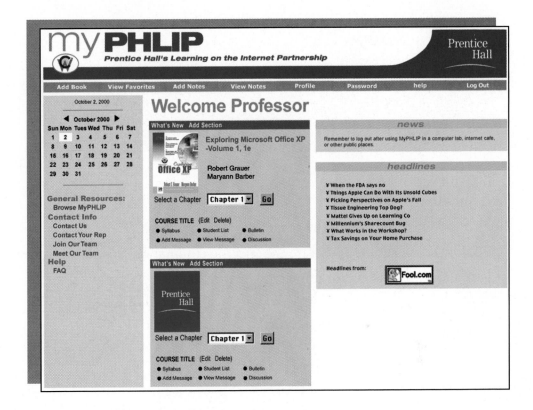

WebCT www.prenhall.com/webct

GOLD LEVEL CUSTOMER SUPPORT available exclusively to adopters of Prentice Hall courses is provided free-of-charge upon adoption and provides you with priority assistance, training discounts, and dedicated technical support.

Blackboard www.prenhall.com/blackboard

Prentice Hall's abundant on-line content, combined with Blackboard's popular tools and interface, result in robust Web-based courses that are easy to implement, manage, and use—taking your courses to new heights in student interaction and learning.

CourseCompass www.coursecompass.com

CourseCompass is a dynamic, interactive on-line course management tool powered by Blackboard. This exciting product allows you to teach with marketing-leading Pearson Education content in an easy-to-use customizable format.

Exploring Microsoft Office XP assumes no prior knowledge of the operating system. A 64-page section introduces the reader to the Essentials of Windows and provides an overview of the operating system. Students are shown the necessary file-management operations to use Microsoft Office successfully.

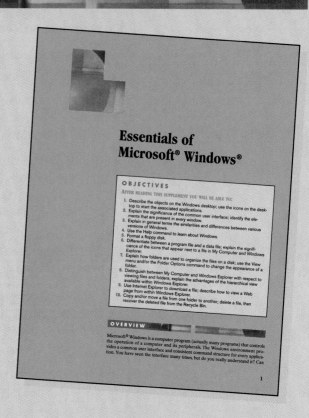

In-depth tutorials throughout all the Office XP applications enhance the conceptual introduction to each task and guide the student at the computer. Every step in every exercise has a full-color screen shot to illustrate the specific commands. Boxed tips provide alternative techniques and shortcuts and/or anticipate errors that students may make.

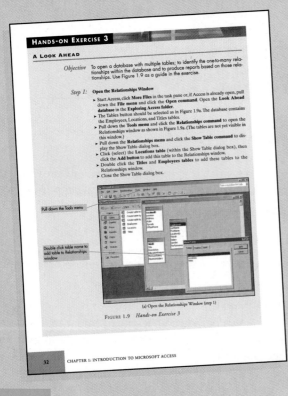

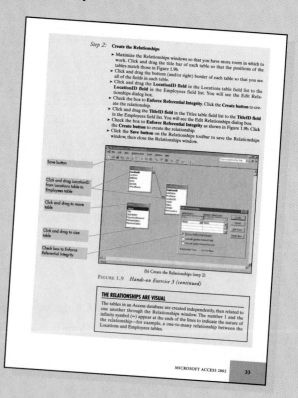

The authors have created an entirely new set of end-of-chapter exercises for every chapter in all of the applications. These new exercises have been written to provide the utmost in flexibility, variety, and difficulty.

Web-based Practice Exercises and On Your Own Exercises are marked by an icon in the margin and allow further exploration and practice via the World Wide Web.

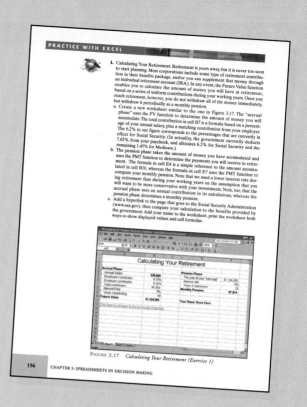

FIGURE 3.17   *Calculating Your Retirement (Exercise 1)*

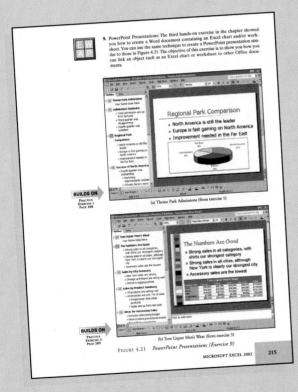

FIGURE 4.21   *PowerPoint Presentations (Exercise 9)*

Integration Exercises are marked by an icon in the margin. These exercises take advantage of the Microsoft Office Suite's power to use multiple applications in one document, spreadsheet, or presentation.

BUILDS ON

Builds On Exercises require students to use selected application files as the starting point in later exercises, thereby introducing new information to students only as needed.

The end-of-chapter material includes multiple-choice questions for self-evaluation plus additional "on your own" exercises to encourage the reader to further explore the application.

We want to thank the many individuals who have helped to bring this project to fruition. David Alexander, senior editor at Prentice Hall, has provided new leadership in extending the series to Office XP. Cathi Profitko did an absolutely incredible job on our Web site. Melissa Whitaker coordinated the myriad details of production and the certification process. Greg Christofferson was instrumental in the acquisition of supporting software. Lynne Breitfeller was the project manager and manufacturing buyer. Greg Hubit has been masterful as the external production editor for every book in the series. Cecil Yarbrough did an outstanding job in checking the manuscript for technical accuracy. Chuck Cox did his usual fine work as copyeditor. Kerri Limpert was the supplements editor. Cindy Stevens, Tom McKenzie, and Michael Olmstead wrote the instructor manuals. Patricia Smythe developed the innovative and attractive design. We also want to acknowledge our reviewers who, through their comments and constructive criticism, greatly improved the series.

Lynne Band, Middlesex Community College
Don Belle, Central Piedmont Community College
Stuart P. Brian, Holy Family College
Carl M. Briggs, Indiana University School of Business
Kimberly Chambers, Scottsdale Community College
Alok Charturvedi, Purdue University
Jerry Chin, Southwest Missouri State University
Dean Combellick, Scottsdale Community College
Cody Copeland, Johnson County Community College
Larry S. Corman, Fort Lewis College
Janis Cox, Tri-County Technical College
Martin Crossland, Southwest Missouri State University
Paul E. Daurelle, Western Piedmont Community College
Carolyn DiLeo, Westchester Community College
Judy Dolan, Palomar College
David Douglas, University of Arkansas
Carlotta Eaton, Radford University
Judith M. Fitspatrick, Gulf Coast Community College
James Franck, College of St. Scholastica
Raymond Frost, Central Connecticut State University
Midge Gerber, Southwestern Oklahoma State University
James Gips, Boston College
Vernon Griffin, Austin Community College
Ranette Halverson, Midwestern State University
Michael Hassett, Fort Hays State University
Mike Hearn, Community College of Philadelphia
Wanda D. Heller, Seminole Community College
Bonnie Homan, San Francisco State University
Ernie Ivey, Polk Community College
Mike Kelly, Community College of Rhode Island
Jane King, Everett Community College

Rose M. Laird, Northern Virginia Community College
John Lesson, University of Central Florida
David B. Meinert, Southwest Missouri State University
Alan Moltz, Naugatuck Valley Technical Community College
Kim Montney, Kellogg Community College
Bill Morse, DeVry Institute of Technology
Kevin Pauli, University of Nebraska
Mary McKenry Percival, University of Miami
Delores Pusins, Hillsborough Community College
Gale E. Rand, College Misericordia
Judith Rice, Santa Fe Community College
David Rinehard, Lansing Community College
Marilyn Salas, Scottsdale Community College
John Shepherd, Duquesne University
Barbara Sherman, Buffalo State College
Robert Spear, Prince George's Community College
Michael Stewardson, San Jacinto College—North
Helen Stoloff, Hudson Valley Community College
Margaret Thomas, Ohio University
Mike Thomas, Indiana University School of Business
Suzanne Tomlinson, Iowa State University
Karen Tracey, Central Connecticut State University
Antonio Vargas, El Paso Community College
Sally Visci, Lorain County Community College
David Weiner, University of San Francisco
Connie Wells, Georgia State University
Wallace John Whistance-Smith, Ryerson Polytechnic University
Jack Zeller, Kirkwood Community College

A final word of thanks to the unnamed students at the University of Miami, who make it all worthwhile. Most of all, thanks to you, our readers, for choosing this book. Please feel free to contact us with any comments and suggestions.

Robert T. Grauer
rgrauer@miami.edu
www.bus.miami.edu/~rgrauer
www.prenhall.com/grauer

Maryann Barber
mbarber@miami.edu
www.bus.miami.edu/~mbarber

CHAPTER 5

One-to-Many Relationships: Subforms and Multiple Table Queries

OBJECTIVES

AFTER READING THIS CHAPTER YOU WILL BE ABLE TO:

1. Explain how a one-to-many relationship is essential in the design of a database; differentiate between a primary key and a foreign key.
2. Use the Relationships window to implement a one-to-many relationship within an Access database.
3. Define referential integrity; explain how the enforcement of referential integrity maintains consistency within a database.
4. Distinguish between a main form and a subform; explain how a subform is used in conjunction with a one-to-many relationship.
5. Create a query based on multiple tables, then create a report based on that query.
6. Create a main form containing two subforms linked to one another

OVERVIEW

The real power of Access stems from its use as a relational database that contains multiple tables, and the objects associated with those tables. We introduced this concept at the end of Chapter 1, when we looked briefly at a database that had three tables. We revisited the concept in the previous chapter when we looked at a second relational database.

This chapter presents an entirely new case study that focuses on a relational database. The case is that of a consumer loan system within a bank. The database contains two tables, one for customers and one for loans. There is a one-to-many relationship between the tables, in that one customer can have many loans, but a loan is tied to only one customer.

The case solution includes a discussion of database concepts. It reviews the definition of a primary key and explains how the primary key of one table exists as a foreign key in a related table. It also reviews the concept of referential integrity, which ensures that the tables within the database are consistent with one another. And most important, it shows how to implement these concepts in an Access database.

The chapter builds on what you already know by expanding the earlier material on forms, queries, and reports. It describes how to create a main form and a corresponding subform that contains data from a related table. It develops a query that contains data from multiple tables, then creates a report based on that query.

Suffice it to say that this is a critically important chapter because it is built around a relational database, as opposed to a single table. Thus, when you complete the chapter, you will have a much better appreciation of what can be accomplished within Access. As always, the hands-on exercises are essential to your understanding of the material.

CASE STUDY: CONSUMER LOANS

Let us assume that you are in the Information Systems department of a commercial bank and are assigned the task of implementing a system for consumer loans. The bank needs complete data about every loan (the amount, interest rate, term, and so on). It also needs data about the customers holding those loans (name, address, telephone, etc.).

The problem is how to structure the data so that the bank will be able to obtain all of the information it needs from its database. The system must be able to supply the name and address of the person associated with a loan. The system must also be able to retrieve all of the loans for a specific individual.

The solution calls for a database with two tables, one for loans and one for customers. To appreciate the elegance of this approach, consider first a single table containing a combination of loan and customer data as shown in Figure 5.1. At first glance this solution appears to be satisfactory. You can, for example, search for a specific loan (e.g., L022) and determine that Lori Sangastiano is the customer associated with that loan. You can also search for a particular customer (e.g., Michelle Zacco) and find all of her loans (L028, L030, and L060).

There is a problem, however, in that the table duplicates customer data throughout the database. Thus, when one customer has multiple loans, the customer's name, address, and other data are stored multiple times. Maintaining the data in this form is a time-consuming and error-prone procedure, because any change to the customer's data has to be made in many places.

A second problem arises when you enter data for a new customer that occurs before a loan has been approved. The bank receives the customer's application data prior to granting a loan, and it wants to retain the customer data even if a loan is turned down. Adding a customer to the database in Figure 5.1 is awkward, however, because it requires the creation of a "dummy" loan record to hold the customer data.

The deletion (payoff) of a loan creates a third type of problem. What happens, for example, when Ted Myerson pays off loan L020? The loan record would be deleted, but so too would Ted's data as he has no other outstanding loans. The bank might want to contact Mr. Myerson about another loan in the future, but it would lose his data with the deletion of the existing loan.

The database in Figure 5.2 represents a much better design because it eliminates all three problems. It uses two different tables, a Loans table and a Customers table. Each record in the Loans table has data about a specific loan (LoanID, Date, Amount, Interest Rate, Term, Type, and CustomerID). Each record in the Customers table has data about a specific customer (CustomerID, First Name, Last Name, Address, City, State, Zip Code, and Phone Number). Each record in the

LoanID	Loan Data (Date, Amount, Interest Rate...)	Customer Data (First Name, Last Name, Address...)
L001	Loan Data for Loan L001	Customer Data for Wendy Solomon
L004	Loan Data for Loan L004	Customer Data for Wendy Solomon
L010	Loan Data for Loan L010	Customer Data for Alex Rey
L014	Loan Data for Loan L014	Customer Data for Wendy Solomon
L020	Loan Data for Loan L020	Customer Data for Tedd Myerson
L022	Loan Data for Loan L022	Customer Data for Lori Sangastiano
L026	Loan Data for Loan L026	Customer Data for Matt Hirsch
L028	Loan Data for Loan L028	Customer Data for Michelle Zacco
L030	Loan Data for Loan L030	Customer Data for Michelle Zacco
L031	Loan Data for Loan L031	Customer Data for Eileen Faulkner
L032	Loan Data for Loan L032	Customer Data for Scott Wit
L033	Loan Data for Loan L033	Customer Data for Alex Rey
L039	Loan Data for Loan L039	Customer Data for David Powell
L040	Loan Data for Loan L040	Customer Data for Matt Hirsch
L047	Loan Data for Loan L047	Customer Data for Benjamin Grauer
L049	Loan Data for Loan L049	Customer Data for Eileen Faulkner
L052	Loan Data for Loan L052	Customer Data for Eileen Faulkner
L053	Loan Data for Loan L053	Customer Data for Benjamin Grauer
L054	Loan Data for Loan L054	Customer Data for Scott Wit
L057	Loan Data for Loan L057	Customer Data for Benjamin Grauer
L060	Loan Data for Loan L060	Customer Data for Michelle Zacco
L062	Loan Data for Loan L062	Customer Data for Matt Hirsch
L100	Loan Data for Loan L100	Customer Data for Benjamin Grauer
L109	Loan Data for Loan L109	Customer Data for Wendy Solomon
L120	Loan Data for Loan L120	Customer Data for Lori Sangastiano

FIGURE 5.1   *Single Table Solution*

Loans table is associated with a matching record in the Customers table through the CustomerID field common to both tables. This solution may seem complicated, but it is really quite simple and elegant.

Consider, for example, how easy it is to change a customer's address. If Michelle Zacco were to move, you would go into the Customers table, find her record (Customer C08), and make the necessary change. You would not have to change any of the records in the Loans table, because they do not contain customer data, but only a CustomerID that indicates who the customer is. In other words, you would change Michelle's address in only one place, and the change would be automatically reflected for every associated loan.

The addition of a new customer is done directly in the Customers table. This is much easier than the approach of Figure 5.1, which required an existing loan in order to add a new customer. And finally, the deletion of an existing loan is also easier than with the single table organization. A loan can be deleted from the Loans table without losing the corresponding customer data.

The database in Figure 5.2 is composed of two tables in which there is a **one-to-many relationship** between customers and loans. One customer (Michelle Zacco) can have many loans (Loan numbers L028, L030, and L060), but a specific loan (L028) is associated with only one customer (Michelle Zacco). The tables are related to one another by a common field (CustomerID) that is present in both the Customers and the Loans table.

Access enables you to create the one-to-many relationship between the tables, then uses that relationship to answer questions about the database. It can retrieve information about a specific loan, such as the name and address of the customer holding that loan. It can also find all loans for a particular customer.

LoanID	Date	Amount	Interest Rate	Term	Type	CustomerID
L001	1/15/01	$475,000	6.90%	15	M	C04
L004	1/23/01	$35,000	7.20%	5	C	C04
L010	1/25/01	$10,000	5.50%	3	C	C05
L014	1/31/01	$12,000	9.50%	10	O	C04
L020	2/8/01	$525,000	6.50%	30	M	C06
L022	2/12/01	$10,500	7.50%	5	O	C07
L026	2/15/01	$35,000	6.50%	5	O	C10
L028	2/20/01	$250,000	8.80%	30	M	C08
L030	2/21/01	$5,000	10.00%	3	O	C08
L031	2/28/01	$200,000	7.00%	15	M	C01
L032	3/1/01	$25,000	10.00%	3	C	C02
L033	3/1/01	$20,000	9.50%	5	O	C05
L040	3/10/01	$129,000	8.50%	15	M	C10
L047	3/11/01	$200,000	7.25%	15	M	C03
L049	3/21/01	$150,000	7.50%	15	M	C01
L052	3/22/01	$100,000	7.00%	30	M	C01
L053	3/31/01	$15,000	6.50%	3	O	C03
L054	4/1/01	$10,000	8.00%	5	C	C02
L057	4/15/01	$25,000	8.50%	4	C	C03
L060	4/18/01	$41,000	9.90%	4	C	C08
L062	4/22/01	$350,000	7.50%	15	M	C10
L100	5/1/01	$150,000	6.00%	15	M	C03
L109	5/3/01	$350,000	8.20%	30	M	C04
L120	5/8/01	$275,000	9.20%	15	M	C07
L121	7/15/01	$20,000	8.00%	3	C	C11

(a) Loans Table

CustomerID	First Name	Last Name	Address	City	State	Zip Code	Phone Number
C01	Eileen	Faulkner	7245 NW 8 Street	Minneapolis	MN	55346	(612) 894-1511
C02	Scott	Wit	5660 NW 175 Terrace	Baltimore	MD	21224	(410) 753-0345
C03	Benjamin	Grauer	10000 Sample Road	Coral Springs	FL	33073	(305) 444-5555
C04	Wendy	Solomon	7500 Reno Road	Houston	TX	77090	(713) 427-3104
C05	Alex	Rey	3456 Main Highway	Denver	CO	80228	(303) 555-6666
C06	Ted	Myerson	6545 Stone Street	Chapel Hill	NC	27515	(919) 942-7654
C07	Lori	Sangastiano	4533 Aero Drive	Santa Rosa	CA	95403	(707) 542-3411
C08	Michelle	Zacco	488 Gold Street	Gainesville	FL	32601	(904) 374-5660
C10	Matt	Hirsch	777 NW 67 Avenue	Fort Lee	NJ	07624	(201) 664-3211

(b) Customers Table

FIGURE 5.2   *Multiple Table Solution*

Use the tables in Figure 5.2 to answer the queries below and gain an appreciation for the power of a relational database.

Query: What are the name, address, and phone number of the customer associated with loan number L010?

Answer: Alex Rey, at 3456 Main Highway is the customer associated with loan L010. His phone number is (303) 555-6666.

To determine the answer, Access searches the Loans table for loan L010 to obtain the CustomerID (C05 in this example). It then searches the Customers table for the customer with the matching CustomerID and retrieves the name, address, and phone number.

Consider a second example, that appears on the next page:

Query: Which loans are associated with Wendy Solomon?

Answer: Wendy Solomon has four loans: loan L001 for $475,000, loan L004 for $35,000, loan L014 for $12,000, and loan L109 for $350,000.

This time Access begins in the Customers table and searches for Wendy Solomon to determine the CustomerID (C04). It then searches the Loans table for all records with a matching CustomerID.

Referential Integrity

Microsoft Access automatically implements certain types of data validation during data entry to ensure that the database will produce accurate information. Access always lets you enter a record in the "one" table, the Customers table in this example, provided that all existing rules for data validation are met. You cannot, however, enter a record in the "many" table (the Loans table in this example) if that record contains an invalid (nonexistent) value for the CustomerID. This type of data validation is known as *referential integrity* and it guarantees that the tables within a database are consistent with one another. Consider:

Query: Can you add a loan to the Loans table (as it presently exists) for Customer C01? Can you add a loan for Customer C20?

Answer: Yes, you can add a loan for Customer C01 provided that the other rules for data validation are met. You cannot add a loan for Customer C20, because that customer is not in the Customers table.

Implementation in Access

Figure 5.3a displays the *Relationships window* that is used to create the one-to-many relationship between customers and loans. Each table stores data about a specific subject, such as customers or loans. Each table has a *primary key*, which is a field (or combination of fields) that uniquely identifies each record. CustomerID is the primary key in the Customers table. LoanID is the primary key in the Loans table.

The one-to-many relationship between the tables is based on the fact that the same field (CustomerID) appears in both tables. The CustomerID is the primary key in the Customers table, where its values are unique, but it is a *foreign key* in the Loans table, where its values are not unique. (A foreign key is simply the primary key of another table.) In other words, multiple records in the Loans table can have the same CustomerID to implement the one-to-many relationship between customers and loans.

To create a one-to-many relationship, you open the Relationships window in Figure 5.3a and add the necessary tables. You then drag the field on which the relationship is built from the field list of the "one" table (Customers) to the matching field in the related table (Loans). Once the relationship has been established, you will see a *relationship line* connecting the tables that indicates the one and many side of the relationship. The line extends from the primary key in the "one" table to the foreign key in the "many" table.

Figure 5.3b displays the Customers table after the one-to-many relationship has been created. A plus (or minus) sign appears to the left of the CustomerID to indicate that there are corresponding records in a related table. You can click the plus sign next to any customer record to display the related records (called a *subdatasheet*) for that customer. Conversely, you can click the minus sign (after the related records have been displayed) and the records are hidden. Look carefully at the related records for customer C04 (Wendy Solomon) and you will see the answer to one of our earlier queries.

CustomerID is the primary
key in the Customers table

Relationships line

CustomerID is the foreign
key in the Loans table

Referential integrity will be
enforced

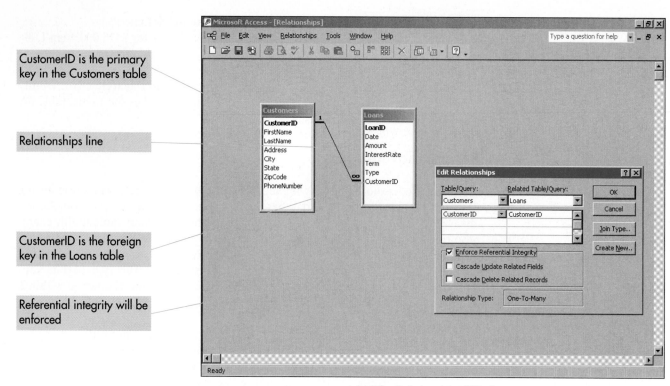

(a) The Relationships Window

+ indicates related records
exist in a related table

Related records are shown
for Wendy Solomon

− indicates subdatasheet is
displayed

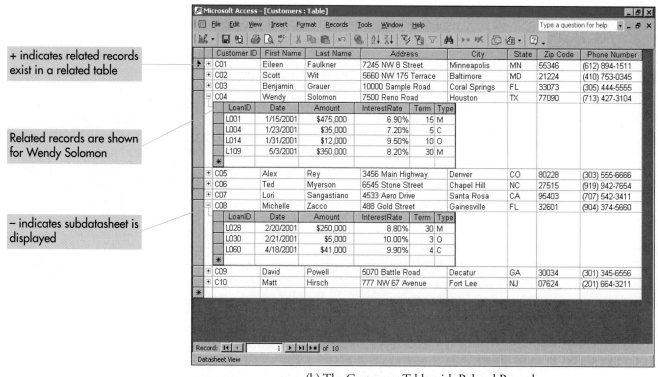

(b) The Customers Table with Related Records

FIGURE 5.3   *One-to-Many Relationship*

ONE-TO-MANY RELATIONSHIPS

Objective To create a one-to-many relationship between existing tables in a database; to demonstrate referential integrity between the tables in a one-to-many relationship. Use Figure 5.4 as a guide in the exercise.

Step 1: **The Relationships Window**

> ➤ Start Access. Open the **National Bank database** in the **Exploring Access folder**. The database contains three tables: for Customers, Loans, and Payments. (The Payments table will be used later in the chapter.)
> ➤ Pull down the **Tools menu** and click **Relationships** to open the Relationships window as shown in Figure 5.4a. (The Customers and Loans tables are not yet visible.) If you do not see the Show Table dialog box, pull down the **Relationships menu** and click the **Show Table command**.
> ➤ The **Tables tab** is selected within the Show Table dialog box. Click (select) the **Customers table**, then click the **Add Command button** to add the table to the Relationships window.
> ➤ Click the **Loans table**, then click the **Add Command button** (or simply double click the **Loans table**) to add this table to the Relationships window.
> ➤ Do *not* add the Payments table at this time. Click the **Close button** to close the Show Table dialog box.

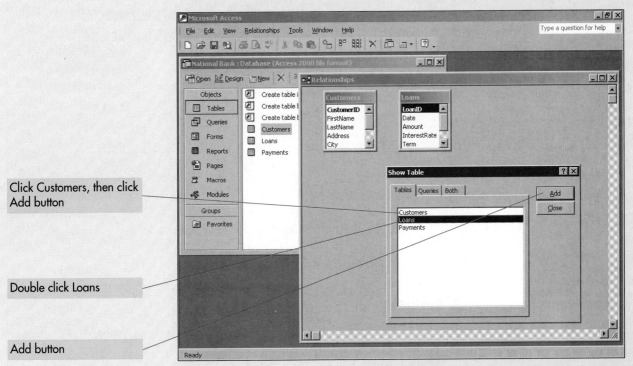

Click Customers, then click Add button

Double click Loans

Add button

(a) The Relationships Window (step 1)

FIGURE 5.4 *Hands-on Exercise 1*

Step 2: **Create the Relationship**

➤ Maximize the Relationships window. Point to the bottom border of the **Customers field list** (the mouse pointer changes to a double arrow), then click and drag the border until all of the fields are visible.

➤ Click and drag the bottom border of the **Loans field list** until all of the fields are visible. Click and drag the title bar of the **Loans field list** so that it is approximately one inch away from the Customers field list.

➤ Click and drag the **CustomerID field** in the Customers field list to the **CustomerID field** in the Loans field list. You will see the Relationships dialog box in Figure 5.4b.

➤ Check the **Enforce Referential Integrity** check box. (If necessary, clear the check boxes to Cascade Update Related Fields and Delete Related Records.)

➤ Click the **Create Command button** to establish the relationship and close the Relationships dialog box. You should see a line indicating a one-to-many relationship between the Customers and Loans tables.

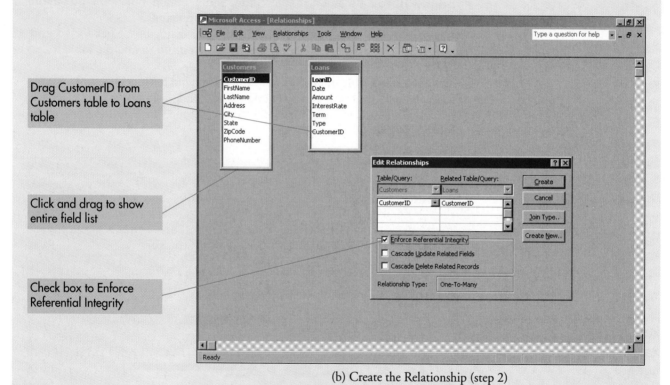

Drag CustomerID from Customers table to Loans table

Click and drag to show entire field list

Check box to Enforce Referential Integrity

(b) Create the Relationship (step 2)

FIGURE 5.4   *Hands-on Exercise 1 (continued)*

THE TABLE ANALYZER WIZARD

Duplicating data within a database results in wasted space, or worse, in erroneous information. Access, however, provides the Table Analyzer Wizard, which will examine the tables within a database to prevent such errors from occurring. The Wizard offers a brief explanation of the consequences of poor design, then it will examine your tables and make the appropriate suggestions. See exercise 10 at the end of the chapter.

Step 3:   **Delete a Relationship**

> ➤ Access displays a relationship line between related tables, containing the number 1 and the infinity symbol (∞), to indicate a one-to-many relationship in which referential integrity is enforced.
> ➤ Point to the line indicating the relationship between the tables, then click the **right mouse button** to select the relationship and display a shortcut menu.
> ➤ Click the **Delete command**. You will see the dialog box in Figure 5.4c, asking whether you are sure you want to delete the relationship.
> ➤ Click **No** since you do *not* want to delete the relationship at this time. (Subsequently, however, it may be necessary for you to delete or edit a relationship.)
> ➤ Close the Relationships window. Click **Yes** if asked whether to save the layout changes.

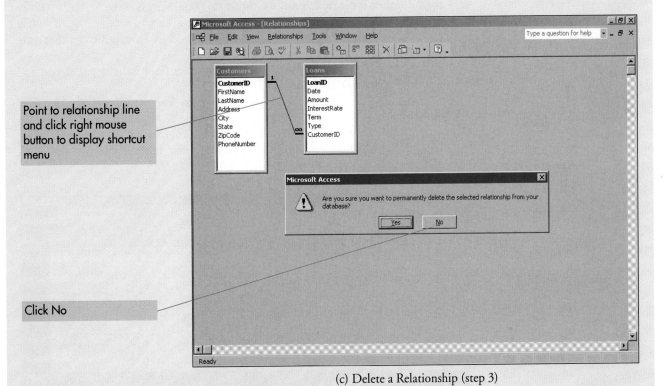

Point to relationship line and click right mouse button to display shortcut menu

Click No

(c) Delete a Relationship (step 3)

FIGURE 5.4   *Hands-on Exercise 1 (continued)*

RELATED FIELDS AND DATA TYPES

The fields on both sides of a relationship must have the same data type; for example, both fields should be text fields or both fields should be number fields. In addition, Number fields must also have the same field size. The exception is an AutoNumber (counter) field in the primary table, which is matched against a Long Integer field in the related table. AutoNumber fields are discussed in Chapter 6.

Step 4: **Add a Customer Record**

➤ The Database window is again visible with the Tables button selected. Open the **Customers table**. If necessary, click the **Maximize button** to give yourself additional room when adding a record. Widen the fields as necessary to see the data.

➤ Click the **New Record button** on the toolbar. The record selector moves to the last record (record 11).

➤ Enter **C11** as the CustomerID as shown in Figure 5.4d. The record selector changes to a pencil as soon as you enter the first character.

➤ Enter data for yourself as the new customer. Data validation has been built into the Customers table, so you must enter the data correctly, or it will not be accepted.

  • The message, *Customer ID must begin with the letter C followed by a two-digit number,* indicates that the CustomerID field is invalid.

  • The message, *The field 'Customers.LastName' can't contain a Null value because the Required property for this field is set to True,* indicates that you must enter a last name.

  • A beep in either the ZipCode or PhoneNumber field indicates that you are entering a nonnumeric character.

  • If you encounter a data validation error, press **Esc** (or Click **OK**), then re-enter the data.

➤ Press **enter** when you have completed your record. Remember your CustomerID (C11) because you will need to enter it in the corresponding loan records.

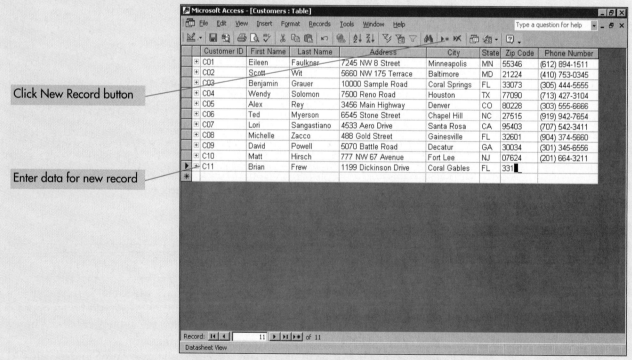

Click New Record button

Enter data for new record

(d) Add a Customer Record (step 4)

FIGURE 5.4 *Hands-on Exercise 1 (continued)*

Step 5: **Add a Loan Record**

➤ Click the **plus sign** next to the record selector for customer C03 (Benjamin Grauer). The plus sign changes to a minus sign and you see the related records as shown in Figure 5.4e. Click the **minus sign** and it changes back to a plus sign. The related records for this customer are no longer visible.

➤ Click the **plus sign** next to your customer record (record C11 in our figure). The plus sign changes to a minus sign but there are no loans as yet. Click in the **LoanID field** and enter data for a new loan record as shown in Figure 5.4e.
  • Use **L121** for the LoanID and enter the terms of the loan as you see fit.
  • Data validation has been built into the Loans table. The term of the loan, for example, cannot exceed 30 years. The interest rate must be entered as a decimal. The type of the loan must be C, M, or O for Car, Mortgage, or Other. Enter **C** for a car loan.

➤ Press **enter** when you have completed the loan record.

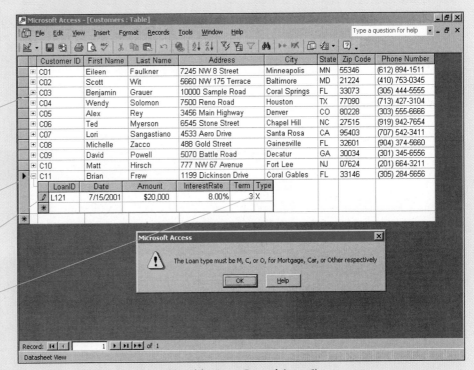

Click + sign to display related records

Click + sign, which then changes to a –

Enter Loan data

Data validation does not permit *X* to be entered

(e) Add a Loan Record (step 5)

FIGURE 5.4   *Hands-on Exercise 1 (continued)*

ADD AND DELETE RELATED RECORDS

Take advantage of the one-to-many relationship that exists between Customers and Loans to add or delete records in the Loans table from within the Customers table. Open the Customers table, then click the plus sign next to the Customer for whom you want to add or delete a loan record. To add a Loan, click in the blank row marked by the asterisk, then enter the new data. To delete a loan, select the Loan record, then click the Delete Record button on the Standard toolbar.

Step 6: **Referential Integrity**

➤ Click the **plus sign** next to the record selector for Customer C09 (David Powell). Click in the CustomerID field for this customer, then click the Delete Record button to (attempt to) delete this customer.

➤ You will see the error message in Figure 5.4f indicating that you cannot delete the customer record because there are related loan records. Click **OK**.

➤ Click in the LoanID for L039 (the loan for this customer). Click the **Delete Record button**. Click **Yes** when warned that you will not be able to undo this operation. The loan disappears.

➤ Click in the CustomerID field, click the **Delete Record button**, then click **Yes** to delete the record. The deletion was permitted because there were no longer any related records in the Loans table.

➤ Close the Customers table. Close the National Bank database. Exit Access if you do not want to continue with the next exercise at this time.

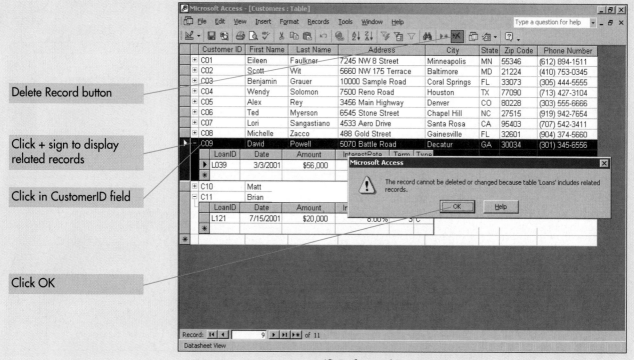

Delete Record button

Click + sign to display related records

Click in CustomerID field

Click OK

(f) Referential Integrity (step 6)

FIGURE 5.4 *Hands-on Exercise 1 (continued)*

CASCADE DELETED RECORDS

The enforcement of referential integrity will prevent the deletion of a record in the primary (Customers) table if there is a corresponding record in the related (Loans) table. (Thus, to delete a customer, you would first have to delete all loans for that customer.) This restriction is relaxed if you modify the relationship by checking the Cascade Delete Related Records option in the Relationships dialog box. The option is discussed further in the next chapter.

A *subform* is a form within a form. It appears inside a main form to display records from a related table. A main form and its associated subform, to display the loans for one customer, are shown in Figure 5.5. The *main form* (also known as the primary form) is based on the primary table (the Customers table). The subform is based on the related table (the Loans table).

The main form and the subform are linked to one another so that the subform displays only the records related to the record currently displayed in the main form. The main form shows the "one" side of the relationship (the customer). The subform shows the "many" side of the relationship (the loans). The main form displays the customer data for one record (Eileen Faulkner with Customer ID C01). The subform shows the loans for that customer. The main form is displayed in the *Form view*, whereas the subform is displayed in the *Datasheet view*. (A subform can also be displayed in the Form view, in which case it would show one loan at a time.)

Each form in Figure 5.5a has its own status bar and associated navigation buttons. The status bar for the main form indicates that the active record is record 1 of 10 records in the Customers table. The status bar for the subform indicates record 1 of 3 records. (The latter shows the number of loans for this customer rather than the number of loans in the Loans table.) Click the navigation button to move to the next customer record and you will automatically see the loans associated with that customer. If, for example, you were to move to the last customer record (C11, which contains the data you entered in the first hands-on exercise), you would see your customer and loan information.

The Loans form also contains a calculated control, the payment due, which is based on the loan parameters. Loan L031, for example (a $200,000 mortgage at 7% with a 15-year term), has a monthly payment of $1,797.66. The amount of the payment is calculated using a predefined function, as will be described in the next hands-on exercise.

Figure 5.5b displays the Design view of the Customers form in Figure 5.5a. The Loans subform control is an object on the Customers form and can be moved and sized (or deleted) just like any other object. It should also be noted that the Loans subform is a form in and of itself, and can be opened in either the Datasheet view or the Form view. It can also be opened in the Design view (to modify its appearance) as will be done in the next hands-on exercise.

Note, too, that reports can be linked to one another in exactly the same way that forms are linked to each other. Thus, you could create a main report/subreport combination to display the same information as the forms in Figure 5.5a. The choice between a form and a report depends on the information requirements of the system. Access, however, gives you the capability to create both. Everything that you learn about creating a subform also pertains to creating a subreport.

THE PMT FUNCTION

The Pmt function is one of several predefined functions built into Access. It calculates the payment due on a loan based on the principal, interest rate, and term and is similar to the PMT function in Excel. The Pmt function is reached most easily through the Expression Builder and can be entered onto any form, query, or report.

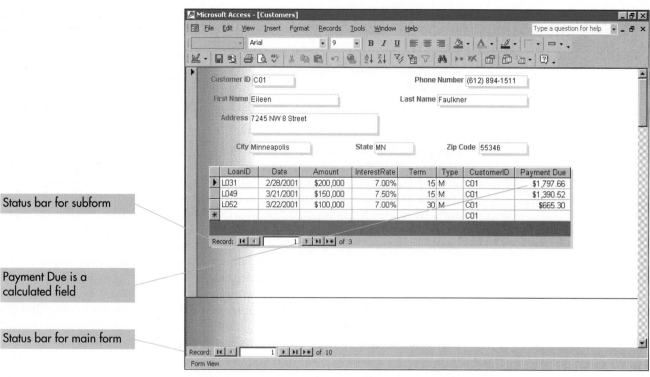

Status bar for subform

Payment Due is a calculated field

Status bar for main form

(a) Form View

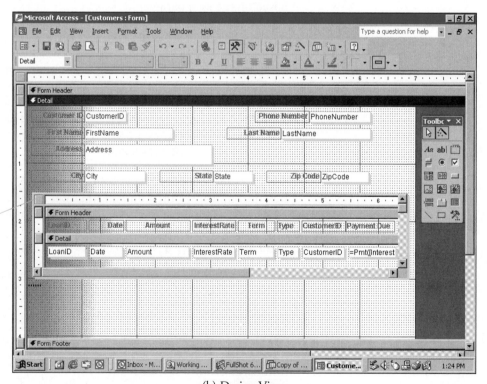

Loans subform control

(b) Design View

FIGURE 5.5   *A Main Form and a Subform*

The Form Wizard

A subform is created in different ways depending on whether or not the main form already exists. The easiest way is to create the two forms at the same time by using the Form Wizard as depicted in Figure 5.6. The Wizard starts by asking you which fields you want to include in your form. You will need to select fields from the Customers table, as shown in Figure 5.6a, as well as from the Loans table as shown in Figure 5.6b, since these tables are the basis for the main form and subform, respectively.

The Wizard will do the rest. It gives you the opportunity to view the records by customer, as shown in Figure 5.6c. (Additional screens, not shown in Figure 5.6, let you choose the style of the forms.) Finally, you save each form as a separate object as shown in Figure 5.6d. You will find that the Wizard provides an excellent starting point, but you usually have to customize the forms after they have been created. This is done in the Form Design view using the identical techniques that were presented earlier to move and size controls and/or modify their properties.

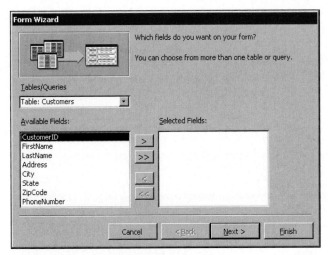

(a) The Customers Table

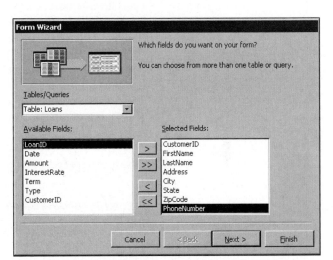

(b) The Loans Table

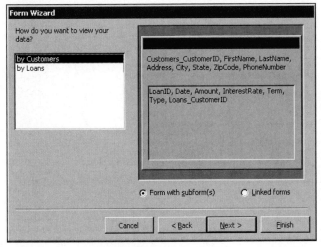

(c) View Data by Customers

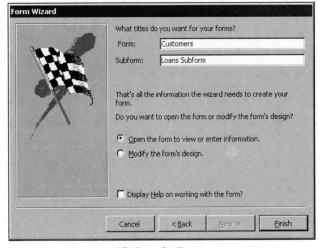

(d) Save the Forms

FIGURE 5.6 *The Form Wizard*

CREATING A SUBFORM

Objective   To create a subform that displays the many records in a one-to-many relationship; to move and size controls in an existing form; to enter data in a subform. Use Figure 5.7 as a guide in doing the exercise.

Step 1:   **Start the Form Wizard**

> ➤ Open the **National Bank database** from the previous exercise. Click the **Forms button** in the Database window, then double click the **Create form by using Wizard button** to start the Form Wizard.
> ➤ You should see the Form Wizard dialog box in Figure 5.7a, except that no fields have been selected.
> ➤ The Customers table is selected by default. Click the **>> button** to enter all of the fields in the Customers table on the form.
> ➤ Click the **drop-down arrow** in the Tables/Queries list box to display the tables and queries in the database.
> ➤ Click **Loans** to select the Loans table as shown in Figure 5.7a. Click the **>> button** to enter all of the fields in the Loans table on the form.
> ➤ Be sure that the Selected Fields area contains the fields from both the Loans form and the Customers form.
> ➤ Click **Next** to continue with the Form Wizard.

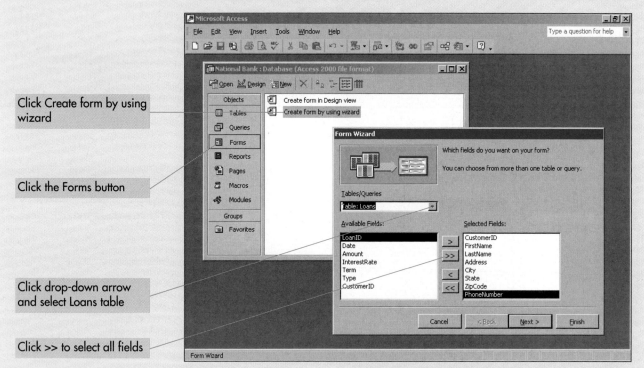

(a) Start the Form Wizard (step 1)

FIGURE 5.7   *Hands-on Exercise 2*

Step 2: **Complete the Forms**

➤ The Wizard will prompt you for the additional information it needs to create the Customers form and the associated Loans subform:
  • The next screen suggests that you view the data by customers and that you are going to create a form with subforms. Click **Next**.
  • The Datasheet option button is selected as the default layout for the subform. Click **Tabular**. Click **Next**.
  • Click **Blends** as the style for your form. Click **Next**.
  • You should see the screen in Figure 5.7b in which the Form Wizard suggests **Customers** as the title of the form and **Loans Subform** as the title for the subform. Click the option button to **Modify the form's design**, then click the **Finish command button** to create the form and exit the Form Wizard.
➤ You should be in the Design view of the Customer form you just created. Click the **Save button** to save the form and continue working.

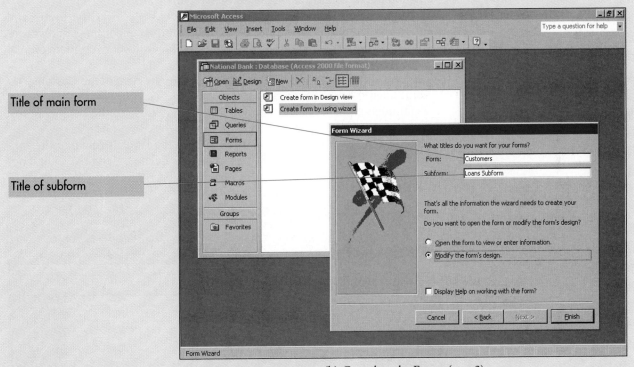

Title of main form

Title of subform

(b) Complete the Forms (step 2)

FIGURE 5.7 *Hands-on Exercise 2 (continued)*

THE NAME'S THE SAME

The Form Wizard automatically assigns the name of the underlying table (or query) to each form (subform) it creates. The Report Wizard works in similar fashion. The intent of the similar naming convention is to help you select the proper object from the Database window when you want to subsequently open the object. This becomes increasingly important in databases that contain a large number of objects.

Step 3: **Modify the Customers Form**

➤ You should see the Customers form in Figure 5.7c. The appearance of your form will be different from our figure, however, as you need to rearrange the position of the fields on the form. Maximize the form window.

➤ Click and drag the bottom of the Detail section down to give yourself additional room in which to work.

➤ It takes time (and a little practice) to move and size the controls within a form. Try the indicated command, then click the **Undo button** if you are not satisfied with the result.

• Move the **City**, **State**, **ZipCode**, **and PhoneNumber** to the bottom of the detail section. (This is only temporary, but we need room to work.)

• Increase the width of the form to seven inches. Click the **LastName** control to select the control and display the sizing handles, then drag the LastName control and its attached label so that it is next to the FirstName control. Align the tops of the LastName and FirstName controls.

• Move the **Address** control up. Place the controls for **City**, **State**, and **ZipCode** on the same line, then move these controls under the Address control. You may need to size some of the other labels to fit everything on one line. Align the tops of these controls as well.

• Click and drag the control for **PhoneNumber** to the right of the CustomerID field. Align the tops of the controls.

• Right align all of the labels so that they appear close to the bound control they identify.

➤ Your form should now match Figure 5.7c. Click the label attached to the subform control and press the **Del key**. Be sure you delete only the label and not the control for the subform. Save the form.

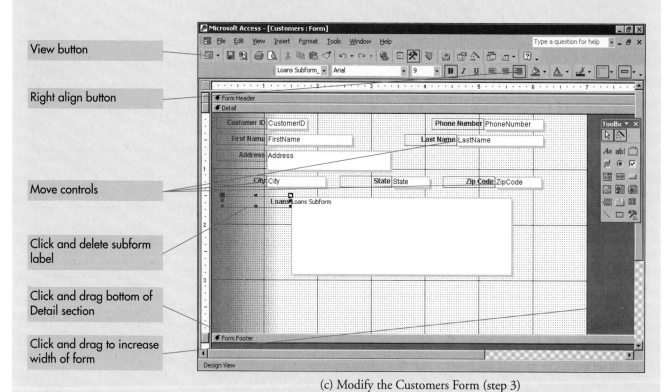

(c) Modify the Customers Form (step 3)

FIGURE 5.7 *Hands-on Exercise 2 (continued)*

Step 4: **View the Customers Form**

➤ You should see the Customers form in the **Form View** as in Figure 5.7d. Do not be concerned about the column widths in the subform or the fact that you may not see all of the fields at this time. Our objective is simply to show the relationship between the main form and the subform.
- The customer information for the first customer (C01) is displayed in the main portion of the form. The loans for that customer are in the subform.
- The status bar at the bottom of the window (corresponding to the main form) displays record 1 of 10 records (you are looking at the first record in the Customers table).
- The status bar for the subform displays record 1 of 3 records (you are on the first of three loan records for this customer).

➤ Click the ▶ **button** on the status bar for the main form to move to the next customer record. The subform is updated automatically to display the two loans belonging to this customer.

➤ Close the Customers form. Click **Yes** if asked to save the changes.

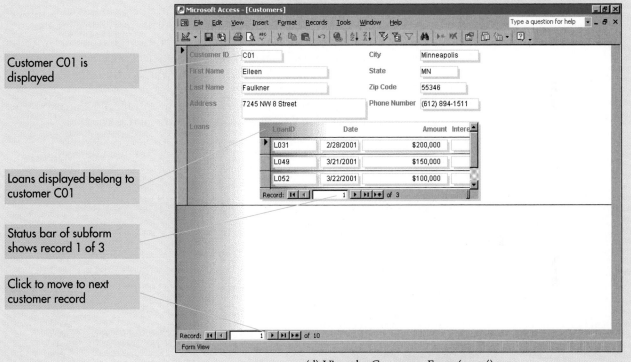

Customer C01 is displayed

Loans displayed belong to customer C01

Status bar of subform shows record 1 of 3

Click to move to next customer record

(d) View the Customers Form (step 4)

FIGURE 5.7 *Hands-on Exercise 2 (continued)*

WHY IT WORKS

The main form (Customers) and subform (Loans) work in conjunction with one another so that you always see all of the loans for a given customer. To see how the link is actually implemented, change to the Design view of the Customers form and point anywhere inside the Loans subform. Click the right mouse button to display a shortcut menu, click Properties to display the Subform/Subreport properties dialog box, and, if necessary, click the All tab within the dialog box. You should see CustomerID next to two properties (Link Child Fields and Link Master Fields).

Step 5: **Add the Payment Amount**

➤ Right click the **Form Selector button** to display a context-sensitive menu, then click **Properties** to display the Properties sheet for the form as a whole.

➤ Click the **All Tab**, click in the **Default View** text box, then select **Datasheet**. Close the Property sheet.

➤ Click the **Forms button** in the Database window. Open the **Loans subform** in Design view. Click and drag the right edge of the form to **7 inches**.

➤ Click the **Label button** on the Toolbox toolbar, then click and drag in the Form Header to create an unbound control. Enter **Payment Due** as the text for the label as shown in Figure 5.7e. Size and align the label.

➤ Click the **Text Box button**, then click and drag in the Detail section to create an unbound control that will contain the amount of the monthly payment. Click the label for the control (e.g., Text 15), then press the **Del key**.

➤ Point to the unbound control, click the **right mouse button**, then click **Properties** to open the properties dialog box. Click the **All tab**.

➤ Click the **Name property**. Enter **Payment Due** in place of the existing label.

➤ Click the **Control Source property**, then click the **Build (...) button**.
  • Double click **Functions** (if there is a plus sign in its icon), then click **Built-In Functions**. Click **Financial** in the second column, then double click **Pmt**.
  • You need to replace each of the arguments in the Pmt function with the appropriate field names from the Loans table. Select the arguments one at a time and enter the replacement for that argument exactly as shown in Figure 5.7e. Click **OK** when finished.

➤ Click the **Format property**, click the **down arrow**, and specify **Currency**. Click the **Decimal Places property**, click the **down arrow**, and select **2**.

➤ Close the Properties dialog box. Change to the Datasheet view and check the column widths, making adjustments as necessary. Close the Loans subform.

➤ Click **Yes** to save the changes.

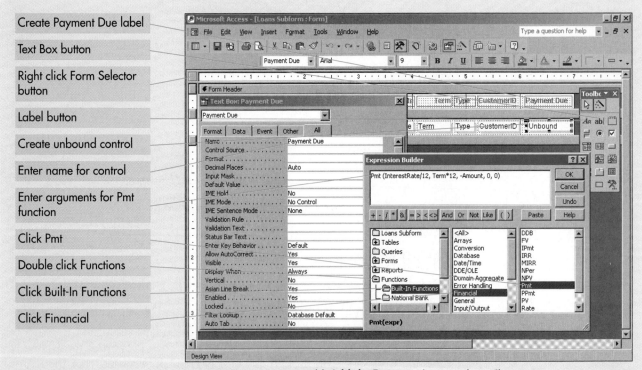

Create Payment Due label
Text Box button
Right click Form Selector button
Label button
Create unbound control
Enter name for control
Enter arguments for Pmt function
Click Pmt
Double click Functions
Click Built-In Functions
Click Financial

(e) Add the Payment Amount (step 5)

FIGURE 5.7 *Hands-on Exercise 2 (continued)*

Step 6: **Change the Column Widths**

➤ Click the **View button** to change to the Form view. You should see the first customer in the database, together with the associated loan information. You may, however, have to adjust the width of the columns within the subform and/or the size and position of the subform within the main form.
➤ To change the width of the columns within the subform:
  • Click the **drop-down arrow** on the **View button** to change to the **Datasheet view**. Click the **plus sign** next to the CustomerID column for the first customer to display the associated records in the Loans table as shown in Figure 5.7f.
  • Click and drag the border between the column headings until you can read all of the information. Click the **Save button** to save the new layout, then close the form. You must close the main form, then reopen the form in order for the changes in the subform to be visible.
  • You should be back in the Database window. Double click the **Customers form** to reopen the form and check the width of the columns in the subform. If necessary, click the **View button** to return to the Datasheet view to further adjust the columns.
➤ It may also be necessary to change the size or position of the subform control within the main form. Click the **View button** and change to the **Design view**.
  • Click the **subform control** to select it, then click and drag a sizing handle to change the size of the subform control.
  • Click and drag a border of the control to change its position.
➤ You will have to switch back and forth between the Form and Design views a few times to get the correct sizing. Save the completed form.

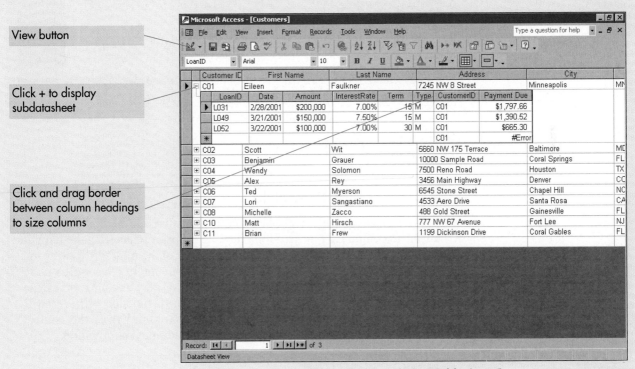

View button

Click + to display subdatasheet

Click and drag border between column headings to size columns

(f) Change the Column Widths (step 6)

FIGURE 5.7   *Hands-on Exercise 2 (continued)*

Step 7:   **Complete the Customers Form**

➤ Select the **Customers form**, then click the **Design button** to reopen the form as shown in Figure 5.7g.

➤ Click the **Tab Order command** to display the Tab Order dialog box. Click the **Auto Order button**, then click **OK** to accept the new tab order and close the dialog box.

➤ Click the **Page Break** tool in the toolbox, then click below the subform control. This will print one customer form per page.

➤ Save the form.

Click the Auto Order button

Click Page Break tool

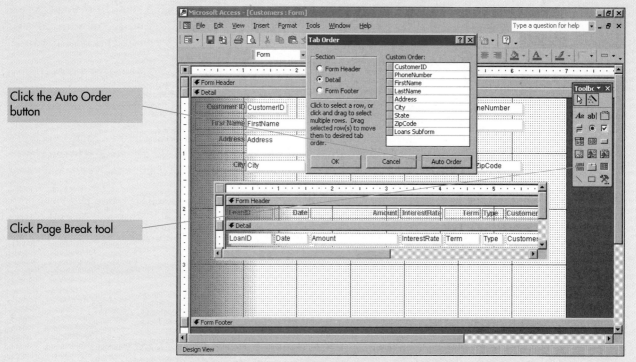

(g) Complete the Customers Form (step 7)

FIGURE 5.7   *Hands-on Exercise 2 (continued)*

#ERROR AND HOW TO AVOID IT

A #Error message will be displayed in the Form view if the Pmt function is unable to compute a payment for a new record prior to entering the term of the loan. You can, however, suppress the display of the message by using the IIf (Immediate If) function to test for a null argument. In other words, if the term of the loan has not been entered, do not display anything; otherwise compute the payment in the usual way. Use the IIf function =IIf([Term] Is Null,"",Pmt([InterestRate]/12, [Term]*12, −[Amount],)) as the control source for the payment amount. See Help for additional information.

Step 8:   **Enter a New Loan**

➤ Click the **View button** to switch to the Form view as shown in Figure 5.7h. (You may have to return to the Design view of the Customers form to increase the space allotted for the Loans subform. You may also have to reopen the Loans subform to adjust the column widths.)

➤ Click the ▶| on the status bar of the main form to move to the last record (customer C11), which is the record you entered in the previous exercise. (Click the **PgUp key** if you are on a blank record.)

➤ Click the **LoanID field** next to the asterisk in the subform. Enter data for the new loan as shown in Figure 5.7h:
  • The record selector changes to a pencil as soon as you begin to enter data.
  • The payment due will be computed automatically as soon as you complete the Term field.
  • You do *not* have to enter the CustomerID since it appears automatically due to the relationship between the Customers and Loans tables.

➤ Press the **down arrow** when you have entered the last field (Type), which saves the data in the current record. (The record selector symbol changes from a pencil to a triangle.)

➤ Check that you are still on the record for customer 11 (the record containing your data), then click the **selection area** at the left of the form.

➤ Pull down the **File menu** and click **Print** (or click the **Print button**) to display the Print dialog box. Click the **Selected Record(s) option button**. Click **OK**. (It may be necessary to use the **Page Setup command** to change the margins, so that the form fits on one page.)

➤ Close the Customers form. Click **Yes** if asked to save the changes to the form. Close the National Bank database. Exit Access if you do not want to continue with the next hands-on exercise at this time.

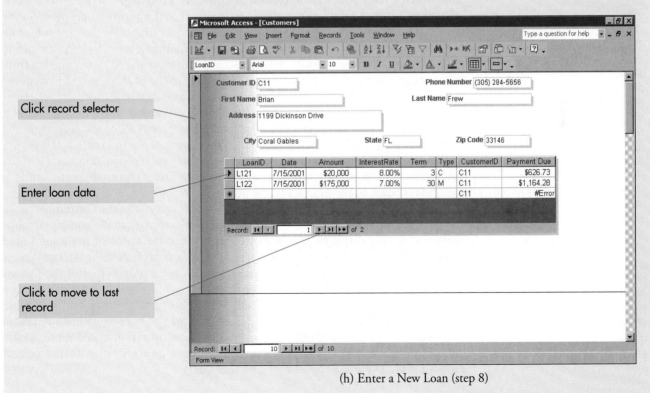

(h) Enter a New Loan (step 8)

FIGURE 5.7   *Hands-on Exercise 2 (continued)*

The chapter began with a conceptual view of the National Bank database, in which we described the need for separate tables to store data for customers and loans. We created a database with sample data, asked several questions about various customers and their loans, then intuitively drew on both tables to derive the answers. Access simply automates the process through creation of a *multiple-table query*. This type of query was introduced in the previous chapter, but it is reviewed in this section because of its importance.

Let's assume that you wanted to know the name of every customer who held a 15-year mortgage that was issued after April 1, 2001. To answer that question, you would need data from both the Customers table and the Loans table, as shown in Figure 5.8. You would create the query using the same grid as for a simple select query, but you would have to add fields from both tables to the query. The Design view of the query is shown in Figure 5.8a. The resulting dynaset is displayed in Figure 5.8b.

The Query window contains the Field, Sort, Show, and Criteria rows that appear in simple select queries. The *Table row* is necessary only in multiple-table queries and indicates the table where the field originates. The customer's last name and first name are taken from the Customers table. All of the other fields are from the Loans table. The one-to-many relationship between the Customers table and the Loans table is shown graphically within the Query window. The tables are related through the CustomerID field, which is the primary key in the Customers table and a foreign key in the Loans table. The line between the two field lists is called a *join line*, and its properties determine how the tables will be accessed within the query.

Figure 5.8 extends the earlier discussion on multiple-table queries to include the SQL statement in Figure 5.8c and the Join Properties dialog box in Figure 5.8d. This information is intended primarily for the reader who is interested in the theoretical concepts of a relational database. *Structured Query Language* (SQL) is the universal way to access a relational database, meaning that the information provided by any database is obtained through SQL queries. Access simplifies the creation of an SQL query, however, by providing the Design grid, then converting the entries in the grid to the equivalent SQL statements. You can view the SQL statements from within Access as we did in Figure 5.8c, by changing to the SQL view, and in so doing you can gain a better appreciation for how a relational database works.

The concept of a "join" is also crucial to a relational database. In essence, Access, or any other relational database, combines (joins) all of the records in the Customers table with all of the records in the Loans table to create a temporary working table. The result is a very large table in which each record contains all of the fields from both the Customers table and the Loans table. The number of records in this table is equal to the product of the number of Customer records times the number of Loans records; for example, if there were 10 records in the Customers table, and 30 records in the Loans table, there would be 300 records in the combined table. However, Access displays only those records where the value of the joined field (CustomerID) is the same in both tables. It sounds complicated (it is), but Access does the work for you. And as we said earlier, you need only to master the Design grid in Figure 5.8a and let Access do the rest.

The power of a relational database is its ability to process multiple-table queries, such as the example in Figure 5.8. The forms and reports within a database also become more interesting when they contain information based on multiple-table queries. Our next exercise has you create a query similar to the one in Figure 5.8, then create a report based on that query.

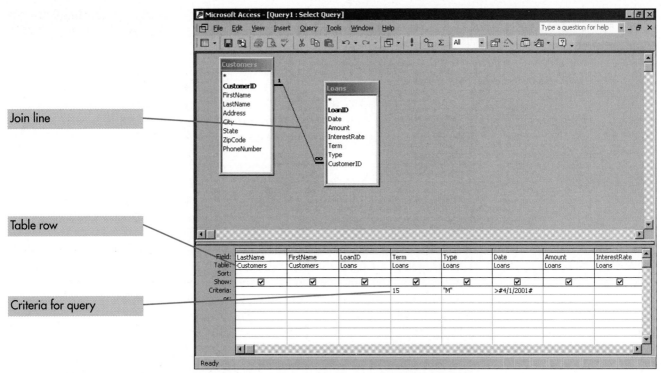

(a) Query Window

Last Name	First Name	LoanID	Term	Type	Date	Amount	InterestRate
Hirsch	Matt	L062	15	M	4/22/2001	$350,000	7.50%
Grauer	Benjamin	L100	15	M	5/1/2001	$150,000	6.00%
Sangastiano	Lori	L120	15	M	5/8/2001	$275,000	9.20%

(b) Dynaset

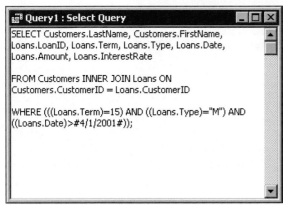

(c) SQL View

Query1 : Select Query

```
SELECT Customers.LastName, Customers.FirstName,
Loans.LoanID, Loans.Term, Loans.Type, Loans.Date,
Loans.Amount, Loans.InterestRate

FROM Customers INNER JOIN Loans ON
Customers.CustomerID = Loans.CustomerID

WHERE (((Loans.Term)=15) AND ((Loans.Type)="M") AND
((Loans.Date)>#4/1/2001#));
```

(d) Join Properties

Join Properties

Left Table Name: Customers
Right Table Name: Loans
Left Column Name: CustomerID
Right Column Name: CustomerID

○ 1: Only include rows where the joined fields from both tables are equal.
○ 2: Include ALL records from 'Customers' and only those records from 'Loans' where the joined fields are equal.
○ 3: Include ALL records from 'Loans' and only those records from 'Customers' where the joined fields are equal.

[OK] [Cancel] [New]

FIGURE 5.8 *A Multiple-Table Query*

QUERIES AND REPORTS

Objective   To create a query that relates two tables to one another, then create a report based on that query; to use the query to update the records in the underlying tables. Use Figure 5.9 as a guide in the exercise.

Step 1:   **Add the Tables**

> ➤ Open the **National Bank database** from the previous exercise.
> ➤ Click the **Queries button** in the Database window. Double click **Create query in Design view**.
> ➤ The Show Table dialog box appears as shown in Figure 5.9a, with the Tables tab already selected. Click the **Customers table,** then click the **Add button** (or double click the **Customers table**) to add the Customers table to the query.
> ➤ Double click the **Loans table** to add the Loans table to the query.
> ➤ Click **Close** to close the Show Table dialog box.

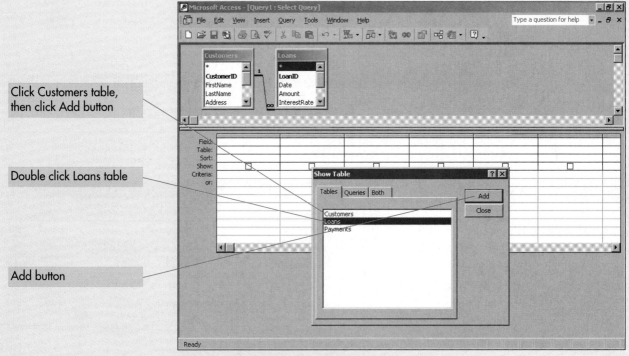

Click Customers table, then click Add button

Double click Loans table

Add button

(a) Add the Tables (step 1)

FIGURE 5.9   *Hands-on Exercise 3*

ADDING AND DELETING TABLES

To add a table to an existing query, pull down the Query menu, click Show Table, then double click the name of the table from the Table/Query list. To delete a table, click anywhere in its field list and press the Del key, or pull down the Query menu and click Remove Table.

Step 2: **Move and Size the Field Lists**

➤ Click the **Maximize button** so that the Query Design window takes the entire desktop.

➤ Point to the line separating the field lists from the design grid (the mouse pointer changes to a cross), then click and drag in a downward direction. This gives you more space to display the field lists for the tables in the query as shown in Figure 5.9b.

➤ Click and drag the bottom of the **Customers table field list** until you can see all of the fields in the Customers table.

➤ Click and drag the bottom of the **Loans table field list** until you can see all of the fields in the Loans table.

➤ Click and drag the title bar of the **Loans table** to the right until you are satisfied with the appearance of the line connecting the tables.

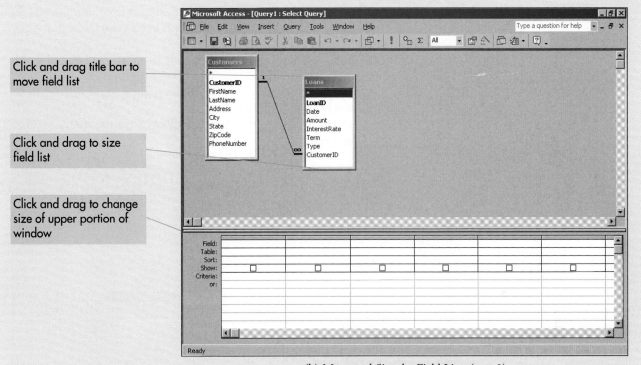

Click and drag title bar to move field list

Click and drag to size field list

Click and drag to change size of upper portion of window

(b) Move and Size the Field Lists (step 2)

FIGURE 5.9 *Hands-on Exercise 3 (continued)*

CONVERSION TO STANDARD FORMAT

Access is flexible in accepting text and date expressions in the Criteria row of a select query. A text entry can be entered with or without quotation marks (e.g., M or "M"). A date entry can be entered with or without pound signs (you can enter 1/1/96 or #1/1/96#). Access does, however, convert your entries to standard format as soon you move to the next cell in the design grid. Thus, text entries are always displayed in quotation marks, and dates are always enclosed in pound signs.

Step 3: **Create the Query**

➤ The Table row should be visible within the design grid. If not, pull down the **View menu** and click **Table Names** to display the Table row in the design grid as shown in Figure 5.9c.

➤ Double click the **LastName** and **FirstName fields**, in that order, from the Customers table to add these fields to the design grid. Double click the **title bar** of the Loans table to select all of the fields, then drag the selected group of fields to the design grid.

➤ Enter the selection criteria (scrolling if necessary) as follows:
  • Click the **Criteria row** under the **Date field**. Type **Between 1/1/01 and 3/31/01**. (You do not have to type the pound signs.)
  • Click the **Criteria row** for the **Amount field**. Type **>200000**.
  • Type **M** in the Criteria row for the **Type field**. (You do not have to type the quotation marks.)

➤ Select all of the columns in the design grid by clicking the column selector in the first column, then pressing and holding the **Shift key** as you scroll to the last column and click its column selector.

➤ Double click the right edge of any column selector to adjust the column width of all the columns simultaneously.

➤ Click the **Sort row** under the LastName field, then click the **down arrow** to open the drop-down list box. Click **Ascending**.

➤ Click the **Save button** on the Query Design toolbar. Save the query as **First Quarter 2001 Jumbo Loans**.

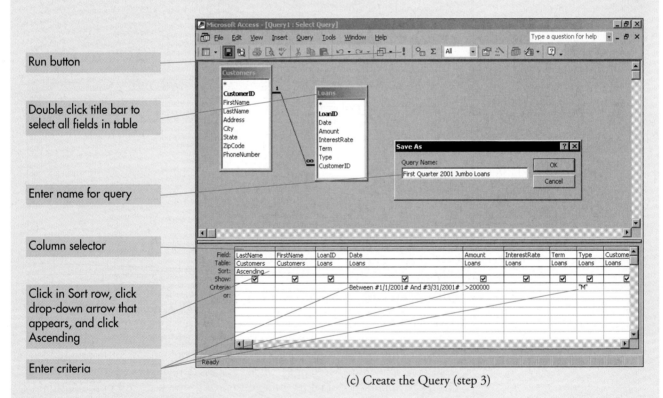

(c) Create the Query (step 3)

FIGURE 5.9 *Hands-on Exercise 3 (continued)*

Step 4:   **The Dynaset**

> ➤ Click the **Run button** (the exclamation point) to run the query and create the dynaset in Figure 5.9d. Three jumbo loans are listed.
> ➤ Click the **Amount field** for loan L028. Enter **100000** as the corrected amount and press **enter**. (This will reduce the number of jumbo loans in subsequent reports to two.)
> ➤ Return to the Design view and rerun the query. Only two loans are listed, because loan L028 is no longer a jumbo loan. Changing a value in a dynaset automatically changes the underlying query.
> ➤ Click the **Close button** to close the query. Click **Yes** if asked whether to save the changes to the query.

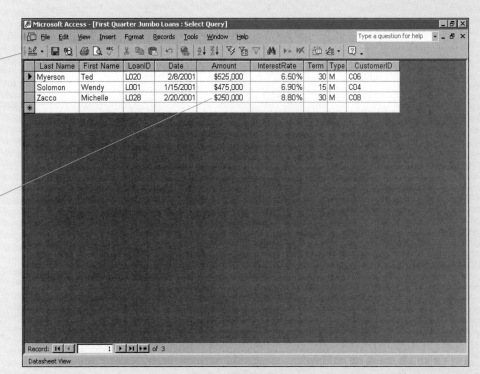

View button

Enter 100000 as new amount

(d) The Dynaset (step 4)

FIGURE 5.9   *Hands-on Exercise 3 (continued)*

DATA TYPE MISMATCH

The data type determines the way in which criteria appear in the design grid. A text field is enclosed in quotation marks. Number, currency, and counter fields are shown as digits with or without a decimal point. Dates are enclosed in pound signs. A Yes/No field is entered as Yes or No without quotation marks. Entering criteria in the wrong format produces a Data Type Mismatch error when attempting to run the query.

Step 5: **Create a Report**

➤ The National Bank database should still be open (although the size of your window may be different from the one in the figure).

➤ Click the **Reports button** in the Database window. Double click **Create report by using Wizard**.

➤ Click the **drop-down arrow** to display the tables and queries in the database to select the one on which the report will be based.

➤ Select **First Quarter 2001 Jumbo Loans** (the query you just created) as the basis of your report as shown in Figure 5.9e.

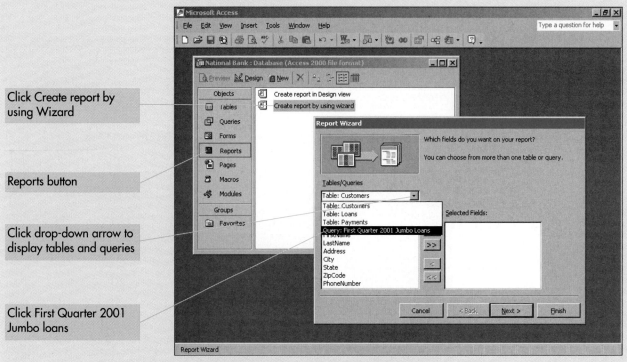

Click Create report by using Wizard

Reports button

Click drop-down arrow to display tables and queries

Click First Quarter 2001 Jumbo loans

(e) Create a Report (step 5)

FIGURE 5.9 *Hands-on Exercise 3 (continued)*

CHANGE THE REPORT PROPERTIES

Do you want the page header or page footer to appear on every page of a report, or would you prefer to suppress the information on pages where there is a report header or footer? You can customize a report to accommodate this and other subtleties by changing the report properties. Open the report in Design view, right click the Report Selector button (the solid square in the upper left corner), then click the Properties command to display the property sheet for the report. Click the All tab, locate the Page Header or Page Footer property, and make the appropriate change.

Step 6:   **The Report Wizard**

➤ Double click **LoanID** from the Available Fields list box to add this field to the report. Add the **LastName**, **FirstName**, **Date**, and **Amount** fields as shown in Figure 5.9f. Click **Next**.

➤ You will be asked how you want to view your data, by Customers or by Loans. Select **Customers**. Click **Next**.

➤ There is no need to group the records. Click **Next**.

➤ There is no need to sort the records. Click **Next**.

➤ The **Tabular layout** is selected, as is **Portrait orientation**. Be sure the box is checked to **Adjust field width so all fields fit on a page**. Click **Next**.

➤ Choose **Soft Gray** as the style. Click **Next**.

➤ Enter **First Quarter 2001 Jumbo Loans** as the title for your report. The option button to **Preview the Report** is already selected.

➤ Click the **Finish Command button** to exit the Report Wizard and preview the report.

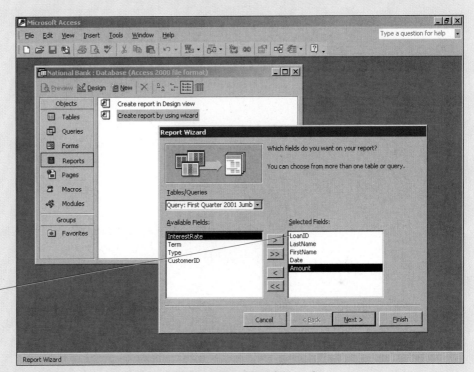

Select fields for report

(f) The Report Wizard (step 6)

FIGURE 5.9   *Hands-on Exercise 3 (continued)*

SYNCHRONIZING REPORTS

The easiest way to link two reports to one another is to create the reports simultaneously through the Report Wizard, by selecting fields from multiple tables. You can, however, add a subreport to an existing report at any time. Open the existing (main) report in Design view, click the Subform/Subreport tool on the Toolbox toolbar, then click and drag on the main report where you want the subreport to go. Supply the information requested by the Wizard and Access will do the rest. See exercise 3 at the end of the chapter.

Step 7: **Print the Completed Report**

➤ Click the **Maximize button**. If necessary, click the **Zoom button** in the Print Preview window so that you can see the whole report as in Figure 5.9g.

➤ The report is based on the query created earlier. Michelle Zacco is *not* in the report because the amount of her loan was updated in the query's dynaset in step 4.

➤ Click the **Print button** to print the report. Close the Preview window, then close the Report window. Click **Yes** if asked to save the changes.

➤ Close the National Bank database and exit Access if you do not want to continue with the next exercise at this time.

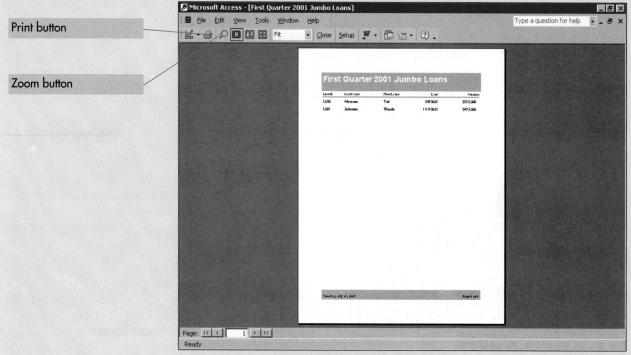

(g) Print the Completed Report (step 7)

FIGURE 5.9 *Hands-on Exercise 3 (continued)*

DATA ACCESS PAGES

The information produced by an Access database can be displayed in a query, form, or printed report. It can also be saved as a data access page that exists as a separate object within an Access database and as an HTML document. The latter can be viewed in Internet Explorer, without having Microsoft Access installed on the client computer. The data within a data access page can be grouped (e.g., by customer), and sorted within a group (e.g., by loan number).

One of the advantages of a relational database is that it can be easily expanded to include additional tables without disturbing the existing tables. The database used throughout the chapter consisted of two tables: a Customers table and a Loans table. Figure 5.10 extends the database to include a partial listing of the Payments table containing the payments received by the bank. Each record in the Payments table has three fields: LoanID, Date (the date the payment was received), and PaymentReceived (the amount sent in).

The original database had a one-to-many relationship between customers and loans. One customer may have many loans, but a given loan is associated with only one customer. The expanded database contains a second one-to-many relationship between loans and payments. One loan has many payments, but a specific payment is associated with only one loan. Thus, the primary key of the Loans table (LoanID) appears as a foreign key in the Payments table.

Look carefully at the Payments table and note that it contains multiple records with the same LoanID. Loan L001, for example, has five payments. In similar fashion, several payments were received on the same date. Payment for two loans, L001 and L002, for example, was received on 2/15/2001. The combination of LoanID and date, however, is unique (e.g., there is only one payment for L001 that was received on 2/15/2001). Thus, *the combination of the two fields*, LoanID and Date, *serves as the primary key*. (This design implies that the system will not accept two payments for the same loan on the same date.)

Query: How many payments have been received for loan L022? What was the date of the most recent payment?

Answer: Four payments have been received for loan L022. The most recent payment was received on 6/12/2001.

The query can be answered with reference to just the Payments table by finding all payments for loan L022. To determine the most recent payment, you would retrieve the records in descending order by Date and retrieve the first record.

Query: How many payments have been received from Michelle Zacco since May 1, 2001?

Answer: Three payments have been received. Two of the payments were for loan L028 on May 20th and June 20th. One payment was for loan L030 on May 21st.

To answer this query, you would look in the Customers table to determine the CustomerID for Ms. Zacco, search the Loans table for all loans for this customer, then retrieve the corresponding payments from the Payments table. (Michelle is also associated with loan L060. The Payments table, however, is truncated in Figure 5.10, and hence the payments for this loan are not visible.)

THE TRANSACTION NUMBER AND AUTONUMBER FIELD TYPE

The use of a concatenated (combined) key, such as LoanID and Date, is one way to create a unique primary key. An alternative technique is to add a new field, such as a transaction number, and assign the AutoNumber field type to that field. Each time a record is added to the Payments table, the value of the transaction number will automatically increase by one, which in turn creates a unique value for that field. This technique is illustrated in the next chapter.

CustomerID	First Name	Last Name	Address	City	State	Zip Code	Phone Number
C01	Eileen	Faulkner	7245 NW 8 Street	Minneapolis	MN	55346	(612) 894-1511
C02	Scott	Wit	5660 NW 175 Terrace	Baltimore	MD	21224	(410) 753-0345
C03	Benjamin	Grauer	10000 Sample Road	Coral Springs	FL	33073	(305) 444-5555
C04	Wendy	Solomon	7500 Reno Road	Houston	TX	77090	(713) 427-3104
C05	Alex	Rey	3456 Main Highway	Denver	CO	80228	(303) 555-6666
C06	Ted	Myerson	6545 Stone Street	Chapel Hill	NC	27515	(919) 942-7654
C07	Lori	Sangastiano	4533 Aero Drive	Santa Rosa	CA	95403	(707) 542-3411
C08	Michelle	Zacco	488 Gold Street	Gainesville	FL	32601	(904) 374-5660
C10	Matt	Hirsch	777 NW 67 Avenue	Fort Lee	NJ	07624	(201) 664-3211

(a) Customers Table

LoanID	Date	Amount	Interest Rate	Term	Type	CustomerID
L001	1/15/01	$475,000	6.90%	15	M	C04
L004	1/23/01	$35,000	7.20%	5	C	C04
L010	1/25/01	$10,000	5.50%	3	C	C05
L014	1/31/01	$12,000	9.50%	10	O	C04
L020	2/8/01	$525,000	6.50%	30	M	C06
L022	2/12/01	$10,500	7.50%	5	O	C07
L026	2/15/01	$35,000	6.50%	5	O	C10
L028	2/20/01	$250,000	8.80%	30	M	C08
L030	2/21/01	$5,000	10.00%	3	O	C08
L031	2/28/01	$200,000	7.00%	15	M	C01
L032	3/1/01	$25,000	10.00%	3	C	C02
L033	3/1/01	$20,000	9.50%	5	O	C05
L040	3/10/01	$129,000	8.50%	15	M	C10
L047	3/11/01	$200,000	7.25%	15	M	C03
L049	3/21/01	$150,000	7.50%	15	M	C01
L052	3/22/01	$100,000	7.00%	30	M	C01
L053	3/31/01	$15,000	6.50%	3	O	C03
L054	4/1/01	$10,000	8.00%	5	C	C02
L057	4/15/01	$25,000	8.50%	4	C	C03
L060	4/18/01	$41,000	9.90%	4	C	C08
L062	4/22/01	$350,000	7.50%	15	M	C10
L100	5/1/01	$150,000	6.00%	15	M	C03
L109	5/3/01	$350,000	8.20%	30	M	C04
L120	5/8/01	$275,000	9.20%	15	M	C07

(b) Loans Table

LoanID	Date	Payment Received
L001	2/15/01	$4,242.92
L001	3/15/01	$4,242.92
L001	4/15/01	$4,242.92
L001	5/15/01	$4,242.92
L001	6/15/01	$4,242.92
L004	2/15/01	$696.35
L004	3/15/01	$696.35
L004	4/15/01	$696.35
L004	5/15/01	$696.35
L004	6/15/01	$696.35
L010	2/25/01	$301.96
L010	3/25/01	$301.96
L010	4/25/01	$301.96

LoanID	Date	Payment Received
L010	5/25/01	$301.96
L010	6/25/01	$301.96
L014	2/28/01	$155.28
L014	3/31/01	$155.28
L014	4/30/01	$155.28
L014	5/30/01	$155.28
L014	6/30/01	$155.28
L020	3/8/01	$3,318.36
L020	4/8/01	$3,318.36
L020	5/8/01	$3,318.36
L020	6/8/01	$3,318.36
L022	3/12/01	$210.40
L022	4/12/01	$210.40

LoanID	Date	Payment Received
L022	5/12/01	$210.40
L022	6/12/01	$210.40
L026	3/15/01	$684.82
L026	4/15/01	$684.82
L026	5/15/01	$684.82
L026	6/15/01	$684.82
L028	3/20/01	$1,975.69
L028	4/20/01	$1,975.69
L028	5/20/01	$1,975.69
L028	6/20/01	$1,975.69
L030	3/21/01	$161.34
L030	4/21/01	$161.34
L030	5/21/01	$161.34

(c) Payments Table (partial list)

FIGURE 5.10 *Expanding the Database*

Multiple Subforms

Subforms were introduced earlier in the chapter as a means of displaying data from related tables. Figure 5.11 continues the discussion by showing a main form with two levels of subforms. The main (Customers) form has a one-to-many relationship with the first (Loans) subform. The Loans subform in turn has a one-to-many relationship with the second (Payments) subform. The Customers form and the Loans subform are the forms you created in the second hands-on exercise. (The Loans subform is displayed in the Form view, as opposed to the Datasheet view.) The Payments subform is new and will be developed in our next exercise.

The records displayed in the three forms are linked to one another according to the relationships within the database. There is a one-to-many relationship between customers and loans so that the first subform displays all of the loans for one customer. There is also a one-to-many relationship between loans and payments so that the second subform (Payments) displays all of the payments for the selected loan. Click on a different loan (for the same customer), and the Payments subform is updated automatically to show all of the payments for that loan.

The status bar for the main form indicates record 5 of 10, meaning that you are viewing the fifth of 10 Customer records. The status bar for the Loans subform indicates record 2 of 2, corresponding to the second of two loan records for the fifth customer. The status bar for the Payments subform indicates record 1 of 3, corresponding to the first of three payment records for this loan for this customer.

The three sets of navigation buttons enable you to advance to the next record(s) in any of the forms. The records move in conjunction with one another. Thus, if you advance to the next record in the Customers form, you will automatically display a different set of records in the Loans subform, as well as a different set of Payment records in the Payments subform.

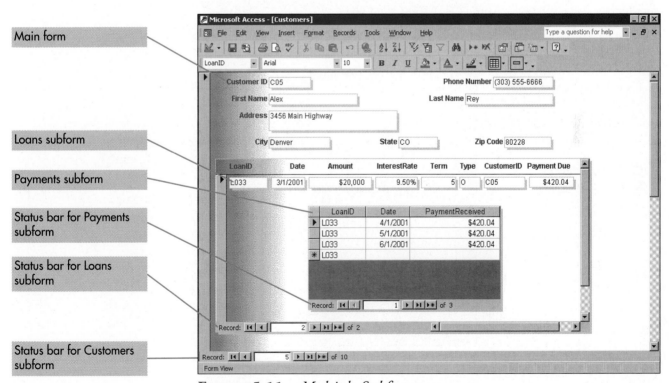

FIGURE 5.11   *Multiple Subforms*

LINKED SUBFORMS

Objective   To create a main form with two levels of subforms; to display a subform in Form view or Datasheet view. Use Figure 5.12 as a guide.

Step 1:   **Add a Relationship**

> ➤ Open the **National Bank database**. Pull down the **Tools menu**. Click **Relationships** to open the Relationships window as shown in Figure 5.12a.
> ➤ Maximize the Relationships window. Pull down the **Relationships menu**. Click **Show Table** to display the Show Table dialog box.
> ➤ The **Tables tab** is selected within the Show Table dialog box. Double click the **Payments table** to add the table to the Relationships window. Close the Show Table dialog box.
> ➤ Click and drag the title bar of the **Payments Field list** so that it is positioned approximately one inch from the Loans table.
> ➤ Click and drag the **LoanID field** in the Loans field list to the **LoanID field** in the Payments field list. You will see the Relationships dialog box.
> ➤ Check the **Enforce Referential Integrity** check box. (If necessary, clear the check boxes to Cascade Update Related Fields and Delete Related Records.)
> ➤ Click the **Create button** to establish the relationship. You should see a line indicating a one-to-many relationship between the Loans and Payments tables.
> ➤ Click the **Save button**, then close the Relationships window.

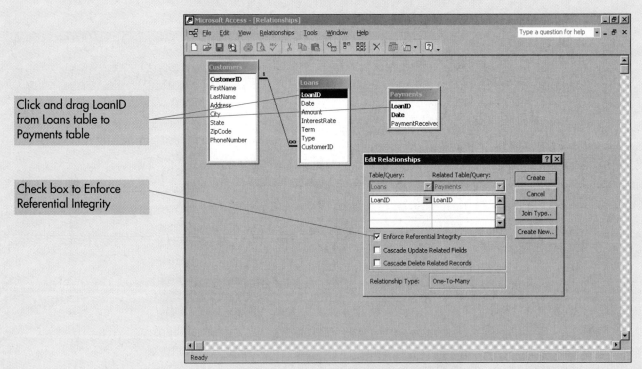

Click and drag LoanID from Loans table to Payments table

Check box to Enforce Referential Integrity

(a) Add a Relationship (step 1)

FIGURE 5.12   *Hands-on Exercise 4*

Step 2: **Create the Payments Subform**

➤ You should be back in the Database window. Click the **Forms button**, then open the **Loans subform** in Design view as shown in Figure 5.12b.

➤ Click and drag the top edge of the **Details section** so that you have approximately 2 to 2½ inches of blank space in the Detail section.

➤ Click the **Subform/Subreport button** on the Toolbox toolbar, then click and drag in the **Loans form** to create the Payments subform. Release the mouse.

➤ The **Use Existing Tables and Queries option button** is selected, indicating that we will build the subform from a table or query. Click **Next**. You should see the Subform/Subreport dialog box in Figure 5.12b.

➤ Click the **drop-down arrow** on the Tables and Queries list box to select the **Payments table**. Click the **>> button** to add all of the fields in the Payments table to the subform. Click **Next**.

➤ The Subform Wizard asks you to define the fields that link the main form to the subform. The option button to **Choose from a list** is selected, as is **Show Payments for each record in Loans using LoanID**. Click **Next**.

➤ **Payments subform** is entered as the name of the subform. Click **Finish**.

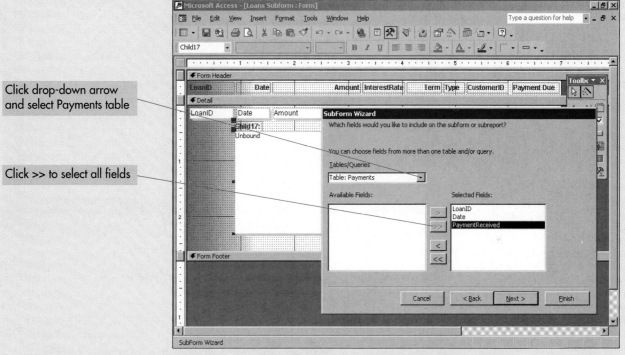

Click drop-down arrow and select Payments table

Click >> to select all fields

(b) Create the Payments Subform (step 2)

FIGURE 5.12 *Hands-on Exercise 4 (continued)*

LINKING FIELDS, FORMS, AND SUBFORMS

Linking fields do not have to appear in the main form and subform but must be included in the underlying table or query. The LoanID, for example, links the Loans form and the Payments form and need not appear in either form. We have, however, chosen to display the LoanID in both forms to emphasize the relationship between the corresponding tables.

Step 3: **Change the Loans Subform**

➤ Maximize the window. Point to the **Form Selector box** in the upper-left corner of the Design window, click the **right mouse button** to display a shortcut menu, and click **Properties** to display the Form Properties dialog box in Figure 5.12c.

➤ The property sheet pertains to the form as a whole, as can be seen from the title bar. Click in the **Default View box**, click the **drop-down arrow** to display the views, then click **Single Form**. Close the Properties dialog box.

➤ Select the label for the Payments subform control, then press the **Del key** to delete the label.

➤ Save the form.

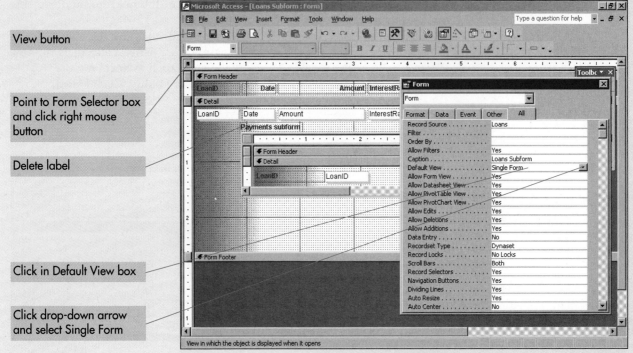

(c) Change the Loans Subform (step 3)

FIGURE 5.12   *Hands-on Exercise 4 (continued)*

THE DEFAULT VIEW PROPERTY

The Default View property determines how a form is dislayed initially and is especially important when working with multiple forms. In general, the highest level form(s) is (are) displayed in the Single Form view and the lowest level in the Datasheet view. In this example, the Customers and Loans forms are both set to the Single Form view, whereas the Payment form is set to the Datasheet view. To change the default view, right click the Form Selector box to display the property sheet, click the All tab, then change the entry in the Default View property.

Step 4:   **The Loans Subform in Form View**

➤ Click the **drop-down arrow** next to the **View button** to switch to the Form view for the Loans subform as shown in Figure 5.12d.

➤ Do not be concerned if the size and/or position of your form is different from ours as you can return to the Design view to make the necessary changes.
  • The status bar of the Loans form indicates record 1 of 26, meaning that you are positioned on the first of 26 records in the Loans table.
  • The status bar for the Payments subform indicates record 1 of 5, corresponding to the first of five payment records for this loan.

➤ Change to the **Datasheet view**, expand the first record, then expand the column widths.

➤ Change to the **Design view** to size and/or move the Payments subform control within the Loans subform. Save, then close, the Loans subform.

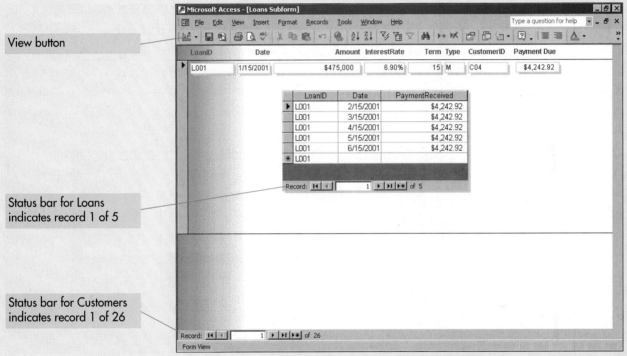

View button

Status bar for Loans indicates record 1 of 5

Status bar for Customers indicates record 1 of 26

(d) The Loans Subform in Form View (step 4)

FIGURE 5.12   *Hands-on Exercise 4 (continued)*

USER-FRIENDLY FORMS

The phrase "user-friendly" appears so frequently that we tend to take it for granted. The intention is clear, however, and you should strive to make your forms as clear as possible so that the user is provided with all the information he or she may need. It may be obvious to the designer that one has to click the navigation buttons to move to a new loan, but a novice unfamiliar with Access may not know that. Adding a descriptive label to the form goes a long way toward making a system successful.

Step 5: **The Customers Form**

➤ You should be back in the Database window. Click the **Forms button** (if necessary), then open the **Customers form** as shown in Figure 5.12e.

➤ Do not be concerned if the sizes of the subforms are different from ours as you can return to the Design view to make the necessary changes.

• The status bar of the Customers form indicates record 1 of 10, meaning that you are positioned on the first of 10 records in the Customers table.

• The status bar for the Loans subform indicates record 1 of 3, corresponding to the first of three records for this customer.

• The status bar for the Payments subform indicates record 1 of 4, corresponding to the first of four payments for this loan.

➤ Change to the **Design view** to move and/or size the control for the Loans subform as described in step 6.

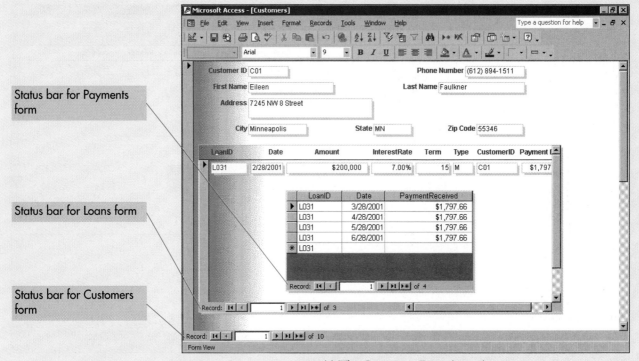

Status bar for Payments form

Status bar for Loans form

Status bar for Customers form

(e) The Customers Form (step 5)

FIGURE 5.12 *Hands-on Exercise 4 (continued)*

THE STARTUP PROPERTY

The Startup property determines how a database will appear when it is opened. One very common option is to open a form automatically so that the user is presented with the form without having to navigate through the Database window. Pull down the Tools menu, click Startup to display the Startup dialog box, then click the drop-down arrow in the Display Form list box. Select the desired form, such as the Customers form created in this exercise, then click OK. The next time you open the database the designated form will be opened automatically.

Step 6: **The Finishing Touches**

➤ You may need to increase the size of the Loans subform control. Click and drag the bottom edge of the **Detail Section** in Figure 5.12f to make the section larger. You may also have to click and drag the Loans subform to the left, then click and drag its right border to make it wider.

➤ We also found it necessary to decrease the size of the Amount field within the Loans subform. Click the label for the **Amount field** in the Form header. Press and hold the **Shift key** as you select the bound control for the Amount field in the detail section, then click and drag the right border to make both controls narrower.

➤ Click the **Interest Rate label**. Press and hold the **Shift key** as you select the remaining controls to the left of the amount field, then click and drag these fields to the left. Save the changes.

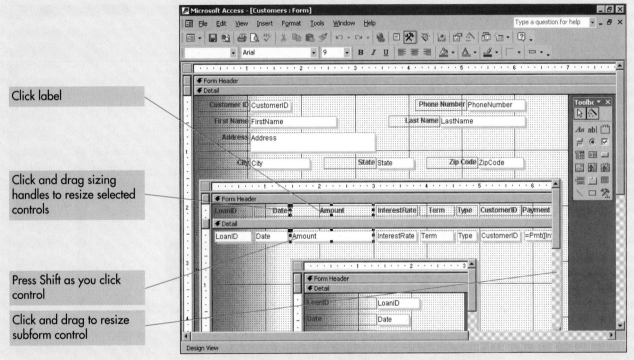

(f) The Finishing Touches (step 6)

FIGURE 5.12 *Hands-on Exercise 4 (continued)*

MULTIPLE CONTROLS AND PROPERTIES

Press and hold the Shift key as you click one control after another to select multiple controls. To view or change the properties for the selected controls, click the right mouse button to display a shortcut menu, then click Properties to display a property sheet. If the value of a property is the same for all selected controls, that value will appear in the property sheet; otherwise the box for that property will be blank. Changing a property when multiple controls are selected changes the property for all selected controls.

Step 7: **Make Your Payments**

➤ Change to the **Form view.** Click the ▶| on the status bar for the Customers form to move to the last record as shown in Figure 5.12g. This should be Customer C11 (your record) that you entered in the earlier exercises in this chapter. You currently have two loans, L121 and L122, the first of which is displayed.

➤ Click in the **Payments subform.** Enter the date of your first payment, press **Tab,** then enter the amount paid. Press **enter** to move to the next payment record and enter this payment as well. Press **enter** and enter a third payment.

➤ Click the **selection area** at the left of the form to select this record. Pull down the **File menu** and click **Print** to display the Print dialog box. Click the **Selected Records Option button.** Click **OK** to print the selected form.

➤ Close the Customers form. Click **Yes** if asked to save the changes to the form.

➤ Close the National Bank database. Exit Access.

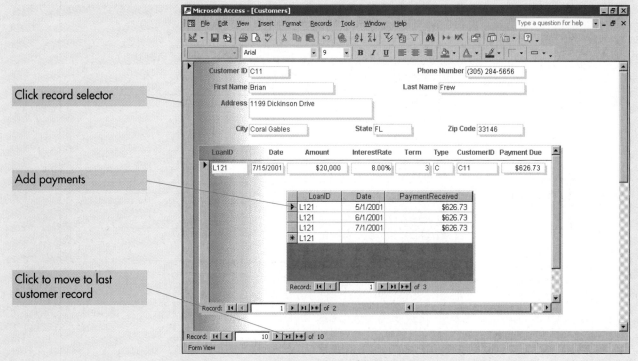

(g) Make Your Payments (step 7)

FIGURE 5.12 *Hands-on Exercise 4 (continued)*

THREE SETS OF NAVIGATION BUTTONS

Each form or subform has its own set of navigation buttons. Thus, in this example you are looking at record 10 of 10 in the Customers form, loan 1 of 2 in the Loans form for this customer, and payment 3 of 3 in the Payments form for this loan. Click the next or previous button in the Customers form and you will be taken to the next or previous customer record, respectively. Click the next button in the Loans form, however, and you are taken to the next loan for the current customer. In similar fashion, clicking the next button in the Payments form takes you to the next payment for the current loan for the current customer.

An Access database may contain multiple tables. Each table stores data about a specific subject. Each table has a primary key, which is a field (or combination of fields) that uniquely identifies each record.

A one-to-many relationship uses the primary key of the "one" table as a foreign key in the "many" table. (A foreign key is simply the primary key of the related table.) The Relationships window enables you to graphically create a one-to-many relationship by dragging the join field from one table to the other.

Referential integrity ensures that the tables in a database are consistent with one another. When referential integrity is enforced, Access prevents you from adding a record to the "many" table if that record contains an invalid foreign key. It also prevents you from deleting a record in the "one" table if there is a corresponding record in the related table. You can, however, always add a record to the "one" table, and you can always delete a record from the "many" table.

A subform is a form within a form and is used to display data from a related table. It is created most easily with the Form Wizard, then modified in the Form Design view just as any other form. A main form can have any number of subforms. Subforms can extend to two levels, enabling a subform to be created within a subform.

The power of a select query lies in its ability to include fields from several tables. The Design view of a query shows the relationships that exist between the tables by drawing a join line that indicates how to relate the data. The Tables row displays the name of the table containing the corresponding field. Once created, a multiple table query can be the basis for a form or report.

The results of a query are displayed in a dynaset, a dynamic subset of the underlying tables that contains the records that satisfy the criteria within the query. Any changes to the dynaset are automatically reflected in the underlying table(s).

Tables can be added to a relational database without disturbing the data in existing tables. A database can have several one-to-many relationships. All relationships are created in the Relationships window.

KEY TERMS

Build button (p. 220)
Control Source property (p. 220)
Datasheet view (p. 213)
Foreign key (p. 205)
Form view (p. 213)
Join line (p. 224)
Main form (p. 213)

Multiple-table query (p. 224)
One-to-many relationship (p. 203)
PMT function (p. 213)
Primary key (p. 205)
Referential integrity (p. 205)
Relationship line (p. 205)
Relationships window (p. 205)

Startup property (p. 240)
Structured Query Language (SQL) (p. 224)
Subdatasheet (p. 205)
Subform (p. 213)
Table row (p. 224)

1. Which of the following will cause a problem of referential integrity when there is a one-to-many relationship between customers and loans?
   (a) The deletion of a customer record that has corresponding loan records
   (b) The deletion of a customer record that has no corresponding loan records
   (c) The deletion of a loan record with a corresponding customer record
   (d) All of the above

2. Which of the following will cause a problem of referential integrity when there is a one-to-many relationship between customers and loans?
   (a) The addition of a new customer prior to entering loans for that customer
   (b) The addition of a new loan that references an invalid customer
   (c) Both (a) and (b)
   (d) Neither (a) nor (b)

3. Which of the following is true about a database that monitors players and the teams to which those players are assigned?
   (a) The PlayerID will be defined as a primary key within the Teams table
   (b) The TeamID will be defined as a primary key within the Players table
   (c) The PlayerID will appear as a foreign key within the Teams table
   (d) The TeamID will appear as a foreign key within the Players table

4. Which of the following best expresses the relationships within the expanded National Bank database as it appeared at the end of the chapter?
   (a) There is a one-to-many relationship between customers and loans
   (b) There is a one-to-many relationship between loans and payments
   (c) Both (a) and (b)
   (d) Neither (a) nor (b)

5. A database has a one-to-many relationship between branches and employees (one branch can have many employees). Which of the following is a true statement about that database?
   (a) The EmployeeID will be defined as a primary key within the Branches table
   (b) The BranchID will be defined as a primary key within the Employees table
   (c) The EmployeeID will appear as a foreign key within the Branches table
   (d) The BranchID will appear as a foreign key within the Employees table

6. Every table in an Access database:
   (a) Must be related to every other table
   (b) Must have one or more foreign keys
   (c) Both (a) and (b)
   (d) Neither (a) nor (b)

7. Which of the following is true of a main form and subform that are created in conjunction with the one-to-many relationship between customers and loans?
   (a) The main form should be based on the Customers table
   (b) The subform should be based on the Loans table
   (c) Both (a) and (b)
   (d) Neither (a) nor (b)

8. Which of the following is true regarding the navigation buttons for a main form and its associated subform?
   (a) The navigation buttons pertain to just the main form
   (b) The navigation buttons pertain to just the subform
   (c) There are separate navigation buttons for each form
   (d) There are no navigation buttons at all

9. How do you open a subform?
   (a) Go to the Design view of the associated main form, click anywhere in the main form to deselect the subform, then double click the subform
   (b) Go to the Database window, select the subform, then click the Open or Design buttons, depending on the desired view
   (c) Either (a) and (b)
   (d) Neither (a) nor (b)

10. Which of the following is true?
    (a) A main form may contain multiple subforms
    (b) A subform may contain another subform
    (c) Both (a) and (b)
    (d) Neither (a) nor (b)

11. Which command displays the open tables in an Access database in equal-sized windows one on top of another?
    (a) The Tile command in the Window menu
    (b) The Cascade command in the Window menu
    (c) The Tile command in the Relationships menu
    (d) The Cascade command in the Relationships menu

12. Which of the following describes how to move and size a field list within the Relationships window?
    (a) Click and drag the title bar to size the field list
    (b) Click and drag a border or corner to move the field list
    (c) Both (a) and (b)
    (d) Neither (a) nor (b)

13. Which of the following is true regarding entries in a Criteria row of a select query?
    (a) A text field may be entered with or without quotation marks
    (b) A date field may be entered with or without surrounding number (pound) signs
    (c) Both (a) and (b)
    (d) Neither (a) nor (b)

14. Which of the following is true about a select query?
    (a) It may reference fields in one or more tables
    (b) It may have one or more criteria rows
    (c) It may sort on one or more fields
    (d) All of the above

15. A report may be based on:
    (a) A table
    (b) A query
    (c) Both (a) and (b)
    (d) Neither (a) nor (b)

ANSWERS

1. a	**6.** d	**11.** b
2. b	**7.** c	**12.** d
3. d	**8.** c	**13.** c
4. c	**9.** c	**14.** d
5. d	**10.** c	**15.** c

1. Widgets of America (database design): Figure 5.13 displays the relationships diagram for a database that is to be used by the Widgets of America Corporation to track the orders generated by its sales staff. Each sales representative has the exclusive rights to his or her customers; that is, each representative has many customers, but a specific customer always deals with the same sales representative. The company needs to know all of the orders placed by a specific customer as well as the total business generated by each sales representative. The data for each order includes the date the order was placed and the amount of the order.

   a. We have designed the database for you. Your task is to implement our design by creating a database that contains the indicated tables and associated relationships.

   b. You do not have to enter data into any of the tables, but you will need to create the tables in order to create a relationships diagram. Pay particular attention to the required field property with respect to the related fields. A customer must have an assigned sales representative to gain access to sales information. And, as you might expect, the company will not accept an order unless it (the order) is associated with a specific customer.

   c. The report in Figure 5.13 is created from the Relationships window after the relationships have been specified. Pull down the Tools menu and click Relationships to open the Relationships window, then pull down the File menu and click the Print Relationships command to display the Print Preview screen of a report that displays the contents of the Relationships window. Change to the Design view and modify the report to include your name. (Our report also includes a label that describes the relationships in the system as well as a clip art image that can serve as a logo for the eventual system.) Print the completed report for your instructor as proof that you did this exercise.

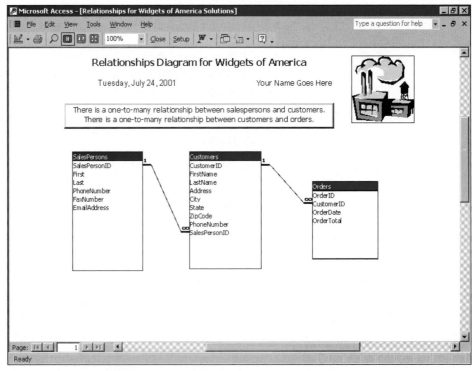

FIGURE 5.13   *Widgets of America (Exercise 1)*

BUILDS ON

HANDS-ON
EXERCISE 3
PAGES 226–232

2. Automobile Loans: Interest rates have come down and National Bank has decided to run a promotion on refinancing all of the existing automobile loans. Your assignment is to create the report in Figure 5.14, which is based on a query that contains fields from both the Customers and Loans tables, and which lists customers in alphabetical order by last name. You need not match our design exactly, but you are required to include your name as well as clip art in the report header. Print the completed report. Add a cover sheet and submit the assignment to your instructor.

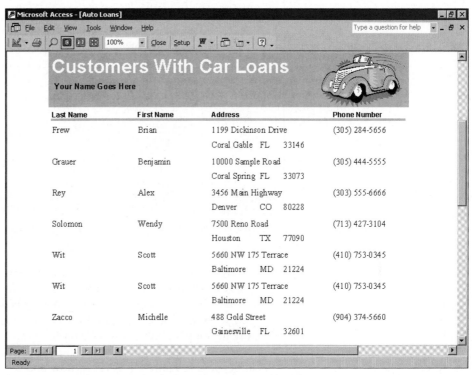

FIGURE 5.14 *Automobile Loans (Exercise 2)*

BUILDS ON

HANDS-ON
EXERCISE 3
PAGES 226–232

3. Customer List: The report in Figure 5.15 displays information about a specific customer, followed by information on all loans for that customer, followed by information about the next customer, his or her loans, and so on. It is similar in concept to the combination of a main form/subform that was created in the chapter. You can create the report in Figure 5.15 by selecting fields from both the Customers table and the Loans table when you start the Report Wizard.

Alternatively, you can create the Customers report initially, change to the Design view, then click and drag the Subform/Subreport tool to start the Subreport Wizard to create the Loan report. This approach creates two separate reports that combine to produce the equivalent information in Figure 5.15. The reports are linked automatically through the CustomerID field that appears in both the Customers and the Loans tables. Which technique do you prefer? Do the same techniques apply to the creation of a main form and a subform? Summarize your thoughts in a brief note to your instructor.

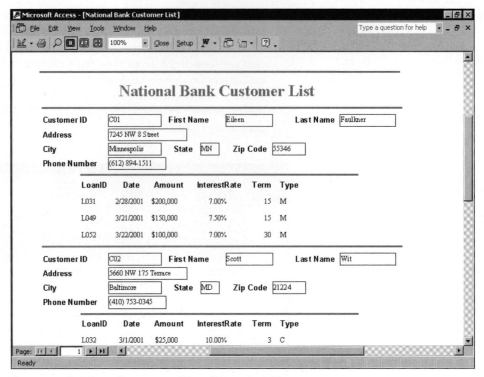

FIGURE 5.15 *Customer List (Exercise 3)*

4. Turkeys To Go Restaurants: Turkeys To Go Restaurants is a small regional chain that builds restaurants to order for individuals seeking a franchise operation. The chain encourages its franchisees to own many restaurants, but a specific restaurant is associated with only one person. A database has been partially developed, but it is up to you to complete the work. Open the *Chapter 5 Practice 4* database and create the one-to-many relationship between franchisees and restaurants. You can now create the main form/subform combination that is shown in Figure 5.16.

a. The database already contains separate forms for both franchises and restaurants, and we want you to use those forms rather than creating the form from scratch. Accordingly, open the existing Franchisee form in Design view and size this form so that you can see the Database window at the same time. Click and drag the existing Restaurants form onto the Franchisee form. Access will automatically link the two forms together, but you will have to go back and forth between the Form view and Design view to size it properly. A restaurant will not be built unless a franchisee is already assigned to the restaurant. Thus, the form in Figure 5.16 is sufficient for all data entry in the database.

b. Use the completed form to enter data for yourself as Franchisee number F010 as shown in Figure 5.16. Use the subform to enter data for two new restaurants, R0100, and R0101 as shown. You can enter any address and restaurant information that you deem appropriate. The annual sales of both restaurants should exceed $500,000. Click the Selector area at the left of the form, then print the record containing your personal information and associated restaurants.

c. Add a cover sheet. Submit the completed assignment to your instructor.

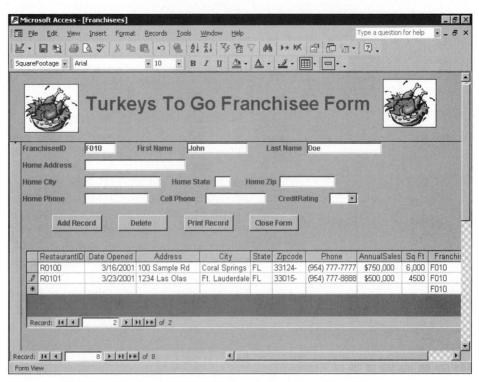

FIGURE 5.16   *Turkeys To Go Restaurants (Exercise 4)*

BUILDS ON

PRACTICE
EXERCISE 4
PAGE 248

5. Turkeys To Go Switchboard: Continue to develop the database for Turkeys To Go Restaurants by creating the switchboard in Figure 5.17. The Data Entry form is the form that you created in the previous exercise. All of the other forms and reports have been created for you, so all that you have to do is build the switchboard. Use the Startup command in the Tools menu to display the switchboard automatically whenever the database is opened. Print the switchboard form and associated table of switchboard items for your instructor.

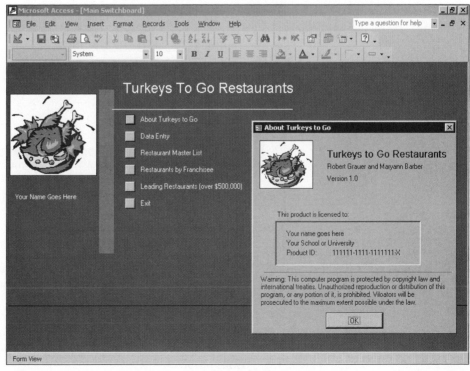

FIGURE 5.17   *Turkeys To Go Switchboard (Exercise 5)*

BUILDS ON

CHAPTER 1
PRACTICE
EXERCISE 5
PAGE 45

6. Employees by Title and Location: The form in Figure 5.18 is developed from the *Look Ahead database* that was first described in Chapter 1. That database contained three tables—Locations, Titles, and Employees. There is a one-to-many relationship between locations and employees (one location can have many employees, but a specific employee is assigned to only one location). There is also a second one-to-many relationship between titles and employees (one title can have many employees, but a specific employee is assigned only one title).

   a. Open the Look Ahead database and check to see if the necessary relationships are in place, based on the earlier work from Chapter 1.

   b. Your name will already be in the database if you have completed the earlier exercises in Chapter 1. If not, add yourself as an Account Rep earning $40,000. Your employee ID is 12345 and you are working in Los Angeles.

   c. Create a main form/subform combination that is similar to Figure 5.18. You need not follow our design exactly, but you are required to include all of the functionality. You can use our clip art or choose a different image. Print the form that displays the information for Account Reps and the associated employees for your instructor.

   d. Create a form parallel to the one in Figure 5.16 that is based on the one-to-many relationship between locations and employees. The main form should display the information for each location, and the subform should display the employees at that location. Print the form for Los Angeles (your location) for your instructor.

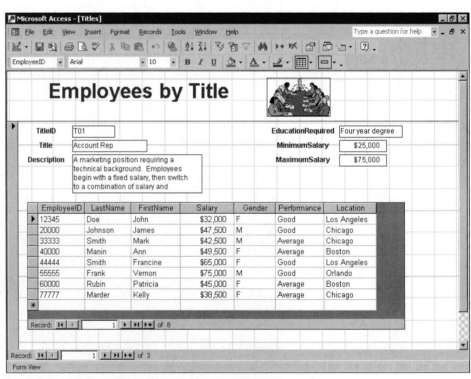

FIGURE 5.18   *Employees by Title (Exercise 6)*

BUILDS ON

PRACTICE
EXERCISE 6
PAGE 250

7. The Look Ahead Switchboard: The switchboard in Figure 5.19 completes the Look Ahead database by providing command buttons for each of the major objects within the database.

   a. Create an "About the Look Ahead database" form similar to the one shown in Figure 5.19. This form is based on similar forms that have appeared throughout the text. Use the same clip art as you did for the form in the previous problem.

b. Add command buttons corresponding to the forms you created in the previous exercise.
c. The three remaining command buttons open reports that are already in the database, and thus do not require any additional work from you. (Do not include a command button for the employee form that is in the database, since that form is now obsolete.)
d. Print the switchboard form as well as the switchboard items table for your instructor as proof that you completed this exercise.

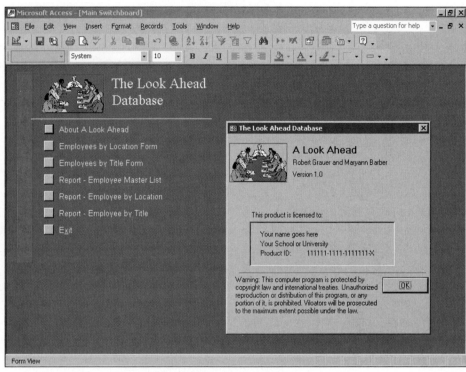

FIGURE 5.19 *The Look Ahead Switchboard (Exercise 7)*

BUILDS ON

HANDS-ON
EXERCISE 3
PAGES 226–232

8. Expanding National Bank: Expand the National Bank database to include a table for Loan Officers, the bank employees who approve each loan before it is granted. One officer will approve many loans, but a specific loan is approved by only one officer, and the loan cannot be granted until the officer approves. (The name of the loan officer will appear in the modified loans subform.) Complete the hands-on exercises in the chapter, then proceed as follows:
a. Open the National Bank database after the third hands-on exercise and create the Loan Officers table. The table contains only four fields—LoanOfficerID, LastName, FirstName, and DateHired. Add two records, Robert Grauer and Maryann Barber, as loan officers one and two, respectively.
b. Modify the Loans table to include a field for the LoanOfficerID. Switch to the Datasheet view, display the loans by LoanID (if they are not yet in this sequence), then assign each loan to an officer. Assign all loans with a LoanID of 50 or less to Bob. Assign the other loans to Maryann.
c. Change to the Design view of the Loans table and make the LoanOfficerID a required field. This ensures that all subsequent loans will be approved by a loan officer.
d. Pull down the Tools menu and expand the Relationships diagram to include the newly created table.

e. Modify the Customer form that was created at the end of the third hands-on exercise to include the Loan Officer information as shown in Figure 5.20. (This requires that you open the existing Loans subform in Design view and insert a control for the Loan Officer.) Pull down the View menu and use the Tab Order command to adjust the order in which the data is entered. In the form header add the additional information that includes your name and today's date.

f. Print the complete record for customer number 1 for your instructor.

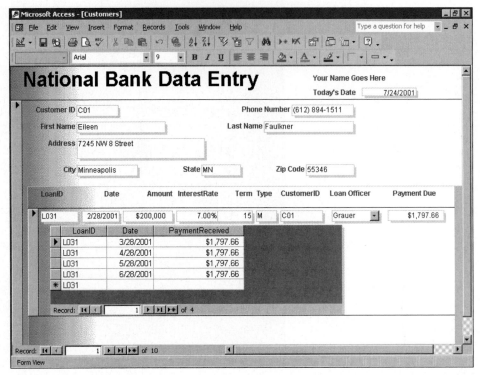

FIGURE 5.20 *Expanding National Bank (Exercise 8)*

9. National Bank Switchboard: Complete the National Bank database by creating the switchboard in Figure 5.21. All of the objects (except for the "About" form) have already been created either in the hands-on exercises in the body of the chapter or in the end-of-chapter exercises. Print the switchboard form as well as the switchboard items table for your instructor.

10. The Table Analyzer Wizard: The *Chapter 5 Practice 10* database is similar to the National Bank example we have used throughout the chapter, except that its design is flawed through duplicate data. The Table Analyzer Wizard will explain how redundant data wastes space and leads to errors, and then it will suggest ways in which to improve your design.

a. Open the database, click the Tables button, and open the Loans table. Can you spot the flaw in the design that leads to redundant data?

b. Pull down the Tools menu, click the Analyze command, then choose Table to display the Table Analyzer Wizard in Figure 5.22. Let the wizard examine the Loans table for you and suggest ways in which to split the data into two or more tables. How does the wizard's design compare to the design of the National Bank database?

c. Close the Fly By Night Banking database, then open the National Bank database you have used throughout the chapter. Start the Table Analyzer Wizard and let it analyze the Customers, Loans, and Payments tables. What suggestions does the Wizard have for changing these tables?

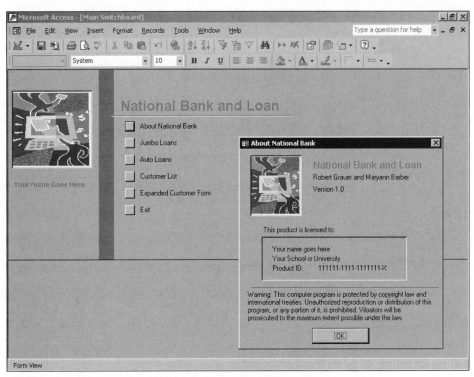

FIGURE 5.21   *National Bank Switchboard (Exercise 9)*

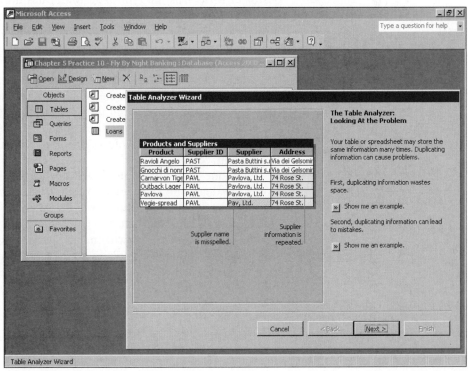

FIGURE 5.22   *The Table Analyzer Wizard (Exercise 10)*

University Apartments

You have just signed your lease for next year at University Apartments, where you have the opportunity to design a database for the complex and thereby save on your rent. The complex has 500 apartments, which are divided into various categories as determined by the number of bedrooms, and additional amenities such as a washer/dryer, patio, and so on. There are many apartments in each category, but a given apartment has only one category.

Your database is to track all apartments in the complex and the students who live in those apartments. Each apartment is leased to one or more students, who sign the identical lease with the same rent and the same starting date for the lease. The lease information is stored within the Apartment record. Each student pays his or her rent individually each month. Your database should produce a report showing the total rent received for each apartment and another report showing the total rent paid by each student.

Design a database that will satisfy the information requirements. You do not have to enter data into the tables, but you do have to create the tables in order to create the relationships diagram, which you will submit to your instructor.

The Automobile Dealership

You have been retained as a database consultant for a local automobile dealership. The dealership has been in the community for fifty years, and it places a premium on customer loyalty, as the typical customer has made repeated purchases over time. The dealership maintains the usual data about its customers—name, address, phone number, credit rating, and so on. It also maintains the usual data about its sales staff. The dealership is large and has several sales managers, each of whom is responsible for multiple salespersons.

The key to the database is the Automobiles table, which contains a record for every car that passes through the dealership. The table contains fields to indicate the date the car was received and the dealer price. It also contains fields for the sale price and sale date, information that is entered when the car is sold. The Automobiles table also contains fields that describe the vehicle such as the make, model, year, color.

Only one salesperson gets credit for each sale and that is the individual who closes the deal. The salesperson receives a commission based on the difference between the sale price and dealer cost. Managers receive an override on all sales generated by their sales staff.

Design a database that will enable the dealership to track its sales by customer, salesperson, and manager. You do not have to enter data into the tables, but you do have to create the tables in order to create the relationships diagram, which you will submit to your instructor.

CHAPTER 6

Many-to-Many Relationships: A More Complex System

OBJECTIVES

AFTER READING THIS CHAPTER YOU WILL BE ABLE TO:

1. Define a many-to-many relationship and explain how it is implemented in Access.
2. Use the Cascade Update and Cascade Delete options in the Relationships window to relax enforcement of referential integrity.
3. Explain how the AutoNumber field type simplifies the entry of a primary key for a new record.
4. Create a main and subform based on a query; discuss the advantage of using queries rather than tables as the basis for a form or report.
5. Create a parameter query; explain how a parameter query can be made to accept multiple parameters.
6. Use aggregate functions in a select query to perform calculations on groups of records.
7. Use the Get External Data command to add external tables to an existing database.

OVERVIEW

This chapter introduces a new case study to give you additional practice in database design. The system extends the concept of a relational database to include both a one-to-many and a many-to-many relationship. The case solution reviews earlier material on establishing relationships in Access and the importance of referential integrity. Another point of particular interest is the use of an AutoNumber field to facilitate the addition of new records.

The chapter extends what you already know about subforms and queries, and uses both to present information from related tables. The forms created in this chapter are based on multiple-table queries rather than tables. The queries themselves are of a more advanced nature. We show you how to create a parameter query, where the user is prompted to enter the criteria when the query is run. We also review queries that use the aggregate functions built into Access to perform calculations on groups of records.

The chapter contains four hands-on exercises to implement the case study. We think you will be pleased with what you have accomplished by the end of the chapter, working with a sophisticated system that is typical of real-world applications.

CASE STUDY: THE COMPUTER SUPER STORE

The case study in this chapter is set within the context of a computer store that requires a database for its customers, products, and orders. The store maintains the usual customer data (name, address, phone, etc.). It also keeps data about the products it sells, storing for each product a product ID, description, quantity on hand, quantity on order, and unit price. And finally, the store has to track its orders. It needs to know the date an order was received, the customer who placed it, the products that were ordered, and the quantity of each product ordered.

Think, for a moment, about the tables that are necessary and the relationships among those tables, then compare your thoughts to our solution in Figure 6.1. You probably have no trouble recognizing the need for the Customers, Products, and Orders tables. Initially, you may be puzzled by the Order Details table, but you will soon appreciate why it is there and how powerful it is.

You can use the Customers, Products, and Orders tables individually to obtain information about a specific customer, product, or order, respectively. For example:

Query: What is Jeffrey Muddell's phone number?
Answer: Jeffrey Muddell's phone is (305) 253-3909.

Query: What is the price of a Pentium III notebook? How many are in stock?
Answer: A Pentium III notebook sells for $2,599. Fifteen systems are in stock.

Query: When was order O0003 placed?
Answer: Order O0003 was placed on April 18, 2001.

Other queries require you to relate the tables to one another. There is, for example, a **one-to-many relationship** between customers and orders. One customer can place many orders, but a specific order can be associated with only one customer. The tables are related through the CustomerID, which appears as the **primary key** in the Customers table and as a foreign key in the Orders table. Consider:

Query: What is the name of the customer who placed order number O0003?
Answer: Order O0003 was placed by Jeffrey Muddell.

Query: How many orders were placed by Jeffrey Muddell?
Answer: Jeffrey Muddell placed five orders: O0003, O0014, O0016, O0024, and C0025.

These queries require you to use two tables. To answer the first query, you would search the Orders table to find order O0003 and obtain the CustomerID (C0006 in this example). You would then search the Customers table for the customer with this CustomerID and retrieve the customer's name. To answer the

(a) Customers Table

CustomerID	FirstName	LastName	Address	City	State	ZipCode	PhoneNumber
C0001	Benjamin	Lee	1000 Call Street	Tallahassee	FL	33340	(904)327-4124
C0002	Eleanor	Milgrom	7245 NW 8 Street	Margate	FL	33065	(305)974-1234
C0003	Neil	Goodman	4215 South 81 Street	Margate	FL	33065	(305)444-5555
C0004	Nicholas	Colon	9020 N.W. 75 Street	Coral Springs	FL	33065	(305)753-9887
C0005	Michael	Ware	276 Brickell Avenue	Miami	FL	33131	(305)444-3980
C0006	Jeffrey	Muddell	9522 S.W. 142 Street	Miami	FL	33176	(305)253-3909
C0007	Ashley	Geoghegan	7500 Center Lane	Coral Springs	FL	33070	(305)753-7830
C0008	Serena	Sherard	5000 Jefferson Lane	Gainesville	FL	32601	(904)375-6442
C0009	Luis	Couto	455 Bargello Avenue	Coral Gables	FL	33146	(305)666-4801
C0010	Derek	Anderson	6000 Tigertail Avenue	Coconut Grove	FL	33120	(305)446-8900
C0011	Lauren	Center	12380 S.W. 137 Avenue	Miami	FL	33186	(305)385-4432
C0012	Robert	Slane	4508 N.W. 7 Street	Miami	FL	33131	(305)635-3454

(a) Customers Table

(b) Products Table

ProductID	Product Name	Units In Stock	Units On Order	Unit Price
P0001	Pentium III/866 MHz	50	0	$1,899.00
P0002	Pentium III/1 GHz	25	5	$1,999.00
P0003	Pentium IV/1.4 GHz	125	15	$2,099.00
P0004	Pentium IV/1.5 GHz	25	50	$2,299.00
P0005	Pentium III notebook/850MHz	15	25	$2,599.00
P0006	17" CRT Monitor	50	0	$499.00
P0007	19" CRT Monitor	25	10	$899.00
P0008	21" CRT Monitor	50	20	$1,599.00
P0009	3 Years On Site Service	15	20	$399.00
P0010	36 GB SCSI Hard Drive	25	15	$799.00
P0011	73.4 GB SCSI Hard Drive	10	0	$1,245.00
P0012	2.6 GB DVD Drive	40	0	$249.00
P0013	Digital Camera	50	15	$449.95
P0014	HD Floppy Disks	500	200	$9.99
P0015	Zip Cartridges	100	50	$14.79
P0016	Digital Scanner	15	3	$179.95
P0017	Serial Mouse	150	50	$69.95
P0018	Trackball	55	0	$59.95
P0019	Joystick	250	100	$39.95
P0020	Cable Modem	35	10	$189.95
P0021	Fax/Modem 56 Kbps	20	0	$65.95
P0022	Digital Photography Package	100	15	$1,395.00
P0023	Ink Jet Printer	50	50	$249.95
P0024	Laser Printer (personal)	125	25	$569.95
P0025	Windows Me	400	200	$95.95
P0026	Windows 98	150	50	$75.95
P0027	Norton Anti-Virus	150	50	$115.95
P0028	Microsoft Scenes Screen Saver	75	25	$29.95
P0029	Microsoft Bookshelf	250	100	$129.95
P0030	Microsoft Cinemania	25	10	$59.95
P0031	Surge Protector	15	0	$45.95

(b) Products Table

(c) Orders Table

OrderID	CustomerID	OrderDate
O0001	C0004	4/15/2001
O0002	C0003	4/18/2001
O0003	C0006	4/18/2001
O0004	C0007	4/18/2001
O0005	C0001	4/20/2001
O0006	C0001	4/21/2001
O0007	C0002	4/21/2001
O0008	C0002	4/22/2001
O0009	C0001	4/22/2001
O0010	C0002	4/22/2001
O0011	C0001	4/24/2001
O0012	C0007	4/24/2001
O0013	C0004	4/24/2001
O0014	C0006	4/25/2001
O0015	C0009	4/25/2001
O0016	C0006	4/26/2001
O0017	C0011	4/26/2001
O0018	C0011	4/26/2001
O0019	C0012	4/27/2001
O0020	C0012	4/28/2001
O0021	C0010	4/29/2001
O0022	C0010	4/29/2001
O0023	C0008	4/30/2001
O0024	C0006	5/1/2001
O0025	C0006	5/1/2001

(c) Orders Table

(d) Order Details Table

OrderID	ProductID	Quantity
O0001	P0013	1
O0001	P0014	4
O0001	P0027	1
O0002	P0001	1
O0002	P0006	1
O0002	P0020	1
O0002	P0022	1
O0003	P0005	1
O0003	P0020	1
O0003	P0022	1
O0004	P0003	1
O0004	P0010	1
O0004	P0022	2
O0005	P0003	2
O0005	P0012	2
O0005	P0016	2
O0006	P0007	1
O0006	P0014	10
O0007	P0028	1
O0007	P0030	3
O0008	P0001	1
O0008	P0004	3
O0008	P0008	4
O0008	P0011	2
O0008	P0012	1
O0009	P0006	1
O0010	P0002	2
O0010	P0022	1
O0010	P0023	1
O0011	P0016	2
O0011	P0020	2
O0012	P0021	10
O0012	P0029	10
O0012	P0030	10
O0013	P0009	4
O0013	P0016	10
O0013	P0024	2
O0014	P0019	2
O0014	P0028	1
O0015	P0018	1
O0015	P0020	1
O0016	P0029	2
O0017	P0019	2
O0018	P0009	1
O0018	P0025	2
O0018	P0026	2
O0019	P0014	25
O0020	P0024	1
O0021	P0004	1
O0022	P0027	1
O0023	P0021	1
O0023	P0028	1
O0023	P0029	1
O0024	P0007	1
O0024	P0013	5
O0024	P0014	3
O0024	P0016	1
O0025	P0012	2
O0025	P0029	2

(d) Order Details Table

FIGURE 6.1 *Super Store Database*

second query, you would begin in the Customers table and search for Jeffrey Muddell to determine the CustomerID (C0006), then search the Orders table for all records with this CustomerID.

The system is more complicated than earlier examples in that there is a ***many-to-many relationship*** between orders and products. One order can include many products, and at the same time a specific product can appear in many orders. The implementation of a many-to-many relationship requires an additional table, the Order Details table, containing (at a minimum) the primary keys of the individual tables.

The Order Details table will contain many records with the same OrderID, because there is a separate record for each product in a given order. It will also contain many records with the same ProductID, because there is a separate record for every order containing that product. However, the *combination* of OrderID and ProductID is unique, and this ***combined key*** becomes the primary key in the Order Details table. The Order Details table also contains an additional field (Quantity) whose value depends on the primary key (the *combination* of OrderID and ProductID). Thus:

Query: How many units of product P0014 were included in order O0001?
Answer: Order O0001 included four units of product P0014. (The order also included one unit of Product P0013 and one unit of P0027.)

The Order Details table has four records with a ProductID of P0014. It also has three records with an OrderID of O0001. There is, however, only one record with a ProductID P0014 *and* an OrderID O0001, which is for four units.

The Order Details table makes it possible to determine all products in a given order or all orders for a given product. You can also use the Products table in conjunction with the Order Details table to determine the names of those products. Consider:

Query: Which orders include a Pentium III/866MHz computer?
Answer: A Pentium III/866MHz computer is found in orders O0002 and O0008.

Query: Which products were included in Order O0003?
Answer: Order O0003 consisted of products P0005 (a Pentium III notebook), P0020 (a cable modem), and P0022 (a digital photography package).

To answer the first query, you would begin in the Products table to find the ProductID for a Pentium III/866MHz (P0001). You would then search the Order Details table for records containing a ProductID of P0001, which in turn identifies orders O0002 and O0008. The second query is processed in similar fashion except that you would search the Order Details table for an OrderID of O0003. This time you would find three records with ProductIDs P0005, P0020, and P0022, respectively. You would then go to the Products table to look up the ProductIDs to return the name of each product.

We've emphasized that the power of a relational database comes from the inclusion of multiple tables and the relationships between those tables. As you already know, you can use data from several tables to compute the answer to more complex queries. For example:

Query: What is the total cost of order O0006? Which products are in the order and how many units of each product?
Answer: The total cost of order O0006 is $998.90. The order consists of one 19-inch monitor at $899 and ten boxes of HD floppy disks at $9.99 each.

To determine the cost of an order, you must first identify all of the products associated with that order, the quantity of each product, and the price of each product. The previous queries have shown how you would find the products in an order and the associated quantities. The price of a specific product is obtained from the Products table, which enables you to compute the invoice by multiplying the price of each product by the quantity. Thus, the total cost of order O0006 is $998.90. (One unit of P0007 at $899.00 and ten units of product P0014 at $9.99.)

The AutoNumber Field Type

Look carefully at the Customer, Order, and Product numbers in their respective tables and note that each set of numbers is consecutive. This is accomplished by specifying the *AutoNumber field* type for each of these fields in the design of the individual tables. The AutoNumber specification automatically assigns the next sequential number to the primary key of a new record. If, for example, you were to add a new customer to the existing Customers table, that customer would be assigned the number 13. In similar fashion, the next order will be order number 26, and the next product will be product number 32. (Deleting a record does not, however, renumber the remaining records in the table; that is, once a value is assigned to a primary key, the primary key will always retain that value.)

The C, O, and P that appear as the initial character of each field, as well as the high-order zeros, are *not* part of the fields themselves, but are displayed through the *Format property* associated with each field. Our Customers table, for example, uses the format \C0000, which displays a "C" in front of the field and pads it with high-order zeros. The Format property determines how a value is displayed, but does not affect how it is stored in the table. Thus, the CustomerID of the first customer is stored as the number 1, rather than C0001. The zeros provide a uniform appearance for that field throughout the table.

The Relationships Window

The *Relationships window* in Figure 6.2 shows the Computer Store database as it will be implemented in Access. The database contains the Customers, Orders, Products, and Order Details tables as per the previous discussion. The field lists display the fields within each table, with the primary key shown in bold. The OrderID and ProductID are both shown in bold in the Order Details table, to indicate that the primary key consists of the combination of these fields.

The many-to-many relationship between Orders and Products is implemented by a *pair* of one-to-many relationships. There is a one-to-many relationship between the Orders table and the Order Details table. There is a second one-to-many relationship between the Products table and the Order Details table. In other words, the Orders and Products tables are related to each other through the pair of one-to-many relationships with the Order Details table.

The *relationship lines* show the relationships among the tables. The number 1 appears next to the Products table on the relationship line connecting the Products table and the Order Details table. The infinity symbol appears at the end of the relationship line next to the Order Details table. The one-to-many relationship between these tables means that each record in the Products table can be associated with many records in the Order Details table. Each record in the Order Details table, however, is associated with only one record in the Products table.

In similar fashion, there is a second one-to-many relationship between the Orders table and the Order Details table. The number 1 appears on the relationship line next to the Orders table. The infinity symbol appears at the end of the line next to the Order Details table. Thus, each record in the Orders table can be associated with many records in the Order Details table, but each record in the Order Details table is associated with only one order.

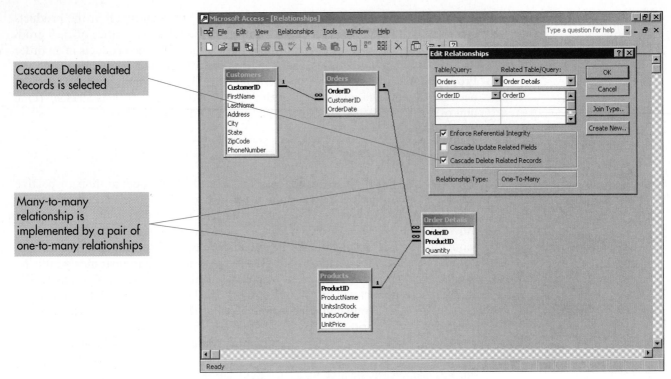

Cascade Delete Related Records is selected

Many-to-many relationship is implemented by a pair of one-to-many relationships

FIGURE 6.2 *The Relationships Window*

Referential integrity ensures that the records in related tables are consistent with one another by preventing you from adding a record to a related table with an invalid foreign key. You could not, for example, add a record to the Order Details table that referenced a nonexistent order in the Orders table. The enforcement of referential integrity will also prevent you from deleting a record in the primary (Orders) table when there are corresponding records in the related (Order Details) table.

There may be times, however, when you want to delete an order and simultaneously delete the corresponding records in the Order Details table. This is accomplished by enabling the *cascaded deletion* of related records (as shown in Figure 6.2), so that when you delete a record in the Orders table, Access automatically deletes the associated records in the Order Details table. If, for example, you were to delete order number O0006 from the Orders table, any records with this OrderID in the Order Details table would be deleted automatically.

You might also want to enable the *cascaded updating* of related fields to correct the value of an OrderID. Enforcement of referential integrity would ordinarily prevent you from changing the value of the OrderID field in the Orders table when there are corresponding records in the Order Details table. You could, however, specify the cascaded updating of related fields so that if you were to change the OrderID in the Orders table, the corresponding fields in the Order Details table would also change.

PRACTICE WITH DATABASE DESIGN

An Access database contains multiple tables, each of which stores data about a specific entity. To use Access effectively, you must be able to relate the tables to one another, which in turn requires knowledge of database design. Appendix B provides additional examples that enable you to master the principles of a relational database.

RELATIONSHIPS AND REFERENTIAL INTEGRITY

Objective To create relationships between existing tables in order to demonstrate referential integrity; to edit an existing relationship to allow the cascaded deletion of related records. Use Figure 6.3 as a guide in the exercise.

Step 1: **Add a Customer Record**

➤ Start Access. Open the **Computer Store database** in the **Exploring Access folder**.

➤ The **Tables button** is already selected in the Database window. Open the **Customers table**, then click the **Maximize button** (if necessary) so that the table takes the entire screen as shown in Figure 6.3a.

➤ Click the **New Record button**, then click in the **FirstName field**. Enter the first letter of your first name (e.g., "J" as shown in the figure):

- The record selector changes to a pencil to indicate that you are in the process of entering a record.
- The CustomerID is assigned automatically as soon as you begin to enter data. *Remember your customer number as you will use it throughout the chapter.* (Your CustomerID is 13, not C0013. The prefix and high-order zeros are displayed through the Format property.)

➤ Complete your customer record, pressing the **Tab key** to move from one field to the next. Press **Tab** after you have entered the last field (phone number) to complete the record. Close the Customers table.

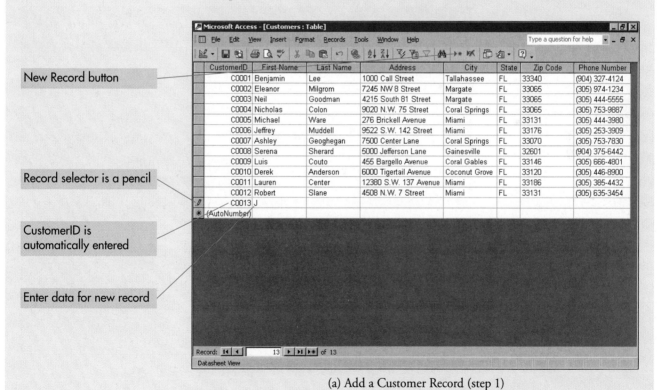

New Record button

Record selector is a pencil

CustomerID is automatically entered

Enter data for new record

(a) Add a Customer Record (step 1)

FIGURE 6.3 *Hands-on Exercise 1*

Step 2:   **Create the Relationships**

> ➤ Pull down the **Tools menu** and click **Relationships** to open the Relationships window as shown in Figure 6.3b. Maximize the Relationships window.
> ➤ Pull down the **Relationships menu** and click **Show Table** (or click the **Show Table button**) to display the Show Table dialog box.
> ➤ The **Tables tab** is selected within the Show Table dialog box, and the **Customers table** is selected. Click the **Add Command button**.
> ➤ Add the **Order Details**, **Orders**, and **Products** tables in similar fashion. Close the Show Table dialog box.
> ➤ Point to the bottom border of the **Customers field list**, then click and drag the border until all of the fields are visible.
> ➤ If necessary, click and drag the bottom border of the other tables until all of their fields are visible. Click and drag the title bars to move the field lists.
> ➤ Click and drag the **CustomerID field** in the Customers field list to the **CustomerID field** in the Orders field list. You will see the Relationships dialog box in Figure 6.3b when you release the mouse.
> ➤ Click the **Enforce Referential Integrity** check box. Click the **Create Command button** to establish the relationship.
> ➤ Click and drag the **OrderID field** in the Orders field list to the **OrderID field** in the Order Details field list. Click the **Enforce Referential Integrity** check box, then click the **Create Command button**.
> ➤ Click and drag the **ProductID field** in the Products field list to the **ProductID field** in the Order Details field list. Click the **Enforce Referential Integrity** check box, then click the **Create Command button**.
> ➤ Click the **Save button**. Close the Relationships window.

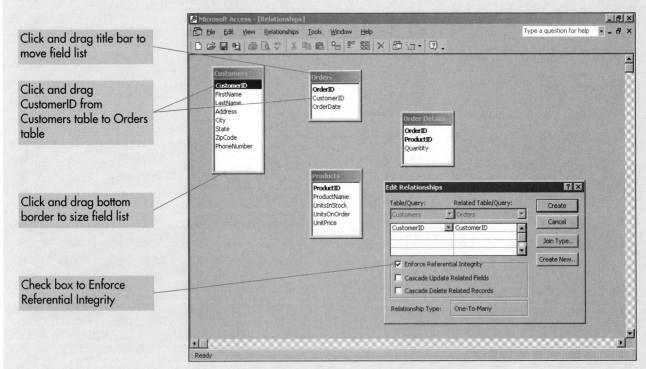

(b) Create the Relationships (step 2)

FIGURE 6.3   *Hands-on Exercise 1 (continued)*

Step 3: **Delete an Order Details Record**

➤ You should be in the Database window. If necessary, click the **Tables button**, then open the **Orders table** as shown in Figure 6.3c.

➤ Click the **plus sign** next to order O0005. The plus sign changes to a minus sign and you see the order details for this record. Click the **row selector column** to select the Order Details record for product **P0016** in order **O0005**.

➤ Press the **Del key**. You will see a message indicating that you are about to delete one record. Click **Yes**. The Delete command works because you are deleting a "many record" in a one-to-many relationship.

➤ Click the **minus sign** next to **Order O0005**. The minus sign changes to a plus sign and you no longer see the order details. Click the **row selector column** to select the record, then press the **Del key** to (attempt to) delete the record.

➤ You will see a message indicating that you cannot delete the record. The Delete command does not work because you are attempting to delete the "one record" in a one-to-many relationship. Click **OK**.

Close button

Click + sign next to order
O0005 to see related
order details records

Click row selector for
product P0016

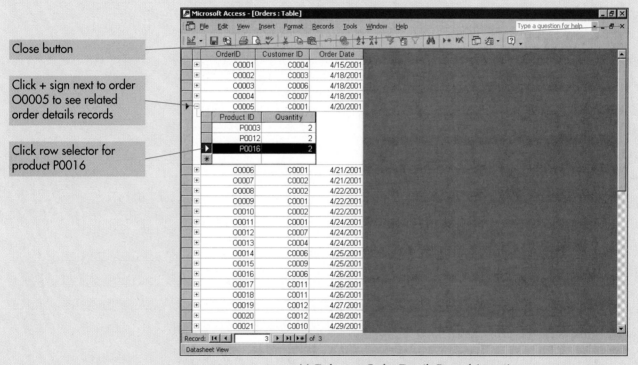

(c) Delete an Order Details Record (step 3)

FIGURE 6.3 *Hands-on Exercise 1 (continued)*

WHAT YOU CAN AND CANNOT DELETE

You can always delete a record from the "many" table, such as the Order Details table in this example. The enforcement of referential integrity, however, will prevent you from deleting a record in the "one" table (i.e., the Orders table) when there are related records in the "many" table (i.e., the Order Details table). Thus you may want to modify the relationship to permit the cascaded deletion of related records, in which case deleting a record from the "one" table will automatically delete the related records.

Step 4:   **Edit a Relationship**

> ➤ Close the Orders table. (The tables in a relationship must be closed before the relationship can be edited.)
> ➤ Pull down the **Tools menu** and click **Relationships** to reopen the Relationships window (or click the **Relationships button** on the toolbar). Maximize the window.
> ➤ Point to the line connecting the Orders and Order Details tables, then click the **right mouse button** to display a shortcut menu. Click **Edit Relationship** to display the Relationships dialog box in Figure 6.3d.
> ➤ Check the box to **Cascade Delete Related Records**, then click **OK** to accept the change and close the dialog box. Click the **Save button** to save the edited relationship. Close the Relationships window.

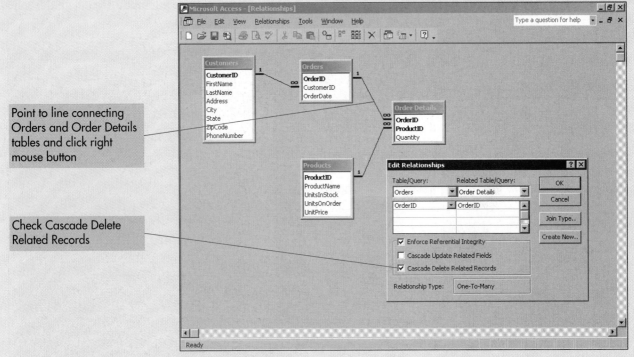

Point to line connecting Orders and Order Details tables and click right mouse button

Check Cascade Delete Related Records

(d) Edit a Relationship (step 4)

FIGURE 6.3   *Hands-on Exercise 1 (continued)*

RELATED FIELDS AND DATA TYPE

The related fields on both sides of a relationship must be the same data type—for example, both number fields or both text fields. (Number fields must also have the same field size setting.) You cannot, however, specify an AutoNumber field on both sides of a relationship. Accordingly, if the related field in the primary table is an AutoNumber field, the related field in the related table must be specified as a number field, with the Field Size property set to Long Integer.

Step 5: **Delete a Record in the Orders Table**

➤ You should be back in the Database window. Open the **Orders table**. Click the **record selector column** for **Order O0005**. Press the **Del key**.

➤ Record O0005 is deleted from the table (although you can cancel the deletion by clicking No in response to the message that is displayed on your screen). We want you to delete the record, however. Thus, click **Yes** in response to the message in Figure 6.3e.

➤ Order O0005 is permanently deleted from the Orders table as are the related records in the Order Details table. The Delete command works this time (unlike the previous attempt in step 3) because the relationship was changed to permit the deletion of related records.

➤ Close the Orders table. Close the database. Click **Yes** if prompted to save the tables or relationships.

➤ Exit Access if you do not want to continue with the next exercise at this time.

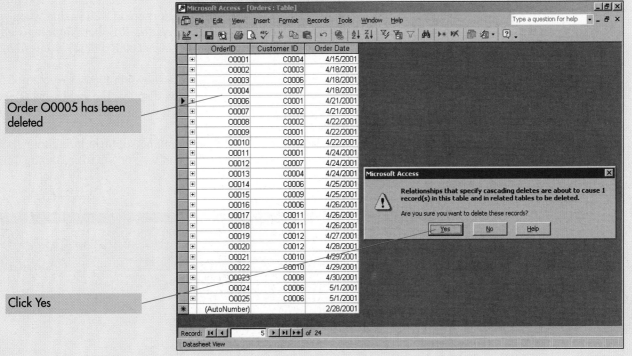

Order O0005 has been deleted

Click Yes

(e) Delete a Record in the Orders Table (step 5)

FIGURE 6.3   *Hands-on Exercise 1 (continued)*

USE WITH CAUTION

The cascaded deletion of related records relaxes referential integrity and eliminates errors that would otherwise occur during data entry. That does not mean, however, that the option should always be selected, and in fact, most of the time it is disabled. What would happen, for example, in an employee database with a one-to-many relationship between branch offices and employees, if cascade deleted records was in effect and a branch office was deleted?

The main and subform combination in Figure 6.4 is used by the store to enter a new order for an existing customer. The forms are based on queries (rather than tables) for several reasons. A query enables you to display data from multiple tables, to display a calculated field, and to take advantage of AutoLookup, a feature that is explained shortly. A query also lets you display records in a sequence other than by primary key.

The *main form* contains fields from both the Orders table and the Customers table. The OrderID, OrderDate, and CustomerID (the join field) are taken from the Orders table. The other fields are taken from the Customers table. The query is designed so that you do not have to enter any customer information other than the CustomerID; that is, you enter the CustomerID, and Access will automatically look up (*AutoLookup*) the corresponding customer data.

The *subform* is based on a second query containing fields from the Order Details table and the Products table. The OrderID, Quantity, and ProductID (the join field) are taken from the Order Details table. The ProductName and UnitPrice fields are from the Products table. AutoLookup works here as well so that when you enter the ProductID, Access automatically displays the Product Name and Unit Price. You then enter the quantity, and the amount (a calculated field) is determined automatically.

The queries for the main form and subform are shown in Figures 6.5a and 6.5b, respectively. The upper half of the Query window displays the field list for each table and the relationship between the tables. The lower half of the Query window contains the design grid.

The following exercise has you create the main and subform in Figure 6.4. We supply the query for the main form (Figure 6.5a), but we ask you to create the query for the subform (Figure 6.5b).

Main form has fields from Orders and Customers tables

Subform has fields from Order Details and Products tables

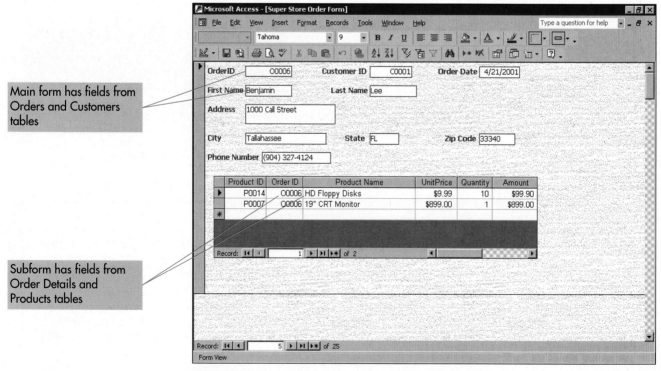

FIGURE 6.4 *The Super Store Order Form*

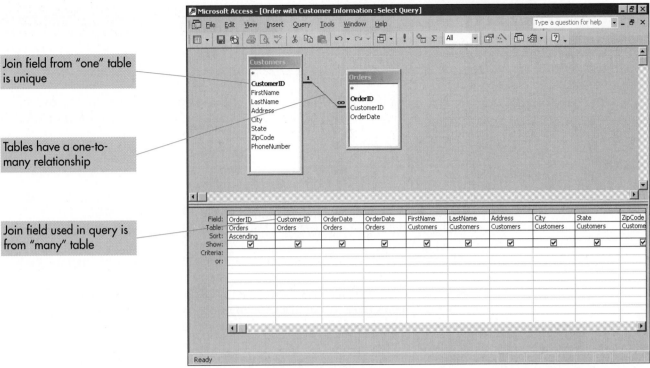

Join field from "one" table is unique

Tables have a one-to-many relationship

Join field used in query is from "many" table

(a) Order with Customer Information Query (used for the main form)

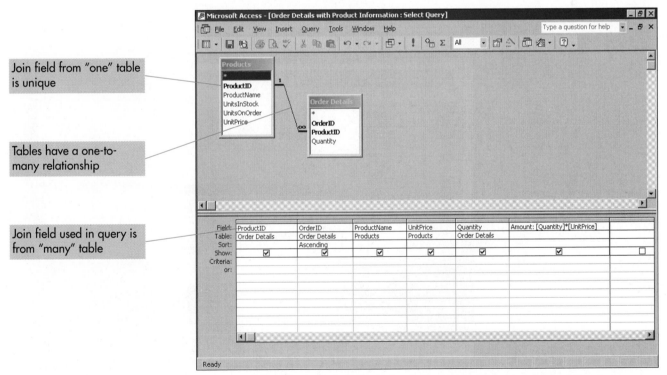

Join field from "one" table is unique

Tables have a one-to-many relationship

Join field used in query is from "many" table

(b) Order Details with Product Information Query (used for subform)

FIGURE 6.5 *Multiple-table Queries*

SUBFORMS AND MULTIPLE TABLE QUERIES

Objective To use multiple-table queries as the basis for a main form and its associated subform; to create the link between a main form and subform manually. Use Figure 6.6 as a guide in the exercise.

Step 1: **Create the Subform Query**

➤ Open the **Computer Store database** from the previous exercise. Click the **Queries button** in the Database window.

➤ Double click **Create query in Design view** to display the Query Design window in Figure 6.6c.

➤ The Show Table dialog box appears as shown in Figure 6.6a with the Tables tab already selected.

➤ Double click the **Products table** to add this table to the query. Double click the **Order Details table** to add this table to the query. A join line showing the one-to-many relationship between the Products and Order Details table appears automatically.

➤ Click **Close** to close the Show Table dialog box. If necessary, click the **Maximize button**. Resize the field lists as necessary.

➤ Click and drag the border separating the two parts of the query window to better display the field list. You are ready to create the query.

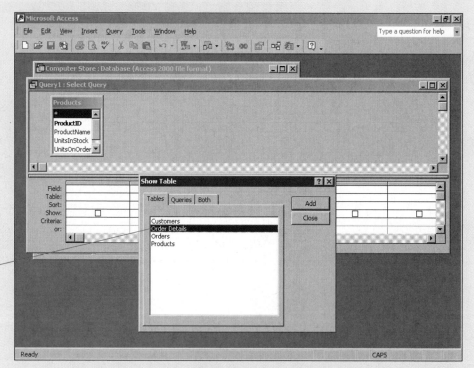

Double click Order Details table to add it to query

(a) Create the Subform Query (step 1)

FIGURE 6.6 *Hands-on Exercise 2*

Step 2: **Create the Subform Query (continued)**

> Add the fields to the query as follows:
>   • Double click the **ProductID** and **OrderID fields** in that order from the Order Details table.
>   • Double click the **ProductName** and **UnitPrice fields** in that order from the Products table.
>   • Double click the **Quantity field** from the Order Details table.
> Click the **Sort row** under the **OrderID field**. Click the **drop-down arrow**, then specify an **ascending** sequence.
> Click the first available cell in the Field row. Type **=[Quantity]*[UnitPrice]**. Do not be concerned if you cannot see the entire expression.
> Press **enter**. Access has substituted Expr1: for the equal sign you typed. Drag the column boundary so that the entire expression is visible as in Figure 6.6b. (You may need to make the other columns narrower to see all of the fields in the design grid.)
> Click and drag to select **Expr1**. (Do not select the colon.) Type **Amount** to substitute a more meaningful field name.
> Point to the expression and click the **right mouse button** to display a shortcut menu. Click **Properties** to display the Field Properties dialog box in Figure 6.6b.
> Click the box for the **Format property**. Click the **drop-down arrow**, then scroll until you can click **Currency**. Close the Properties dialog box.
> Save the query as **Order Details with Product Information**. Click the **Run button** to test the query so that you know the query works prior to using it as the basis of a form.

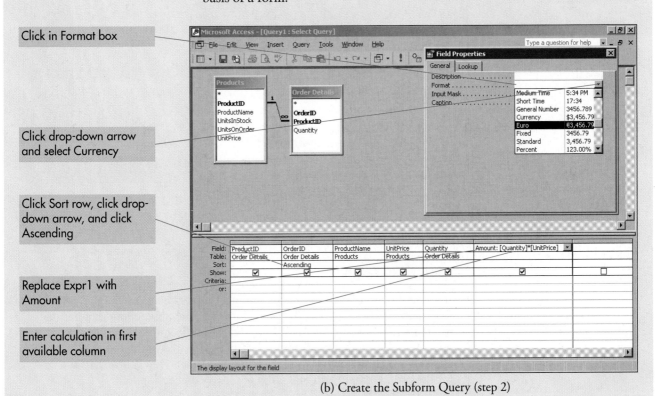

Click in Format box

Click drop-down arrow and select Currency

Click Sort row, click drop-down arrow, and click Ascending

Replace Expr1 with Amount

Enter calculation in first available column

(b) Create the Subform Query (step 2)

FIGURE 6.6 *Hands-on Exercise 2 (continued)*

Step 3: **Test the Query**

➤ You should see the dynaset shown in Figure 6.6c. (See the boxed tip if the dynaset does not appear.)

➤ Enter **1** (not P0001) to change the ProductID to 1 (from 14) in the very first record. (The Format property automatically displays the letter P and the high-order zeros.)

➤ Press **enter**. The Product Name changes to a Pentium III/866MHz system as you hit the enter key. The unit price also changes, as does the computed amount.

➤ Click the **Undo button** to cancel the change. The ProductID returns to P0014, and the Product Name changes back to HD Floppy Disks. The unit price also changes, as does the computed amount.

➤ Close the query. Save the changes to the query design if prompted to do so.

Undo button

Enter 1

Product data will change when you press enter key

Computed amount will also change

Product ID	Order ID	Product Name	UnitPrice	Quantity	Amount
1	O0001	HD Floppy Disks	$9.99	4	$39.96
P0027	O0001	Norton Anti-Virus	$115.95	1	$115.95
P0013	O0001	Digital Camera	$449.95	1	$449.95
P0001	O0002	Pentium III/866 MHz	$1,899.00	1	$1,899.00
P0006	O0002	17" CRT Monitor	$499.00	1	$499.00
P0020	O0002	Cable Modem	$189.95	1	$189.95
P0022	O0002	Digital Photography Package	$1,395.00	1	$1,395.00
P0005	O0003	Pentium III notebook/850MHz	$2,599.00	1	$2,599.00
P0020	O0003	Cable Modem	$189.95	1	$189.95
P0022	O0003	Digital Photography Package	$1,395.00	1	$1,395.00
P0003	O0004	Pentium IV/1.4 GHz	$2,099.00	1	$2,099.00
P0010	O0004	36 GB SCSI Hard Drive	$799.00	1	$799.00
P0022	O0004	Digital Photography Package	$1,395.00	2	$2,790.00
P0007	O0006	19" CRT Monitor	$899.00	1	$899.00
P0014	O0006	HD Floppy Disks	$9.99	10	$99.90
P0030	O0007	Microsoft Cinemania	$59.95	3	$179.85
P0028	O0007	Microsoft Scenes Screen Saver	$29.95	1	$29.95
P0001	O0008	Pentium III/866 MHz	$1,899.00	1	$1,899.00
P0004	O0008	Pentium IV/1.5 GHz	$2,299.00	3	$6,897.00
P0008	O0008	21" CRT Monitor	$1,599.00	4	$6,396.00
P0011	O0008	73.4 GB SCSI Hard Drive	$1,245.00	2	$2,490.00
P0012	O0008	2.6 GB DVD Drive	$249.00	1	$249.00
P0006	O0009	17" CRT Monitor	$499.00	1	$499.00
P0002	O0010	Pentium III/1 GHz	$1,999.00	2	$3,998.00
P0022	O0010	Digital Photography Package	$1,395.00	1	$1,395.00
P0023	O0010	Ink Jet Printer	$249.95	1	$249.95

Record: 1 of 56

Datasheet View

(c) Test the Query (step 3)

FIGURE 6.6 *Hands-on Exercise 2 (continued)*

A PUZZLING ERROR

If you are unable to run a query, it is most likely because you misspelled a field name in the design grid. Access interpets the misspelling as a parameter query (discussed later in the chapter) and asks you to enter a parameter value (the erroneous field name is displayed in the dialog box). Press the Esc key to exit the query and return to the Design view. Click the field row for the problem field and make the necessary correction.

Step 4: **Create the Orders Form**

➤ Click the **Forms button** in the Database window, then double click the **Create form by using wizard icon** to start the Form Wizard. You should see the dialog box in Figure 6.6d except that no tables have been selected at this time.

➤ Click the **drop-down arrow** on the Tables/Queries list box to display the tables and queries in the database. Select **Order with Customer Information** (the query we provided), then click the **>> button** to enter all of the fields from the query onto the form.

➤ Click the **drop-down arrow** to redisplay the tables and queries in the database. Click **Order Details with Product Information** to select this query as shown in Figure 6.6d. Click the **>> button**.

➤ Be sure that the Selected Fields area contains the fields from both queries. Click **Next**. The wizard will prompt you for the additional information it needs to create the form and its associated subform:

• The next screen suggests that you view the data by **Order with Customer Information** and that you create a form with subforms. Click **Next**.

• The **Datasheet option button** is selected as the default layout for the subform. Click **Next**.

• Click **Sumi Painting** as the style for your form. Click **Next**.

• Enter **Super Store Order form** as the title of the form, but accept the wizard's suggestion for the name of the subform (**Order Details with Product Information subform**).

• Click the option button to **Modify the form's design**, then click the **Finish command button** to create the form and exit the Form Wizard.

➤ You should be in the Design view of the Super Store Order form you just created. Click the **Save button** to save the form and continue working.

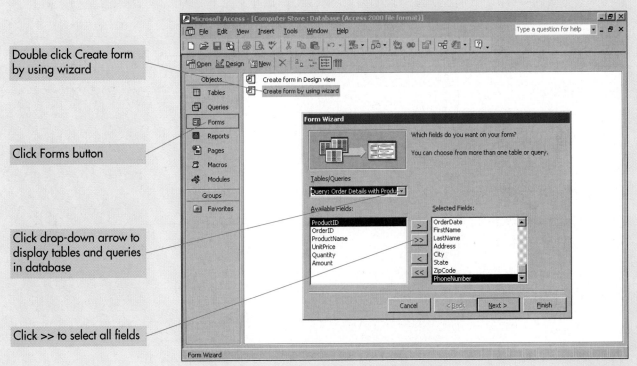

Double click Create form by using wizard

Click Forms button

Click drop-down arrow to display tables and queries in database

Click >> to select all fields

(d) Create the Orders Form (step 4)

FIGURE 6.6 *Hands-on Exercise 2 (continued)*

Step 5: **Modify the Orders Form**

➤ You are in the Design view. Maximize the window (if necessary), then **click and drag the bottom of the Details section** down to give yourself additional room in which to work.

➤ It takes time (and a little practice) to move and size the controls within a form. Try the indicated command, then click the **Undo button** if you are not satisfied with the result.

➤ Click and drag the control for the subform and its label toward the form footer. Select the label of the subform control, then press the **Del key** to delete the label as shown in Figure 6.6e. Click and drag the left border of the subform control toward the left to make the subform wider.

➤ Click the **PhoneNumber control** to select the control and display the sizing handles, then drag the control above the subform control.

➤ Click and drag the controls for **City**, **State**, and **ZipCode** (one at a time) on the line above the PhoneNumber control.

➤ Click and drag the **LastName control** so that it is next to the FirstName control. Click and drag the **Address control** under the control for FirstName.

➤ Move the **CustomerID control** to the right of the OrderID control. Click and drag the **OrderDate control** so that it is next to the CustomerID. The width of the form will change automatically if the form is not wide enough. You may, however, need to extend the width a little further when you release the mouse.

➤ Select the **Page Break tool** then click below the subform control to insert a page break on the form. The page break will print one order per page.

➤ Adjust the size, spacing, and alignment of the labels as necessary, switching back and forth between Form view and Design view. Save the form.

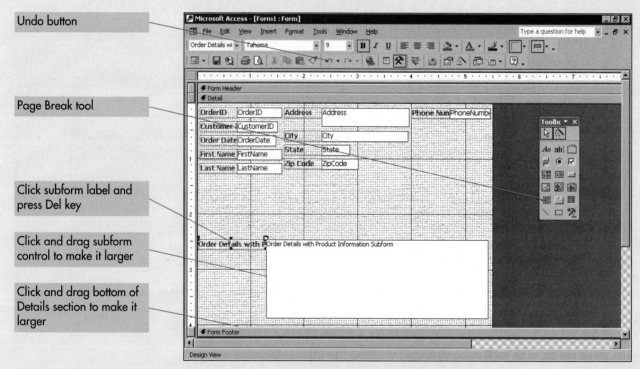

(e) Modify the Orders Form (step 5)

FIGURE 6.6 *Hands-on Exercise 2 (continued)*

Step 6:   **Change the Column Widths**

➤ Click the **View button** to change to the Form view. You should see the first order in the database together with the associated product information. You may, however, have to adjust the width of the columns within the subform and/or change the size and position of the subform within the main form.

➤ To change the width of the columns within the subform:
- Click the **down arrow** on the **View button** and change to the **Datasheet view**. Click the **plus sign** next to the OrderID column for the first order to display the related records as shown in Figure 6.6f.
- Click and drag the various column headings until you can read all of the information. Click the **Save button** to save the new layout, then close the form. You must close the main form, then reopen the form for the changes in the subform to be visible.
- You should be back in the Database window. Double click the **Super Store Order form** to reopen the form and check the width of the columns in the subform. If necessary, click the **down arrow** on the **View button** to return to the Datasheet view to further adjust the columns.

➤ It may also be necessary to change the size or position of the subform within the main form. Click the **View button** and change to the **Design view**.

➤ Click and drag a sizing handle to change the size of the subform. Click and drag the subform control to change its position. If necessary, extend the width of the form.

➤ The process is one of trial and error, but it should take only a few minutes to size the subform properly. Save the completed form.

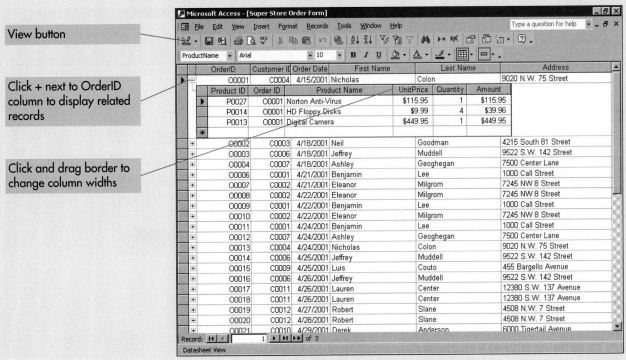

View button

Click + next to OrderID column to display related records

Click and drag border to change column widths

(f) Change the Column Widths (step 6)

FIGURE 6.6   *Hands-on Exercise 2 (continued)*

Step 7: **Enter a New Order**

➤ Change to the **Form view** of the Orders form as shown in Figure 6.6g. The navigation buttons on the main form let you move from one order to the next. The navigation buttons on the subform move between products in an order.

➤ Click the **New Record button** on the main form to display a blank form so that you can place an order.

➤ Click in the **Customer ID** text box. Enter **13** (your customer number from exercise 1), then press the **Tab** or **enter key** to move to the next field.

• The OrderID is entered automatically as it is an AutoNumber field and assigned the next sequential number.

• All of your customer information (your name, address, and phone number) is entered automatically because of the AutoLookup feature that is built into the underlying query.

• Today's date is entered automatically because of the default value (=Date( ) that is built into the Orders table.

➤ Click the **Product ID** text box in the subform. Enter **1** (not P0001) and press the **enter key** to move to the next field. The OrderID (O0026) is entered automatically, as are the Product Name and Unit Price.

➤ Press the **Tab key** three times to move to the Quantity field, enter **1**, and press the **Tab key** twice more to move to the ProductID field for the next item. (The amount is calculated automatically.)

➤ Complete your order as shown in Figure 6.6g. The navigation buttons in the figure show that you are currently working in the third (of three) order detail records, in the 25th (of twenty-five) orders.

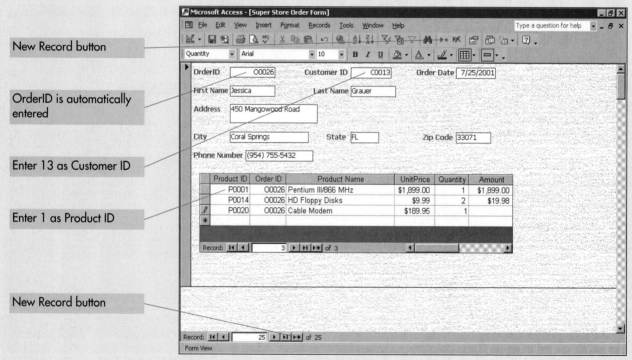

(g) Enter a New Order (step 7)

FIGURE 6.6 *Hands-on Exercise 2 (continued)*

Step 8: **Print the Completed Order**

➤ Click the **Selection Area** to select the current record (the order you just completed).

➤ Pull down the **File menu**. Click **Page Setup** to display the Page Setup dialog box as shown in Figure 6.6h. Click the **Page tab**, then click the **Landscape option** button so that your form will fit on the page. (Alternatively, you could click the **Margins tab** and decrease the left and right margins.) Click **OK**.

➤ Pull down the **File menu**, click **Print** to display the Print dialog box, then click the option button to specify **Selected Record(s)** as the print range. (You should not click the Print button on the toolbar, as that will print every record.)

➤ Click **OK** to print the form. Close the form, then close the database. Answer **Yes** if asked to save the changes.

➤ Exit Access if you do not want to continue with the next exercise at this time.

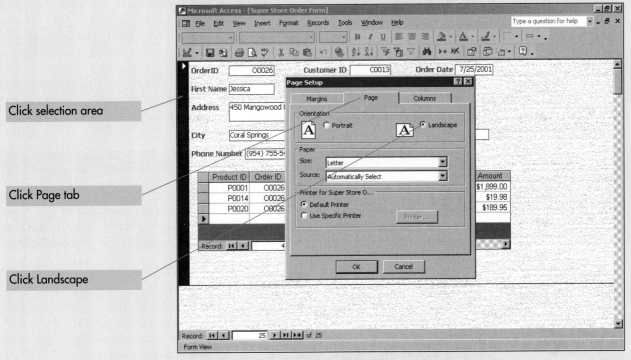

Click selection area

Click Page tab

Click Landscape

(h) Print the Completed Order (step 8)

FIGURE 6.6 *Hands-on Exercise 2 (continued)*

ADDING CUSTOMERS

The order form enables you to add an order for a new customer in the process of creating an order for that customer. Click the New Record button to add a new order, leave the CustomerID field blank, then complete the customer information (name, address, etc.) in the upper part of the form. (You need to enter at least one field, after which the CustomerID will be created automatically since it was defined as an AutoNumber field.) Press the enter key after you have entered the last field (telephone number) of customer information.

A select query, powerful as it is, has its limitations. It requires you to enter the criteria directly into the query, which means you have to change the query every time you vary the criteria. What if you wanted to use a different set of criteria (e.g., a different customer's name) every time you ran the "same" query?

A **parameter query** prompts you for the criteria each time you execute the query. It is created in similar fashion to a select query and is illustrated in Figure 6.7. The difference between a parameter query and an ordinary select query is the way in which the criteria are specified. A select query contains the actual criteria. A parameter query, however, contains a **prompt** (message) that will request the criteria when the query is executed.

The design grid in Figure 6.7a creates a parameter query that will display the orders for a particular customer. The query does not contain the customer's name, but a prompt for that name. The prompt is enclosed in square brackets and is displayed in a dialog box in which the user enters the requested data when the query is executed. Thus, the user supplies the customer's name in Figure 6.7b, and the query displays the resulting dynaset in Figure 6.7c. This enables you to run the same query with different criteria; that is, you can enter a different customer name every time you execute the query.

A parameter query may prompt for any number of variables (parameters), which are entered in successive dialog boxes. The parameters are requested in order from left to right, according to the way in which they appear in the design grid.

TOTAL QUERIES

A **total query** performs calculations on a *group* of records using one of several summary (aggregate) functions available within Access. These include the Sum, Count, Avg, Max, and Min functions to determine the total, number of, average, maximum, and minimum values, respectively. Figure 6.8 illustrates the use of a total query to compute the total amount for each order.

Figure 6.8a displays the dynaset from a select query with fields from both the Products and Order Details tables. (The dynaset contains one record for each product in each order and enables us to verify the results of the total query in Figure 6.8c.) Each record in Figure 6.8a contains the price of the product, the quantity ordered, and the amount for that product. There are, for example, three products in order O0001. The first product costs $449.95, the second product costs $39.96 (four units at $9.99 each), and the third product costs $115.95). The total for the order comes to $605.86, which is obtained by (manually) adding the amount field in each of the records for this order.

Figure 6.8b shows the Design view of the total query to calculate the cost of each order. The query contains only two fields, OrderID and Amount. The QBE grid also displays a **Total row** in which each field in the query has either a Group By or aggregate entry. The **Group By** entry under OrderID indicates that the records in the dynaset are to be grouped (aggregated) according to the like values of OrderID; that is, there will be one record in the total query for each distinct value of OrderID. The **Sum function** specifies the arithmetic operation to be performed on that field for each group of records.

The dynaset in Figure 6.8c displays the result of the total query and contains *aggregate* records, as opposed to *individual* records. There are three records for order O0001 in Figure 6.8a, but only one record in Figure 6.8c. This is because each record in a total query contains a calculated result for a group of records.

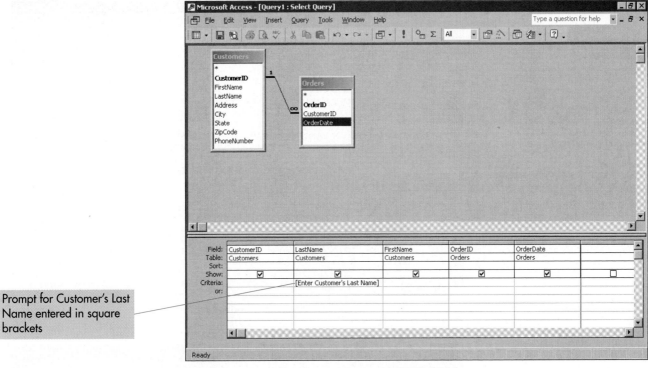

Prompt for Customer's Last Name entered in square brackets

(a) Design Grid

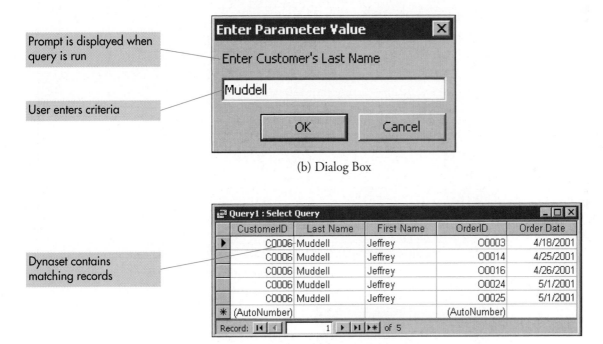

Prompt is displayed when query is run

User enters criteria

(b) Dialog Box

Dynaset contains matching records

(c) Dynaset

FIGURE 6.7   *Paramter Query*

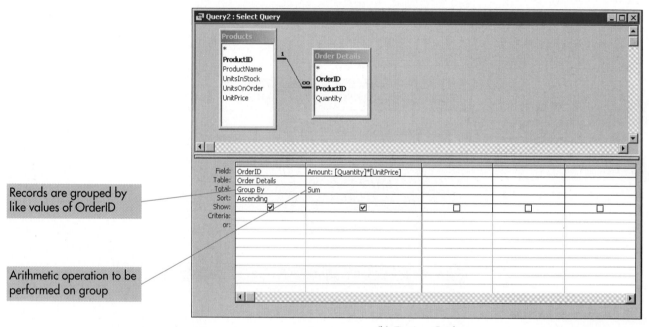

Three products are included in order O0001

Amount for each product in order O0001

(a) Order Details with Product Information Dynaset

Records are grouped by like values of OrderID

Arithmetic operation to be performed on group

(b) Design Grid

(c) Dynaset

FIGURE 6.8 *Total Query*

The exercise that follows begins by having you create the report in Figure 6.9. The report is a detailed analysis of all orders, listing every product in every order. The report is based on a query containing fields from the Orders, Customers, Products, and Order Details tables. The exercise also provides practice in creating parameter queries and total queries.

Sales Analysis by Order

Prepared by Jessica Grauer

			Product Name	Quantity	UnitPrice	Amount
O0001	Colon	4/15/2001				
			Digital Camera	1	$449.95	$449.95
			HD Floppy Disks	4	$9.99	$39.96
			Norton Anti-Virus	1	$115.95	$115.95
					Sum	$605.86
O0002	Goodman	4/18/2001				
			17" CRT Monitor	1	$499.00	$499.00
			Cable Modem	1	$189.95	$189.95
			Digital Photography	1	$1,395.00	$1,395.
			Pentium III/866 MHz	1	$1,899.00	$1,899.
					Sum	$3,982.95
O0003	Muddell	4/18/2001				
			Cable Modem	1	$189.95	$189.95
			Digital Photography	1	$1,395.00	$1,395.
			Pentium III	1	$2,599.00	$2,599.
					Sum	$4,183.95
O0004	Geoghegan	4/18/2001				
			36 GB SCSI Hard	1	$799.00	$799.00
			Digital Photography	2	$1,395.00	$2,790.
			Pentium IV/1.4 GHz	1	$2,099.00	$2,099.
					Sum	$5,688.00
O0006	Lee	4/21/2001				
			19" CRT Monitor	1	$899.00	$899.00
			HD Floppy Disks	10	$9.99	$99.90
					Sum	$998.90
O0007	Milgrom	4/21/2001				
			Microsoft Cinemania	3	$59.95	$179.85
			Microsoft Scenes	1	$29.95	$29.95

Wednesday, July 25, 2001   **Page 1 of 4**

FIGURE 6.9   *Sales Analysis by Order*

ADVANCED QUERIES

Objective   To copy an existing query; to create a parameter query; to create a total
query using the Aggregate Sum function. Use Figure 6.10 as a guide.

Step 1:   **Create the Query**

➤ Open the **Computer Store database** from the previous exercise. Click the
Queries button in the Database window. Double click **Create query in Design
view** to display the Query Design window.

➤ By now you have had sufficient practice creating a query, so we will just outline
the steps:

• Add the **Customers**, **Orders**, **Products**, and **Order Details** tables. Move and
size the field lists within the Query window to match Figure 6.10a. Maximize
the window.

• Add the indicated fields to the design grid. Be sure to take each field from
the appropriate table.

• Add the calculated field to compute the amount by multiplying the quantity
by the unit price. Point to the expression, click the **right mouse button** to display a shortcut menu, then change the Format property to **Currency**.

• Check that your query matches Figure 6.10a. Save the query as **Sales
Analysis by Order**.

➤ Click the **Run button** (the exclamation point) to run the query. The dynaset
contains one record for every item in every order. Close the query.

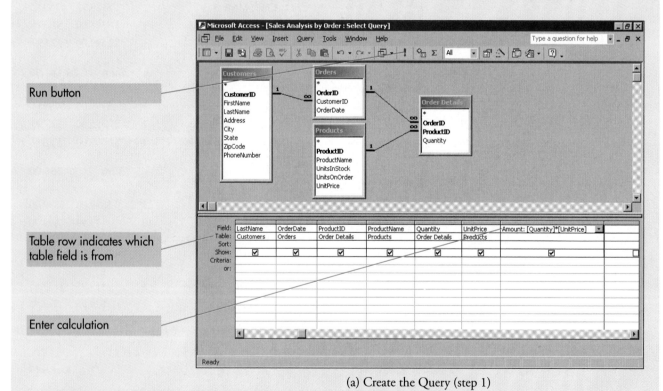

(a) Create the Query (step 1)

FIGURE 6.10   *Hands-on Exercise 3*

Step 2:   **The Report Wizard**

➤ Click the **Reports button** in the Database window. Double click the **Create report by using Wizard** icon to start the Report Wizard.

➤ Click the **drop-down arrow** to display the tables and queries in the database, then select **Sales Analysis by Order** (the query you just created).

➤ By now you have had sufficient practice using the Report Wizard, so we will just outline the steps:

 • Select all of the fields in the query *except* the ProductID. Click the **>> button** to move every field in the Available Fields list box to the Selected Fields list.

 • Select the **ProductID field** in the Selected Fields list and click the **< button** to remove this field. Click **Next**.

 • Group the report by **OrderID**. Click **Next**.

 • Sort the report by **ProductName**. Click the **Summary Options button** to display the Summary Options dialog box in Figure 6.10b. Check **Sum** under the Amount field. The option button to **Show Detail and Summary** is selected. Click **OK** to close the Summary Options dialog box. Click **Next**.

 • The **Stepped Layout** is selected, as is **Portrait orientation**. Be sure the box is checked to **Adjust field width so all fields fit on a page**. Click **Next**.

 • Choose **Bold** as the style. Click **Next**.

 • **Sales Analysis by Order** is entered as the title of the report. The option button to **Preview the Report** is selected. Click **Finish**.

➤ The report you see approximates the finished report, but requires several modifications to improve the formatting. The OrderDate and LastName, for example, are repeated for every product in an order, when they should appear only once in the group (OrderID) header.

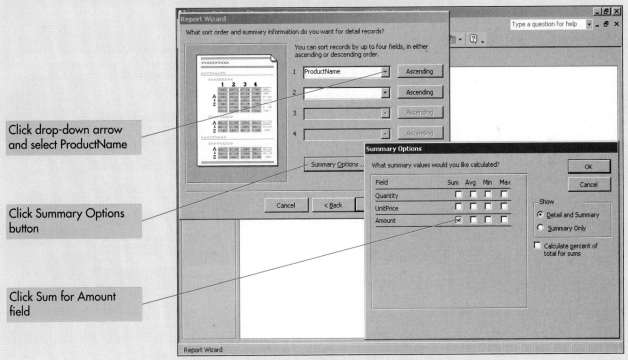

(b) The Report Wizard (step 2)

FIGURE 6.10   *Hands-on Exercise 3 (continued)*

Step 3: **Modify the Report Design**

➤ Click the **Close button** to change to the Design view to modify the report as shown in Figure 6.10c.

➤ Press and hold the **Shift key** as you click the **OrderDate** and **LastName** controls to select both controls, then drag the controls to the group header next to the OrderID.

➤ Click anywhere in the report to deselect the controls after they have been moved. Press and hold the **Shift key** to select the **OrderID**, **OrderDate**, and **LastName** labels in the Page Header. Press the **Del key** to delete the labels.

➤ Size the **Quantity**, **UnitPrice**, and **Amount controls** (and their **labels**). Move the **ProductName control** and its **label** closer to the other controls.

➤ Click the **OrderID control** in the OrderID header. Click the **right mouse button**, click **Properties**, and change the Border Style to **Transparent**. Close the Properties dialog box.

➤ Click the **Label** tool, then click and drag in the report header to create an unbound control under the title of the report. Type **Prepared by:** followed by your name as shown in Figure 6.10c.

➤ Select (click) the first control in the OrderID footer (which begins with "Summary for"). Press the **Del key**.

➤ Click and drag the unbound control containing the word **Sum** to the right of the group footer so that the label is next to the computed total for each order. Do the same for the Grand Total label in the Report footer.

➤ Click the **Save button** to save the report, then click the **View button** to preview the report.

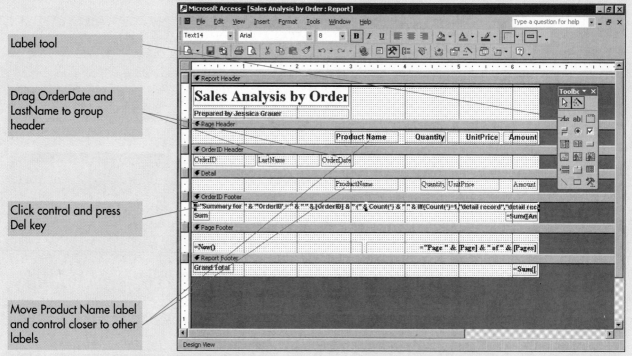

Label tool

Drag OrderDate and LastName to group header

Click control and press Del key

Move Product Name label and control closer to other labels

(c) Modify the Report Design (step 3)

FIGURE 6.10   *Hands-on Exercise 3 (continued)*

Step 4: **Print the Report**

➤ You should see the report in Figure 6.10d, which groups the reports by OrderID. The products are in alphabetical order within each order.
➤ Click the **Zoom button** to see the entire page. Click the **Zoom button** a second time to return to the higher magnification.
➤ Use the navigation buttons at the bottom of the window to see other pages in the report.
➤ Click the **Printer button** if you are satisfied with the appearance of the report, or return to the Design view to make any needed changes.
➤ Pull down the **File menu** and click **Close** to close the report. Click **Yes** if asked whether to save the changes.

Printer button

Zoom button

Report is grouped by OrderID

Products within each order are in alphabetical order

Click forward button to see next page

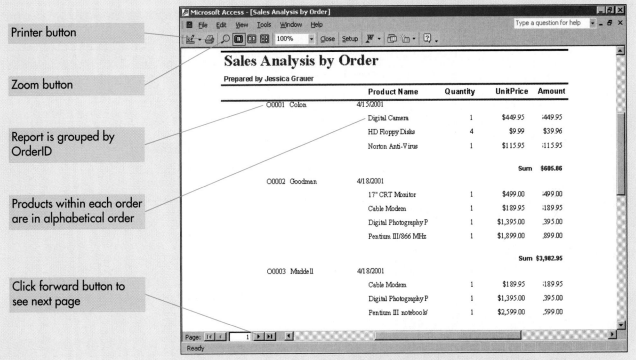

(d) Print the Report (step 4)

FIGURE 6.10   *Hands-on Exercise 3 (continued)*

Products within each order are in alphabetical order

THE UNMATCHED QUERY WIZARD

The cost of inventory is a significant expense for every business. It is one thing to maintain inventory of products that are selling well, and quite another to stock products that have never been ordered. The Unmatched Query Wizard identifies records in one table (such as the Products table) that do not have matching records in another table (such as the Order Details table). In other words, it will tell you which products (if any) have never been ordered. See exercise 2 at the end of the chapter.

Step 5: **Copy an Existing Query**

➤ If necessary, return to the Database window, then click the **Queries button** in the Database window.

➤ Click the **Sales Analysis by Order query** to select the query as shown in Figure 6.10e.

➤ Pull down the **Edit menu** and click **Copy** (or use the **Ctrl+C** shortcut) to copy the query to the clipboard.

➤ Pull down the **Edit menu** and click **Paste** (or use **Ctrl+V** shortcut) to produce the Paste As dialog box in Figure 6.10e. Type **Sales Totals**. Click **OK**.

➤ The Database window contains the original query (Sales Analysis by Order) as well as the copied version (Sales Totals) you just created.

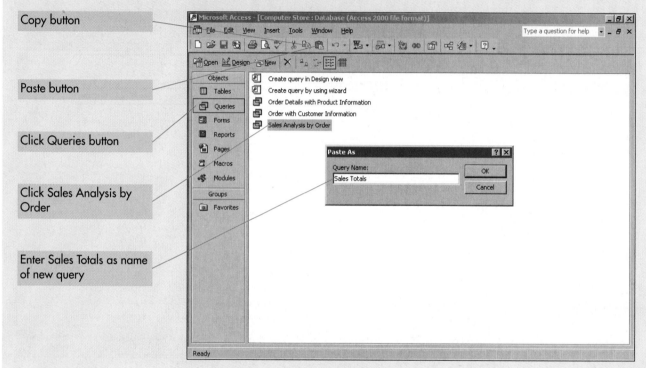

Copy button

Paste button

Click Queries button

Click Sales Analysis by Order

Enter Sales Totals as name of new query

(e) Copy an Existing Query (step 5)

FIGURE 6.10   *Hands-on Exercise 3 (continued)*

COPY, DELETE, OR RENAME A REPORT

The Database window enables you to copy, delete, or rename any object (a table, form, query, or report) in an Access database. To copy an object, select the object, pull down the Edit menu, and click Copy. Pull down the Edit menu a second time, click Paste, then enter the name of the copied object. To delete or rename an object, point to the object, then click the right mouse button to display a shortcut menu, and select the desired operation.

Step 6: **Create a Total Query**

➤ Select the newly created **Sales Totals query**. Click the **Design button** to open the Query Design window in Figure 6.10f.
➤ Click the **column selector** for the **OrderDate field** to select the column. Press the **Del key** to delete the field from the query. Delete the **ProductID**, **ProductName**, **Quantity**, and **UnitPrice fields** in similar fashion.
➤ Pull down the **View menu** and click **Totals** to display the Total row (or click the **Totals button** on the toolbar).
➤ Click the **Total row** under the Amount field, then click the **drop-down arrow** to display the summary functions. Click **Sum** as shown in the figure.
➤ Save the query.

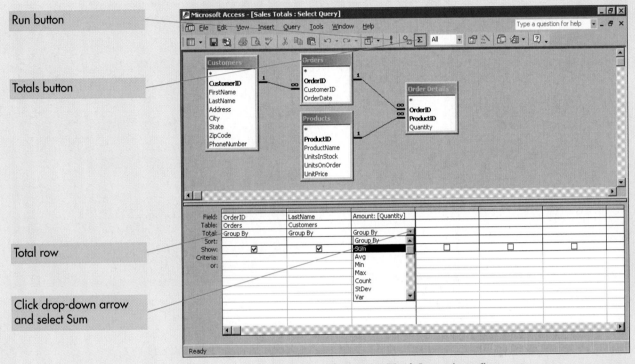

Run button

Totals button

Total row

Click drop-down arrow and select Sum

(f) Create a Total Query (step 6)

FIGURE 6.10 *Hands-on Exercise 3 (continued)*

THE DESCRIPTION PROPERTY

A working database will contain many different objects of the same type, making it all too easy to forget the purpose of the individual objects. The Description property helps you to remember. Point to any object within the Database window, click the right mouse button to display a shortcut menu, click Properties to display the Properties dialog box, enter an appropriate description, then click OK to close the Properties sheet. Once a description has been created, you can right click any object in the Database window, then click the Properties command from the shortcut menu to display the information.

Step 7:   **Run the Query**

➤ Pull down the **Query menu** and click **Run** (or click the **Run button**) to run the query. You should see the datasheet in Figure 6.10g, which contains one record for each order with the total amount of that order.
➤ Click any field and attempt to change its value. You will be unable to do so as indicated by the beep and the message in the status bar, indicating that the recordset is not updatable.
➤ Click the **Design View button** to return to the Query Design view.

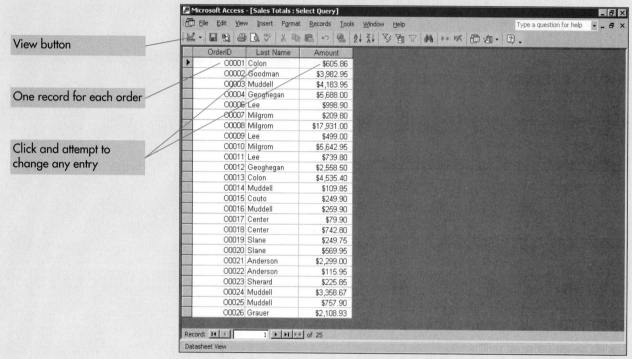

(g) Run the Query (step 7)

FIGURE 6.10   *Hands-on Exercise 3 (continued)*

UPDATING THE QUERY

The changes made to a query's dynaset are automatically made in the underlying table(s). Not every field in a query is updatable, however, and the easiest way to determine if you can change a value is to run the query, view the dynaset, and attempt to edit the field. Access will prevent you from updating a calculated field, a field based on an aggregate function (such as Sum or Count), or the join field on the "one side" of a one-to-many relationship. If you attempt to update a field you cannot change, the status bar will display a message indicating why the change is not allowed.

Step 8: **Create a Parameter Query**

➤ Click the **Criteria row** under **LastName**. Type **[Enter Customer's Last Name]**. Be sure to enclose the entry in square brackets.

➤ Pull down the **File menu**. Click **Save As**. Enter **Customer Parameter Query** in the Save Query "Sales Total" To box. Click **OK**.

➤ Run the query. Access will display the dialog box in Figure 6.10h, asking for the Customer's last name. Type **your name** and press **enter**. Access displays the information for your order(s). Close the query.

Run button

Enter your name in response to prompt

Enter prompt in square brackets

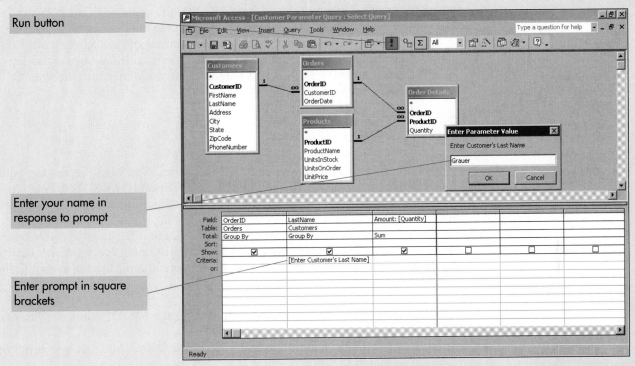

(h) Create a Parameter Query (step 8)

FIGURE 6.10   *Hands-on Exercise 3 (continued)*

THE TOPVALUES PROPERTY

The TopValues property returns a designated number of records rather than the entire dynaset. Open the query in Design view, then click the right mouse button *outside* the design grid to display a shortcut menu. Click Properties, click the box for TopValues, and enter the desired value as either a number or a percent; for example, 5 to list the top five records, or 5% to display the records that make up the top five percent. The dynaset must be in sequence according to the desired field for the TopValues property to work properly.

Step 9: **Exit Access**

➤ Exit Access if you do not want to continue with the next exercise. (Do not be concerned if Access indicates it will empty the clipboard.)

One of the advantages of an Access database is that it can be easily expanded to include additional data without disturbing the existing tables. The database used throughout the chapter consisted of four tables: a Customers table, a Products table, an Orders table, and an Order Details table. Figure 6.11 extends the database to include a Sales Persons table with data about each member of the sales staff.

The salesperson helps the customer as he or she comes into the store, then receives a commission based on the order. There is a one-to-many relationship between the salesperson and orders. One salesperson can generate many orders, but an order can have only one salesperson. The Sales Persons and Orders tables are joined by the SalesPersonID field, which is common to both tables.

Figure 6.11 is similar to Figure 6.1 at the beginning of the chapter except that the Sales Persons table has been added and the Orders table has been expanded to include a SalesPersonID. This enables management to monitor the performance of the sales staff. Consider:

Query: How many orders has Cori Rice taken?
Answer: Cori has taken five orders.

The query is straightforward and easily answered. You would search the Sales Persons table for Cori Rice to determine her SalesPerson ID (S03). You would then search the Orders table and count the records containing S03 in the SalesPersonID field.

The Sales Persons table is also used to generate a report listing the commissions due to each salesperson. The store pays a 5% commission on every sale. It's easy to determine the salesperson for each order. It's more complicated to compute the commission. Consider:

Query: Which salesperson is associated with order O0003? When was this person hired?
Answer: Cori Rice is the salesperson for order O0003. Ms. Rice was hired on March 15, 1993.

The determination of the salesperson is straightforward, as all you have to do is search the Orders table to locate the order and obtain the SalesPerson ID (S03). You then search the Sales Persons table for this value (S03) and find the corresponding name (Cori Rice) and hire date (3/15/93).

Query: What is the commission on order O0003?
Answer: The commission on order O0003 is $209.20.

The calculation of the commission requires a fair amount of arithmetic. First, you need to compute the total amount of the order. Thus, you would begin in the Order Details table, find each product in order O0003, and multiply the quantity of that product by its unit price. The total cost of order O0003 is $4,183.95, based on one unit of product P0005 at $2,599, one unit of product P0020 at $189.95, and one unit of product P0022 at $1,395. (You can also refer to the sales report in Figure 6.9 that was developed in the previous exercise to check these calculations.)

Now that you know the total cost of the order, you can compute the commission, which is 5% of the total order, or $209.20 (.05 × $4,183.95). The complete calculation is lengthy, but Access does it automatically, and therein lies the beauty of a relational database.

(a) Customers Table

CustomerID	FirstName	LastName	Address	City	State	ZipCode	PhoneNumber
C0001	Benjamin	Lee	1000 Call Street	Tallahassee	FL	33340	(904)327-4124
C0002	Eleanor	Milgrom	7245 NW 8 Street	Margate	FL	33065	(305)974-1234
C0003	Neil	Goodman	4215 South 81 Street	Margate	FL	33065	(305)444-5555
C0004	Nicholas	Colon	9020 N.W. 75 Street	Coral Springs	FL	33065	(305)753-9887
C0005	Michael	Ware	276 Brickell Avenue	Miami	FL	33131	(305)444-3980
C0006	Jeffrey	Muddell	9522 S.W. 142 Street	Miami	FL	33176	(305)253-3909
C0007	Ashley	Geoghegan	7500 Center Lane	Coral Springs	FL	33070	(305)753-7830
C0008	Serena	Sherard	5000 Jefferson Lane	Gainesville	FL	32601	(904)375-6442
C0009	Luis	Couto	455 Bargello Avenue	Coral Gables	FL	33146	(305)666-4801
C0010	Derek	Anderson	6000 Tigertail Avenue	Coconut Grove	FL	33120	(305)446-8900
C0011	Lauren	Center	12380 S.W. 137 Avenue	Miami	FL	33186	(305)385-4432
C0012	Robert	Slane	4508 N.W. 7 Street	Miami	FL	33131	(305)635-3454
C0013	Jessica	Grauer	450 Mangowood Road	Coral Springs	FL	33071	(305)755-5432

(a) Customers Table

(b) Products Table

ProductID	Product Name	Units In Stock	Units On Order	Unit Price
P0001	Pentium III/866 MHz	50	0	$1,899.00
P0002	Pentium III/1 GHz	25	5	$1,999.00
P0003	Pentium IV/1.4 GHz	125	15	$2,099.00
P0004	Pentium IV/1.5 GHz	25	50	$2,299.00
P0005	Pentium III notebook/850MHz	15	25	$2,599.00
P0006	17" CRT Monitor	50	0	$499.00
P0007	19" CRT Monitor	25	10	$899.00
P0008	21" CRT Monitor	50	20	$1,599.00
P0009	3 Years On Site Service	15	20	$399.00
P0010	36 GB SCSI Hard Drive	25	15	$799.00
P0011	73.4 GB SCSI Hard Drive	10	0	$1,245.00
P0012	2.6 GB DVD Drive	40	0	$249.00
P0013	Digital Camera	50	15	$449.95
P0014	HD Floppy Disks	500	200	$9.99
P0015	Zip Cartridges	100	50	$14.79
P0016	Digital Scanner	15	3	$179.95
P0017	Serial Mouse	150	50	$69.95
P0018	Trackball	55	0	$59.95
P0019	Joystick	250	100	$39.95
P0020	Cable Modem	35	10	$189.95
P0021	Fax/Modem 56 Kbps	20	0	$65.95
P0022	Digital Photography Package	100	15	$1,395.00
P0023	Ink Jet Printer	50	50	$249.95
P0024	Laser Printer (personal)	125	25	$569.95
P0025	Windows Me	400	200	$95.95
P0026	Windows 98	150	50	$75.95
P0027	Norton Anti-Virus	150	50	$115.95
P0028	Microsoft Scenes Screen Saver	75	25	$29.95
P0029	Microsoft Bookshelf	250	100	$129.95
P0030	Microsoft Cinemania	25	10	$59.95
P0031	Surge Protector	15	0	$45.95

(b) Products Table

(c) Orders Table

OrderID	CustomerID	OrderDate	SalesPersonID
O0001	C0004	4/15/2001	S01
O0002	C0003	4/18/2001	S02
O0003	C0006	4/18/2001	S03
O0004	C0007	4/18/2001	S04
O0006	C0001	4/21/2001	S05
O0007	C0002	4/21/2001	S01
O0008	C0002	4/22/2001	S02
O0009	C0001	4/22/2001	S03
O0010	C0002	4/22/2001	S04
O0011	C0001	4/24/2001	S05
O0012	C0007	4/24/2001	S01
O0013	C0004	4/24/2001	S02
O0014	C0006	4/25/2001	S03
O0015	C0009	4/25/2001	S04
O0016	C0006	4/26/2001	S05
O0017	C0011	4/26/2001	S01
O0018	C0011	4/26/2001	S02
O0019	C0012	4/27/2001	S03
O0020	C0012	4/28/2001	S04
O0021	C0010	4/29/2001	S05
O0022	C0010	4/29/2001	S01
O0023	C0008	4/30/2001	S02
O0024	C0006	5/1/2001	S03
O0025	C0006	5/1/2001	S04
O0026	C0013	7/25/2001	S05

(c) Orders Table

(d) Order Details Table

OrderID	ProductID	Quantity
O0001	P0013	1
O0001	P0014	4
O0001	P0027	1
O0002	P0001	1
O0002	P0006	1
O0002	P0020	1
O0002	P0022	1
O0003	P0005	1
O0003	P0020	1
O0003	P0022	1
O0004	P0003	1
O0004	P0010	1
O0004	P0022	2
O0005	P0003	2
O0005	P0012	2
O0005	P0016	2
O0006	P0007	1
O0006	P0014	10
O0007	P0028	1
O0007	P0030	3
O0008	P0001	1
O0008	P0004	3
O0008	P0008	4
O0008	P0011	2
O0008	P0012	1
O0009	P0006	1
O0010	P0002	2
O0010	P0022	1
O0010	P0023	1
O0011	P0016	2
O0011	P0020	2
O0012	P0021	10
O0012	P0029	10
O0012	P0030	10
O0013	P0009	4
O0013	P0016	10
O0013	P0024	2
O0014	P0019	2
O0014	P0028	1
O0015	P0018	1
O0015	P0020	1
O0016	P0029	2
O0017	P0019	2
O0018	P0009	1
O0018	P0025	2
O0018	P0026	2
O0019	P0014	25
O0020	P0024	1
O0021	P0004	1
O0022	P0027	1
O0023	P0021	1
O0023	P0028	1
O0023	P0029	1
O0024	P0007	1
O0024	P0013	5
O0024	P0014	3
O0024	P0016	1
O0025	P0012	2
O0025	P0029	2
O0026	P0001	1
O0026	P0014	2
O0026	P0020	1

(d) Order Details Table

(e) Sales Persons Table

SalesPersonID	FirstName	LastName	WorkPhone	HireDate
S01	Linda	Black	(305) 284-6105	02/03/93
S02	Michael	Vaughn	(305) 284-3993	02/10/93
S03	Cori	Rice	(305) 284-2557	03/15/93
S04	Karen	Ruenheck	(305) 284-4641	01/31/94
S05	Richard	Linger	(305) 284-4662	01/31/94

(e) Sales Persons Table

FIGURE 6.11 *Super Store Database*

The Sales Commission Query

Figure 6.12a displays the design view of a parameter query to calculate the commissions for a specific salesperson. (This query determines the commissions for Cori Rice, which you computed manually in the previous discussion.) Enter the last name of the sales associate, Rice, and the query returns the dynaset in Figure 6.12b, showing all of her commissions. Note, too, that the commission returned for order O0003 is $209.20, which corresponds to the amount we arrived at earlier.

The query in Figure 6.12a includes fields from all five tables in the database. The relationships are shown graphically in the top half of the query window and reflect the earlier discussion—for example, the one-to-many relationship between salespersons and orders. These tables are joined through the SalesPersonID field, which is the primary key in the Sales Persons table but a foreign key in the Orders table. (The Orders table has been modified to include this field.)

The following exercise has you import the Sales Persons table from another Access database. It then directs you to modify the existing Orders table to include a SalesPerson ID, which references the records in the Sales Persons table, and to modify the Super Store Order Form to include the salesperson data.

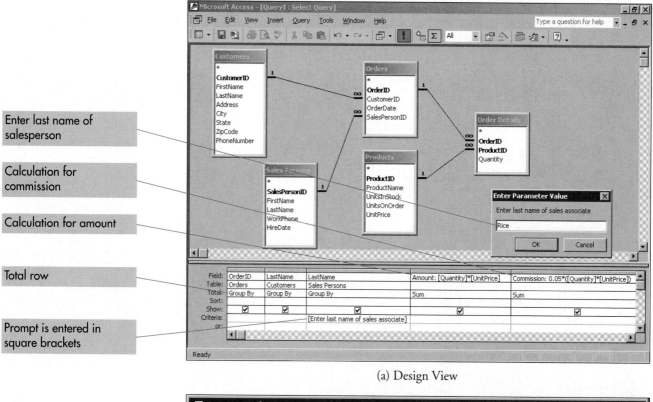

(a) Design View

(b) Dynaset

FIGURE 6.12   *Sales Commission*

EXPANDING THE DATABASE

Objective To import a table from another database; to modify the design of an existing table. Use Figure 6.13 as a guide in the exercise.

Step 1: **Import the Sales Persons Table**

> ➤ Open the **Computer Store database**. Click the **Tables button**. Pull down the **File menu**. Click **Get External Data**, then click the **Import** command.
> ➤ Click (select) the **Sales Persons database** from the **Exploring Access folder**, then click **Import** to display the Import Objects dialog box in Figure 6.13a.
> ➤ If necessary, click the **Tables button**, click **SalesPersons** (the only table in this database), then click **OK**. A dialog box will appear briefly on your screen as the Sales Persons table is imported into the Computer Store database.

Click Tables tab

Click Sales Persons

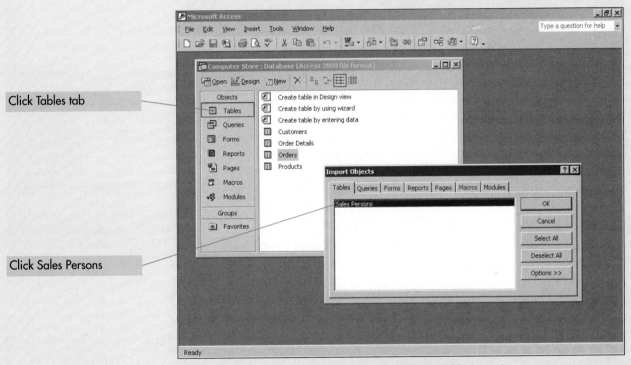

(a) Import the Sales Persons Table (step 1)

FIGURE 6.13 *Hands-on Exercise 4*

THE DOCUMENTS SUBMENU

The Documents menu contains shortcuts to the last 15 files that were opened. Click the Start button, click (or point to) the Documents menu, then click the document you wish to open (e.g., Computer Store), assuming that it appears on the menu. Windows will start the application, then open the indicated document.

Step 2: **Modify the Orders Table Design**

➤ Select the **Orders table** from the Database window as shown in Figure 6.13b. Click the **Design button**.

➤ Click in the first available row in the **Field Name** column. Enter **SalesPersonID** as shown in Figure 6.13b. Choose **Number** as the data type. The Field Size property changes to Long Integer by default.
  • Click the **Format** property. Enter **\S00**.
  • Click the **Default Value** property and delete the **0**.

➤ Click the **Save button** to save the modified design of the Orders table.

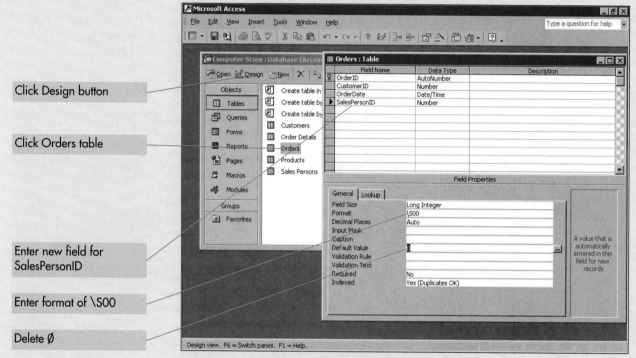

Click Design button

Click Orders table

Enter new field for
SalesPersonID

Enter format of \S00

Delete 0

(b) Modify the Orders Table Design (step 2)

FIGURE 6.13 *Hands-on Exercise 4 (continued)*

RELATIONSHIPS AND THE AUTONUMBER FIELD TYPE

The join fields on both sides of a relationship must be the same data type—for example, both number fields or both text fields. The AutoNumber field type, however, cannot be specified on both sides of a relationship. Thus, if the join field (SalesPersonID) in the primary table (Sales Persons) is an AutoNumber field, the join field in the related table (Orders) must be specified as a Number field, with the Field Size property set to Long Integer.

Step 3:   **Add the Sales Person to Existing Orders**

➤ Click the **Datasheet View button** to change to the Datasheet view as shown in Figure 6.13c. Maximize the window.

➤ Enter the **SalesPersonID** for each existing order as shown in Figure 6.13c. (You can now modify the Required property for the SalesPersonID in the Orders table to make this a required field for new orders.)

➤ Enter only the number (e.g., 1, rather than S01) as the S and leading 0 are displayed automatically through the Format property. We are adding the data in random fashion so that we will be able to generate meaningful reports later on in the exercise.

➤ Close the Orders table.

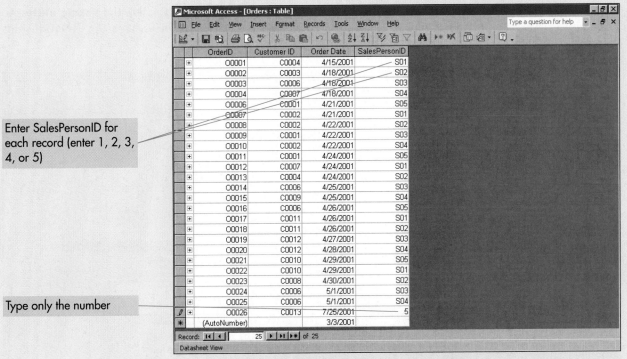

Enter SalesPersonID for each record (enter 1, 2, 3, 4, or 5)

Type only the number

(c) Add the Sales Person to Existing Orders (step 3)

FIGURE 6.13   *Hands-on Exercise 4 (continued)*

HIDE THE WINDOWS TASKBAR

The Windows taskbar is great for novices because it makes task switching as easy as changing channels on a TV. It also takes up valuable real estate on the desktop, and hence you may want to hide the taskbar when you don't need it. Point to an empty area on the taskbar, click the right mouse button to display a shortcut menu, and click Properties to display the Taskbar Properties dialog box. Click the Taskbar Options tab (if necessary), check the box to Autohide the taskbar, and click OK. The taskbar should disappear. Now point to the bottom of the screen (or the edge where the taskbar was last displayed), and it will reappear.

Step 4: **Create the Relationship**

➤ Pull down the **Tools menu**. Click **Relationships** to open the Relationships window as shown in Figure 6.13d. (The Sales Persons table is not yet visible.) Click the **Maximize button**.

➤ If necessary, drag the bottom border of the **Orders table** until you see the SalesPersonID (the field you added in step 2).

➤ Pull down the **Relationships menu**. Click **Show Table**. Click the **Tables button** if necessary, select the **Sales Persons table**, then click the **Add button**. Close the Show Table dialog box.

➤ Drag the title bar of the **SalesPersons table** to position the table as shown in Figure 6.13d. Drag the **SalesPersonID field** from the Sales Persons table to the SalesPersonID in the Orders table.

➤ Check the box to **Enforce Referential Integrity**. Click the **Create button** to create the relationship. Click the **Save button** to save the Relationships window. Close the Relationships window.

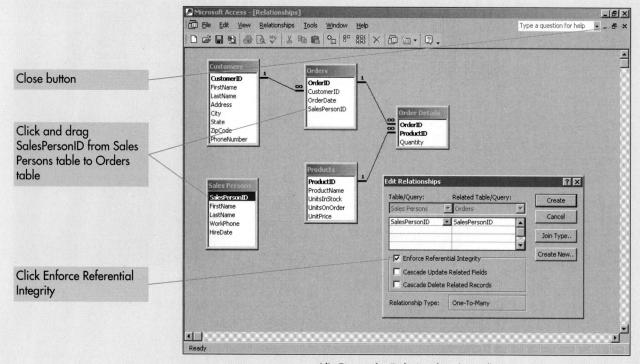

Close button

Click and drag SalesPersonID from Sales Persons table to Orders table

Click Enforce Referential Integrity

(d) Create the Relationship (step 4)

FIGURE 6.13 *Hands-on Exercise 4 (continued)*

PRINT THE RELATIONSHIPS

Pull down the Tools menu and click the Relationships command to open the Relationships window, then pull down the File menu and click the Print Relationships command. You will see the Print Preview screen of a report that displays the contents of the Relationships window. Click the Print button to print the report, or change to the Design view to modify the report, perhaps by adding your name. Save the report after printing so that it will be available at a later time.

Step 5: **Modify the Order with Customer Information Query**

➤ You should be back in the Database window. Click the **Queries button**, select the **Order with Customer Information query**, then click the **Design button** to open the query in the Design view as shown in Figure 6.13e.

➤ If necessary, click and drag the border of the **Orders table** so that the newly added SalesPersonID field is displayed. Click the **horizontal scroll arrow** until a blank column in the design grid is visible.

➤ Click and drag the **SalesPersonID** from the Orders table to the first blank column in the design grid.

➤ Save the query. Close the query.

Drag SalesPersonID to first blank column

Click arrow until blank column is visible

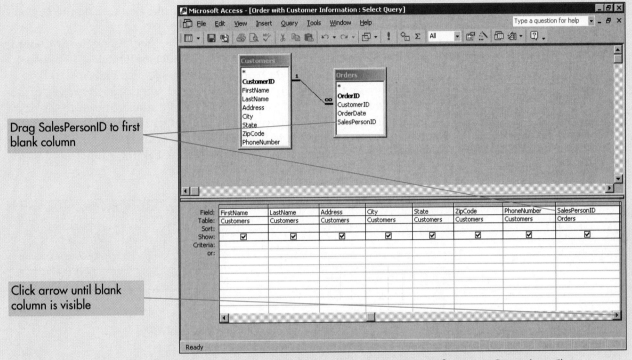

(e) Modify the Order with Customer Information Query (step 5)

FIGURE 6.13 *Hands-on Exercise 4 (continued)*

OPTIMIZE QUERIES USING INDEXES

The performance of a database becomes important as you progress from a "student" database with a limited number of records to a real database with large tables. Thus it becomes advantageous to optimize the performance of individual queries by creating indexes in the underlying tables. Indexes should be specified for any criteria field in a query, as well as for any field that is used in a relationship to join two tables. To create an index, open the table in Design view and set the indexed property to Yes.

Step 6: Modify the Order Form

➤ You should be back in the Database window. Click the **Forms button**, select the **Super Store Order Form**, then click the **Design** button.

➤ Move and size the controls on the first line to make room for the SalesPersonID as shown in Figure 6.13f.

➤ Click the **Combo Box** tool, then click and drag in the form where you want the combo box to go. Release the mouse to start the Combo Box Wizard.

- Check the option button that indicates you want the combo box to look up values in a table or query. Click **Next**.
- Choose the **Sales Persons table** in the next screen. Click **Next**.
- Select the **SalesPersonID** and **LastName**. Click **Next**.
- Adjust the column width if necessary. Be sure the box to hide the key column is checked. Click **Next**.
- Click the option button to store the value in the field. Click the **drop-down arrow** to display the fields and select the **SalesPersonID field**. Click **Next**.
- Enter **Salesperson** as the label for the combo box. Click **Finish**.

➤ Move and/or size the combo box and its label so that it is spaced attractively on the form. Point to the combo box, click the **right mouse button** to display a shortcut menu, and click **Properties**. Click the **Other tab**.

➤ Change the name of the box to **Sales Person.** Close the dialog box.

➤ Pull down the **View menu** and click **Tab Order**. Click the **AutoOrder button**. Click **OK**. Save the form. Change to the Form view.

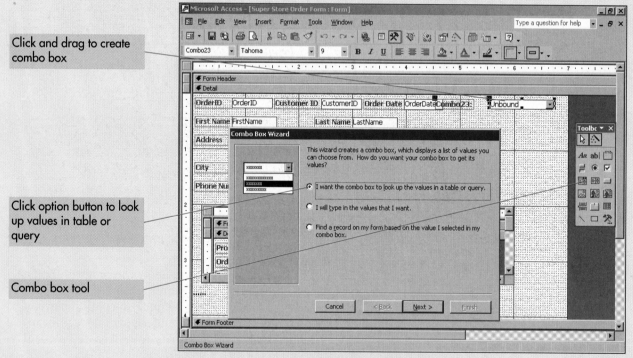

Click and drag to create combo box

Click option button to look up values in table or query

Combo box tool

(f) Modify the Order Form (step 6)

FIGURE 6.13   *Hands-on Exercise 4 (continued)*

Step 7: **The Completed Order Form**

➤ You should see the completed form as shown in Figure 6.13g. Click the **New Record button** on the Form View toolbar to display a blank form so that you can place an order.

➤ Click in the **Customer ID text box**. Enter **13** (your customer number from the first exercise), then press the **Tab key** to move to the next field.
  • The OrderID is entered automatically as it is an AutoNumber field and assigned the next sequential number.
  • All of your customer information (your name, address, and phone number) is entered automatically because of the AutoLookup feature that is built into the underlying query.
  • Today's date is entered automatically because of the default value (=Date( )) that is built into the Orders table.

➤ Click the **drop-down arrow** on the Sales Person combo box. Select **Black** (or click in the box and type **B**), and the complete name is entered automatically.

➤ Click the **ProductID text box** in the subform. Enter **2** (not P0002) and press the **enter key** to move to the next field. The OrderID (O0027) is entered automatically, as are the Product Name and Unit Price.

➤ Press the **Tab key** three times to move to the Quantity field and enter **1**. The amount is computed automatically.

➤ Move to the ProductID field for the next item. Choose any item and enter a quantity.

➤ Close the Order form.

Click the New Record button

OrderID is automatically entered

Enter 13

Click drop-down arrow and select Black

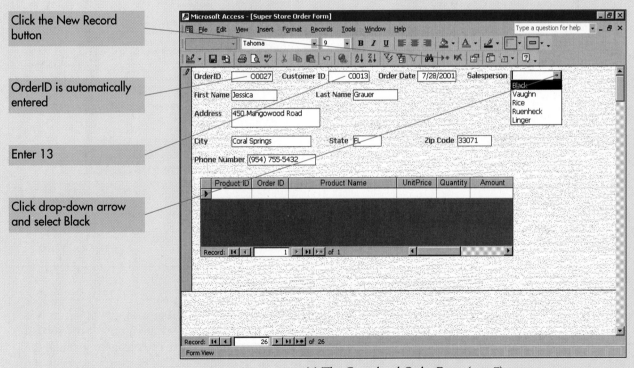

(g) The Completed Order Form (step 7)

FIGURE 6.13 *Hands-on Exercise 4 (continued)*

Step 8: **Database Properties**

➤ You should be back in the Database window. Pull down the **File menu** and click **Database Properties** to display the dialog box in Figure 6.13h. Click the **Contents tab** to display the contents of the Computer Store database.
- There are five tables (Customers, Order Details, Orders, Products, and Sales Persons).
- There are five queries, which include the Total and Parameter queries you created in exercise 3.
- There are two forms—the main form, which you have completed in this exercise, and the associated subform.
- There is one report, the report you created in exercise 3.

➤ Click **OK** to close the dialog box. Close the Computer Store database. Exit Access.

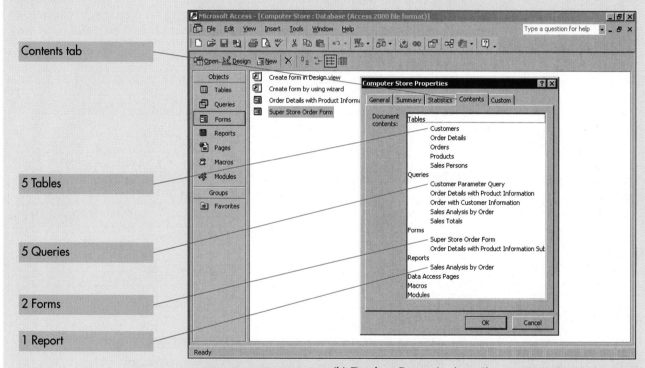

(h) Database Properties (step 8)

FIGURE 6.13   *Hands-on Exercise 4 (continued)*

THE STARTUP PROPERTY

The Startup property determines how a database will appear when it is opened. One very common option is to open a form automatically so that the user is presented with the form without having to navigate through the Database window. Pull down the Tools menu, click Startup to display the Startup dialog box, then click the drop-down arrow in the Display Form list box. Select the desired form (e.g., the Super Store Order form developed in this exercise), then click OK. The next time you open the database the designated form will be opened automatically.

The implementation of a many-to-many relationship requires an additional table whose primary key consists of (at least) the primary keys of the individual tables. The many-to-many table may also contain additional fields whose values are dependent on the combined key. All relationships are created in the Relationships window by dragging the join field from the primary table to the related table. A many-to-many relationship in the physical system is implemented by a pair of one-to-many relationships in an Access database.

Enforcement of referential integrity prevents you from adding a record to the related table if that record contains an invalid value of the foreign key. (You cannot, for example, add a record to the Orders table that contains an invalid value for CustomerID.) Referential integrity also prevents the deletion and/or updating of records on the "one" side of a one-to-many relationship when there are matching records in the related table. The deletion (updating) can take place, however, if the relationship is modified to allow the cascaded deletion (updating) of related records (fields).

Referential integrity does not prevent you from adding a record to the "many" table that omits a value for the field from the "one" table. You could, for example, add a record to the Orders table that omitted CustomerID. If this does not make sense in the physical situation, then you have to make the CustomerID a required field in the Orders table.

There are several reasons to base a form (or subform) on a query rather than a table. A query can contain a calculated field; a table cannot. A query can contain fields from more than one table and take advantage of AutoLookup. A query can also contain selected records from a table and/or display those records in a different sequence from that of the table on which it is based.

A parameter query prompts you for the criteria each time you execute the query. The prompt is enclosed in square brackets and is entered in the Criteria row within the Query Design view. Multiple parameters may be specified within the same query.

Aggregate functions (Avg, Min, Max, Sum, and Count) perform calculations on groups of records. Execution of the query displays an aggregate record for each group, and individual records do not appear. Updating of individual records is not possible in this type of query.

Tables may be added to an Access database without disturbing the data in existing tables. The Get External Data command enables you to import an object(s) from another database.

KEY TERMS

AutoLookup (p. 266)
AutoNumber field (p. 259)
Cascaded deletion (p. 260)
Cascaded updating (p. 260)
Combined key (p. 258)
Description property (p. 285)
Format property (p. 259)
Get External Data command (p. 291)

Group By (p. 276)
Main form (p. 266)
Many-to-many relationship (p. 258)
One-to-many relationship (p. 256)
Parameter query (p. 276)
Primary key (p. 256)
Prompt (p. 276)
Referential integrity (p. 260)
Relationship lines (p. 259)

Relationships window (p. 259)
Startup property (p. 298)
Subform (p. 266)
Sum function (p. 276)
TopValues property (p. 287)
Total query (p. 276)
Total row (p. 276)
Unmatched Query Wizard (p. 283)

1. Which table(s) is(are) necessary to implement a many-to-many relationship between students and the courses they take?
   (a) A Students table
   (b) A Courses table
   (c) A Students-Courses table
   (d) All of the above

2. Which of the following would be suitable as the primary key in a Students-Courses table, where there is a many-to-many relationship between Students and Courses, and further, when a student is allowed to repeat a course?
   (a) The combination of StudentID and CourseID
   (b) The combination of StudentID, CourseID, and semester
   (c) The combination of StudentID, CourseID, semester, and grade
   (d) All of the above are equally appropriate

3. Which of the following is necessary to add a record to the "one" side in a one-to-many relationship in which referential integrity is enforced?
   (a) A unique primary key for the new record
   (b) One or more matching records in the many table
   (c) Both (a) and (b)
   (d) Neither (a) nor (b)

4. Which of the following is necessary to add a record to the "many" side in a one-to-many relationship in which referential integrity is enforced?
   (a) A unique primary key for the new record
   (b) A matching record in the primary table
   (c) Both (a) and (b)
   (d) Neither (a) nor (b)

5. Under which circumstances can you delete a "many" record in a one-to-many relationship?
   (a) Under all circumstances
   (b) Under no circumstances
   (c) By enforcing referential integrity
   (d) By enforcing referential integrity with the cascaded deletion of related records

6. Under which circumstances can you delete the "one" record in a one-to-many relationship?
   (a) Under all circumstances
   (b) Under no circumstances
   (c) By enforcing referential integrity
   (d) By enforcing referential integrity with the cascaded deletion of related records

7. Which of the following would be suitable as the primary key in a Patients-Doctors table, where there is a many-to-many relationship between patients and doctors, and where the same patient can see the same doctor on different visits?
   (a) The combination of PatientID and DoctorID
   (b) The combination of PatientID, DoctorID, and the date of the visit
   (c) Either (a) or (b)
   (d) Neither (a) nor (b)

8. How do you implement the many-to-many relationship between patients and doctors described in the previous question?
   (a) Through a one-to-many relationship between the Patients table and the Patients-Doctors table
   (b) Through a one-to-many relationship between the Doctors table and the Patients-Doctors table
   (c) Both (a) and (b)
   (d) Neither (a) nor (b)

9. A database has a one-to-many relationship between teams and players. Which data type and field size should be assigned to the TeamID field in the Players table, if TeamID is defined as an AutoNumber field in the Teams table?
   (a) AutoNumber and Long Integer
   (b) Number and Long Integer
   (c) Text and Long Integer
   (d) Lookup Wizard and Long Integer

10. Which of the following is true about a main form and an associated subform?
    (a) The main form can be based on a query
    (b) The subform can be based on a query
    (c) Both (a) and (b)
    (d) Neither (a) nor (b)

11. A parameter query:
    (a) Displays a prompt within brackets in the Criteria row of the query
    (b) Is limited to a single parameter
    (c) Both (a) and (b)
    (d) Neither (a) nor (b)

12. Which of the following is available as an aggregate function within a select query?
    (a) Sum and Avg
    (b) Min and Max
    (c) Both (a) and (b)
    (d) Neither (a) nor (b)

13. A query designed to take advantage of AutoLookup requires:
    (a) A unique value for the join field in the "one" side of a relationship
    (b) The join field to be taken from the "many" side of a one-to-many relationship
    (c) Both (a) and (b)
    (d) Neither (a) nor (b)

14. Which of the following can be imported from another Access database?
    (a) Tables and forms
    (b) Queries and reports
    (c) Both (a) and (b)
    (d) Neither (a) nor (b)

15. Which of the following is true of the TopValues query property?
    (a) It can be used to display the top 10 records in a dynaset
    (b) It can be used to display the top 10 percent of the records in a dynaset
    (c) Both (a) and (b)
    (d) Neither (a) nor (b)

ANSWERS

1. d	**6.** d	**11.** a
2. b	**7.** b	**12.** c
3. a	**8.** c	**13.** c
4. a	**9.** b	**14.** c
5. a	**10.** c	**15.** c

BUILDS ON

HANDS-ON
EXERCISE 4
PAGES 291–298

1. Sales Commission Report: This problem continues the Computer Store database that was developed in the chapter. Complete the four hands-on exercises in the chapter, after which you will be able to develop the Sales Commission Report in Figure 6.14. The report is based on a query that is similar to the query in Figure 6.12. The Report Wizard was used to create the report after the query was completed. (The query uses fields from all five tables in the database.) You need not match our design exactly, but you have to display equivalent information. Add your name to the report header, then print the result for your instructor.

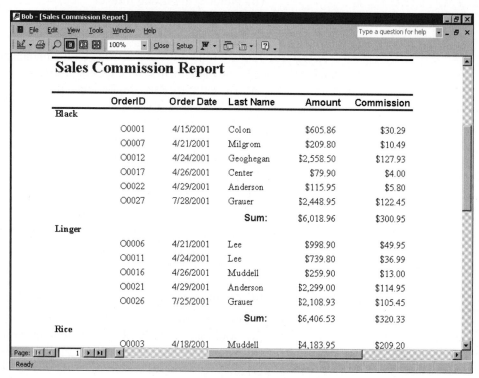

FIGURE 6.14   Sales Commission Report (Exercise 1)

BUILDS ON

HANDS-ON
EXERCISE 4
PAGES 291–298

2. Unmatched Query Wizard: Figure 6.15 displays a query created by the Unmatched Query Wizard to determine those products that have never been ordered. This type of information is very valuable to management, which can realize significant cost savings by eliminating these products from inventory. Proceed as follows:
   a. Complete the four hands-on exercises in this chapter.
   b. Click the Queries button in the Database window. Click the New button, select the Find Unmatched Query Wizard, and click OK. Choose Products as the table whose records you want to see in the query results. Click Next. Choose Order Details as the table that contains the related records.
   c. Product ID is selected automatically as the matching field. Click Next. Select every field from the Available Fields list. Click Next. Products without Matching Order Details is entered as the name of the query.
   d. Click Finish. You will see a list of the products (if any) that have never been ordered. Print the results of the query for your instructor. What advice would you give to management regarding the inventory of these items?
   e. Add a cover sheet to complete the assignment.

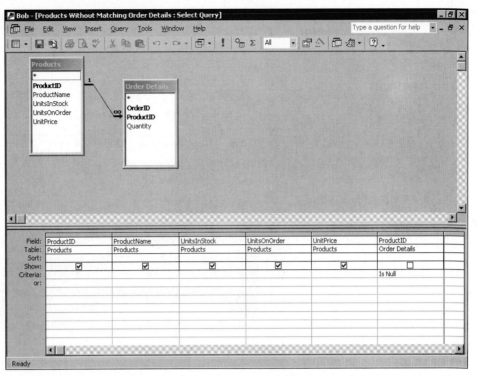

FIGURE 6.15   *Unmatched Query Wizard (Exercise 2)*

BUILDS ON

HANDS-ON
EXERCISE 4
PAGES 291–298

3. **An Improved Order Form:** The order form in Figure 6.16 builds on the order form that was developed in the fourth hands-on exercise in the chapter. A header has been added that includes clip art and a label for your name. Two command buttons to add a new order and close the form have also been added. The most significant change, however, is the inclusion of a Product Name combo box on the subform in place of the Product ID. Proceed as follows:

   a. Open the Order Details subform in Design view. Delete the controls and associated labels for ProductID and Product Name. Click the Combo Box Wizard tool, then click and drag in the Detail area of the subform to create a combo box (where the ProductName control was previously).

   b. Supply the information requested by the Wizard. Click the option button to indicate that you want the combo box to look up values in a table or query. Click Next. Specify the Products table. Click Next. Select the ProductID and ProductName fields. Click Next. Adjust the column width of the ProductName field. Click Next. Click the option button to store the value in a field and specify ProductID. Click Finish.

   c. Adjust the size, position, and alignment of the newly created control. Right click the combo box, click Properties, and change the name of the combo box to Product Name.

   d. Pull down the View menu, click the Tab Order command, and specify AutoOrder. Save the form.

   e. Open the Super Store Order form, which should now contain a drop-down list box to facilitate data entry of new products. Adjust the column width of this field within the subform if necessary.

   f. Click the add button to add a new order to demonstrate the functionality in the completed form. Click in the CustomerID and enter your CustomerID, then tab to the combo box where you can select a salesperson. Complete the order by going to the subform and selecting the individual products. Click in the Product Name list box, then click the down arrow to select the product by name, rather than by product ID. Tab to the quantity field to enter the quantity. Enter at least three products, then print the completed order.

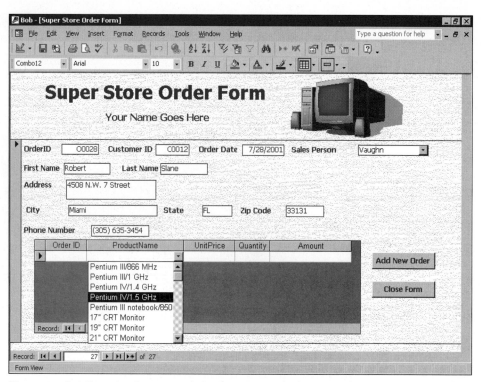

FIGURE 6.16   *An Improved Order Form (Exercise 3)*

BUILDS ON

PRACTICE
EXERCISES 1, 2, AND 3
PAGES 302–304

4. Super Store Switchboard: The switchboard in Figure 6.17 provides access to the various objects that were created for the Computer Super Store. You do not have to match our design exactly, but you should try for consistency and simplicity. The computer logo that appears in the switchboard and in the About form is the same logo as in the order form from the previous example. Print the completed switchboard as well as the table of switchboard items.

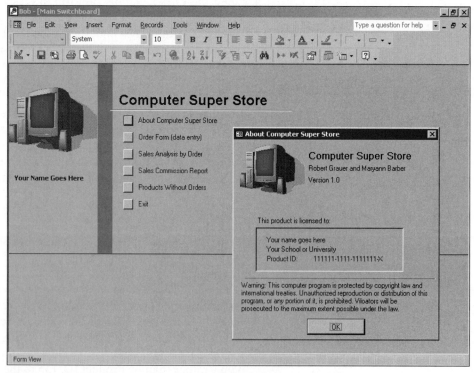

FIGURE 6.17   *Super Store Switchboard (Exercise 4)*

BUILDS ON

CHAPTER 5
PRACTICE
EXERCISE 9
PAGE 252

5. National Bank Advanced Queries: The dynaset in Figure 6.18 is the result of a total query that is associated with the National Bank database from the previous chapter. There was a one-to-many relationship between customers and loans (one customer has many loans). The amount that is displayed represents the sum of all the loans for each customer. Ted Myerson, for example, has borrowed a total of $525,000.

The query also reflects the one-to-many relationship between loan officers and loans (one loan officer is responsible for many loans) for a specific loan officer (Grauer). The name of the loan officer is entered as the query is executed since it (the officer's name) is specified as a parameter. Your assignment is to develop the query and print the dynaset shown in Figure 6.18. Add a cover sheet to complete the assignment.

LoanOfficers.LastName	LoanOfficers.FirstName	Last Name	First Name	SumOfAmount
Grauer	Robert	Myerson	Ted	$525,000.00
Grauer	Robert	Solomon	Wendy	$522,000.00
Grauer	Robert	Faulkner	Eileen	$350,000.00
Grauer	Robert	Grauer	Benjamin	$200,000.00
Grauer	Robert	Hirsch	Matt	$164,000.00
Grauer	Robert	Zacco	Michelle	$105,000.00
Grauer	Robert	Rey	Alex	$30,000.00
Grauer	Robert	Wit	Scott	$25,000.00
Grauer	Robert	Sangastiano	Lori	$10,500.00

FIGURE 6.18   *National Bank Advanced Queries (Exercise 5)*

BUILDS ON

PRACTICE
EXERCISE 5
PAGE 305

6. Expanded National Bank Switchboard: The switchboard in Figure 6.19 is an expanded version of the switchboard developed in the preceding chapter. The last two items (above the Exit button) have been added to complete the switchboard. The Loans by Loan Officer button runs the query of the previous problem and displays the parameter value of the loan officer (Grauer in this example). The Loans Without Payments button uses the Unmatched Query Wizard to display all loans that have not received any payments. Only one loan should appear, and it will contain your name as the customer, provided you have followed all of the instructions in the hands-on exercises from the previous chapter. Print this loan for your instructor.

The completed switchboard ties together all of the objects that were created in the various exercises. Print the switchboard itself, together with the table of switchboard items. Add a cover sheet to complete the assignment.

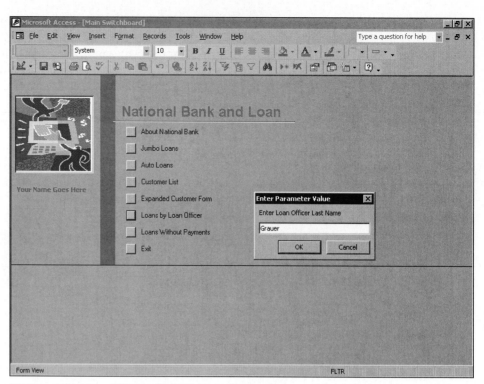

FIGURE 6.19 *Expanded National Bank Switchboard (Exercise 6)*

7. Medical Research Database Design: Figure 6.20 displays the relationships diagram for a database that is to be used by a medical research project that will track volunteers (subjects) and/or the research studies with which they are associated. A study will require several subjects, but a specific person may participate in only one study. The system should also be able to track the physicians who do the research. Many physicians can work on the same study, and a given physician may work on multiple studies.
   a. The system should be able to display all facts about a particular volunteer (subject) such as name, birth date, sex, height, weight, blood pressure, cholesterol level, and so on. It should be able to display all characteristics associated with a particular study such as the title, beginning date, ending date, as well as the names of all physicians who work on that study. It should also show whether the physician is a primary or secondary investigator in each study.
   b. Open the partially completed database in *Chapter 6 Practice 7* and implement our design. The report in Figure 6.20 is created from the Relationships window after the relationships have been specified. Print the completed report for your instructor.

BUILDS ON

PRACTICE
EXERCISE 7
PAGE 306

8. Medical Research Switchboard: The switchboard in Figure 6.21 contains several potential commands for the medical research database. Your assignment is to implement the indicated database design, then create the appropriate object for each button on the switchboard.

   Start by creating a basic switchboard that contains your name and a logo (selected clip art) for the application. The initial switchboard should contain three items—one command, to display the "About Medical Research" form that is similar to the various forms, one command to print the relationships diagram, and a command to exit the application. Print this switchboard and table of switchboard items for your instructor. Add the additional objects as directed by your instructor.

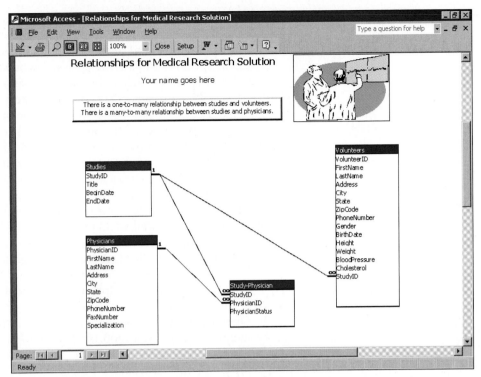

FIGURE 6.20 *Medical Research Database Design (Exercise 7)*

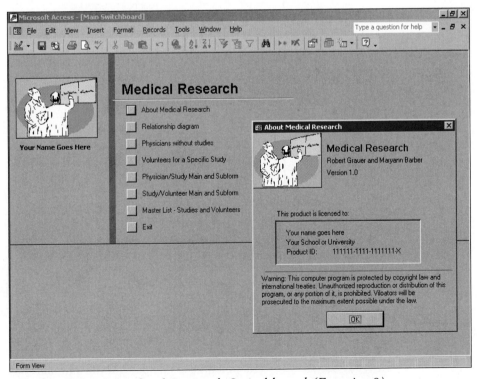

FIGURE 6.21 *Medical Research Switchboard (Exercise 8)*

9. National Conference Database Design: You have been retained as a consultant to design a database for the national conference of a professional organization. This is an annual event and the planning is extensive. Your assignment is to track the speakers and associated sessions at which they will appear in order to create a program for the conference. One speaker can participate in many sessions, and one session can have many speakers. You need to maintain the information for each speaker (name, address, telephone, e-mail, and so on). You also need to maintain information about each session (the title, a more detailed synopsis of up to 500 words, the date, starting time, duration, and the room).

a. Your database also has to track the available rooms within the hotel to facilitate the session assignments. During the course of the conference, one room will host many sessions, but a particular session will be held in only one room. The program should print the name of the session, its location, date, and starting time, as well as all of the scheduled speakers. The capacity of each room should be stored in the database so that sessions can be assigned to an appropriate room. Some rooms have large screens and/or the ability to serve refreshments, and this information should be stored as well. The database should also produce an alphabetical list of all speakers that shows all sessions at which the individual is speaking.

b. Open the partially completed database in *Chapter 6 Practice 9* and implement our design. The report in Figure 6.22 is created from the Relationships window after the relationships have been specified. Print the completed report for your instructor.

FIGURE 6.22 *National Conference Database Design (Exercise 9)*

BUILDS ON

PRACTICE
EXERCISE 9
PAGE 308

10. National Conference Switchboard: The switchboard in Figure 6.23 contains several potential commands for the national conference database. Your assignment is to implement the indicated database design, then create the appropriate object for each button on the switchboard. Print the switchboard form and table of switchboard items for your instructor.

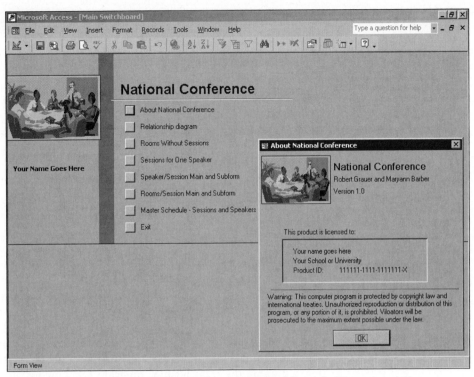

FIGURE 6.23 *National Conference Switchboard (Exercise 10)*

BUILDS ON

PRACTICE
EXERCISE 4
PAGE 304

11. A Look Ahead: Open the Computer Store database. Pull down the Tools menu, click (or point to) the Database Utilities command, then select the Database Splitter to display a screen similar to Figure 6.24. Click the button to Split the Database, then follow the onscreen instructions. Be sure to store the back end (the database containing the tables) in the same folder as the original database. You will learn the rationale for splitting a database in this fashion in Chapter 7.

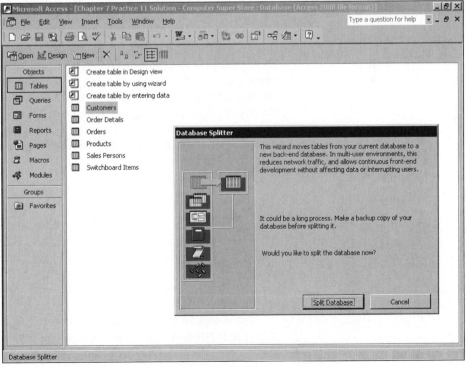

FIGURE 6.24 *Splitting a Database (Exercise 11)*

Health Clubs

Your interest in physical fitness has led to a part-time job at a local health club where you have been asked to design a database for its members and trainers. The health club runs promotions periodically, and so individuals join under different membership plans. Each plan specifies the initial fee (if any), monthly payment (if any), and duration. One plan can have many members, but a specific member has only one plan.

The health club needs to track the number of hours that each employee works, which is accomplished through time cards that record the date, time in, and time out. The health club also wants to know how often members work out, and which trainer they use—thus all members complete a simple workout form each time they are at the club. The form contains the member's identification number, date, and length of the workout (in hours). The workout form also indicates the specific facilities that were used in that session. One member can work out with different trainers, and one trainer will work out with many different members.

The database should be capable of computing the total revenue that is received by the health club. One report should show the sum of all initial fees that have been paid by all members. A second report should show the projected revenue each month, based on the monthly payment due from each member. Print the report containing the relationships diagram for your instructor as proof that you completed this exercise.

The Morning Paper

We take the delivery of our morning paper for granted, but there is a lot of planning to ensure that we receive it each day. You are to design a database for a large metropolitan newspaper that is printed at a central location within the area. Once printed, the papers are delivered to multiple warehouses. Each warehouse services multiple carriers, each of whom goes to the assigned warehouse to pick up the requisite number of papers for his or her customers. One carrier has many customers, but a particular customer has only one carrier.

The database is further complicated by the fact that the newspaper has several editions such as a Spanish edition, a daily (Monday through Saturday) edition, and a Sunday edition. One edition can go to many customers, and one customer can order many editions. There is a specific price associated with each edition. You are to design a database that will enable the paper to determine how many of each edition is to be sent to each warehouse. The database should also be capable of producing a report that shows the total amount of business that each carrier brings in. Print the report containing the relationships diagram for your instructor as proof that you completed this exercise.

The College Bookstore

The manager of a college bookstore has asked for your help in improving its database. The bookstore needs to know which books are used in which courses. One course may require several books, and the same book can be used in different courses. A book may be required in one course and merely recommended in another. The bookstore has a list of all courses taught by the university, with the faculty coordinator for each course.

The design of this database begins with the creation of a Books table that contains the ISBN for each book, its title and author, price, and publisher. Books are ordered directly from the publisher, so it is necessary to know the address and telephone for each publisher. One publisher has many books, but a specific book has only one publisher.

The bookstore places multiple orders with each publisher. One order can specify many books, and the same book can appear in multiple orders. The manager must know the date that each order was placed and the total cost of each order. The manager must also be able to create a report showing the books that are used in each course and its status for that course (i.e., whether the book is required or suggested). Your assignment is to design a database that will fulfill all of the requirements of the bookstore manager. Print the report containing the relationships diagram for your instructor as proof that you completed this exercise.

Bob's Burgers

The corporate office of Bob's Burgers has asked you to design a database to track its restaurants and managers. The database is to produce reports that show the sales of each restaurant and the performance of each manager, as measured by the total sales of all restaurants for that manager. Each restaurant has one manager, but a manager is responsible for multiple restaurants. The company stores the typical personnel data (name, salary, and so on) for each manager as well as basic data for each restaurant such as the telephone and address of each restaurant, its size in square feet, and annual sales for last year. The company would like objective ways to measure the performance of a manager such as the total revenue for which he or she is responsible, the average revenue per restaurant, the average revenue per square foot, and so on.

The database also tracks the orders that are placed by the individual restaurants to the corporate office for various food supplies. Each order is associated with a specific restaurant, and of course, one restaurant will place multiple orders during the course of the year. The company uses a standard set of product numbers, product descriptions, and associated prices that applies to every restaurant. Each order can specify multiple products, and one product may appear in several orders. The database should be capable of computing the total cost of each order. Print the report containing the relationships diagram for your instructor as proof that you completed this exercise.

The Medical Practice

Design a database for a small medical practice that has five physicians. Any patient may see any physician, and, over time, one patient will see many physicians. A patient may complain about multiple ailments, all of which can be treated in a single appointment. (The patient sees only one physician per appointment.) The practice is very efficient in its billing practices and stores all of the ailment information (description, treatment, charge, and so on) in a separate ailments table. As indicated, one appointment can deal with multiple ailments, and the same ailment (e.g., a broken arm) can be treated in different appointments.

Your solution should include separate tables for patients and physicians, with appropriate fields in each table. There is also an ailments table. Additional tables are also required to accommodate the many-to-many relationships that exist within the system. Create a database that contains all of the required tables (you do not have to enter any data) in order to print the relationships diagram for your design. Include a simple switchboard that incorporates a basic logo and color scheme.

CHAPTER 7

Building Applications: Macros and a Multilevel Switchboard

OBJECTIVES

AFTER READING THIS CHAPTER YOU WILL BE ABLE TO:

1. Use the Switchboard Manager to create and/or modify a switchboard; explain why multiple switchboards may be required within one application.
2. Use the Link Tables command to associate tables in one database with objects in a different database.
3. Describe how macros are used to automate an application; explain the special role of the AutoExec macro.
4. Describe the components of the Macro window; distinguish between a macro action and an argument.
5. Explain how prototyping facilitates the development of an application; use the MsgBox action as the basis of a prototype macro.
6. Use the Unmatched Query Wizard to identify records in one table that do not have a corresponding record in another table.
7. Create a macro group; explain how macro groups simplify the organization of macros within a database.

OVERVIEW

This chapter revisits the concept of a user interface (or switchboard) that ties the objects in a database together, so that the database is easy to use. The switchboard displays a menu, often a series of menus, which enables a nontechnical person to move easily from one Access object to another. Any database containing a switchboard is known as an application and, unlike an ordinary Access database, it does not require knowledge of Microsoft Access on the part of the user.

The development of an application may also entail the splitting of a database into two files—one containing the tables and the other containing the remaining objects (the forms, reports, queries, and macros). The tables are then linked to the other objects through the Link Tables command. It sounds complicated, but this approach has several advantages, as you will see.

The chapter also covers macros and prototypes, two techniques that are used by developers in creating applications. A macro automates common command sequences and further simplifies the system for the end user. Prototypes are used in conjunction with developing the various switchboards to demonstrate the "look and feel" of an application, even before the application is complete. Three hands-on exercises are included in the chapter to progressively build the application as you develop your skills in Access.

CASE STUDY: A RECREATIONAL SPORTS LEAGUE

You have probably played in a sports league at one time or another, whether in Little League as a child or in an intramural league at school or work. Whatever the league, it had teams, players, and coaches. The typical league registers the players and coaches individually, then holds a draft among the coaches to divide the players into teams according to ability. The league may have been organized informally, with manual procedures for registering the participants and creating the teams. Now we automate the process.

Let's think for a moment about the tables and associated relationships that will be necessary to create the database. There are three tables, one each for players, coaches, and teams. There is a one-to-many relationship between teams and players (one team has many players, but a player is assigned to only one team). There is also a one-to-many relationship between teams and coaches (one team has many coaches, but a coach is assigned to only one team).

In addition to the tables, the database will contain multiple forms, queries, and reports based on these tables. A Players form is necessary in order to add a new player, or edit or delete the record of an existing player. A similar form should exist for Coaches. There might also be a sophisticated main and subform combination for the Teams table that displays the players and coaches on each team, and through which data for any table (Team, Player, or Coach) can be added, edited, or deleted. And, of course, there will be a variety of reports and queries.

Let's assume that this database has been created. It would not be difficult for a person knowledgeable in Access to open the database and select the various objects as the need arose. He or she would know how to display the Database window and how to select the various buttons to open the appropriate objects. But what if the system is to be used by someone who does not know Access, which is typically the case? You can see that the user interface becomes the most important part of the system, at least from the viewpoint of the end user. An interface that is intuitive and easy to use will be successful. Conversely, a system that is difficult to use or visually unappealing is sure to fail.

Figure 7.1a displays the *switchboard* that will be created for this application. We have added a soccer ball as a logo, but the application applies to any type of recreational sports league. The interface is intuitive and easy to use. Click the About Sports button, the first button on our menu, and the system displays the informational screen we like to include in all of our applications. Click any other button, and you display the indicated form. Click the Teams button, for example, and you see the form in Figure 7.1b, where you can add a new team, view, edit, or print the data for any existing team, then click the Close Form button to return to the main menu.

The switchboard in Figure 7.1a exists as a form within the database. Look closely, however, and you will see it is subtly different from the forms you have developed in previous chapters. The record selector and navigation buttons, for example, have been suppressed because they are not needed. In other words, this

Click About Sports button to display informational message

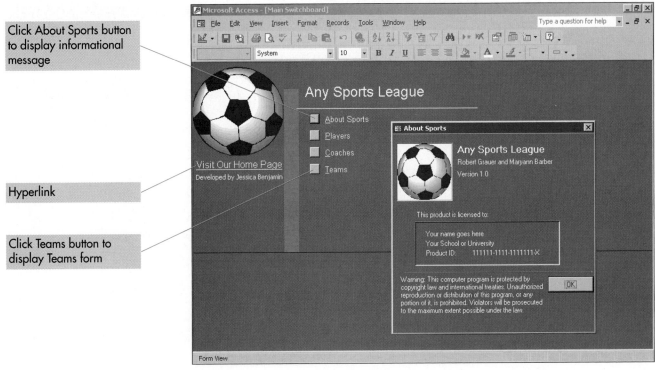

Hyperlink

Click Teams button to display Teams form

(a) The Main Menu

Add, edit, or delete a team

Add, edit, or delete a coach

Add, edit, or delete a player

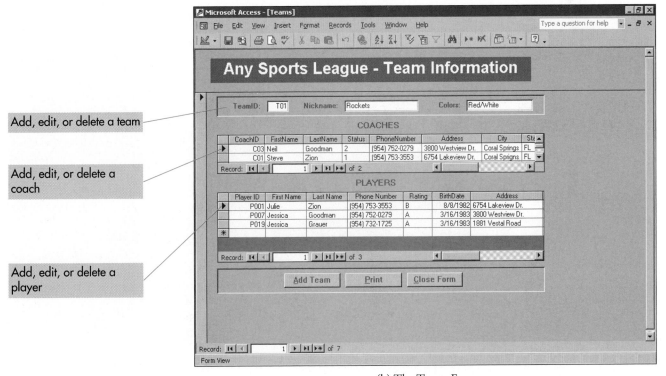

(b) The Teams Form

FIGURE 7.1   *Building a User Interface*

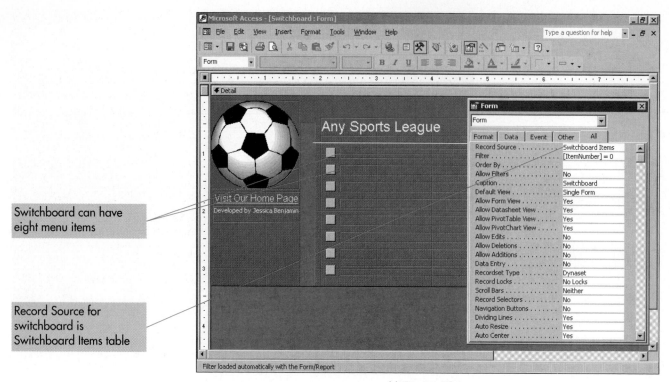

Switchboard can have
eight menu items

Record Source for
switchboard is
Switchboard Items table

(c) Design View

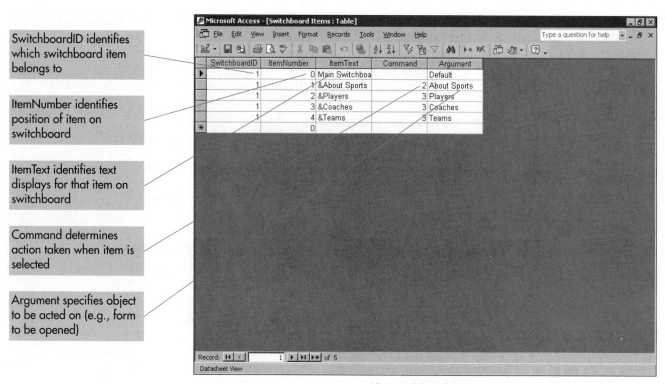

SwitchboardID identifies
which switchboard item
belongs to

ItemNumber identifies
position of item on
switchboard

ItemText identifies text
displays for that item on
switchboard

Command determines
action taken when item is
selected

Argument specifies object
to be acted on (e.g., form
to be opened)

(d) Switchboard Items

FIGURE 7.1 *Building a User Interface (continued)*

form is not used for data entry, but as the basis of a menu for the user. You can even visit the league's Web site by clicking the indicated hyperlink.

The essence of the form, however, lies in the command buttons that enable the user to open the other objects in the database. Thus, when a user clicks a button, Access interprets that action as an *event* and responds with an action that has been assigned to that event. Clicking the Teams button, for example, causes Access to open the Teams form. Clicking the Players button is a different event, and causes Access to open the Players form.

The Switchboard Manager

The *Switchboard Manager* creates a switchboard automatically, by prompting you for information about each menu item. You supply the text of the item as it is to appear on the switchboard, together with the underlying command. Access does the rest. It creates a *switchboard form* that is displayed to the user and a *Switchboard Items table* that stores information about each command.

The switchboard form is shown in both the Form view and the Design view, in Figures 7.1a and 7.1c, respectively. At first, the views do not appear to correspond to one another, in that text appears next to each button in the Form view, but it is absent in the Design view. This, however, is the nature of a switchboard, because the text for each button is taken from the Switchboard Items table in Figure 7.1d, which is the record source for the form, as can be inferred from the Form property sheet. In other words, each record in the Switchboard Items table has a corresponding menu item in the switchboard form. Note, too, that you can modify the switchboard form after it has been created, perhaps by inserting a picture or a hyperlink as was done in Figure 7.1.

As indicated, the Switchboard Items table is created automatically and can be modified through the Switchboard Manager or by directly opening the table. It helps, therefore, to have an appreciation for each field in the table. The SwitchboardID field identifies the number of the switchboard, which becomes important in applications with more than one switchboard. Access limits each switchboard to eight items, but you can create as many switchboards as you like, each with a different value for the SwitchboardID. Every application has a main switchboard by default, which can in turn display other switchboards as necessary.

The ItemNumber and ItemText fields identify the position and text of the item, respectively, as it appears on the switchboard form. (The & that appears within the ItemText field will appear as an underlined letter on the switchboard to enable a keyboard shortcut; for example, &Teams is displayed as Teams and recognizes the Alt+T keyboard shortcut in lieu of clicking the button.) The Command and Argument fields determine the action that will be taken when the corresponding button is clicked. Command number 3, for example, opens a form.

The Linked Tables Manager

Every application consists of tables *and* objects (forms, queries, reports, macros, and modules) based on those tables. The tables and objects may be stored in the same database (as has been done throughout the text), or they may be stored in separate databases, as will be done for the soccer application. Look closely at the Database window in Figure 7.2a. The title bar displays "Sports Objects" and indicates the name of the database that is currently open. Note, however, the arrows that appear next to the icons for the Players, Teams, and Coaches tables to indicate that the tables are stored in a different database. The name of the second database, "Sports Tables," is seen in the Linked Table Manager dialog box in Figure 7.2b.

The tables and objects are associated with one another through the *Link Tables command* and/or through the *Linked Table Manager*. Once the linking has been established, however, it is as though the Players, Coaches, and Teams tables were in the Sports Objects database with respect to maintaining the data. In other words, you can add, edit, and delete a record in any of the three tables as if the tables were physically in the Sports Objects database.

The advantage to storing the tables and objects in separate databases is that you can enhance an application by creating a new version of the Sports Objects database, without affecting the underlying tables. The new version has the improved features, such as a new form or report, but attaches to the original data, and thus retains all of the transactions that have been processed.

Open database is Sports Objects

Arrow indicates tables are linked

(a) The Database Window

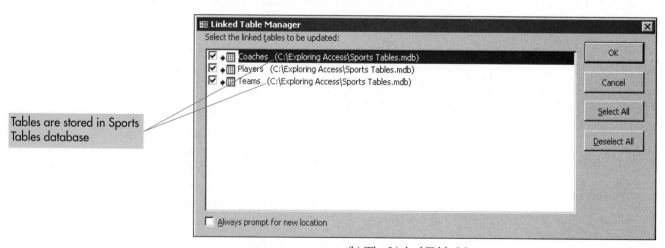

Tables are stored in Sports Tables database

(b) The Linked Table Manager

FIGURE 7.2 *Linking Tables*

THE SWITCHBOARD MANAGER

Objective   To create a switchboard; to use the Link Tables command to associate tables in one database with the objects in a different database. Use Figure 7.3 as a guide in the exercise.

Step 1:   **The Sports Objects Database**

➤ Start Access. Change to the **Exploring Access folder** as you have been doing throughout the text.

➤ Open the **Sports Objects database** as shown in Figure 7.3a, then click the various buttons in the Database window to view the contents of this database. This database contains the various objects (forms, queries, and reports) in the soccer application, but not the tables.

- Click the **Tables button**. There are currently no tables in the database.
- Click the **Queries button**. There is one query in the database.
- Click the **Forms button**. There are six forms in the database.
- Click the **Reports button**. There is one report in the database.

➤ Pull down the **File menu**, click **Database Properties**, then click the **Contents tab** to see the contents of the database as shown in Figure 7.3a. The Database Properties command enables you to see all of the objects on one screen.

➤ Click **OK** to close the dialog box.

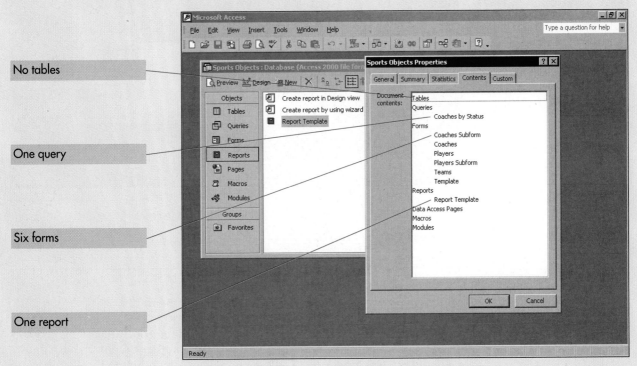

No tables

One query

Six forms

One report

(a) The Sports Objects Database (step 1)

FIGURE 7.3   *Hands-on Exercise 1*

Step 2:   **The Link Tables Command**

➤ Pull down the **File menu**. Click **Get External Data**, then click **Link Tables** from the cascaded menu. You should see the Link dialog box (which is similar in appearance to the Open dialog box).

➤ Select the **Exploring Access folder**, the folder you have been using throughout the text. Scroll (if necessary) until you can select the **Sports Tables database**, then click the **Link command button**.

➤ You should see the Link Tables dialog box in Figure 7.3b. Click the **Select All command button** to select all three tables, then click **OK**.

➤ The system (briefly) displays a message indicating that it is linking the tables, after which the tables should appear in the Database window.

➤ Click the **Tables button** in the Database window. The arrow next to each table indicates that the table physically resides in another database. (You may have to relink the tables if you move the database to another computer.)

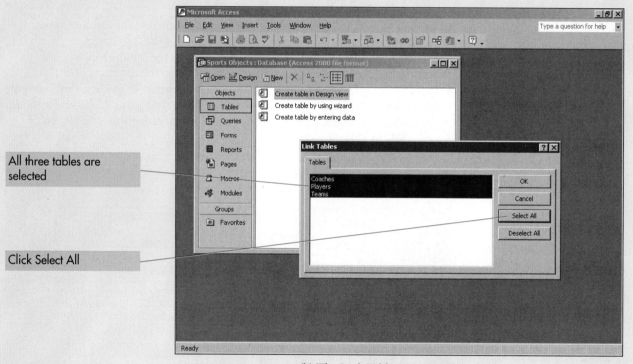

All three tables are selected

Click Select All

(b) The Link Tables Command (step 2)

FIGURE 7.3   *Hands-on Exercise 1 (continued)*

THE DATABASE SPLITTER

The tables and associated objects should always be stored in separate databases. But what if you created the application prior to learning about the ability to link tables and objects to one another? Open the existing database, pull down the Tools menu, click (or point to) the Database Utilities, select the Database Splitter command, and follow the onscreen instructions. You will wind up with two separate databases, a back end that contains the tables, and a front end that contains the other objects.

Step 3: **Import the About Sports Form**

➤ Pull down the **File menu,** click the **Get External Data command,** then click **Import** to display the Import dialog box. Select the **Exploring Access folder**, the folder you have been using throughout the text.

➤ Scroll (if necessary) until you can select the **About Sports database**, then click the **Import button** to display the Import Objects dialog box in Figure 7.3c. Click the **Forms button**, select the **About Sports** form, and click **OK**. The system pauses as the About Sports form is brought into this database.

➤ Once the importing is complete, the Database window changes to display the forms in this database, which now includes the About Sports form. Open the form in the Design view, then modify its contents to include your name and school. Save your changes, then close the form.

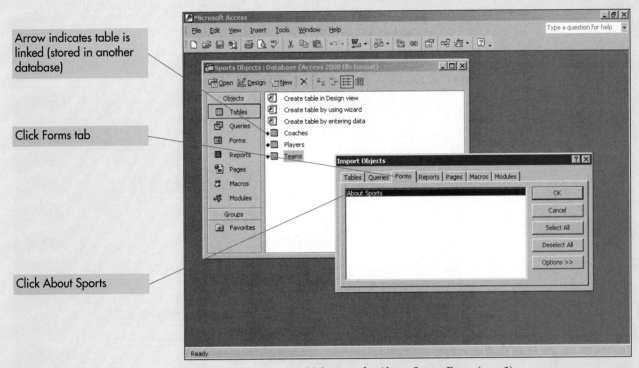

Arrow indicates table is linked (stored in another database)

Click Forms tab

Click About Sports

(c) Import the About Sports Form (step 3)

FIGURE 7.3 *Hands-on Exercise 1 (continued)*

IMPORTING VERSUS LINKING

The Get External Data command displays a cascaded menu to import or link an object from another database. Importing a table brings a copy of the table into the current database and does not maintain a tie to the original table. Linking, on the other hand, does not bring the table into the database but only a pointer to the table. All changes are stored in the original table and are reflected automatically in any database that is linked to the original table. Any type of object can be *imported* into a database. A table is the only type of object that can be *linked*.

Step 4: **Start the Switchboard Manager**

➤ Minimize the Database window. Pull down the **Tools menu**, click the **Database Utilities command**, and choose **Switchboard Manager**.

➤ Click **Yes** if you see a message indicating that there is no valid switchboard. You should see the Switchboard Manager dialog box in Figure 7.3d.

➤ Click the **Edit command button** to display the Edit Switchboard Page dialog box. Click the **New command button** to add an item to this page, which in turn displays the Edit Switchboard Item dialog box.

➤ Click in the **Text** list box and type **&About Sports**, which is the name of the command as it will appear in the switchboard.

➤ Click the **drop-down arrow** on the Command list box. Choose the command to open the form in either Add or Edit mode (it doesn't matter for this form).

➤ Click the **drop-down arrow** in the Form list box and choose **About Sports**.

➤ Click **OK** to create the switchboard item. The Edit Switchboard Item dialog box closes and the About Sports item appears in the Main Switchboard.

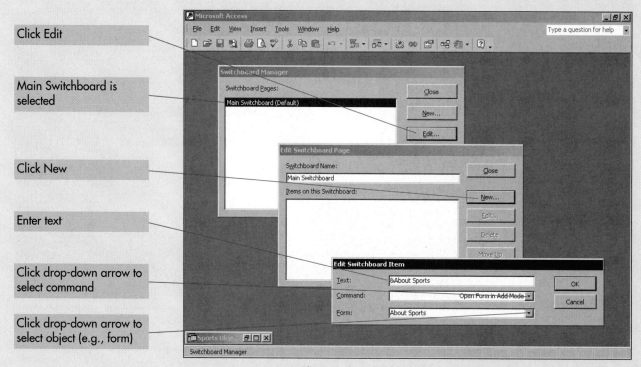

Click Edit

Main Switchboard is selected

Click New

Enter text

Click drop-down arrow to select command

Click drop-down arrow to select object (e.g., form)

(d) Start the Switchboard Manager (step 4)

FIGURE 7.3 *Hands-on Exercise 1 (continued)*

CREATE A KEYBOARD SHORTCUT

The & has special significance when used within the name of an Access object because it creates a keyboard shortcut to that object. Enter "&About Sports", for example, and the letter A (the letter immediately after the ampersand) will be underlined and appear as "About Sports" on the switchboard. From there, you can execute the item by clicking its button, or you can use the Alt+A keyboard shortcut.

Step 5:   **Complete the Switchboard**

> Click the **New command button** in the Edit Switchboard Page dialog box to add a second item to the switchboard. Once again, you see the Edit Switchboard dialog box.
> Click in the **Text** list box and type **&Players**. Click the **drop-down arrow** on the Command list box and choose **Open Form in Edit Mode**. Click the **drop-down arrow** in the Form list box and choose **Players**.
> Click **OK** to close the Edit Switchboard Item dialog box. The &Players command appears as an item on the switchboard.
> Create two additional switchboard items for **&Coaches** and **&Teams** in similar fashion. Your switchboard should contain four items as shown in Figure 7.3e. Click **Close** to close the Edit Switchboard Page dialog box. Click **Close** to close the Switchboard Manager dialog box.

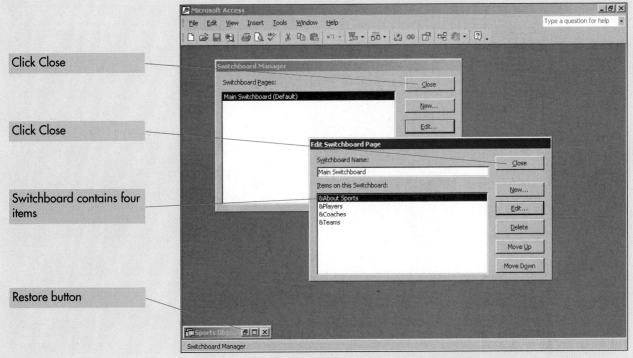

Click Close

Click Close

Switchboard contains four items

Restore button

(e) Complete the Switchboard (step 5)

FIGURE 7.3   *Hands-on Exercise 1 (continued)*

ADD MODE VERSUS EDIT MODE

It's easy to miss the difference between opening a form in the Add mode versus the Edit mode. The Add mode lets you add new records to a table, but it precludes you from viewing records that are already in the table. The Edit mode is more general and lets you add new records and/or edit existing records. Select the Add mode if you want to prevent a user from modifying existing data. Choose the Edit mode to give the user unrestricted access to the table.

Step 6:   **Test the Switchboard**

➤ Click the **Restore button** in the Database window to view the objects in the database, then click the **Forms tab**. The Switchboard form has been created automatically by the Switchboard Manager.

➤ Double click the **Switchboard form** to open the Main Switchboard. Do not be concerned about the design of the switchboard at this time, as your immediate objective is to make sure that the buttons work. (We modify the design of the switchboard at the end of the exercise.) Maximize the window.

➤ Click the **About Sports button** (or use the **Alt+A** shortcut) to display the About Sports form as shown in Figure 7.3f. Click the **OK button** to close the form.

➤ Click the **Players button** (or use the **Alt+P** shortcut) to open the Players form. Click the **Maximize button** so that the Players form takes the entire window.

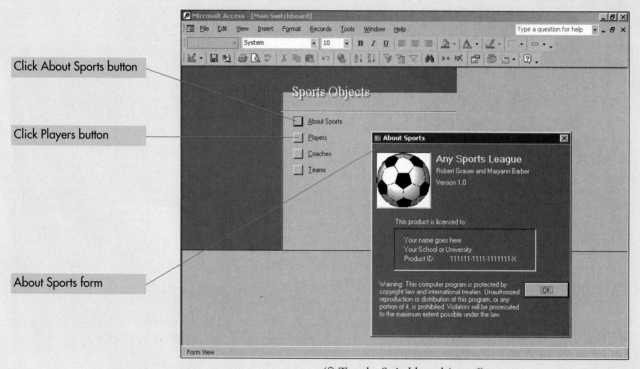

(f) Test the Switchboard (step 6)

FIGURE 7.3   *Hands-on Exercise 1 (continued)*

THE SWITCHBOARD ITEMS TABLE

You can modify an existing switchboard in one of two ways—by using the Switchboard Manager or by making changes directly in the underlying table of switchboard items. Press the F11 key to display the Database window, click the Tables button, then open the Switchboard Items table, where you can make changes to the various entries on the switchboard. We encourage you to experiment, but start by changing one entry at a time. The ItemText field is a good place to begin.

Step 7: **Add Your Record**

➤ Click the **Add Player button** on the bottom of the form (or use the **Alt+A** shortcut) to display a blank record where you will enter data for yourself as shown in Figure 7.3g.

➤ Click the **text box** to enter your first name. (The PlayerID is an AutoNumber field that is updated automatically.) Enter your name, then press the **Tab key** to move to the next field.

➤ Continue to enter the appropriate data for yourself, but please assign yourself to the **Comets team**. The team is entered via a drop-down list. Type **C** (the first letter in Comets) and Comets is entered automatically from the drop-down list for teams.

➤ The player rating is a required field (all players are evaluated for ability in order to balance the teams) and must be A, B, C, or D.

➤ Click the **Close Form button** to return to the switchboard.

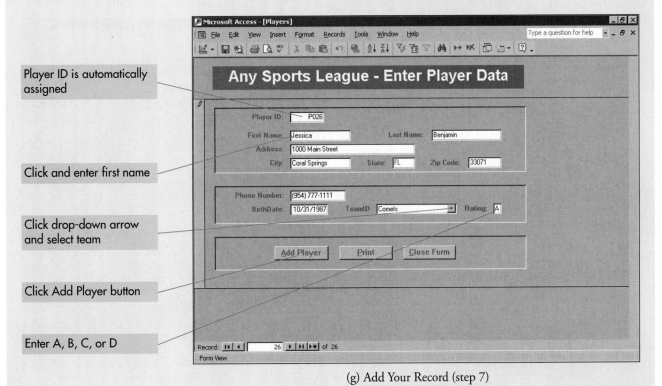

(g) Add Your Record (step 7)

FIGURE 7.3 *Hands-on Exercise 1 (continued)*

A LOOK AHEAD

The Add Record button in the Players form was created through the Command Button Wizard. The Wizard in turn creates a VBA *event procedure* that creates a blank record at the end of the underlying table and enables you to add a new player. The procedure does not, however, position you at a specific control within the Players form; that is, you still have to click in the First Name text box to start entering the data. You can, however, add a VBA statement that automatically moves to the First Name control. See exercise 2 at the end of the chapter.

Step 8:   **Complete the Data Entry**

➤ You should once again see the switchboard. Click the **Coaches button** (or use the **Alt+C** shortcut) to open the Coaches form.

➤ Click the **Add Coach button** at the bottom of the form. Click the **text box** to enter the coach's first name. (The CoachID is entered automatically.)

➤ Enter data for your instructor as the coach. Click the appropriate **option button** to make your instructor a **Head Coach**. Assign your instructor to the Comets. Click the **Close Form button** to return to switchboard.

➤ Click the **Teams command button** on the switchboard to open the Teams form and move to Team T02 (the Comets). You should see your instructor as the head coach and yourself as a player as shown in Figure 7.3h.

➤ Pull down the **Edit menu** and click **Select Record** (or click the selection area), then click the **Print button** to print the roster for your team.

➤ Click the **Close Form button** to return to the switchboard.

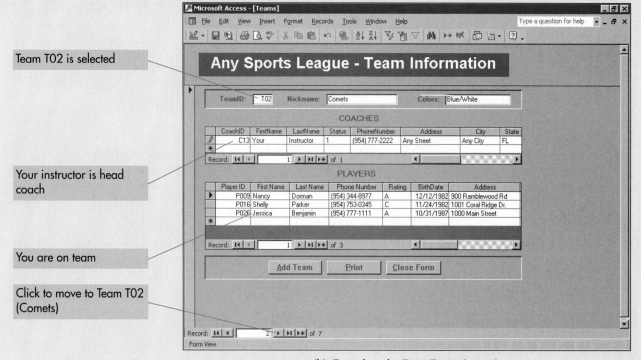

(h) Complete the Data Entry (step 8)

FIGURE 7.3   *Hands-on Exercise 1 (continued)*

THE DISPLAY WHEN PROPERTY

The Add, Print, and Close Form command buttons appear on the various forms (Team, Player, or Coach) when the forms are displayed on the screen, but not when the forms are printed. Open a form in Design view, point to an existing command button, then click the right mouse button to display a shortcut menu. Click the Properties command, click on the line for the Display When property, and choose when you want the button to appear— that is, when the form is displayed, printed, or both.

Step 9: **Insert the Clip Art**

➤ Change to the Design view. **Right click** in the Picture area of the form to display a context-sensitive menu, then click the **Properties command** to display the Property sheet. Click the **All tab**.

➤ The Picture property is currently set to "none" because the default switchboard does not contain a picture. Click in the **Picture box**, then click the **Build button** to display the Insert Picture dialog box.

➤ Click the **down arrow** in the Look In box to change to the **Exploring Access folder**, then select the **SoccerBall** as shown in Figure 7.3i. Click **OK**.

➤ Size the picture as appropriate. The dimensions of the soccer ball should be changed to a square—for example, 1.7 inches × 1.7 inches. Close the property sheet.

➤ Right click below the picture in the Detail area of the form. Point to the **Fill/Back Color command** from the context-sensitive menu to display a color palette. Choose the same shade as appears on the rest of the form. (It is the fifth square from the left in the second row.)

➤ Click the **Undo button** if the color does not match. Save the form.

Click in Picture box, then click Build button

Right click in Picture area to display shortcut menu

Click to select Exploring Access folder

Click SoccerBall

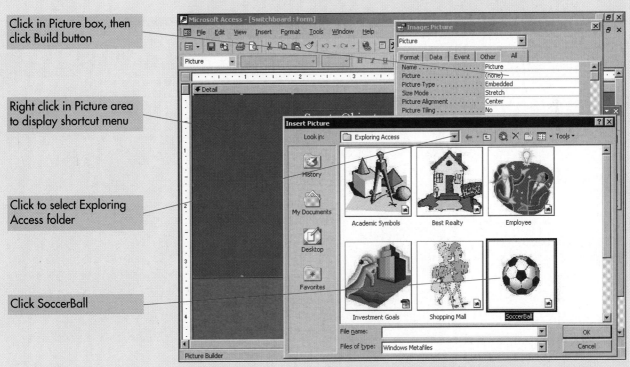

(i) Insert the Clip Art (step 9)

FIGURE 7.3 *Hands-on Exercise 1 (continued)*

THE OBJECT BOX

The easiest way to familiarize yourself with the design of the switchboard is to click the down arrow on the object box on the Formatting toolbar, scrolling as necessary to see the various objects. Select (click) any object in the Object box and it is selected automatically in the form. Right click the selected object to display its property sheet.

Step 10: **Complete the Design**

➤ Delete the label that contains the title of the switchboard, "Sports Objects". (You will have to delete two labels, because the switchboard manager automatically creates a shadow.)

➤ Click and drag the Label tool to create a new unbound control for the title of the switchboard. Enter **Any Sports League** as the title. Use 18-point Arial bold, in white for the formatting.

➤ Click the **Label** tool, then click and drag to create a text box under the picture. Enter your name in an appropriate font, point size, and color. Move and/or size the label containing your name as appropriate.

➤ Press and hold the **Shift key** as you click each text box in succession. The boxes appear to be empty, but the text will be drawn from the Switchboard Items table.

➤ Be sure that you selected all text boxes. Click the **drop-down arrow** on the Font/Fore Color button and change the color to white as shown in Figure 7.3j. Change the font and point size to **Arial** and **10pt**, respectively. Save the form.

➤ Change to the Form view to see the result of your changes. Exit Access if you do not want to continue with the next exercise at this time.

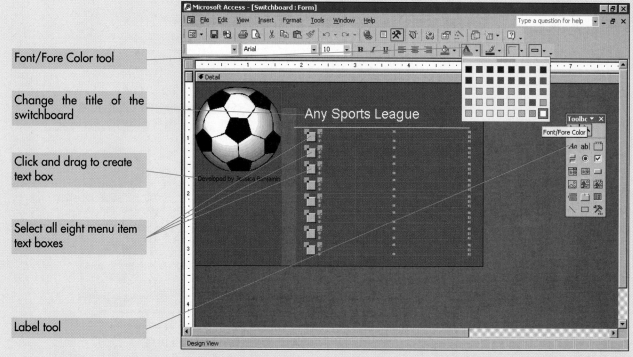

Font/Fore Color tool

Change the title of the switchboard

Click and drag to create text box

Select all eight menu item text boxes

Label tool

(j) Complete the Design (step 10)

FIGURE 7.3 *Hands-on Exercise 1 (continued)*

SET A TIME LIMIT

It's easy to spend an hour or more on the design of the switchboard, but that is counterproductive. The objective of this exercise was to develop a user interface that provides the "look and feel" of a system by selecting various menu options. That has been accomplished. Yes, it is important to fine-tune the interface, but within reason. Set a time limit for your design, then move on to the next exercise.

The exercise just completed created a switchboard that enabled a nontechnical user to access the various tables within the database. It did not, however, automate the application completely in that the user still has to open the form containing the switchboard to get started, and further may have to maximize the switchboard once it is open. You can make the application even easier to use by including macros that perform these tasks automatically.

A *macro* automates a command sequence. Thus, instead of using the mouse or keyboard to execute a series of commands, you store the commands (actions) in a macro and execute the macro. You can create a macro to open a table, query, form, or report. You can create a macro to display an informational message, then beep to call attention to that message. You can create a macro to move or size a window, or to minimize, maximize, or restore a window. In short, you can create a macro to execute any command (or combination of commands) in any Access menu and thus make an application easier to use.

The Macro Window

A macro is created in the *Macro window,* as shown in Figure 7.4. The Macro window is divided into two sections. The *actions* (commands) that comprise the macro are entered at the top. The *arguments,* or information for those actions, are entered in the lower section. Access macros are different from those in Word or Excel, in that Access lacks the macro recorder that is common to those applications. Hence, you have to enter the actions explicitly in the Macro window rather than have the recorder do it for you. In any event, macros are stored as separate objects in a database. The macro name can contain up to 64 characters (letters, numbers, and spaces), and it appears in the title bar of the Macro window (e.g., Back Up in Figure 7.4).

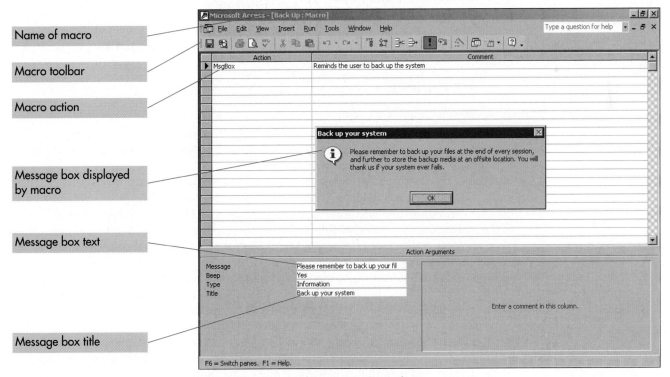

FIGURE 7.4   *The Macro Window*

To create a macro, select the Macros button in the Database window, then click the New button to display the Macro window. You add actions to a macro by clicking in Action area, then choosing the action from a drop-down list, or by typing the name of the action. The arguments for an action are entered in similar fashion—that is, by choosing from a drop-down list (when available) or by typing the argument directly. The macro in Figure 7.4 consists of a single action with four arguments. As indicated, you specify the action, *MsgBox* in this example, in the top portion of the window, then you enter the values for the various arguments (Message, Beep, Type, and Title) in the bottom half of the window.

After the macro is created, you can execute it whenever the application is open. Execution of the macro in Figure 7.4, for example, will display the dialog box shown in the figure, to remind the user to back up his or her data. The contents of the dialog box are determined by the value of the arguments. The text of the dialog box is specified in the Message argument, only a portion of which is visible in the Macro window. The value of the Type argument determines the icon that is displayed within the dialog box (Information in this example). The Title argument contains the text that appears in the title bar of the dialog box.

The *macro toolbar* is displayed at the top of the Macro window and contains buttons that help create and test a macro. Many of the buttons (e.g., the Database window, Save, and Help buttons) are common to other toolbars you have used in conjunction with other objects. Other buttons are specific to the Macro window and are referenced in the hands-on exercises. As with other toolbars, you can point to a button to display its ScreenTip and determine its purpose.

The AutoExec Macro

The *AutoExec macro* is unique in that it is executed automatically whenever the database in which it is stored is opened. The macro is used to automate a system for the end user. It typically contains an OpenForm action to open the form containing the main switchboard. It may also perform other housekeeping chores, such as maximizing the current window.

Every database can have its own AutoExec macro, but there is no requirement for the AutoExec macro to be present. We recommend, however, that you include an AutoExec macro in every application to help the user get started.

Debugging

Writing a macro is similar to writing a program, in that errors occur if the actions and/or the associated arguments are specified incorrectly. Should Access encounter an error during the execution of a macro, it displays as much information as it can to help you determine the reason for the error.

Figure 7.5 contains an erroneous version of the AutoExec macro that attempts to open the Switchboard form. The macro contains two actions, Maximize and OpenForm. The Maximize action maximizes the Database window and affects all subsequent screens that will be displayed in the application. The OpenForm macro is intended to open the switchboard from the previous exercise. The name of the form is deliberately misspelled.

When the AutoExec macro is executed, Access attempts to open a form called "Switchboards", but is unable to do so, and hence it displays the informational message in the figure. Click OK, and you are presented with another dialog box, which attempts to step you through the macro and discover the cause of the error. As indicated, the error is due to the fact that the name of the form should have been "Switchboard" rather than "Switchboard*s*". The errors will not always be this easy to find, and hopefully, you will not make any. Should a bug occur, however, you will know where to begin.

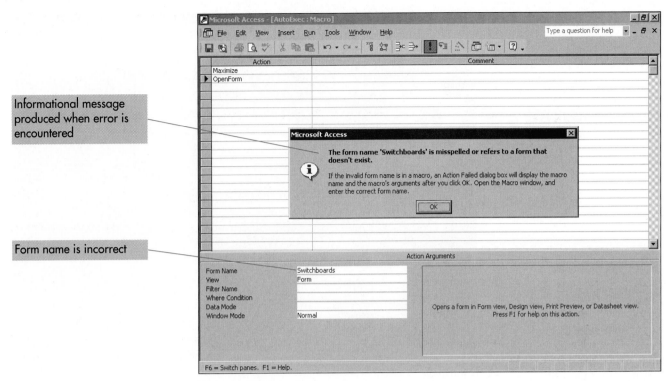

Informational message produced when error is encountered

Form name is incorrect

FIGURE 7.5 *Debugging*

APPLICATION DEVELOPMENT

Application development is an iterative process that entails continual dialog between the end user (client) and the developer. In essence, the developer presents the client with multiple versions of the application, with each successive version containing additional functionality. The user tests and evaluates each version and provides comments to the developer, who incorporates the feedback and delivers a new version (release) of the application. The process continues with each successive release containing increased functionality until the system is complete.

The user is presented with a working system (or ***prototype***) at every stage of testing that captures the "look and feel" of the finished application. The switchboard in Figure 7.6a, for example, is an updated version of the main switchboard from the first hands-on exercise. Look closely and you will see a menu option to display the report switchboard in Figure 7.6b, which was created using the Switchboard Manager. The corresponding Switchboard Items table is shown in Figure 7.6c. The SwitchboardID field assumes significance in this version because there are now two different switchboards, the Main Switchboard and the Report Switchboard, with values of one and two, respectively.

The reports, however, have not yet been created, nor do they need to be, because the user can click any of the buttons on the report switchboard and see the indicated message, which was created by a simple macro. The application is "complete" in the sense that every button on the switchboard works, but it is incomplete in that the reports have not been fully developed. Nevertheless, the prototype lets the user see a working system and enables the user to provide immediate feedback.

The Report Switchboard also provides access to the report template that appears in Figure 7.6d. The purpose of the ***template*** is to provide additional feedback to the user with respect to the appearance of the eventual reports. It is just as easy to create an attractive report as an ugly one, and a uniform report header adds to the professional look of an application. The sooner the user communicates the requested changes to the developer, the easier (and less costly) it is for the developer to incorporate those changes.

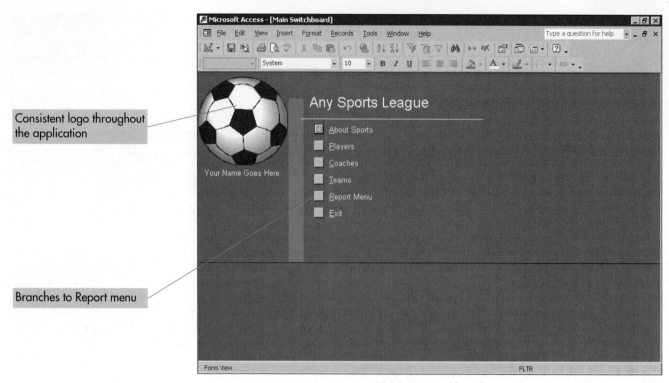

Consistent logo throughout the application

Branches to Report menu

(a) Main Switchboard

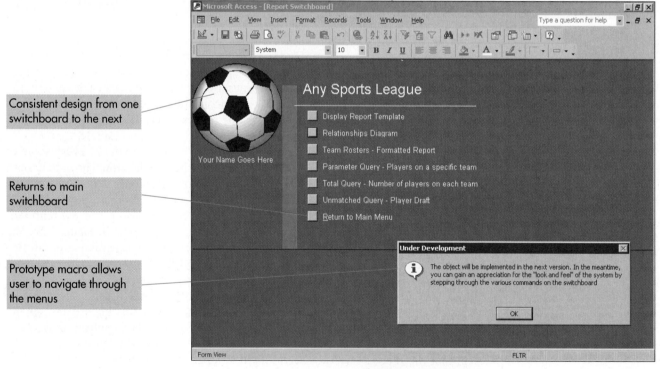

Consistent design from one switchboard to the next

Returns to main switchboard

Prototype macro allows user to navigate through the menus

(b) Report Switchboard

FIGURE 7.6 *Application Development*

Value of SwitchboardID indicates two different switchboards

Executes prototype macro to indicate report is not yet implemented

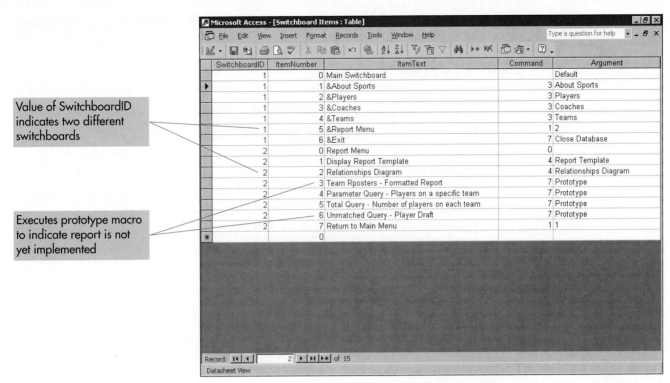

(c) Switchboard Items Table

Consistent design adds to visual appeal

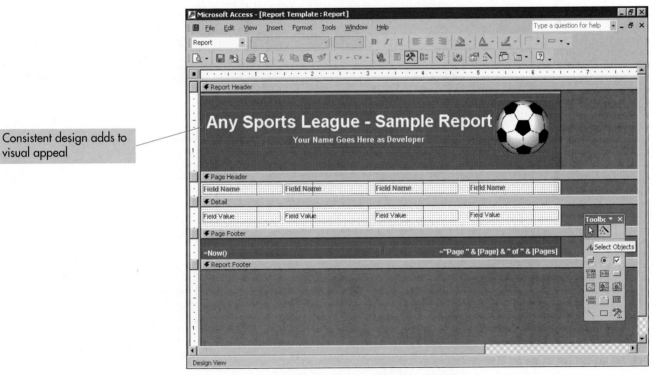

(d) Report Template

FIGURE 7.6 *Application Development (continued)*

MACROS AND PROTOTYPING

Objective To create an AutoExec and a Close Database macro; to create a subsidiary switchboard. Use Figure 7.7 as a guide in the exercise.

Step 1: **Create the AutoExec Macro**

➤ Start Access. Open the **Sports Objects database** from the previous exercise. Click the **Macros button** in the Database window.

➤ Click the **New button** to create a new macro. If necessary, click the **Maximize button** so that the Macro window takes the entire screen as in Figure 7.7a.

➤ Click the **drop-down arrow** to display the available macro actions. Scroll until you can select **Maximize**. (There are no arguments for this action.)

➤ Click the **Action box** on the second line, click the **drop-down arrow** to display the macro actions, then scroll until you can click the **OpenForm action**. Click the text box for the **Form Name** argument in the lower section of the Macro window.

➤ Click the **drop-down arrow** to display the list of existing forms and select **Switchboard** (the form you created in the previous exercise).

➤ Click the **Save button** to display the Save As dialog box in Figure 7.7a. Type **AutoExec** as the macro name and click **OK**. Click the **Run button** to run the macro and open the switchboard.

➤ Close the switchboard. Close the AutoExec macro.

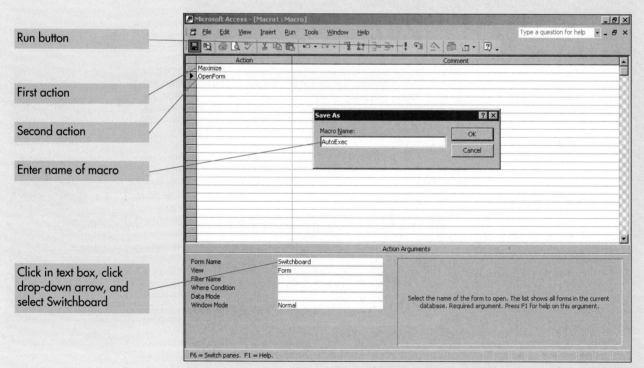

(a) Create the AutoExec Macro (step 1)

FIGURE 7.7 *Hands-on Exercise 2*

Step 2: Create the Prototype Macro

➤ You should be back in the Database window, which should display the name of the AutoExec macro. Click the **New button** to create a second macro.

➤ Type **Ms** (the first two letters in the MsgBox action), then press **enter** to accept this action. Enter the comment shown in Figure 7.7b.

➤ Click the text box for the **Message** argument, then press **Shift+F2** to display the zoom box so that you can see the contents of your entire message. Enter the message in Figure 7.7b. Click **OK**.

➤ Click the text box for the **Type** argument, click the **drop-down arrow** to display the list of message types, and select **Information**.

➤ Click in the text box for the **Title** argument, and enter "**Under Development**".

➤ Click the **Run button** to test the macro. You will see a message indicating that you have to save the macro. Click **Yes** to save the macro, type **Prototype** as the name of the macro, and click **OK**.

➤ You will see a dialog box containing the message you just created. Click **OK**. Close the macro.

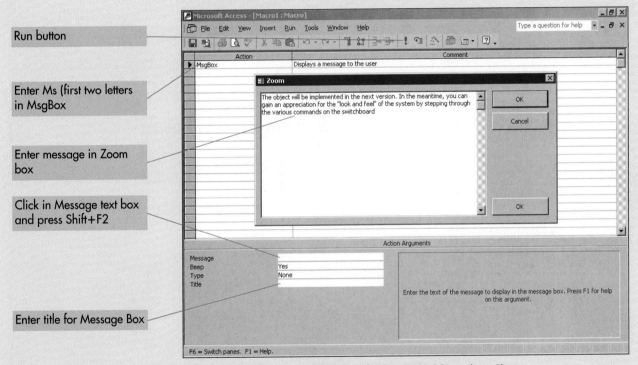

(b) Create the Prototype Macro (step 2)

FIGURE 7.7 *Hands-on Exercise 2 (continued)*

TYPE ONLY THE FIRST LETTER(S)

Click the Action box, then type the first letter of a macro action to move immediately to the first macro action beginning with that letter. Type an M, for example, and Access automatically enters the Maximize action. If necessary, type the second letter of the desired action; for example, type the letter i (after typing an M), and Access selects the Minimize action.

Step 3:   **Create the Close Database Macro**

➤ Click the **New button** once again to create the third (and last) macro for this exercise. Specify the **MsgBox** action as the first command in the macro. Enter the comment shown in Figure 7.7c.

➤ Enter an appropriate message that stresses the importance of backup. Select Warning as the message type. Enter an appropriate title for the message box.

➤ Click the **Action box** on the second line. Type **Cl** (the first two letters in Close) and press **enter**. Enter the indicated comment as shown in Figure 7.7c.

➤ Click the text box for the **Object Type** argument. Click the **drop-down arrow** and choose **Form** as the Object type. Click the **Object Name** argument, click the **drop-down arrow**, and choose **Switchboard** as the Object (form) name.

➤ Click the **Action box** on the third line. Type **Cl** (the first two letters in Close) and press **enter**. Click the **comments line** for this macro action and enter the comment shown in the figure. No arguments are necessary.

➤ Save the macro as **Close Database**, then close the macro. If necessary, press the **F11 key** to return to the Database window, where you should see three macros: AutoExec, Close Database, and Prototype.

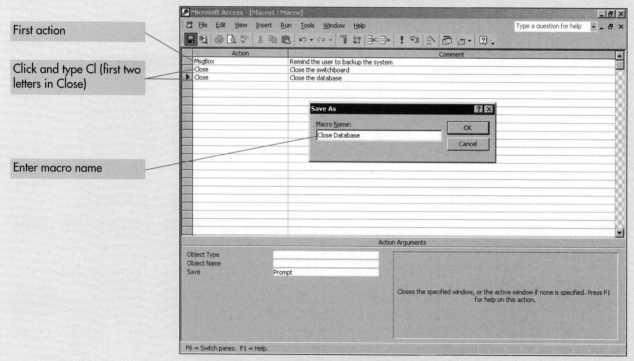

First action

Click and type Cl (first two letters in Close)

Enter macro name

(c) Create the Close Database Macro (step 3)

FIGURE 7.7   *Hands-on Exercise 2 (continued)*

USE KEYBOARD SHORTCUTS—F6, F11, AND SHIFT+F2

Use the F6 key to move back and forth between the top and bottom halves of the Macro window. Press Shift+F2 to display a zoom box that enables you to view long arguments in their entirety. Use the F11 key at any time to display the Database window.

Step 4:   **Create the Report Switchboard**

➤ Minimize the Database window to give yourself more room in which to work. Pull down the **Tools menu**, click the **Database Utilities command**, and choose **Switchboard Manager** to display the Switchboard Manager dialog box.

➤ Click **New**. Enter **Report Switchboard** as the name of the switchboard page. Click **OK**. The Create New dialog box closes and the Report Switchboard page appears in the Switchboard Manager dialog box.

➤ Select the **Report Switchboard**, click **Edit** to open the Edit Switchboard Page dialog box. Click **New** to open the Edit Switchboard Item dialog box.

➤ Add the first switchboard item. Click in the **Text** list box and type **Display Report Template** as shown in Figure 7.7d.

➤ Press the **Tab key** to move to the Command list box and type the **Open R** (the first several letters in Open Report). Press **Tab** to move to the Report list box and type **R** (the first letter in the report name, "Report Template").

➤ Click **OK** to create the switchboard item. The Edit Switchboard Item dialog box closes and Display Report Template appears on the Report Switchboard page.

➤ Add **Report 1** as the next switchboard item. Specify the **Run macro command** and choose **Prototype** as the macro. Add additional buttons for Reports 2 and 3.

➤ Add an additional item that will return the user to the main switchboard. Click **New** to open the Edit Switchboard Item dialog box. Click in the **Text** list box and type "**&Return to Main Menu . . .**"

➤ Press the **Tab key** to move to the Command list box, where the Go to Switchboard command is entered by default. Press the **Tab key** to move to the Switchboard list box, and type **M** (the first letter in the "Main Switchboard"). Click **OK** to create the switchboard item. Close the Edit Switchboard Page.

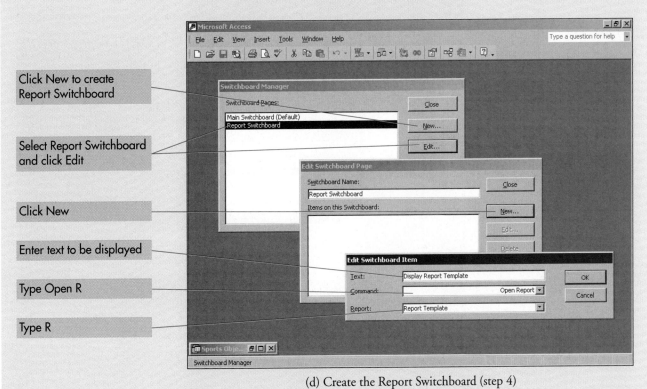

Click New to create Report Switchboard

Select Report Switchboard and click Edit

Click New

Enter text to be displayed

Type Open R

Type R

(d) Create the Report Switchboard (step 4)

FIGURE 7.7   *Hands-on Exercise 2 (continued)*

Step 5:   **Modify the Main Switchboard**

➤ Select the **Main Switchboard** in the Switchboard Manager dialog box, click the **Edit button** to open the Edit Switchboard Page dialog box, then click **New** to open the Edit Switchboard Item dialog box as shown in Figure 7.7d.

➤ Add a new switchboard item to open the Report Switchboard. Click in the **Text** list box and type "**&Report Menu . . .**", the name of the command as it will appear in the switchboard.

➤ Press the **Tab key** to move to the Command list box, where "Go to Switchboard" is already entered, then press the **Tab key** a second time to move to the Switchboard list box. Type **R** (the first letter in the "Report Switchboard"). Click **OK** to create the switchboard item.

➤ The Edit Switchboard Item dialog box closes and "&Report Menu" appears on the main switchboard.

➤ The main switchboard needs one last command to close the database. Thus, click **New** to open the Edit Switchboard Item dialog box. Type **&Exit** as the name of the command.

➤ Press the **Tab key** to move to the Command list box and type **R** (the first letter in "Run Macro"). Press the **Tab key** a second time to move to the Macro list box, and type **C** (the first letter in the "Close Database" macro). Click **OK** to create the switchboard item.

➤ The main switchboard should contain six items—&About Sports, &Players, &Coaches, and &Teams from the first exercise, and &Report Menu and &Exit from this exercise.

➤ Close the Edit Switchboard Page dialog box. Close the Switchboard Manager.

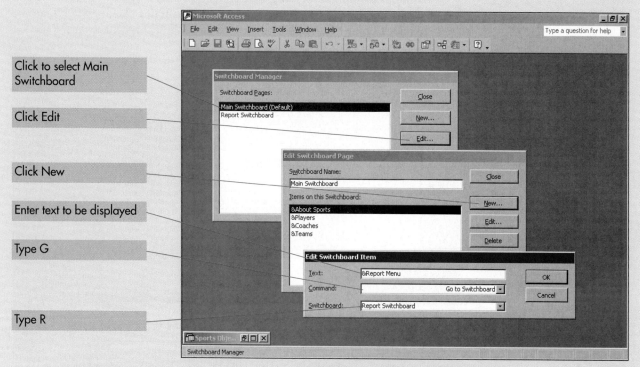

Click to select Main Switchboard

Click Edit

Click New

Enter text to be displayed

Type G

Type R

(e) Modify the Main Switchboard (step 5)

FIGURE 7.7   *Hands-on Exercise 2 (continued)*

Step 6: **Test the Main Switchboard**

➤ Click the **Restore button** in the Database window to view the objects in the database, click the **Forms button**, then double click the **Switchboard form** to open the main switchboard.
➤ Click the **Exit button** (or use the **Alt+E** shortcut):
  • You should see an informational message similar to the one shown in the figure. (The message is displayed by the MsgBox action in the Close Database macro.)
  • Click **OK** to accept the message. The Close Database macro then closes the database.
➤ Pull down the **File menu**, then click **Sports Objects** from the list of recently opened databases. The AutoExec macro executes automatically, maximizes the current window, and displays the main switchboard.

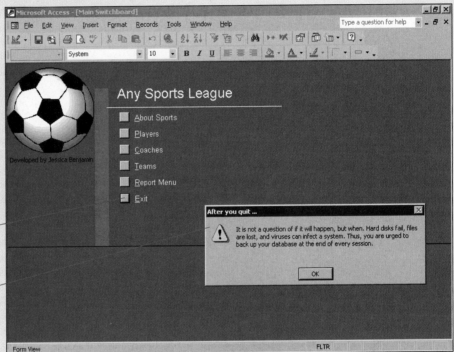

(f) Test the Main Switchboard (step 6)

FIGURE 7.7 *Hands-on Exercise 2 (continued)*

ADD A HYPERLINK

You can enhance the appeal of your switchboard through inclusion of a hyperlink. Open the switchboard form in Design view, then click the Insert Hyperlink button to display the Insert Hyperlink dialog box. Enter the text to be displayed and the Web address, then click OK to close the dialog box and return to the Design view. Right click the hyperlink to display a shortcut menu, click the Properties command to display the Properties dialog box, then change the font and/or point size as appropriate.

Step 7: **Test the Report Switchboard**

➤ Click the **Report Menu button** (or use the **Alt+R** keyboard shortcut) on the main switchboard to display the Report switchboard in Figure 7.7g.

➤ Click the button to **Display the Report Template**. Click the **Print button** to print a copy of this report for your instructor. Close the Report Preview window to return to the Report switchboard. Click the buttons for Reports 1, 2, and 3, which should display the message in Figure 7.7g.

➤ Click the **Return to Main Menu button** to exit the Report Menu and return to the main switchboard.

- To continue working, click the **Close button** on the title bar (or pull down the **File menu** and click the **Close command**) to close the form and continue working on this database. (You should not click the Exit command button as that would close the database.) You should be back in the Database window, where you can continue with the next hands-on exercise.

- To close the database, click the **Exit button** (or use the **Alt+E** shortcut).

➤ Either way, you have demonstrated the "look and feel" of the system to the extent that you can step through the various menus. Good work.

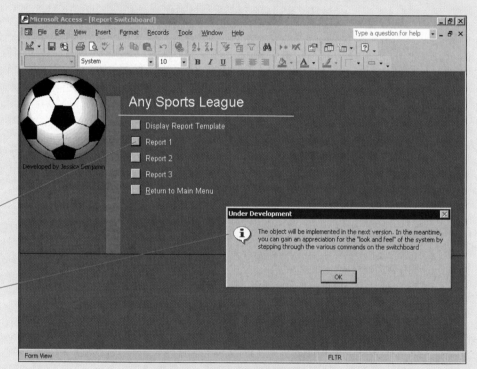

Click button for Report 1

Informational message is displayed

(g) Test the Report Switchboard (step 7)

FIGURE 7.7 *Hands-on Exercise 2 (continued)*

BE CONSISTENT

Consistency within an application is essential to its success. Similar functions should be done in similar ways to facilitate learning and build confidence in the application. The sports application, for example, has similar screens for the Players, Coaches, and Teams forms, each of which contains the identical buttons to add or print a record and close the form.

A player draft is essential to the operation of the league. Players sign up for the coming season at registration, after which the coaches meet to select players for their teams. All players are rated as to ability, and the league strives to maintain a competitive balance among teams. This is accomplished through a draft in which the coaches take turns selecting players from the pool of unassigned players.

The player draft is implemented through the form in Figure 7.8, which is based on a query that identifies players who have not yet been assigned to a team. The easiest way to create the underlying query is through the **Unmatched Query Wizard** that identifies records in one table (the Players table) that do not have matching records in another table (the Teams table). The Wizard prompts you for the necessary information, then it creates the required query as you will see in the next hands-on exercise. A **combo box** within the query simplifies data entry in that the user is able to click the drop-down list box to display the list of teams, rather than having to remember the TeamID.

In addition to displaying the list of unassigned players, the form in Figure 7.8 also contains three command buttons that are used during the player draft. The Find Player button moves directly to a specific player, and enables a coach to see whether a specific player has been assigned to a team, and if so, to which team. The Update List button refreshes the underlying query on which the list of unassigned players is based. It is used periodically during the draft as players are assigned to teams, to remove those players from the list of unassigned players. The End Draft button closes the form and returns to the Switchboard. Note, too, that the appearance of the form matches the other forms in the application. This type of consistency is important to give your application a professional look.

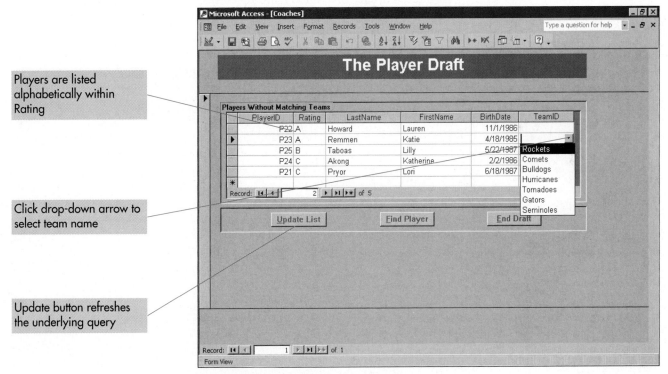

Players are listed alphabetically within Rating

Click drop-down arrow to select team name

Update button refreshes the underlying query

FIGURE 7.8 *The Player Draft*

Macro Groups

Implementation of the player draft requires three macros, one for each command button. Although you could create a separate macro for each button, it is convenient to create a ***macro group*** that contains the individual macros. The macro group has a name, as does each macro in the group. Only the name of the macro group appears in the Database window.

Figure 7.9 displays a Player Draft macro group containing three individual macros (Update List, Find Player, and End Draft), which run independently of one another. The name of each macro appears in the Macro Name column (which is displayed by clicking the Macro Names button on the Macro toolbar). The actions and comments for each macro are shown in the corresponding columns to the right of the macro name.

The advantage of storing related macros in a macro group, as opposed to storing them individually, is purely organizational. Large systems often contain many macros, which can overwhelm the developer as he or she tries to locate a specific macro. Storing related macros in macro groups limits the entries in the Database window, since only the (name of the) macro group is displayed. Thus, the Database window would contain a single entry (Player Draft, which is the name of the macro group), as opposed to three individual entries (Update List, Find Player, and End Draft, which correspond to the macros in the group).

Access must still be able to identify the individual macros so that each macro can be executed at the appropriate time. If, for example, a macro is to be executed when the user clicks a command button, the ***On Click property*** of that command button must specify both the individual macro and the macro group. The two names are separated by a period; for example, Player Draft.Update List to indicate the Update List macro in the Player Draft macro group.

As indicated, each macro in Figure 7.9 corresponds to a command button in the Player Draft form. The macros are created in the following hands-on exercise that implements the player draft.

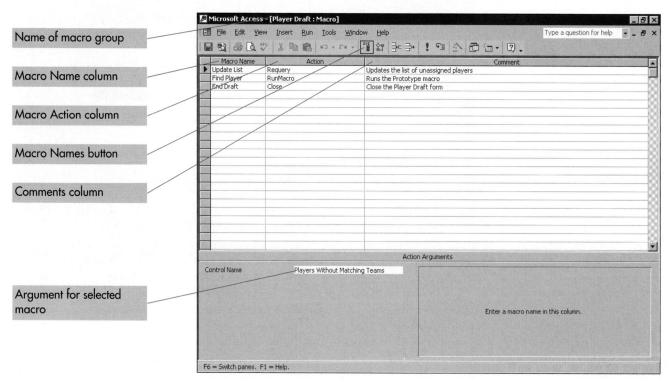

FIGURE 7.9   *Macro Group*

THE PLAYER DRAFT

Objective Create a macro group containing three macros to implement a player draft. Use Figure 7.10 as a guide in the exercise.

Step 1: **The Unmatched Query Wizard**

➤ Start Access and open the **Sports Objects database**. Pull down the **File menu** and click **Close** (or click the **Close button**) to close the Main Menu form but leave the database open.

➤ Click the **Queries button** in the Database window. Click **New**, select the **Find Unmatched Query Wizard**, then click **OK** to start the wizard:

• Select **Players** as the table whose records you want to see in the query results. Click **Next**.

• Select **Teams** as the table that contains the related records. Click **Next**.

• **TeamID** is automatically selected as the matching field. Click **Next**.

• Select the following fields from the Available Fields list: **PlayerID**, **Rating**, **LastName**, **FirstName**, **BirthDate**, and **TeamID**. Click **Next**.

• **Players Without Matching Teams** is entered as the name of the query. Check that the option button to **View the results** is selected, then click **Finish** to exit the wizard and see the results of the query.

➤ You should see a dynaset containing five players (Pryor, Howard, Remmen, Akong, and Taboas) as shown in Figure 7.10a. The TeamID field for each of these players is blank, indicating that these players have not yet been assigned.

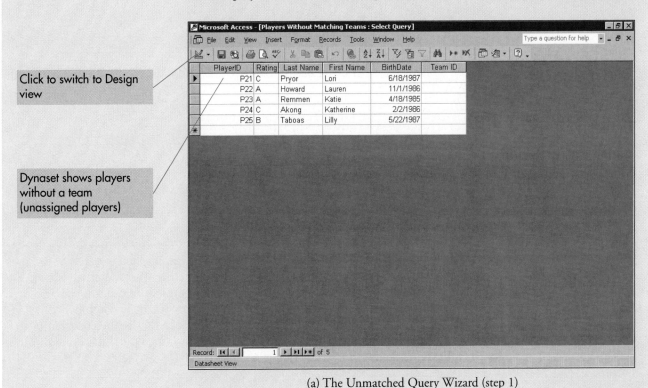

Click to switch to Design view

Dynaset shows players without a team (unassigned players)

(a) The Unmatched Query Wizard (step 1)

FIGURE 7.10 *Hands-on Exercise 3*

Step 2: **Modify the Query**

➤ Change to Design view to see the underlying query as displayed in Figure 7.10b.
➤ Click and drag the line separating the upper and lower portions of the window. If necessary, click and drag the field lists to match the figure.
➤ Click in the **Sort row** for **Rating**, then click **Ascending** from the drop-down list. Click in the **Sort row** for **LastName**, then click **Ascending** from the drop-down list.
➤ Click the **Run button** to view the revised query, which lists players according to their player rating and alphabetically within rating.
➤ Close the query. Click **Yes** if asked whether to save the changes to the Players Without Matching Teams query.

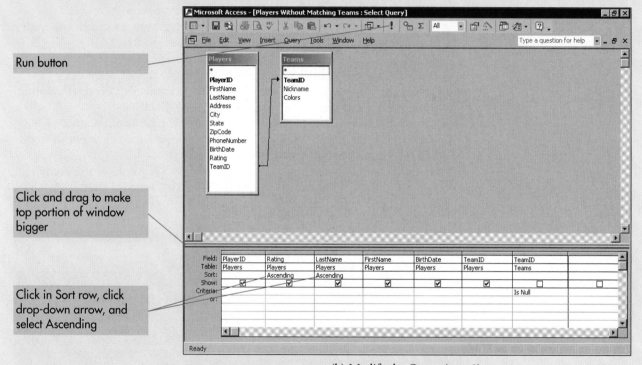

Run button

Click and drag to make top portion of window bigger

Click in Sort row, click drop-down arrow, and select Ascending

(b) Modify the Query (step 2)

FIGURE 7.10 *Hands-on Exercise 3 (continued)*

THE IS NULL CRITERION

The Is Null criterion selects those records that do not have a value in the designated field. It is the essence of the Unmatched Query Wizard, which uses the criterion to identify the records in one table that do not have a matching record in another table. The NOT operator can be combined with the Is Null criterion to produce the opposite effect; that is, the criterion Is Not Null will select records with any type of entry (including spaces) in the specified field.

Step 3:   **Create the Unmatched Players Form**

➤ Click the **Forms button** in the Database window, click **New** to display the New Form dialog box and select **AutoForm:Tabular**.

➤ Click the **drop-down arrow** to choose a table or query. Select the **Players Without Matching Teams** (the query created in steps 1 and 2). Click **OK**.

➤ Maximize the window if necessary, then change to the Design view. Select the **TeamID control** in the Detail section, then press the **Del key**.

➤ Click the **Combo Box** tool. Click and drag in the Detail section, then release the mouse to start the Combo Box Wizard:

  • Check the option button that indicates you want the combo box to **look up values in a table or query**. Click **Next**.

  • Choose the **Teams** table in the next screen. Click **Next**.

  • Select the **TeamID** and **Nickname** fields. Click **Next**.

  • Adjust the column width if necessary. Be sure the box to **Hide the key column** is checked. Click **Next**.

  • Click the option button to store the value in the field. Click the **drop-down arrow** to display the fields and select the **TeamID** field. Click **Next**.

  • Enter **TeamID** as the label for the combo box. Click **Finish**.

➤ Click (select) the label next to the control you just created. Press the **Del key**.

➤ Point to the combo box, click the **right mouse button** to display a shortcut menu, and click **Properties**. Change the name of the control to **TeamID**.

➤ Right click the **Form Selector** box and click the **Properties command**. Click the **Default View** text box, click the **drop-down arrow**, and select **Datasheet**. Close the Properties sheet.

➤ Click the **Save button** to display the Save As dialog box in Figure 7.10c. (Players Without Matching Teams is already entered as the default name.)

➤ Click **OK** to save the form, then close the form.

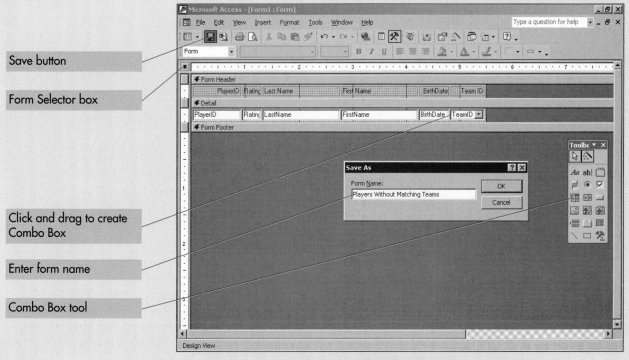

(c) Create the Unmatched Players Form (step 3)

FIGURE 7.10   *Hands-on Exercise 3 (continued)*

Step 4: Create the Player Draft Macro Group

➤ Click the **Macros button** in the Database window. Click **New** to create a new macro. Click the **Maximize button** to maximize the Macro window.

➤ If you do not see the Macro Names column, pull down the **View menu** and click **Macro Names** to display the column.

➤ Enter the macro names, comments, and actions, as shown in Figure 7.10d.

• The Requery action (in the Update List macro) has a single argument in which you specify the control name (the name of the query). Type **Players Without Matching Teams**, which is the query you created in step 1.

• The Find Player macro will be implemented as an assignment (see practice exercise 3), but in the interim, it will access the Prototype macro developed earlier. Choose **RunMacro** as the action and specify **Prototype**.

• The arguments for the End Draft macro are visible in Figure 7.10d. The Player Draft form will be created in the next step. (You must enter the name manually since the form has not yet been created.)

➤ Save the Macro group as **Player Draft**. Close the Macro window.

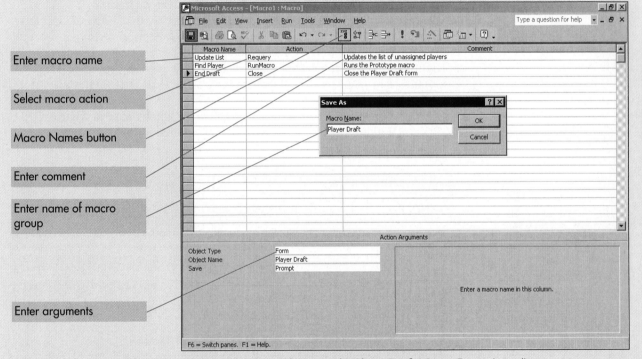

(d) Create the Player Draft Macro Group (step 4)

FIGURE 7.10   *Hands-on Exercise 3 (continued)*

REQUERY COMMAND NOT AVAILABLE

The macros in the Player Draft group are designed to run only when the Player Draft form is open. Do not be concerned, therefore, if you attempt to test the macros at this time and the Action Failed dialog box appears. The macros will work correctly at the end of the exercise, when the entire player draft is in place.

Step 5:   **Create the Player Draft Form**

➤ Click the **Forms button** in the Database window. Select the **Template form**, click the **Copy button** to copy the form to the clipboard, then click the **Paste button** to complete the copy operation. Type **Player Draft** as the name of the copied form. Click **OK**.

➤ Open the Player Draft form in Design view. Pull down the **Window menu** and click **Tile Horizontally** to arrange the windows as shown in Figure 7.10e. (If necessary, close any open windows besides the two in our figure, then retile the windows.)

➤ Click in the **Player Draft** form. Delete the labels and text boxes for fields 1 and 2.

➤ Click in the **Database window**. Click and drag the **Players Without Matching Teams** form into the Detail section of the Player Draft form as shown in Figure 7.10e. Maximize the Player Draft window.

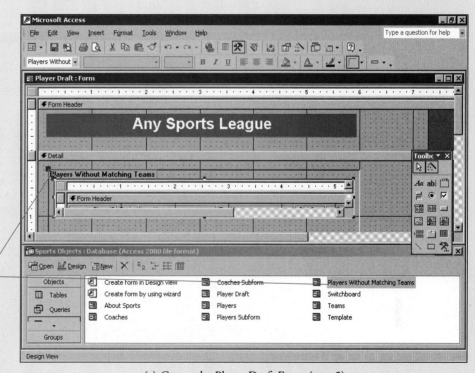

Click and drag Players Without Matching Teams to Detail section of Player Draft form

(e) Create the Player Draft Form (step 5)

FIGURE 7.10   *Hands-on Exercise 3 (continued)*

USE A TEMPLATE

Avoid the routine and repetitive work of creating a new form by basing all forms for a given application on the same template. A template is a partially completed form or report that contains graphic elements and other formatting specifications. A template does not, however, have an underlying table or query. We suggest that you create a template for your application and store it within the database, then use that template whenever you need to create a new form. It saves you time and trouble. It also promotes a consistent look that is critical to the application's overall success.

Step 6: **Modify the Player Draft Form**

➤ Click and drag the decorative box so that it is larger than the Players Without Matching Forms control. Move the control within the decorative box.

➤ Select the control for the form, then click and drag the **sizing handles** in the Players Without Matching Team form so that its size approximates the form in Figure 7.10f.

➤ Select (click) the label, **Players Without Matching Teams**, as shown in Figure 7.10f, then press the **Del key** to remove the label. Change the text in the Form header to say **The Player Draft**.

➤ Change to the Form view. You should see the Form view of the subform, which displays the players who have not yet been assigned to a team. Change the column widths if necessary.

➤ Return to the Form Design view to change the width of the subform. Continue to switch back and forth between the Form view and the Design view until you are satisfied. Save the form.

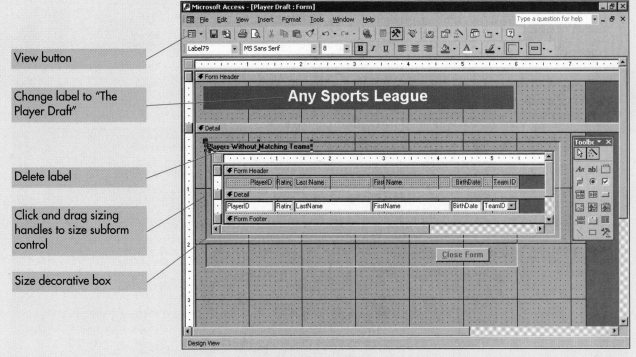

(f) Modify the Player Draft Form (step 6)

FIGURE 7.10 *Hands-on Exercise 3 (continued)*

SUPPRESS THE RECORD SELECTOR AND NAVIGATION BUTTONS

You can suppress the Record Selector and Navigation buttons on the Player Draft form, which have no active function and only confuse the user. Change to the Design view, right click the Form selector box to the left of the ruler, then click the Properties command to display the Properties dialog box. Click the Record Selectors text box and click No to disable it. Click the Navigation Buttons text box and click No to disable it. Close the Properties dialog box, then return to the Form view to see the effect of these changes, which are subtle but worthwhile.

Step 7: **Add the Command Buttons**

➤ Click and drag the **Command Button** tool to create a command button, as shown in Figure 7.10g. Click **Miscellaneous** in the Categories list box. Select **Run Macro** from the list of actions. Click **Next**.

➤ Select **Player Draft.Update List** from the list of existing macros. Click **Next**.

➤ Click the **Text option button**. Click and drag to select the default text (Run Macro), then type **&Update List** as the text to display. Click **Next**.

➤ Enter **Update List** (in place of the button number). Click **Finish**.

➤ Create a second command button to find a player. The caption of the button should be **&Find Player** and it should run the Find Player macro.

➤ Change the caption property of the existing button on the template that closes the form to **&End Draft**.

➤ Size, align, space, and color the command buttons. Save the form.

➤ Change to the Form view. Click the **End Draft button** to close the form.

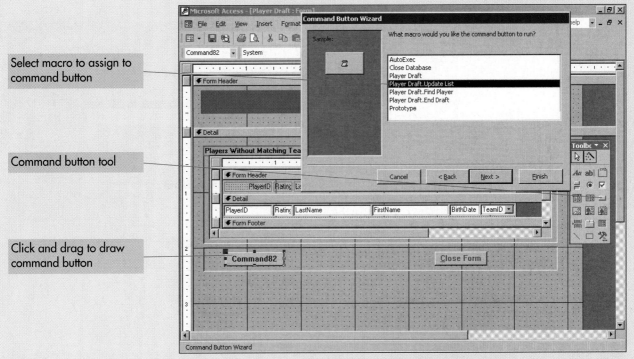

Select macro to assign to command button

Command button tool

Click and drag to draw command button

(g) Add the Command Buttons (step 7)

FIGURE 7.10 *Hands-on Exercise 3 (continued)*

ASSIGN MACROS TO CONTROLS AND COMMAND BUTTONS

Right click any command button or control to display a context-sensitive menu in which you click the Properties command, then click the Event tab in the resulting property sheet. Click in the text box of the desired event, then click the down arrow to assign an existing macro to the control or command button. Note, too, that you can click the Build button, instead of the down arrow, to select the Macro Builder and create a macro if it does not yet exist.

Step 8: **Modify the Main Switchboard**

➤ Pull down the **Tools menu**, click the **Database Utilities command**, and choose **Switchboard Manager**. Select the **Main Switchboard** in the Switchboard Manager dialog box, then click the **Edit button**.

➤ Click **New** to open the Edit Switchboard Item dialog box. Click in the **Text** list box and type **Player &Draft**. (The ampersand in front of the letter "D" establishes Alt+D as a shortcut for this button.)

➤ Press the **Tab key** to move to the Command list box. Select the command to open the form in the Edit mode. Press the **Tab key** to move to the Form list box and select the Player Draft form as shown in Figure 7.10h.

➤ Click **OK** to create the switchboard item. The Edit Switchboard Item dialog box closes and Player &Draft appears on the Main Switchboard. Select the **Player &Draft** entry, then click the **Move Up button** to move this command above the &Exit command.

➤ Close the Edit Switchboard page, then close the Switchboard Manager.

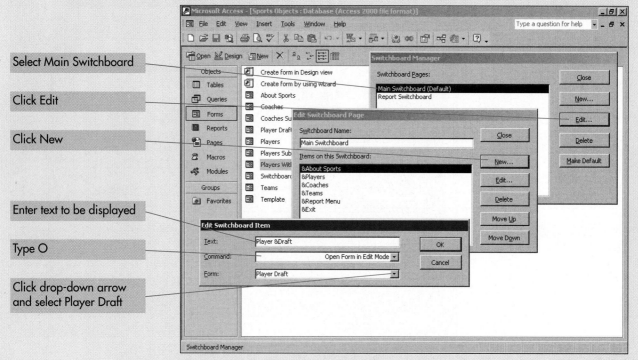

(h) Modify the Main Switchboard (step 8)

FIGURE 7.10 *Hands-on Exercise 3 (continued)*

REPLICATE THE DATABASE

You can create a copy of a database, known as a replica, then take the replica with you on a laptop computer. This lets you work with the database even if you are not connected to the network, but you will eventually have to synchronize your replica with the network version. Start Windows Explorer, click and drag the Access database to the My Briefcase icon on the desktop, then follow the onscreen instructions. Use the Access Help facility for additional information. See practice exercise 12 at the end of the chapter.

Step 9:   **Test the Completed System**

➤ Click the **Macros button** in the Database window. Double click the **AutoExec macro** to execute this macro, as though you just opened the database.

➤ Click the **Player Draft button** on the Main Switchboard to display the form you just created, as shown in Figure 7.10i.

➤ Click the **TeamID field** for Katie Remmen. Type **R** (the first letter in Rockets) and Katie is assigned automatically to this team. Click the **Update List command button**. Katie disappears from the list of unassigned players.

➤ Click the **Find Player button**. Click **OK** when you see the message indicating this function has not been implemented. Click the **End Draft button**.

➤ Click the **Teams command button** to view the team rosters. Team T01 (Rockets) is the first team you see, and Katie Remmen is on the roster. Click the **Close Form button** to return to the switchboard.

➤ Click the **Exit button**. Click **OK** in response to the message for backup.

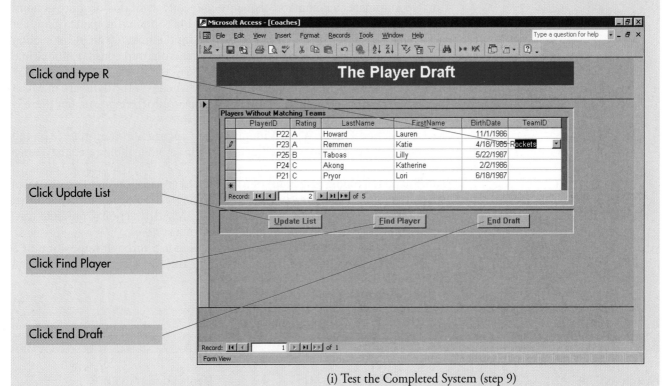

Click and type R

Click Update List

Click Find Player

Click End Draft

(i) Test the Completed System (step 9)

FIGURE 7.10   *Hands-on Exercise 3 (continued)*

PASSWORD PROTECT A DATABASE

Protect your database from unauthorized access through imposition of a password. It's a two-step process. First, close the database, then pull down the File menu, click the Open command to display the Open dialog box, select the database, then click the drop-down Open button and choose Open Exclusive. Next, pull down the Tools menu, click Security, click Set Database password, and follow the onscreen prompts. Be careful, however, because you cannot open the database if you forget the password. See practice exercse 5 at the end of the chapter.

An Access application is different from an ordinary database in that it contains an intuitive user interface known as a switchboard. The switchboard can be created automatically using the Switchboard Manager, a tool that prompts you for each item you want to include. You supply the text of the menu item, as it is to appear on the switchboard, together with the underlying command. Access does the rest and creates the switchboard form and associated table of switchboard items.

The tables in a database can be separated from the other objects to enable the distribution of updated versions of the application without disturbing the data. The tables are stored in one database and the objects in another. The Link Tables command associates the tables with the objects.

A template is a partially completed report or form that contains graphical elements and other formatting specifications. It is used as the basis for other objects and helps to promote a consistent look throughout an application.

A macro automates a command sequence and consists of one or more actions. The Macro window has two sections. The upper section contains the name (if any) of the macro and the actions (commands) that make up the macro. The lower section specifies the arguments for the various actions. A macro group consists of multiple macros and is used for organizational purposes.

The AutoExec macro is executed automatically whenever the database in which it is stored is opened. Each database can have its own AutoExec macro, but there is no requirement for an AutoExec macro to be present.

The Unmatched Query Wizard identifies the records in one table (e.g., the Players table) that do not have matching records in another table (e.g., the Teams table).

A prototype is a model (mockup) of a completed application that demonstrates the "look and feel" of the application. Prototypes can be developed quickly and easily through the use of simple macros containing the MsgBox action. Continual testing through prototyping is essential to the success of a system.

A database can be protected from unauthorized use through imposition of a password. Once a password has been implemented, the database cannot be opened without it.

Action (p. 329)
Argument (p. 329)
AutoExec macro (p. 330)
Combo box (p. 341)
Database properties (p. 319)
Database splitter (p. 320)
Debugging (p. 330)
Display When property (p. 326)
Event (p. 317)
Event procedure (p. 325)
Get External Data command
    (p. 320)

Is Null criterion (p. 344)
Linked Table Manager (p. 318)
Link Tables command (p. 318)
Macro (p. 329)
Macro group (p. 342)
Macro toolbar (p. 330)
Macro window (p. 329)
MsgBox action (p. 330)
On Click property (p. 342)
Password protection (p. 351)
Prototype (p. 331)

Replication (p. 350)
Requery command (p. 346)
Switchboard (p. 314)
Switchboard form (p. 317)
Switchboard Items table (p. 317)
Switchboard Manager (p. 317)
Template (p. 331)
Unmatched Query Wizard (p. 341)

1. Which of the following is created by the Switchboard Manager?
   (a) A form to hold the switchboard
   (b) A table containing the commands associated with the switchboard
   (c) Both (a) and (b)
   (d) Neither (a) nor (b)

2. Which of the following describes the storage of the tables and objects for the application developed in the chapter?
   (a) Each table is stored in its own database
   (b) Each object is stored in its own database
   (c) The tables are stored in one database and the objects in another
   (d) The tables and objects are stored in the same database

3. Which of the following is true regarding the Link Tables command as it was used in the chapter?
   (a) It was executed from the Sports Objects database
   (b) It was executed from the Sports Tables database
   (c) Both (a) and (b)
   (d) Neither (a) nor (b)

4. What happens when an Access database is opened initially?
   (a) Access executes the AutoExec macro if the macro exists
   (b) Access opens the AutoExec form if the form exists
   (c) Both (a) and (b)
   (d) Neither (a) nor (b)

5. Which statement is true regarding the AutoExec macro?
   (a) Every database must have an AutoExec macro
   (b) A database may have more than one AutoExec macro
   (c) Both (a) and (b)
   (d) Neither (a) nor (b)

6. Which of the following are examples of arguments?
   (a) MsgBox and OpenForm
   (b) Message type (e.g., critical) and Form name
   (c) Both (a) and (b)
   (d) Neither (a) nor (b)

7. Which of the following can be imported from another Access database?
   (a) Tables and forms
   (b) Queries and reports
   (c) Both (a) and (b)
   (d) Neither (a) nor (b)

8. How do you change the properties of a command button on a form?
   (a) Open the form in Form view, then click the left mouse button to display a shortcut menu
   (b) Open the form in Form view, then click the right mouse button to display a shortcut menu
   (c) Open the form in Form Design view, then click the left mouse button to display a shortcut menu
   (d) Open the form in Form Design view, then click the right mouse button to display a shortcut menu

9. Which of the following is true regarding the Unmatched Query Wizard with respect to the Sports league database?
   (a) It can be used to identify teams without players
   (b) It can be used to identify players without teams
   (c) Both (a) and (b)
   (d) Neither (a) nor (b)

10. Which of the following can be associated with the On Click property of a command button?
    (a) An event procedure created by the Command Button Wizard
    (b) A macro created by the user
    (c) Either (a) or (b)
    (d) Neither (a) nor (b)

11. Which of the following was suggested as essential to a backup strategy?
    (a) Backing up files at the end of every session
    (b) Storing the backup file(s) at another location
    (c) Both (a) and (b)
    (d) Neither (a) nor (b)

12. Which of the following is true if the On Click property of a command button contains the entry, *Player Draft.Update List*?
    (a) Update List is an event procedure
    (b) Player Draft is an event procedure
    (c) Player Draft is a macro in the Update List macro group
    (d) Update List is a macro in the Player Draft macro group

13. Which of the following is true?
    (a) An existing database may be split into two separate databases, one containing the tables, and one containing the other objects
    (b) Once the objects in a database have been linked to the tables in another database, the name and/or location of the latter database can never be changed
    (c) Both (a) and (b)
    (d) Neither (a) nor (b)

14. The F6 and F11 function keys were introduced as shortcuts. Which of the following is true about these keys?
    (a) The F6 key switches between the top and bottom sections of the Macro window
    (b) The F11 key makes the Database window the active window
    (c) Both (a) and (b)
    (d) Neither (a) nor (b)

15. Which of the following was suggested as a way to organize macros and thus limit the number of macros that are displayed in the Database window?
    (a) Avoid macro actions that have only a single argument
    (b) Avoid macros that contain only a single action
    (c) Create a macro group
    (d) All of the above

ANSWERS

1. c	**6.** b	**11.** c
2. c	**7.** c	**12.** d
3. a	**8.** d	**13.** a
4. a	**9.** c	**14.** c
5. d	**10.** c	**15.** c

BUILDS ON

HANDS-ON
EXERCISE 3
PAGES 343–351

1. Report Design: Complete the three hands-on exercises in the chapter, then create the report shown in Figure 7.11. The report prints the team rosters, which shows all the players on each team. The teams are listed alphabetically, and by last name within each team.

    a. Create a Team Rosters query that contains fields from the Teams table and the Players table. This query includes a concatenated field that contains the player's first and last name as follows, = [LastName] & ", " & [FirstName], where LastName and FirstName are field names within the Players table. The ampersands concatenate (join) the two fields together with a comma to separate the first and last names.

    b. The Report Wizard is the easiest way to create the initial report based on the query from part a. The report header can be copied directly from the Report template that appears in the database.

    c. Print the completed report for your instructor as proof that you did this exercise.

FIGURE 7.11 *Report Design (Exercise 1)*

BUILDS ON

HANDS-ON
EXERCISE 3
PAGES 343–351

2. A Look Ahead: Open the Players form, click the button to add a player, then note that to add a player you must first click the First Name text box. You can automate the process by adding a VBA statement to the event procedure that was created by the Command Button Wizard. (VBA—Visual Basic for Applications—is a powerful programming language that is covered in the next chapter.) Proceed as follows.

    a. Open the Players form in Design view. Point to the Add Player command button, then click the right mouse button to display a shortcut menu. Click Properties to display the Properties dialog box. Click the down arrow on the vertical scroll bar until you can see the On Click property, which contains the entry [Event Procedure]. Click this entry, then click the Build Button (the three dots to the right of the box) to display the associated VBA code.

b. Click under the DoCmd statement and add the line FirstName.SetFocus as shown in Figure 7.12. This tells Access to go to the control called FirstName after inserting a new record. Click the Save button, then close the VBA window.

c. Click the Form View button to switch to Form view and test the Add Player macro. Click the Add Player command button. You should be positioned in the First Name box and can start typing immediately.

d. Click the Close Form command button when you have completed the record. Click Yes if prompted to save the changes to the Players form.

e. This may seem like a lot of trouble, but the end user appreciates this type of convenience. You can modify the Coaches form in similar fashion, then submit the completed disk to your instructor as proof you completed the exercise.

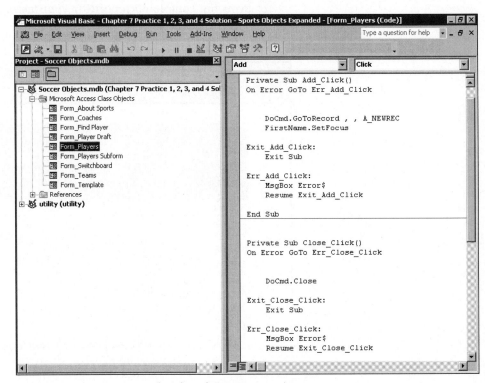

FIGURE 7.12   *A Look Ahead (Exercise 2)*

BUILDS ON

HANDS-ON
EXERCISE 3
PAGES 343–351

3. The Find Player Query: The player draft was only partially completed in the third hands-on exercise in that the Find Player button displayed the prototype macro, as opposed to locating a specific player. You can add the additional functionality in Figure 7.13 as follows:

a. Create a parameter query that requests the last name of a player, then displays all fields for that player.

b. Copy the existing Players form to a new form called Find Player. Change the Record Source property of the Find Player form to the parameter query you created in part a.

c. Change the Find Player macro in the Player Draft group so that it opens the Find Player form you just created.

d. Test the Find Player button. The player draft is now complete.

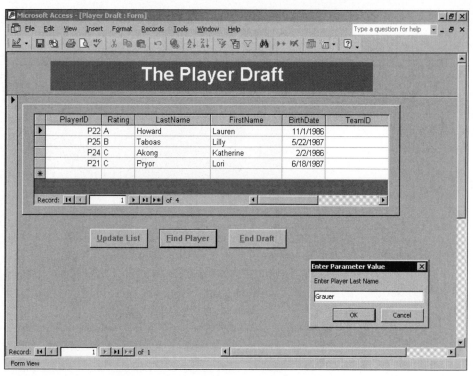

FIGURE 7.13   *The Find Player Query (Exercise 3)*

HANDS-ON
EXERCISE 3
PAGES 343–351

4. The Report Switchboard: The switchboard in Figure 7.14 is an expanded version of the switchboard from the third hands-on exercise. Your assignment is to create the indicated reports and queries, then modify the switchboard to display those objects. The Team Rosters report corresponds to the report that was created in exercise 1.

   a. The parameter query is to display the players on a specific team. Note, however, that you cannot run a query directly through the Switchboard Manager. There are two alternatives. You can create a macro to run a query, then run the macro from the Switchboard Manager. Alternatively, you can create a report based on the parameter query, and open the report from the Switchboard Manager.

   b. The Totals query is to display the team name and number of players.

   c. The Unmatched query (player draft) was implemented in the third hands-on exercise.

   d. Complete the Report Switchboard as indicated, then print each object for your instructor. Print the switchboard form itself as well as the table of switchboard items.

5. Password Protection: Close the Sports Objects database. Pull down the File menu, click the Open command to display the Open dialog box, click the Sports Objects database, then click the drop-down Open button and choose Open Exclusive. You must open the database in this way or else you will not be able to set a password. Next pull down the Tools menu, click Security, click Set Database Password, and follow the on-screen prompts as shown in Figure 7.15. Be careful, however because once you save a database with a password, you cannot open it if you forget the password.

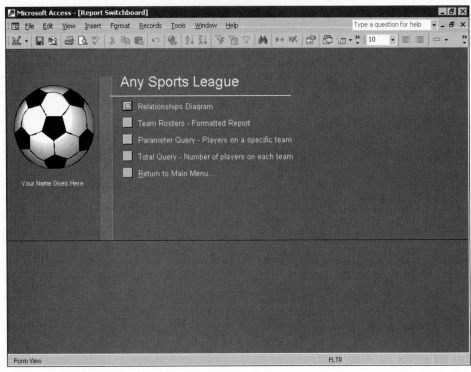

FIGURE 7.14 *The Report Switchboard (Exercise 4)*

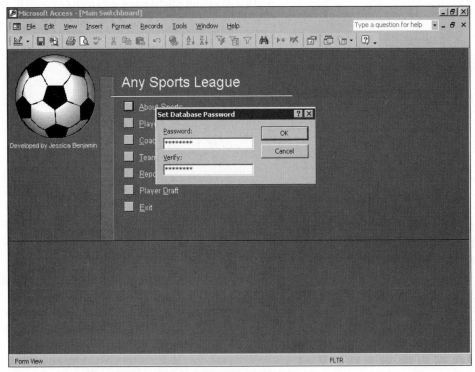

FIGURE 7.15 *Password Protection (Exercise 5)*

6. Class Scheduling: Figure 7.16 represents a database intended for class scheduling at a typical college or university. The scheduling process entails the coordination of course offerings as published in a registration schedule together with faculty assignments. The university may offer multiple sections of any given course at different times. The information about when a class meets is stored within the one-letter section designation; for example, section A meets from 9:00 to 9:50 on Mondays, Wednesdays, and Fridays.

a. The database contains separate tables for courses, sections, and faculty as can be seen in Figure 7.16. There are many-to-many relationships between courses and sections, between courses and faculty, and between faculty and sections. The key to the design is the creation of an additional Offerings table that includes the CourseID, SectionID, and FacultyID. The combination of these three fields could serve as the primary key of the Offerings table, but it is easier to add an additional field, the OfferingID with the AutoNumber field type. The additional fields, Building and Room, provide information as to where the specific course will meet.

b. We have designed the database for you. Your task is to implement our design by creating a database that contains the indicated tables and associated relationships. You do not have to enter data into any of the tables, but you will need to create the tables in order to create a relationships diagram.

c. We have embellished the report containing the relationships diagram to include a report header, with a modified font and selected clip art. These elements will be used in the next two practice exercises that develop the switchboard and a report template. The cosmetic design of a system is an important consideration that should be given careful attention. Print the completed report for your instructor.

d. Would this design be applicable to the comparable database at your school or university? Summarize your thoughts in a short note to your instructor.

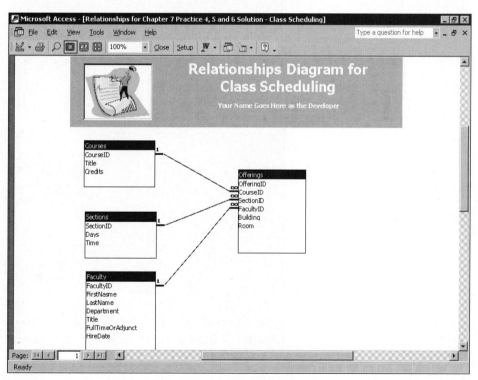

FIGURE 7.16   *Class Scheduling (Exercise 6)*

BUILDS ON

PRACTICE
EXERCISE 6
PAGE 359

7. Class Scheduling Prototype: The switchboard in Figure 7.17 continues the development of the class scheduling database and represents Version 1 of the completed system. You do not have to follow our design exactly, but you are required to include the indicated functionality. It is important, however, that you use a consistent design so that all of the objects in your database have a uniform look. This attention to detail enhances the visual appeal of a database and gives it a more professional appearance. Note the following:

a. The switchboard should open automatically whenever the database is opened. This can be accomplished through the Startup property or through the creation of an AutoExec macro.

b. The About Class Scheduling form contains the same logo that appears on the switchboard and is similar to the other forms that have appeared throughout the text.

c. The second menu option should print the report containing the relationships diagram from the previous exercise.

d. Create a prototype macro to indicate items under development as shown in Figure 7.17. The associated message box will appear upon clicking either of the data entry forms, which are not yet developed.

e. The Report Switchboard button should display a secondary switchboard that contains several reports that will be available in the completed system. Clicking any of the report buttons displays the message from the prototype macro. The Report Switchboard should also contain a button to return to the main switchboard.

f. The Exit button should display a message to the user to back up the system.

g. Print each switchboard and the table of switchboard items for your instructor. Add a cover sheet to complete the assignment.

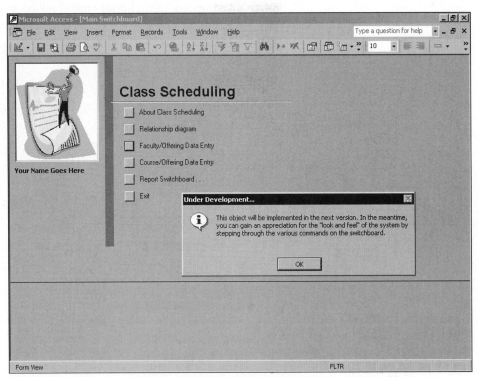

FIGURE 7.17   *Class Scheduling Prototype (Exercise 7)*

BUILDS ON

PRACTICE
EXERCISE 7
PAGE 360

8. Class Scheduling Template: Create a template for the class scheduling application that is consistent with the switchboard you developed in the previous exercise. Our template is shown in Figure 7.18. It was created in Form Design view without benefit of the Form Wizard, and it (the template) is not based on a table or query. The fields that appear in the template are labels (unbound controls) and are there to show the user the proposed color scheme that will appear on the finished form. Modify the data entry buttons on the main switchboard to display the template you just created, as opposed to the prototype macro. Print the template for your instructor.

   a. Create a simple faculty form based on the template. Start in the Database window. Select the template, press Ctrl+C to copy the template to the clipboard, press Ctrl+V to paste the contents of the clipboard into the database, then name the copied form Faculty.

   b. Go to the Design view of the newly created Faculty form as shown in Figure 7.18. Right click the Form Selector button of the form to display the Properties sheet, then change the Record Source to the Faculty table. Close the Properties sheet.

   c. The field list for the Faculty table opens automatically. Delete the dummy fields from the original template, then click and drag the fields from the field list to the form. Add the necessary command buttons and save the form.

   d. Add your instructor to the Faculty table and print the associated form.

   e. Create a report template that is based on the relationships diagram created earlier. Copy the existing report and use the duplicated object as the basis of the report template. The consistent design enhances the visual appeal of your database and gives it a professional look. Print the template for your instructor.

   f. Add a cover sheet to complete the assignment.

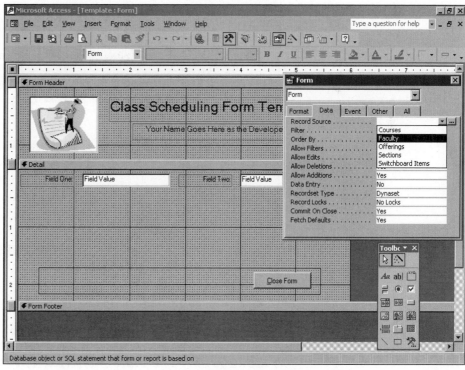

FIGURE 7.18 *Class Scheduling Template (Exercise 8)*

9. The Video Store: You have an internship at the local video store, which rents and/or sells tapes to customers. The store maintains the usual information about every customer (name, address, phone number, and so on). It also has detailed information about every movie such as its duration, rating, rental price, and purchase price. There is a subtlety in the design because the video store stocks multiple copies (tapes) of the same movie. Customers rent tapes (that contain movies), as opposed to renting movies.

a. The Movies table contains the detailed information about each movie. There is a one-to-many relationship between movies and tapes; that is, one movie can have many tapes, but a specific tape is associated with only one movie.

b. There is a many-to-many relationship between customers and tapes; that is, one customer can rent several tapes, and the same tape will (over time) be rented to many customers. This in turn gives rise to the Customer-Tape or Rentals table as shown in Figure 7.19.

c. We have designed the database for you. Your task is to implement our design by creating a database that contains the indicated tables and associated relationships. You do not have to enter data into any of the tables, but you will need to create the tables in order to create a relationships diagram for your instructor.

d. We have embellished the report containing the relationships diagram to include a report header, with a modified font and selected clip art. These elements will be used in the next two practice exercises that develop the switchboard and a report template. The cosmetic design of a system is an important consideration that should be given careful attention. Print the completed report for your instructor.

e. Add a cover sheet to complete the assignment.

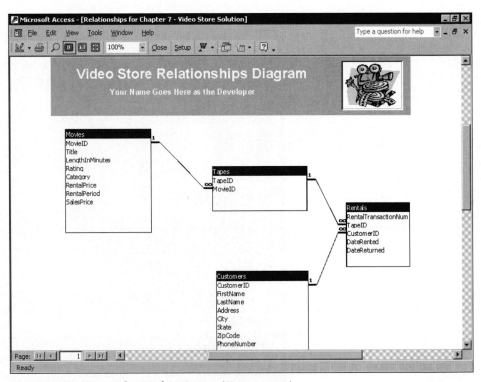

FIGURE 7.19   *The Video Store (Exercise 9)*

BUILDS ON

PRACTICE
EXERCISE 9
PAGE 362

10. Video Store Prototype: The switchboard in Figure 7.20 continues the development of the Video Store database and represents Version 1 of the completed system. You do not have to follow our design exactly, but you are required to include the indicated functionality. It is important, however, that you use a consistent design so that all of the objects in your database have a uniform look. This attention to detail enhances the visual appeal of a database and gives it a more professional appearance.

a. The switchboard should open automatically whenever the database is opened. This can be accomplished through the Startup property or through the creation of an AutoExec macro.

b. The About Video Store form contains the same logo that appears on the switchboard and is similar to the other forms that have appeared throughout the text.

c. The second menu option should print the report containing the relationships diagram from the previous exercise.

d. Create a prototype macro to indicate items under development as shown in Figure 7.20. The associated message box will appear upon clicking either of the data entry forms, which are not yet developed.

e. The Report Switchboard button should display a secondary switchboard that contains several reports that will be available in the completed system. Clicking any of the report buttons displays the message from the prototype macro. The Report Switchboard should also contain a button to return to the main switchboard.

f. The Exit button should display a message to the user to back up the system.

g. Print each switchboard and the table of switchboard items for your instructor. Add a cover sheet to complete the assignment.

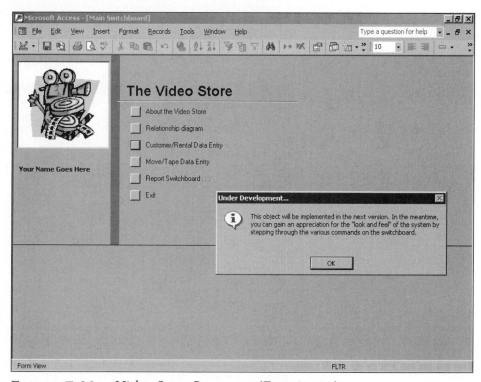

FIGURE 7.20 *Video Store Prototype (Exercise 10)*

BUILDS ON

PRACTICE
EXERCISE 10
PAGE 363

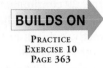

11. Video Store Templates: Continue the development of the Video Store database by creating the report and form templates shown in Figures 7.21a and 7.21b, respectively. Both templates are created in Design view, without benefit of the associated Wizard. The fields that appear are text boxes as opposed to specific controls. You do not have to follow our design exactly, but you should be consistent with the switchboard developed earlier.

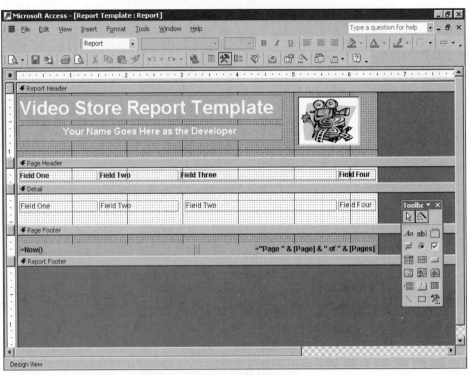

(a) Report Template

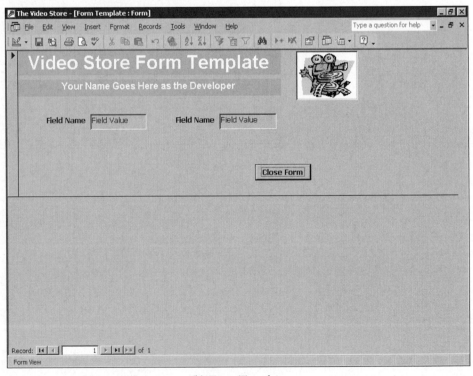

(b) Form Template

FIGURE 7.21 *Video Store Templates (Exercise 11)*

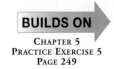

BUILDS ON

CHAPTER 5
PRACTICE EXERCISE 5
PAGE 249

12. **Replicating a Database:** A replica is a copy of a database that can be synchronized with other replicas to coordinate changes to the underlying data. Open the Turkeys To Go database from Chapter 5, pull down the Tools menu, click Replication, then click the Create Replica command. Click Yes when asked whether to close the database and create a replica. You will see a message suggesting that Access create a backup copy of your database. Click Yes.

a. Access creates a replica of the database and displays the Location of New Replica dialog box in which you specify the name and folder for the replica. Use the default name, but save the replica in the Exploring Access folder.

b. You will see a message similar to Figure 7.22 in which Access indicates that it converted the original database to the Design master, and further that it has created a replica. Note that the last sentence in the message indicating only the Design master can accept changes to the database structure, but that changes to the data can be made in either the Design master or the replica. Click OK. Look at the title bar of the Database window and note that "Database Master" has been appended to the name of the database.

c. Click the Data entry button on the switchboard. Add Jessica Benjamin as a new franchisee, with FranchiseeID F011. Complete the other information as you see fit. Close the data entry form. Click the Exit button on the switchboard to close this database.

d. Start Windows Explorer and open the Replica of the Turkeys To Go database in the Exploring Access folder. Pull down the Tools menu, click Replication, then click the Synchronize Now command. Click Yes when Access asks if you want to close the open objects.

e. You should see a Synchronize Database dialog box. The option button to synchronize directly with the replica is selected. Click OK. Click Yes when asked whether to close the database, after which you should get a message that the synchronization was successful. Note that the title bar indicates you are working in the replica, not the Design master.

f. Click the Data entry button on the switchboard. Locate the record for Jessica Benjamin, the franchisee you just added. Use the form to add a new restaurant (RestaurantID 8765) with any parameters you like.

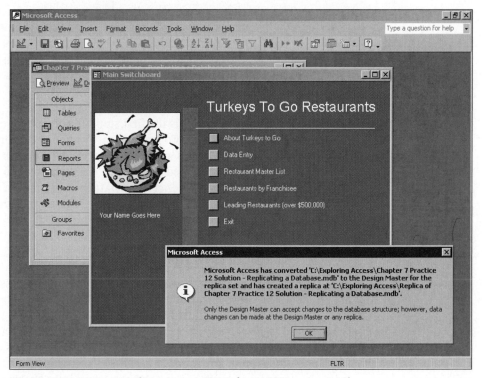

FIGURE 7.22 *Replicating a Database (Exercise 12)*

Computer Repair

The Director of the Administrative Services has come to you for assistance in implementing a system to track the repairs associated with the computers on campus. The data about each computer—such as the make and model, operating system, location on campus, and so on—is stored in a Computers table within an Access database. The faculty or staff member responsible for that computer is also indicated. The data about the faculty and staff is stored in a separate table. (One individual, such as the director of a specific computer lab, can be responsible for many computers, but a given computer is the responsibility of one person.)

Problems inevitably occur, and when they do, the faculty or staff member responsible for that computer calls the Director's office to report the problem. The nature of the problem is recorded, and a technician is assigned to fix it. (Technicians are employed as independent contractors and do not appear in the Faculty/Staff table.) One technician can work on many computers, and a specific computer may be worked on by different technicians. Your assignment is to design a database that will maintain this data and produce the associated reports. The database should be able to list all computers that are currently under repair. It should also provide a report that shows all completed repairs. Other reports might include all problems for a specific technician, or all problems reported by a particular faculty member. Your instructor has asked for a report containing the relationships diagram.

Find a Mate Dating Service

The Find a Mate Dating Service employs dating counselors to match its clients to one another. Each counselor works with many clients, but a specific client always works with the same counselor. All clients complete extensive questionnaires that describe themselves and the qualities they wish to find in a mate. The counselors evaluate this information and pair the agency's clients with one another to create a date. One client can have many dates, and a date has many (actually two) clients. Feedback is important, and each client is asked for his or her reaction to the date.

Your assignment is to design a database that will track counselors, clients, and dates. It should be able to list all dates for a specific client as well as all dates arranged by a specific counselor. Print the relationships diagram.

Security Options

Setting a password is the first step in protecting a database. You can also set different levels of password protection, by giving different permissions to different users. Pull down the Tools menu, click Security, then click User and Group Permissions to display the associated dialog box. Use help to explore the options within this dialog box. You can also encrypt a database through a different command within the Security menu. Explore the various security options, then summarize your findings in a short note to your instructor.

Compacting versus Compressing

The importance of adequate backup has been stressed throughout the text. As a student, however, your backup may be limited to what you can fit on a single floppy disk, which in turn creates a problem if the size of your database grows beyond 1.4Mb. Two potential solutions involve compacting and/or compressing the database. Compacting is done from within Access, whereas compressing requires additional software. In addition, you can split a database in two, then compact and/or compress each database. Investigate both of these techniques with respect to the Sports league database created in the chapter. Be sure to indicate to your instructor the reduction in file size that you were able to achieve.

Creating More Powerful Applications: Introduction to VBA

AFTER READING THIS CHAPTER YOU WILL BE ABLE TO:

1. Describe the relationship of VBA to Microsoft Office; list several reasons to use VBA in creating an Access application.
2. Describe the components of the Module window; differentiate between the Procedure view and the Full Module view.
3. Describe two different ways to create an event procedure; explain how to navigate between existing procedures.
4. Explain how the Quick Info and Complete Word features facilitate the entry of VBA statements.
5. Create a combo box to locate a record on a form; explain why an event procedure is required for the combo box to function properly.
6. Describe the parameters associated with the MsgBox statement; explain how MsgBox can be used as a function to return a value from the user.
7. Create an event procedure to facilitate data entry through keyboard shortcuts.
8. Create an event procedure that substitutes application-specific messages for the standard Access error messages.
9. Describe several types of data validation; create an event procedure that warns the user a field has been omitted, giving the user the option to save the record without entering the data.

You can accomplish a great deal in Access without using Visual Basic. You can create an Access database consisting of tables, forms, queries, and reports, by executing commands from pull-down menus. You can use macros to create menus that tie those objects together so that the database is easier to use. Nevertheless, there comes a point where you need the power of a programming language to develop a truly useful application. Hence, this introduction to *Visual Basic for Applications* (or *VBA*), a subset of Visual Basic that is accessible from every application in Microsoft Office.

VBA is different from traditional programming languages in that it is event-driven. An *event* is any action that is recognized by Access. Opening or closing a form is an event. So is clicking a button in a form or entering data in a text box or other control on the form. The essence of VBA is the creation of *procedures* (or sets of VBA statements) that respond to specific events. Hence, the term *event procedure* will be used throughout the chapter.

To enhance an application through VBA, you decide which events are significant and what is to happen when those events occur. Then you develop the appropriate event procedures. You can, for example, create an event procedure that displays a splash (introductory) screen for the application every time a user opens the database. You can write an event procedure that creates a keyboard shortcut for data entry that executes when the user presses a particular keystroke combination. You can create an event procedure to display a specific message in place of the standard error message supplied by Access. In all instances, the execution of your procedures depends entirely on the user, because he or she triggers the underlying events through an appropriate action.

You can also use VBA to modify the event procedures that Access has created for you. If, for example, you used the Command Button Wizard to create a button to close a form, Access created the event procedure for you. The user clicks the button, and the event procedure closes the form. You can, however, use VBA to improve the procedure created by Access by adding a statement that reminds the user to back up the database after closing the form.

This chapter provides a general introduction to VBA through four hands-on exercises that enhance an application in different ways. Our approach is very different from that of other texts that run several hundred pages and cover the subject in extended detail. Our objective is to provide you with an appreciation for what can be accomplished, rather than to cover VBA in detail. We will show you how to create and modify simple procedures. We will also provide you with the conceptual framework to explore the subject in greater detail on your own.

One last point before we begin is that VBA is common to every application in Microsoft Office, and thus anything that you learn about VBA from within Access is applicable to the other applications as well. If, for example, you create a macro in Word or Excel, the macro recorder captures the keystrokes and then generates a VBA procedure that is accessible through the Word document or Excel workbook, respectively. You can modify the procedure by changing existing statements and/or by adding additional statements using the techniques in this chapter.

THE VBA PRIMER

There are two ways to learn the rudiments of VBA. You can begin your study with this chapter, which has you look at typical VBA procedures within an Access form, then proceed to the VBA primer at the end of the text to study the syntax more precisely. Alternatively, you may want to start with the primer, then return to this chapter to see the application of the various VBA statements within Access. Either way, the two chapters reinforce each other and provide a solid foundation in this important programming language.

The form in Figure 8.1 will be used throughout the chapter as the basis of our VBA examples. The form itself is unremarkable and parallels many of the forms that were developed throughout the text. It was created initially through the Form Wizard, then modified by moving and sizing controls as appropriate. What then is so special about the form, and how does it utilize VBA?

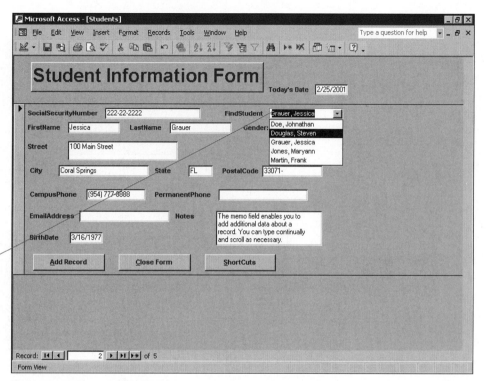

Find Student combo box

FIGURE 8.1   *User Form*

The answer lies beneath the surface and is best explained in conjunction with the dialog boxes in Figure 8.2. At first glance, the dialog boxes look like typical messages displayed by Microsoft Access. Look closely at the title bar of any message, however, and note that it has been changed to reflect the authors' introduction to Visual Basic. This is a subtle change that is easily implemented through VBA, and it gives your application a personal touch. Note, too, the different icons that are displayed in the various messages. This, too, is a subtle touch that further customizes the application and its messages.

Look closely at the content of each dialog box to learn more about the underlying VBA capability. The message in Figure 8.2a indicates that the user has omitted the e-mail address, then asks if the record should be saved anyway. This is an improvement over the built-in routines for data validation, which use the Required property to reject any record that omits the e-mail address. Should this occur, the user is notified that the field is required, but he or she cannot save the record unless a value is specified. Through VBA, however, the user has a choice and can opt to save the record even when there is no e-mail address.

The dialog box in Figure 8.2b is displayed as a result of clicking the Shortcuts command button on the form. The message implies that the user can use keyboard shortcuts to enter the city, state, and zip code for Miami or Coral Springs. True, the user could enter the data manually, but think how much time can be saved when there is extensive data entry.

Title bar is customized

Icon prompts user for further action

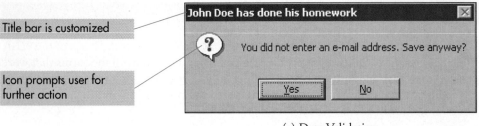

(a) Data Validation

Icon indicates an informational message

Keyboard shortcuts facilitate data entry

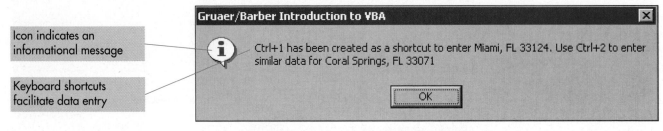

(b) Facilitating Data Entry

Icon indicates a warning

Simplified error message

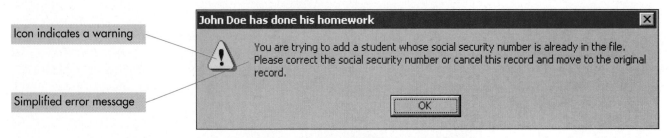

(c) Error Trapping

Icon indicates a critical event

Message alerts the user to subsequent action

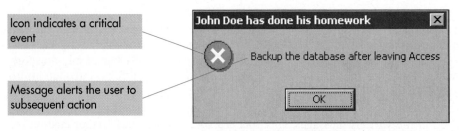

(d) Enhanced Communication with User

FIGURE 8.2 *Dialog Boxes*

Figure 8.2c displays a message indicating that one is attempting to add a student whose social security number is already in the file. The text is very straightforward and that is exactly the point. The default Access error message would not be as clear, and would have indicated that changes to the table were not successful because they would have created a duplicate value of the primary key. In other words, we used VBA to first detect the error, and then substituted a more explicit message. Finally, the message in Figure 8.2d simply reminds the user to back up the database upon exiting Access.

Modules and Procedures

There are, in essence, two different ways to learn VBA. The first is to immerse yourself in the theory and syntax before you attempt to develop any applications on your own. The second, and the one we follow, is to start with an overall appreciation of what it can do, then plunge right in. You need some basic vocabulary, but after that you can model your procedures on ours and create some very powerful applications in the process.

Visual Basic code is developed in units called procedures. There are two types of procedures, general procedures and event procedures. *Event procedures* are the essence of an Access application and run automatically in response to an event such as clicking a button or opening a form. *General procedures* do not run automatically, but are called explicitly from within another procedure. We focus exclusively on event procedures.

All (general and event) procedures are stored in modules; that is, one module contains one or more procedures. Every form in an Access database has its own module (known as a *class module*), which contains the procedures for that form. A procedure is either public or private. A *private procedure* is accessible only from within the module in which it is contained. A *public procedure* is accessible from anywhere.

The procedures in a module are displayed and edited through the *Module window* within the Visual Basic editor. Figure 8.3, for example, displays the Module window for the student form shown earlier in Figure 8.1. Four different procedures are visible, each of which is associated with a different event. Each procedure begins with a procedure header that names the procedure. This is followed by the executable statements within the procedure, followed by the End Sub statement to mark the end of the procedure. Do not be concerned if you do not understand the precise syntax of every statement. Try, instead, to gain an overall appreciation for what the procedures do.

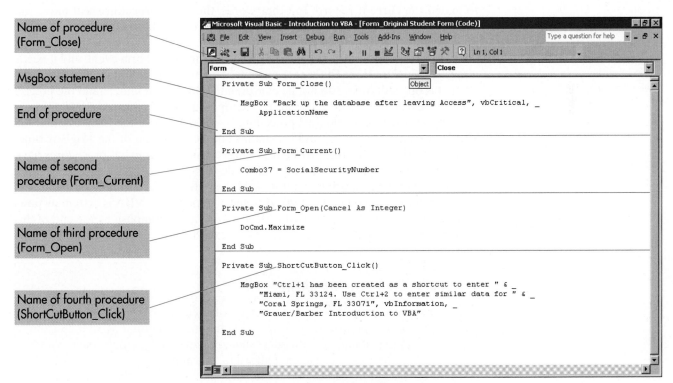

FIGURE 8.3 *The Module Window*

The first event procedure is for the **Close Form event**. The procedure header contains the key word Sub, followed by the procedure name (Form_Close). The **MsgBox statement** within the procedure displays the message box (shown earlier in Figure 8.2d) when the event occurs. Thus whenever the user closes the form, either by clicking the Close button on the form or by clicking the Close button in the document window, the event procedure is triggered and one is reminded to back up the database. (See boxed tip.)

The syntax of the MsgBox function is typical of many VBA statements and is best understood if you view the statement as it might appear in a help screen *MsgBox (prompt, buttons, title)*. The entries in parentheses are known as **arguments** (or **parameters**) and determine the contents of the message box. The first argument is contained in quotation marks, and it specifies the prompt (or message text) that appears within the message box. The second argument indicates the type of command buttons (if any) and the associated icon that appear within the dialog box. This argument is specified as an **intrinsic** (or previously defined) **constant** (vbCritical in this example), and it determines the icon that is to appear in the message box. The third argument contains the text that appears in the title bar of the message box. It, too, appears in quotation marks.

The second event procedure is associated with the **Current event** of the form and is the focus of our first hands-on exercise. The nature of this procedure is much less intuitive than the previous example, yet this event procedure is critical to the success of the form. Return to the Student Form shown in Figure 8.1 and note the presence of a combo box to find a specific student. The user clicks the drop-down arrow on the combo box and selects a student from the displayed list, after which the data for that student is displayed in the form.

The combo box was created through the Combo Box Wizard, and it works well, but it does have one limitation. If the user elects to move from one record to the next by clicking a navigation button at the bottom of the form, the combo box is out of sync in that it does not reflect the name of the new student. Hence the need to write a VBA procedure for the Current event to change the value in the combo box to match the current record. In other words, the VBA procedure will move the SocialSecurityNumber of the current record to the combo box control whenever the record changes.

The third event procedure is associated with the Open Form event, and it needs almost no explanation. The single executable statement will maximize the form when it is opened. Again, do not be concerned if you do not understand the precise syntax of every statement in our initial examples as we add further explanation in the chapter. The fourth and final procedure is associated with the Click event of the ShortCut command button, and it contains another example of the MsgBox function. Note, too, that for this procedure to make sense, other event procedures have to be created to implement the shortcuts as described.

We would be misleading you if we said that VBA is easy. It's not, but neither is it as complicated as you might think. And more importantly, VBA is extremely powerful. We think you will be pleased with what you can accomplish by the end of this chapter. Once again, it is time for a hands-on exercise.

A SIMPLE STRATEGY FOR BACKUP

We cannot overemphasize the importance of adequate backup. Backup procedures are personal and vary from individual to individual as well as from installation to installation. Our suggested strategy is very simple, namely that you back up whatever you cannot afford to lose and that you do so at the end of every session. Be sure to store the backup at a different location from the original file.

CREATE A COMBO BOX AND ASSOCIATED VBA PROCEDURE

Objective To create a combo box to locate a record; to create a VBA procedure to synchronize the combo box with the current record. Use Figure 8.4.

Step 1: **Open the Introduction to VBA Database**

➤ Start Access. Open the **Introduction to VBA database** in the **Exploring Access folder** as shown in Figure 8.4a.

➤ If necessary, click the **Forms button**. Select (click) the **Original Student Form**. Pull down the **Edit menu** and click the **Copy command** (or click the **Copy button** on the Database toolbar). The form is copied to the clipboard.

➤ Pull down the **Edit menu** a second time and click the **Paste command** (or click the **Paste button** on the Database toolbar) to display the Paste As dialog box. Type **Completed Student Form** and press **enter**.

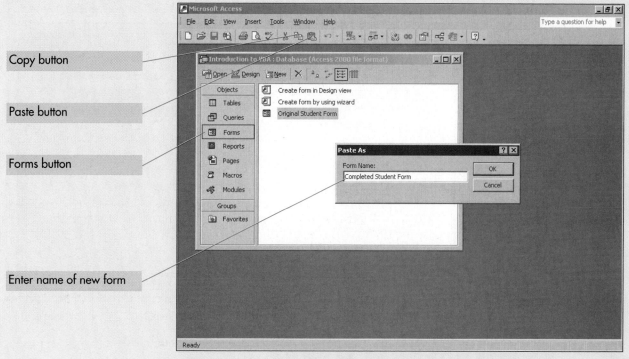

Copy button

Paste button

Forms button

Enter name of new form

(a) Open the Introduction to VBA Database (step 1)

FIGURE 8.4 *Hands-on Exercise 1*

KEYBOARD SHORTCUTS—CUT, COPY, AND PASTE

Ctrl+X, Ctrl+C, and Ctrl+V are shortcuts to cut, copy, and paste, respectively, and apply to Windows applications in general. The shortcuts are easier to remember when you realize that the operative letters X, C, and V are next to each other at the bottom-left side of the keyboard.

Step 2: **The Combo Box Wizard**

> ➤ Open the newly created **Completed Student Form** in Design view. Maximize the window.
> ➤ Click the **Combo Box** tool on the Toolbox toolbar, then click and drag on the form next to the SSN control to create a combo box and start the Wizard.
> ➤ Select the option button to **Find a record on my form based on the value I selected in my combo box** as shown in Figure 8.4b. Click **Next**.
> ➤ Double click the **SocialSecurityNumber field** to move it from the list box of available fields (on the left of the Combo Box Wizard) to the list of selected fields. Double click the **LastName field** to move this field as well. Click **Next**.
> ➤ You should see the columns in the combo box as they will appear in the form. Be sure the Check box to Hide key column is checked. Click **Next**.
> ➤ Change the label of the combo box to **FindStudent** (do not use a space in the label). Click **Finish** to exit the Combo Box Wizard.

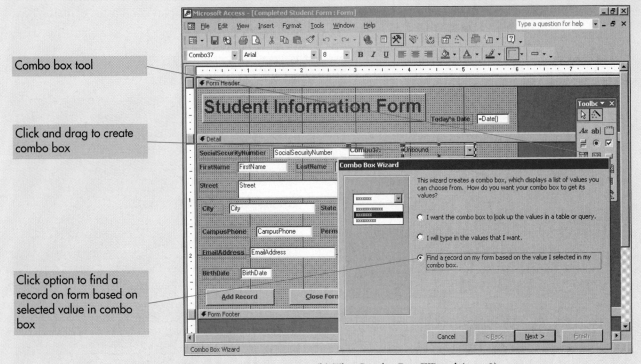

Combo box tool

Click and drag to create combo box

Click option to find a record on form based on selected value in combo box

(b) The Combo Box Wizard (step 2)

FIGURE 8.4 *Hands-on Exercise 1 (continued)*

SIZING AND MOVING A COMBO BOX AND ITS LABEL

A combo box is always created with an attached label. Select (click) the combo box, and it will have sizing handles and a move handle, but the label has only a move handle. Select the label (instead of the combo box) and the opposite occurs. To move a combo box and its label, click and drag the border of either object. To move either the combo box or its label, click and drag the move handle (a tiny square in the upper left corner) of the appropriate object.

Step 3:   **Move and Size the Combo Box**

➤ Move and size the newly created combo box to match the layout in Figure 8.4c. The Properties sheet is not yet visible. You will most likely have to decrease the size of the combo box and/or increase the size of the label.

➤ To align the combo box and/or its label with the other controls on the same row of the form, press and hold the **Shift key** to select the controls you want to align. Pull down the **Format menu**, click **Align**, then click **Top** to align the top of all selected elements.

➤ Point to the combo box, click the **right mouse button** to display a shortcut menu, then click **Properties** to display the Properties dialog box in Figure 8.4c. If necessary, click the **All tab**.

➤ Write down the name of the combo box (Combo37 in our figure) as you will need it in step 7. The name of your control may be different from ours.

➤ Click the **Row Source property** to select it, then click the **Build button** (the button with three dots) that appears when the row is selected.

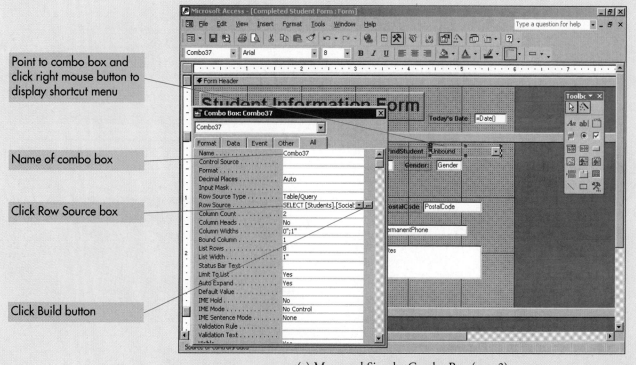

Point to combo box and click right mouse button to display shortcut menu

Name of combo box

Click Row Source box

Click Build button

(c) Move and Size the Combo Box (step 3)

FIGURE 8.4   *Hands-on Exercise 1 (continued)*

THE PROPERTY DIALOG BOX

You can change the appearance or behavior of a control in two ways—by changing the actual control on the form itself or by changing the underlying properties. Anything you do to the control automatically changes the associated property, and conversely, any change to the property sheet is reflected in the appearance or behavior of the control. We find ourselves continually switching back and forth between the two techniques.

Step 4: **Update the Row Source**

➤ You should see the query in Figure 8.4d, except that your query has not yet been completed. Click in the second column of the Field row, immediately after the LastName control.

➤ Press the **space bar** then type **&", "& FirstName**. Leave a space after the comma within the quotation marks. Press **enter**.

➤ Double click the border between this cell and the next to increase the column width so that you can see the entire expression. Note that Expr1: has been entered automatically in front of the expression.

➤ Click in the **Sort row** of the same column, click the **down arrow** if necessary, then click **Ascending** to display the records in alphabetical order by last name.

➤ Close the query. Click **Yes** when asked whether to save the changes that were made to the SQL statement. Close the Properties sheet.

➤ Click the **View button** to return to Form view.

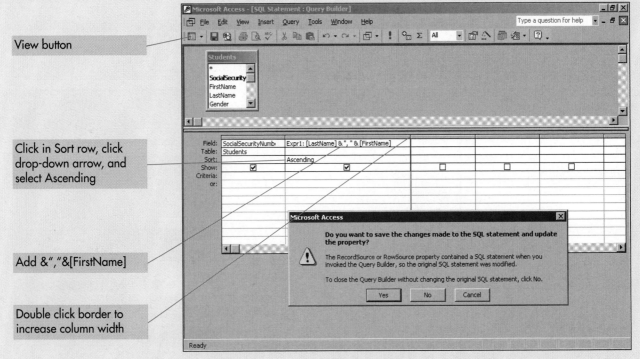

(d) Update the Row Source (step 4)

FIGURE 8.4 *Hands-on Exercise 1 (continued)*

CONCATENATING A STRING

The ampersand (&), or concatenation operator, indicates that the elements on either side of an expression are to appear adjacent to one another when the expression is displayed. You can also concatenate a literal and a field name such as "The employee's last name is" & LastName to display "The employee's last name is Smith," assuming that Smith is the current value in the LastName field.

Step 5:   **Test the Find Student Combo Box**

➤ If necessary, click the **navigation button** above the status bar to return to the first record in the table, Maryann Jones, as shown in Figure 8.4e.

➤ Click the **drop-down arrow** on the combo box you just created to display a list of students in alphabetical order. (If you do not see the list of students, press **Esc** to cancel whatever operation is in effect, then return to Design view to repeat the instructions in the previous steps.)

➤ Select (click) **Grauer, Jessica** from the list of names in the combo box. The form is updated to display the information for this student. Click the **drop-down arrow** a second time and select **Douglas, Steven** from the combo box. Again the form is updated.

➤ Click the **navigation button** to return to the first student. The form displays the record for Maryann Jones, but the combo box is *not* updated; it still displays Douglas, Steven.

➤ Click the **View button** to return to Design view.

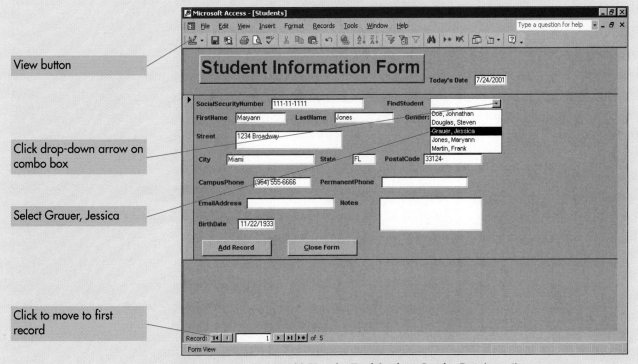

(e) Test the Find Student Combo Box (step 5)

FIGURE 8.4   *Hands-on Exercise 1 (continued)*

WHY USE VBA?

The combo box enables you to select a name from an alphabetical list, then updates the form to display the data for the corresponding record. All of this has been accomplished without the use of VBA. The problem is that the combo box is not updated automatically when records are selected via the navigation buttons. The only way to correct this problem is by writing a VBA procedure.

Step 6: Create an Event Procedure

➤ Point to the **form selector** box (the tiny square at the upper left of the form), click the **right mouse button** to display a shortcut menu, then click **Properties** to display the Form property sheet.

➤ Click the **Event tab**. Click the **On Current** event, then click the **Build button** to display the Choose Builder dialog box as shown in Figure 8.4f.

➤ Click (select) **Code Builder**, then click **OK**. A VBA window will open containing the module for the Completed Student Form.

➤ If necessary, maximize the VBA window and/or click the **Procedure View button** above the status bar. The insertion point is positioned automatically within a newly created event procedure.

➤ You should see a statement beginning Private Sub Form_Current( ) corresponding to the On Current event. You should also see the line ending End Sub, but no code appears between the Sub and End Sub statements.

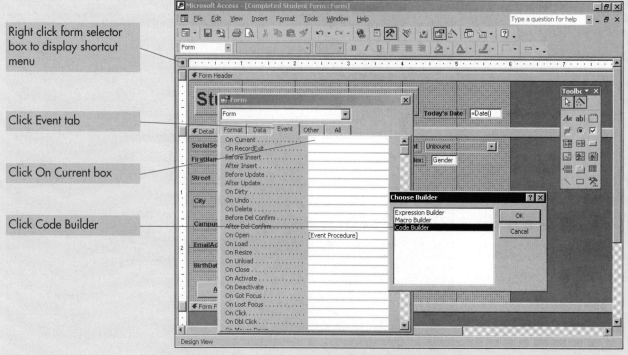

Right click form selector box to display shortcut menu

Click Event tab

Click On Current box

Click Code Builder

(f) Create an Event Procedure (step 6)

FIGURE 8.4 *Hands-on Exercise 1 (continued)*

CREATING AN EVENT PROCEDURE

There is only one correct way to create an event procedure, and that is the technique used in this exercise. Thus, you right click the form selector box to display the form properties, click the Event tab to select the desired event, click the Build button, and click the Code Builder. This in turn takes you to the VBA editor, where you enter the procedure. Do *not* create the event directly in the module window (without first clicking the Event tab). The latter technique appears reasonable, but it will not create the necessary association between the event and the code.

Step 7: **Complete the On Current Event Procedure**

➤ The insertion point should be on a blank line, between the Sub and End Sub statements. If not, click on the blank line. Press the **Tab key** to indent the statements within the procedure. Indentation makes your code easier to read, but is not a syntactical requirement.

➤ Type **Combo37** (use the number of your combo box as determined in step 3).

➤ If you do not remember the name of the combo box, click the button on the taskbar to return to the Form window, click in the combo box and click the **All tab**. Look at the entry in the **Name property**.

➤ Press the **space bar** after you have entered the name of your combo box, type an **equal sign**, and press the **space bar** a second time. Type **Social** (the first several letters in the name of the SocialSecurityNumber control).

➤ Pull down the **Edit menu** and click **Complete Word** (or press **Ctrl+Space**) to display all of the objects, properties, and methods that start with these letters.

➤ SocialSecurityNumber is already selected as shown in Figure 8.4g. Press the **space bar** to copy the selected item and complete the statement.

➤ Click the **Save button** on the Visual Basic toolbar. Close the VBA window.

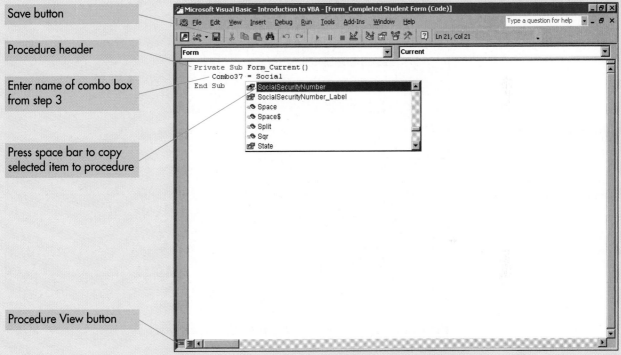

Save button

Procedure header

Enter name of combo box from step 3

Press space bar to copy selected item to procedure

Procedure View button

(g) Complete the On Current Event Procedure (step 7)

FIGURE 8.4 *Hands-on Exercise 1 (continued)*

USE THE RIGHT MOUSE BUTTON

The Quick Info and AutoList features are activated automatically as you create a VBA statement. The features can also be activated at any time by pulling down the Edit menu and selecting the Quick Info or List Properties/Methods commands, respectively. You can also point to any portion of a VBA statement and click the right mouse button to display a shortcut menu with options to display this information.

Step 8:   **Add Your Record**

➤ If necessary, click the button for the Access form on the task bar. Close the properties sheet. Click the **View button** to return to Form view.
➤ You should see the Student Information form. Click the **navigation button** to move to the next record. The data in the form is updated.
➤ Click the **navigation button** to return to the first record. Once again the data in the form is updated, as is the name in the combo box.
➤ Click the form's **Add Record command button**. You should see a blank form as shown in Figure 8.4h.
➤ Click in the **SocialSecurityNumber** text box and enter your Social Security number. Continue to enter your personal data.
➤ Close the form when you have finished entering data. Exit Access if you do not want to continue with the next exercise at this time.

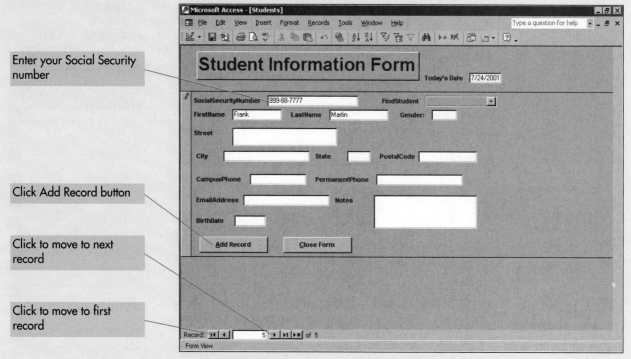

Enter your Social Security number

Click Add Record button

Click to move to next record

Click to move to first record

(h) Add Your Record (step 8)

FIGURE 8.4   *Hands-on Exercise 1 (continued)*

THE SET FOCUS METHOD

Ideally, clicking the Add Record button should position you in the SocialSecurityNumber field, without your having to click in the field to begin entering data. Open the Student form in Design view, right click the Add Record button and display the Properties dialog box. Click the Event tab, click the On Click property, then click the Build button. Insert the statement SocialSecurityNumber.SetFocus immediately after the DoCmd statement. Go to Form view, then click the Add button. You should be positioned in the SocialSecurityNumber field.

One of the most useful things you can accomplish through VBA is to provide the user with shortcuts for data entry. Many forms, for example, require the user to enter the city, state, and zip code for incoming records. In certain systems, such as a local store or company, this information is likely to be repeated from one record to the next. One common approach is to use the *Default property* in the table definition to specify default values for these fields, so that the values are automatically entered into a record.

What if, however, there are several sets of common values? Our local store, for example, may draw customers from two or three different cities, and we need to constantly switch among the different cities. The Default property is no longer effective because it is restricted to a single value. A better solution is to use VBA to provide a set of keyboard shortcuts such as Ctrl+1 for the first city, state, and zip code, Ctrl+2 for the next set of values, and so on. The user selects the appropriate shortcut, and the city, state, and zip code are entered automatically. The VBA code is shown in Figure 8.5.

Figure 8.5a displays the *KeyDown event* procedure to implement two shortcuts, Ctrl+1 and Ctrl+2, corresponding to Miami and Coral Springs, respectively. Figure 8.5b displays the *Click event* procedure for the shortcut button on the data entry form (which was shown in Figure 8.1). The user clicks the button, and a message is displayed that describes the shortcuts. The latter is very important because the system must communicate the availability of the shortcuts to the user, else how is he or she to know that they exist?

KeyCode argument

SetFocus method

```
Private Sub Form_KeyDown(KeyCode As Integer, Shift As Integer)
'The Key Preview Property of the form must be set to Yes
    If KeyCode = vbKey1 And Shift = acCtrlMask Then 'Ctrl+1 was pressed
        City = "Miami"
        State = "FL"
        PostalCode = "33124"
        CampusPhone.SetFocus
    End If
    If KeyCode = vbKey2 And Shift = acCtrlMask Then 'Ctrl+2 was pressed
        City = "Coral Springs"
        State = "FL"
        PostalCode = "33071"
        CampusPhone.SetFocus
    End If
End Sub
```

(a) Form KeyDown Event Procedure

MsgBox function

```
Private Sub ShortCutButton_Click()
    MsgBox "Ctrl+1 has been created as a shorcut to enter " & _
        "Miami, FL 33124. Use Ctrl+2 to enter similar data for " & _
        "Coral Springs, FL 33071.", vbInformation, _
        "Grauer/Barber Introduction to VBA"
End Sub
```

(b) ShortCutButton Click Event Procedure

FIGURE 8.5   *Procedure for Exercise 2*

Consider now the event procedure in Figure 8.5a and think about what it takes to implement a keyboard shortcut. In essence, the procedure must determine whether the user has used any of the existing shortcuts, and if so, enter the appropriate values in the form. There are different ways to accomplish this, the easiest being through a series of If statements, each of which checks for a specific shortcut. In other words, check to see if the user pressed Ctrl+1, and if so, enter the appropriate data. Then check to see if the user pressed Ctrl+2, etc. (If you have a previous background in programming, you may recognize alternate ways to implement this logic, either through the Else clause in the If statement, or through a Case statement. We explore these alternate structures later in the chapter, but for the time being, we want to keep our statements as simple as possible.)

Once again, we ask that you try to gain an overall appreciation for the procedure, as opposed to concerning yourself with every detail in every statement. You should recognize, for example, that the KeyDown event procedure requires two arguments, KeyCode and Shift, as can be seen from the parenthetical information in the **procedure header**. (The procedure header is created automatically as you shall see in the following hands-on exercise.)

The **KeyCode argument** tests for a specific number or letter; for example, KeyCode = vbKey1 determines whether the number 1 has been pressed by the user. (VBA defines several intrinsic constants such as vbKey1 or vbKeyA corresponding to the number 1 and letter A, respectively.) In similar fashion, the Shift argument tests for the Ctrl, Shift, or Alt key by checking for the intrinsic constants acCtrlMask, acShiftMask, and acAltMask, respectively. The And operator ensures that both keys (Ctrl and the number 1) have been pressed simultaneously.

Once a determination has been made as to whether a shortcut has been used, the corresponding values are moved to the indicated controls (City, State, and PostalCode) on the form. The **SetFocus method** then moves the insertion point to the CampusPhone control, where the user can continue to enter data into the form.

The Click event procedure in Figure 8.5b contains a single MsgBox statement which displays information about the shortcuts to the user when he or she clicks the Shortcuts button. The MsgBox statement has three parameters—a literal that is continued over two lines containing the text of the message, an intrinsic constant (vbInformation) indicating the icon that is to be displayed with the message, and a second literal indicating the text that is to appear in the title bar of the message dialog box.

The statement is straightforward, but it does illustrate the rules for continuing a VBA statement from one line to the next. To continue a statement, leave a space at the end of the line to be continued, type the underscore character, then continue the statement on the next line. You may not, however, break a line in the middle of a character string. Thus you need to complete the character string with a closing quotation mark, add an ampersand (as the concatenation operator to display this string with the character string on the next line), then leave a space followed by the underscore to indicate continuation.

BUILD CODE BY OBSERVATION AND INFERENCE

VBA is a powerful language with a subtle syntax and an almost endless variety of intrinsic constants. The expertise required to build the procedures for the keyboard shortcuts is beyond the novice, but once you are given the basic code, it is relatively easy to extend or modify the code to accommodate a specific application. Look at the code in Figure 8.5, for example, and decide how you would change the existing Ctrl+1 keyboard shortcut to reflect a different city. Can you add a third If statement to create a Ctrl+3 shortcut for a new city?

FACILITATING DATA ENTRY

Objective Create keyboard shortcuts to facilitate data entry. Use Figure 8.6 as a guide in the exercise.

Step 1: **Create the KeyDown Event Procedure**

➤ Open the **Introduction to VBA database** from the previous exercise. Click the **Forms button**, then open the **Completed Student Form** in Design view.

➤ Pull down the **View menu** and click **Code** (or click the **Code button** on the Database toolbar).

➤ If necessary, pull down the **View menu** and click **Project Explorer** to display the Project Explorer pane at the left of the window. If you are in Full Module view, click within any procedure, then click the **Procedure View button**.

➤ Click the **down arrow** in the Event list box and select **Form**.

➤ Click the **down arrow** in the Procedure list box to display the list of events for the form. Click **KeyDown** to create a procedure for this event.

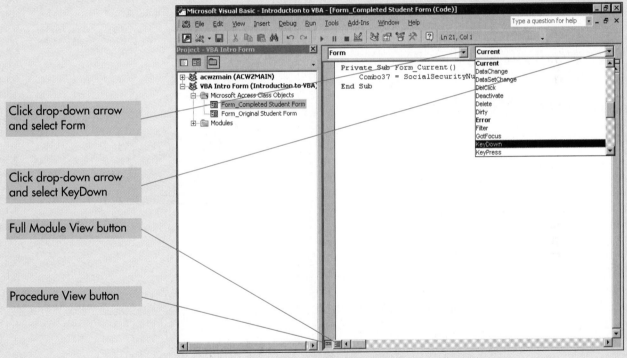

Click drop-down arrow and select Form

Click drop-down arrow and select KeyDown

Full Module View button

Procedure View button

(a) Create the KeyDown Event Procedure (step 1)

FIGURE 8.6 *Hands-on Exercise 2*

PROCEDURE VIEW VERSUS FULL MODULE VIEW

Procedures can be displayed individually, or multiple procedures can be viewed simultaneously. Click the Procedure View button to display one procedure, or click the Full Module View button to show multiple procedures. Either way, you can press Ctrl+PgDn and Ctrl+PgUp to move between procedures in the Module window.

Step 2: **Correct the Compile Error**

➤ The Procedure header and End Sub statements for the KeyDown event procedure are created automatically as shown in Figure 8.6b. The insertion point is positioned on the blank line between these two statements.

➤ Type an **apostrophe** (to indicate a comment), then enter the text of the comment as shown in the figure. Press **enter** when you have completed the comment. The line turns green to indicate it is a comment.

➤ Press the **Tab key** to indent the first line of code, then enter the statement exactly as it appears in the figure. Press **enter**. You should see the error message because we made a (deliberate) error in the If statement to illustrate what happens when you make an error.

➤ Click **OK** if you know the reason for the error, or click **Help** to display a screen describing the error, then close the Help window.

➤ Now return to the VBA statement, type a space at the end of the line, and add the key word **Then** to correct the error. Press **enter** to complete the statement. The error message should not appear.

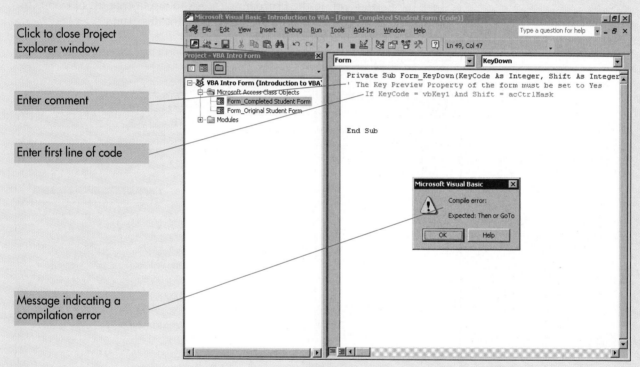

Click to close Project Explorer window

Enter comment

Enter first line of code

Message indicating a compilation error

(b) Correct the Compile Error (step 2)

FIGURE 8.6 *Hands-on Exercise 2 (continued)*

RED, GREEN, AND BLUE

Visual Basic for Applications uses different colors for different types of statements (or a portion of those statements). Any statement containing a syntax error appears in red. Comments appear in green. Key words, such as Sub and End Sub, appear in blue.

Step 3: **Complete the KeyDown Event Procedure**

➤ Close the Project Explorer window and complete the KeyDown procedure as shown in Figure 8.6c. Use what you know about the Cut, Copy, and Paste commands to facilitate entering the code.

➤ You could, for example, copy the first If statement, then modify the code as appropriate, rather then typing it from scratch. Select the statements to cut or copy to the clipboard, then paste them elsewhere in the module.

➤ If the results are different from what you expected or intended, click the Undo command immediately to reverse the effects of the previous command.

➤ Be sure that your code matches the code in Figure 8.6c. The indentation is not a syntactical requirement of VBA, per se, but is used to make the statements easier to read.

➤ Click the **Save button** to save the module.

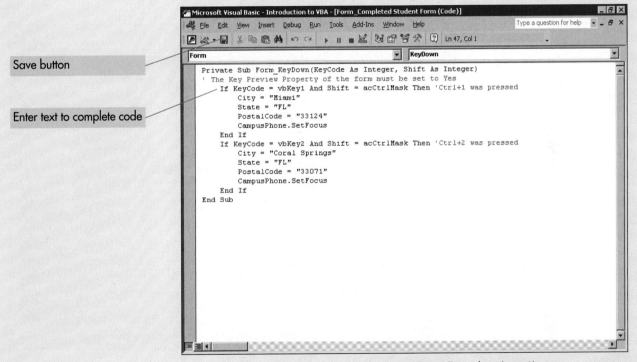

(c) Complete the KeyDown Event Procedure (step 3)

FIGURE 8.6 *Hands-on Exercise 2 (continued)*

THE COMPLETE WORD TOOL

You know that your form contains a control to reference the postal code, but you are not quite sure of the spelling. The Complete Word tool can help. Enter the first several characters, then press Ctrl+Space (or pull down the Edit menu and click Complete Word). VBA will complete the term for you if you have entered a sufficient number of letters, or it will display all of the objects, properties, and methods that begin with the letters you have entered. Use the down arrow to scroll through the list until you find the item, then press the space bar to complete the entry.

Step 4: **Set the Key Preview Property**

➤ The Key Preview property of the form must be set to Yes to complete the keyboard shortcut. Click the taskbar button to return to the **Completed Student Form**.

➤ Point to the **form selector box** (the tiny square at the upper left of the form). Click the **right mouse button** to display a context-sensitive menu with commands for the entire form.

➤ Click **Properties** to display the Form Properties dialog box. Click the **Event tab** and scroll until you can click the **Key Preview property**. Change the property to **Yes** as shown in Figure 8.6d.

➤ Close the Form Property dialog box. Save the form, which now contains the new procedure for the keyboard shortcut. The procedure should be tested as soon as it completed.

➤ Click the **View button** on the Form Design toolbar to return to Form view.

Click Event tab

Point to form selector box and click right mouse button to display shortcut menu

Click KeyPreview box

Click drop-down arrow and click Yes

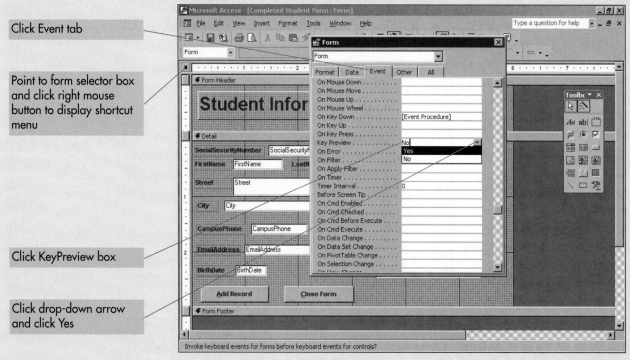

(d) Set the Key Preview Property (step 4)

FIGURE 8.6 *Hands-on Exercise 2 (continued)*

USE THE PROPERTY SHEET

Every object on a form has its own property sheet. This enables you to change the appearance or behavior of a control in two ways—by changing the control through application of a menu command or toolbar button, or by changing the underlying property sheet. Anything you do to the control changes the associated property, and conversely, any change to the property sheet is reflected in the appearance or behavior of the control.

Step 5: **Test the Procedure**

➤ Click the **navigation button** to move to the first record in the table as shown in Figure 8.6e. Press **Ctrl+2** to change the City, State, and Postal Code to reflect Coral Springs, as per the shortcut you just created.

➤ The data changes automatically, and you are automatically positioned on the CampusPhone field. The record selector changes to a pencil to indicate that the data has been edited, but not yet saved.

➤ If the shortcut does not work, return to step 4 and check that the Key Preview property has been set to Yes. If the shortcut still does not work, return to the module for the form and check the VBA statements.

➤ Press **Ctrl+1** to change the city to Miami. The data should change automatically, after which you are positioned in the CampusPhone field.

➤ Click the **View button** to return to the Design view of the form.

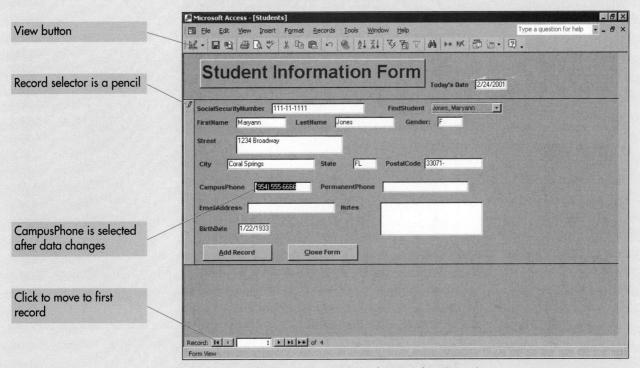

(e) Test the Procedure (step 5)

FIGURE 8.6 *Hands-on Exercise 2 (continued)*

CHANGE THE TAB ORDER

The Tab key provides a shortcut in the finished form to move from one field to the next; that is, you press Tab to move forward to the next field and Shift+Tab to return to the previous field. The order in which fields are selected corresponds to the sequence in which the controls were entered onto the form, and need not correspond to the physical appearance of the actual form. To restore a left-to-right, top-to-bottom sequence, pull down the View menu, click Tab Order, then select AutoOrder.

Step 6: **Create the ShortCut Command Button**

➤ Click and drag the **Command Button** tool on the Toolbox toolbar to create a new command button as shown in Figure 8.6f.

➤ The Command Button Wizard starts automatically. This time, however, you want to create the Click event procedure for this button yourself.

➤ Click the **Cancel button** as soon as you see the wizard. Right click the newly created command button and display its property sheet. Click the **All tab**.

➤ Change the Name property to **ShortCutButton**. Change the Caption property to **&ShortCuts**.

➤ Click the **Event tab**. Click the **On Click property**, click the **Build button**, click **Code Builder**, then click **OK** to display the Module window.

Change Name property

Change Caption property

Click command button tool

Click and drag to create command button

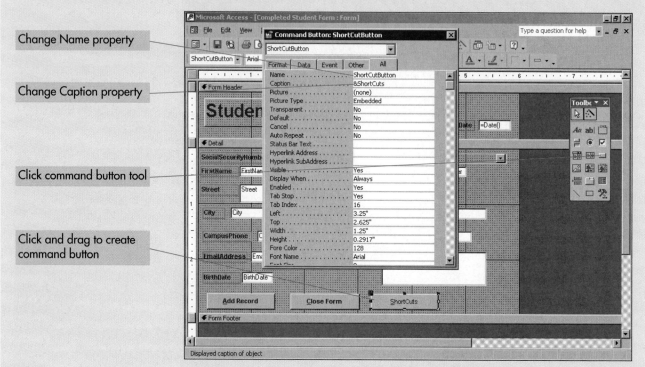

(f) Create the ShortCut Command Button (step 6)

FIGURE 8.6   *Hands-on Exercise 2 (continued)*

ACCELERATOR KEYS AND THE CAPTION PROPERTY

The Caption property enables you to create a keyboard shortcut for a command button. Right click the button in the Form Design view to display the Properties dialog box for the command button. Click the All tab, then modify the Caption property to include an ampersand immediately in front of the letter that will be used in the shortcut (e.g., &Help if you have a Help button). Close the dialog box, then go to Form view. The command button will contain an underlined letter (e.g., Help) that can be activated in conjunction with the Alt key (e.g., Alt+H) as a shortcut or accelerator key.

Step 7: **Create the OnClick Procedure**

➤ You should be positioned on the blank line in the ShortCutButton_Click procedure, as shown in Figure 8.6g. Press the **Tab key** to indent, then enter the VBA statement exactly as it is shown in the figure. Note the following:

- A tip (known as "Quick Info") appears as soon as you type the left parenthesis after the MsgBox function. The tip displays the syntax of the function and lists its arguments.

- Indentation is not a requirement of VBA per se, but is done to make the VBA code easier to read. Continuation is also optional and is done to make the code easier to read.

➤ Complete the statement exactly as shown in the figure, except substitute your name for Grauer/Barber. Click the **Save button**. Close the Module window.

➤ Return to the Access Design view. Close the property sheet. Size and align the new button. Save the form.

➤ Click the **View button** to change to Form view.

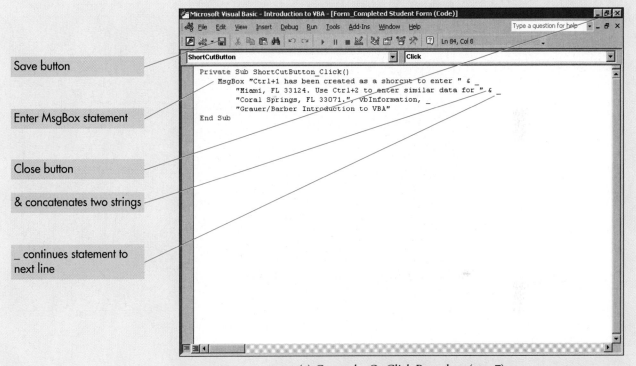

Save button

Enter MsgBox statement

Close button

& concatenates two strings

_ continues statement to next line

(g) Create the OnClick Procedure (step 7)

FIGURE 8.6 *Hands-on Exercise 2 (continued)*

THE MSGBOX STATEMENT

The MsgBox statement has three parameters—the text of the message to be displayed, the number of buttons and type of message, and the text that appears on the title bar. The message itself is divided into multiple character strings, which continue from one line to the next. The ampersand concatenates the two character strings to display a single message. The underscore character indicates that the statement is continued to the next line.

Step 8:   **Test the ShortCuts Button**

➤ Click the **ShortCuts button**. You can also use the keyboard shortcut, **Alt+S**, as indicated by the underlined letter on the button name that was established through the Caption property for the button.

➤ You should see the message box that is displayed in Figure 8.6h. Your name should appear in the title bar of the dialog box rather than ours. Click **OK** to close the dialog box.

➤ Try the other shortcuts that have been built into the form. Press **Ctrl+1** and **Ctrl+2** to switch back and forth between Miami and Coral Springs, respectively. Press **Alt+C** to close the form. Not everyone prefers the keyboard to the mouse, but you have nonetheless created a powerful set of shortcuts.

➤ Exit Access if you do not want to continue with the next exercise at this time.

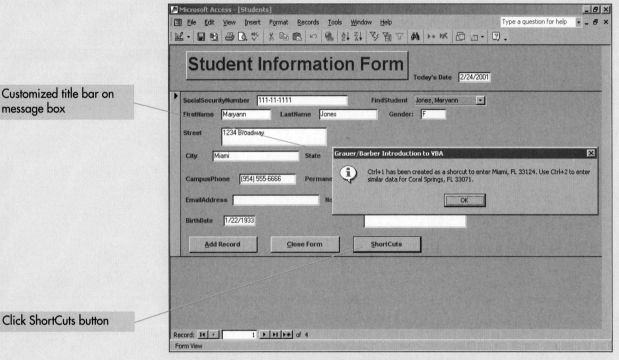

Customized title bar on message box

Click ShortCuts button

(h) Test the ShortCuts Button (step 8)

FIGURE 8.6   *Hands-on Exercise 2 (continued)*

CREATE UNIFORM COMMAND BUTTONS

A form is made more appealing if all of its command buttons have similar properties. Change to Design view, then press and hold the Shift key as you select each of the command buttons. Pull down the Format menu, click Size, then choose the desired parameters for all of the buttons such as widest and tallest. (You have to execute the command once for each parameter.) Leave the buttons selected, pull down the Format menu, select the Align command, then choose the desired alignment. Pull down the Format menu a final time, select the Horizontal Spacing command, then implement the desired (e.g., uniform) spacing for the buttons.

It is not a question of whether errors in data entry will occur, but rather how quickly a user will understand the nature of those errors in order to take the appropriate corrective action. If, for example, a user attempts to add a duplicate record for an existing customer, Access will display an error message of the form, "changes to the table were not successful because they would create duplicate values of the primary key." The issue is whether this message is clear to the nontechnical individual who is doing the data entry.

An experienced Access programmer will realize immediately that Access is preventing the addition of the duplicate record because another record with the same primary key (e.g., a Social Security or account number) is already in the file. A nontechnical user, however, may not understand the message because he or she does not know the meaning of "primary key." Wouldn't it be easier if the system displayed a message indicating that a customer with that Social Security or account number is already in the file? In other words, errors invariably occur, but it is important that the message the user sees clearly indicates the problem.

Figure 8.7 displays the event procedure that is developed in the next hands-on exercise to display application-specific error messages in place of the standard messages provided by Access. The procedure is triggered any time there is an error in data entry. Realize, however, that there are literally hundreds of errors, and it is necessary to test for each error for which we want a substitute message. Each error has a unique error number, and thus the first task is to determine the number associated for the error you want to detect. This is accomplished by forcing the error to occur, then printing the error number in the *Immediate window* (a special window within the VBA editor that enables you to display results of a procedure as it is executing). It's easier than it sounds, as you will see in the hands-on exercise.

Once you know the error numbers, you can complete the procedure by checking for the errors that you wish to trap, then displaying the appropriate error messages. One way to implement this logic is through a series of individual If statements, with one *If statement* for each error. It is more efficient, however, to use a Case statement as shown in Figure 8.7.

The *Case statement* tests the value of an incoming variable (DataErr in our example, which contains the error number), then goes to the appropriate set of statements, depending on the value of that variable. Our procedure tests for two errors, but it could be easily expanded to check for additional errors. Error 2237 occurs if the user attempts to find a record that is not in the table. Error 3022 results when the user attempts to add a duplicate record. Once an error is detected, the MsgBox statement is used to display the error message we create, after which Access will continue processing without displaying the default error message.

Note, too, the last case (Else), which is executed when Access detects an error other than 2237 or 3022. This time we do not display our own message because we do not know the nature of the error. Instead we set the Response variable to the intrinsic constant acDataErrContinue, which causes Access to display the default error message for the error that occurred.

Figure 8.7b displays the *General Declarations section*, which contains statements that apply to every procedure in the form. The section defines the constant ApplicationName as a string and sets it to the literal value "John Doe did his homework." Note, too, how the two MsgBox statements in Figure 8.7a reference this constant as the third argument, and recall that this argument contains the text that is displayed on the title bar of the message box. In other words, we can change the value of the ApplicationName constant in one place, and have that change reflected automatically in every MsgBox function.

```
Private Sub Form_Error(DataErr As Integer, Response As Integer)
' You need to determine the specific error number
'    1. Create the error in Access to determine the error number
'    2. Use the Print method of the Debug object to display the error
'    3. Press Ctrl+G to open the Immediate window

    Debug.Print "Error Number = ", DataErr

    Select Case DataErr
        Case 2237
            MsgBox "The student is not in our file. Please " & _
                "check the spelling and reenter correctly, or click the " & _
                "Add button to enter a new record.", vbExclamation, _
                ApplicationName
            Response = acDataErrContinue
        Case 3022
            MsgBox "You are trying to add a student whose " & _
                "social security number is already in the file. Please " & _
                "correct the social security number or cancel this " & _
                "record and move to the original record.", vbExclamation, _
                ApplicationName
            Response = acDataErrContinue
        Case Else
            Response = acDataErrDisplay
    End Select
End Sub
```

Error numbers

MsgBox statement
displays an
improved error
message

(a) Form Error Event Procedure

ApplicationName
constant

```
Option Compare Database
Option Explicit

Const ApplicationName As String = "John Doe has done his homework"
```

(b) General Declarations Section

FIGURE 8.7   *Procedure for Exercise 3*

THE CASE STATEMENT

The Case statement tests the value of a variable, then branches to one of several sets of statements, depending on the value of that variable. You may not be able to write a Case statement intially, but once you see the statement, you can extend the code to accommodate any application. Look at the code in Figure 8.7, for example, and decide the required modifications to reflect employees rather than students. How would you extend the existing Case statement to include an additional error message?

ERROR TRAPPING

Objective   To create an event procedure that substitutes application-specific messages for the standard Access error messages. Use Figure 8.8 as a guide.

Step 1:   **Force the Error Message**

➤ Open the **Introduction to VBA database**. If necessary, click the **Forms button**, then open the **Completed Student Form** in Form view.

➤ Click and drag to select the name in the Find Student combo box. Type **XXXX** (an obviously invalid name). Press **enter**. You should see the error message in Figure 8.8a, which may be confusing to a nontechnical user.

➤ Click **OK** to close the message box. Press the **Esc key** to erase the XXXX, since we are not interested in finding this student.

➤ Change to Design view.

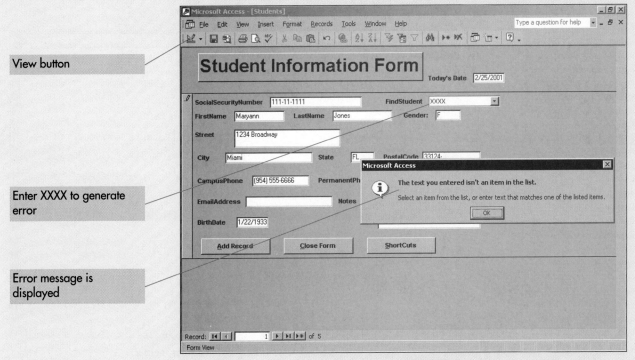

View button

Enter XXXX to generate error

Error message is displayed

(a) Force the Error Message (step 1)

FIGURE 8.8   *Hands-on Exercise 3*

EVENT-DRIVEN VERSUS TRADITIONAL PROGRAMMING

A traditional program is executed sequentially, beginning with the first line of code and continuing in order through the remainder of the program. VBA, however, is event driven, meaning that its procedures are executed when designated events occur. Thus, it is the user, and not the program, who determines which procedures are executed and when. This exercise creates a procedure that will run if specified errors occur during data entry.

Step 2: **Determine the Error Number**

➤ Pull down the **View menu** and click **Code** (or click the **Code button** on the Form Design toolbar) to display the Module window. If necessary, click the **down arrow** for the Object box and select the **Form object**.

➤ Click the **down arrow** in the Procedure box and click **Error** to display the event procedure that will execute when an error occurs in the form. Click the **Procedure View button** as shown in Figure 8.8b.

➤ We created this procedure for you. It consists of a single executable statement, to print a literal, followed by the number of the error. The comments explain how to use the procedure.

➤ Pull down the **View menu** and click **Immediate window** (or press **Ctrl+G**) to open the Immediate window. You should see number 2237.

➤ This is the error number reserved by Access to indicate that the value that was entered in the text portion of a combo box does not match any of the entries in the associated list.

➤ Close the Immediate window.

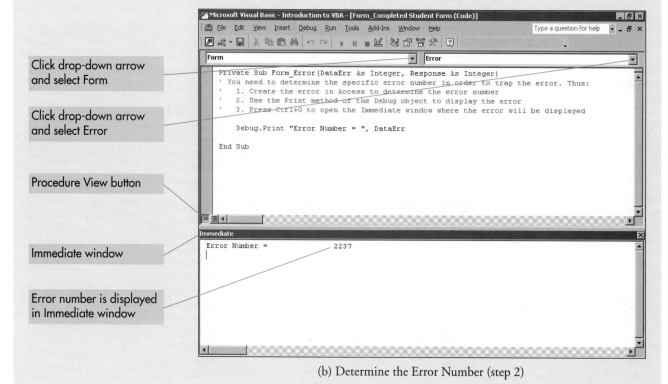

(b) Determine the Error Number (step 2)

FIGURE 8.8 *Hands-on Exercise 3 (continued)*

INSTANT CALCULATOR

Use the Print method (action) in the Immediate window to use VBA as a calculator. Press Ctrl+G at any time to display the Immediate window. Type the statement Debug.Print, followed by your calculation, for example, Debug.Print 2+2, then press enter. The answer is displayed on the next line in the Immediate window.

Step 3: **Trap the First Error**

➤ Click in the event procedure at the end of the Debug statement, press the **enter key** twice, then enter the VBA statements in Figure 8.8c. Note the following:
- Comments appear at the beginning of the procedure.
- The Case statement tests the value of an incoming variable (DataErr), then goes to the appropriate set of statements, depending on the value of that variable. The procedure currently tests for only one error, but it will be expanded later in the exercise to check for additional errors.
- The indentation and blank lines within the procedure are not requirements of VBA per se, but are used to make the code easier to read.
- A "Quick Info" tip appears as soon as you type the space after MsgBox. The tip displays the syntax of the statement.

➤ Complete the statement exactly as shown in Figure 8.8c. Save the procedure.

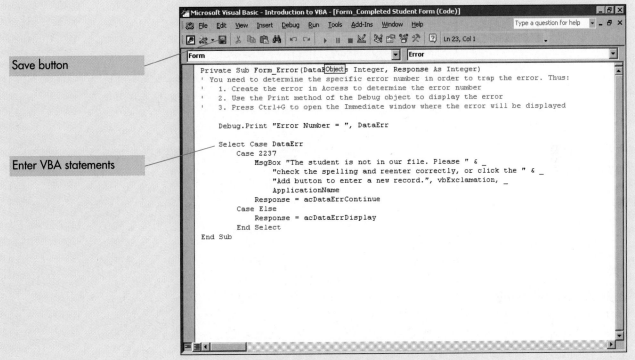

Save button

Enter VBA statements

(c) Trap the First Error (step 3)

FIGURE 8.8 *Hands-on Exercise 3 (continued)*

CONTINUING A VBA STATEMENT—THE & AND THE UNDERSCORE

A VBA statement can be continued from one line to the next by leaving a space at the end of the line to be continued, typing the underscore character, then continuing on the next line. You may not, however, break a line in the middle of a literal (character string). Thus you need to complete the character string with a closing quotation mark, add an ampersand (as the concatenation operator to display this string with the character string on the next line), then leave a space followed by the underscore to indicate continuation.

Step 4: **Test the Error Event Procedure**

➤ Click the taskbar button to return to the **Completed Student Form**. Change to the Form view. Click and drag to select the name in the Find Student combo box. Type **XXXX** (an obviously invalid name). Press **enter**.

➤ This time you should see the error message in Figure 8.8d corresponding to the text you entered in the previous step. (Note the title bar on the dialog box indicating that your name goes here. We tell you how to modify the title bar later in the exercise.)

➤ Click **OK** to close the message box. Press the **Esc key** to erase the XXXX. Return to Design view.

➤ Pull down the **View menu** and click **Code** (or click the **Code button** on the Form Design toolbar) to display the Module window.

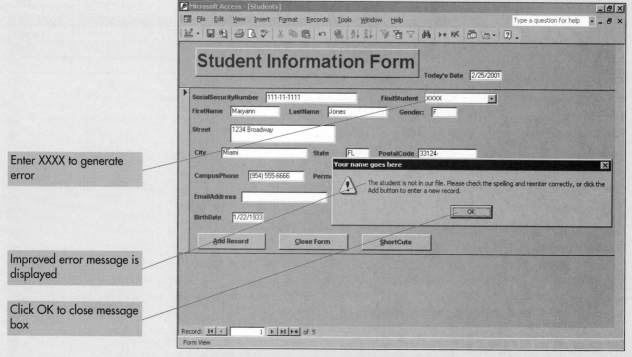

Enter XXXX to generate error

Improved error message is displayed

Click OK to close message box

(d) Test the Error Event Procedure (step 4)

FIGURE 8.8 *Hands-on Exercise 3 (continued)*

THE FIRST BUG

A bug is a mistake in a computer program; hence debugging refers to the process of correcting program errors. According to legend, the first bug was an unlucky moth crushed to death on one of the relays of the electromechanical Mark II computer, bringing the machine's operation to a halt. The cause of the failure was discovered by Grace Hopper, who promptly taped the moth to her logbook, noting, "First actual case of bug being found."

Step 5: **Change the Application Name**

➤ Click the **down arrow** for the Object box and select **(General)** at the beginning of the list of objects.

➤ We have defined the Visual Basic constant **ApplicationName**, and initialized it to "Your name goes here." This was the text that appeared in the title bar of the dialog box in the previous step.

➤ Click and drag to select **Your name goes here**. Enter **John Doe has done his homework**, substituting your name for John Doe.

➤ Pull down the **Edit menu**, click the **Find command** to display the Find dialog box. Enter **ApplicationName** in the Find What text box. Specify the option to search the **Current module** and specify **All** as the direction.

➤ Click the **Find Next command button** to locate all occurrences of the ApplicationName constant. Can you appreciate the significance of this technique to customize your application? Save the procedure.

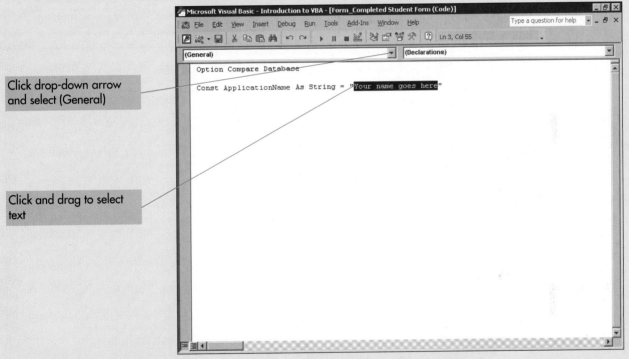

Click drop-down arrow and select (General)

Click and drag to select text

(e) Change the Application Name (step 5)

FIGURE 8.8 *Hands-on Exercise 3 (continued)*

THE MSGBOX STATEMENT—CONSTANTS VERSUS LITERALS

The third parameter in the MsgBox statement can be entered as a literal such as "John Doe's Application." It's preferable, however, to specify the argument as a constant such as ApplicationName, then define that constant in the Declarations section. That way, you can change the name of the application in one place, and have the change automatically reflected in every MsgBox statement that references the constant.

Step 6: **Complete the Error Event Procedure**

➤ Click the **down arrow** for the Object box and select the **Form object**. Click the **down arrow** for the Procedure box and click the **Error procedure**.

➤ Click immediately before the Case Else statement, then enter the additional code shown in Figure 8.8f. Use the Copy and Paste commands to enter the second Case statement. Thus:

- Click and drag to select the first Case statement, click the **Copy button**, click above the Case Else statement, and click the **Paste button**.
- Modify the copied statements as necessary, rather than typing the statements from scratch. Use the **Ins key** to toggle between insertion and replacement. Be sure that your code matches ours.

➤ Click the **Save button** to save the procedure. Click the taskbar button to return to the **Completed Student Form**.

Click drop-down arrow and select Form

Click drop-down arrow and select Error

Enter VBA satatements

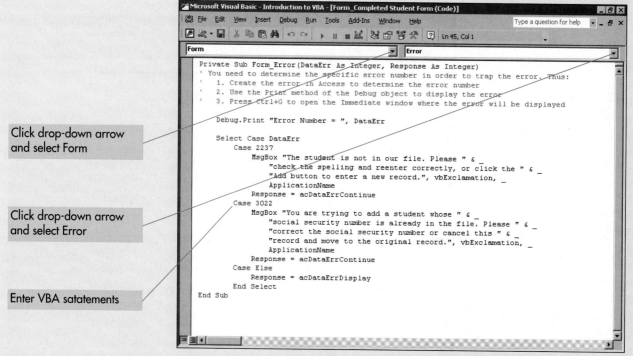

(f) Complete the Error Event Procedure (step 6)

FIGURE 8.8 *Hands-on Exercise 3 (continued)*

THE OBJECT AND PROCEDURE BOXES

The Object box at the top left of the Module window displays the current object, such as a form or a control on the form. The Procedure box displays the name of the current procedure for the selected object. To create or navigate between events for a form, click the down arrow on the Object box to select the Form object, then click the down arrow on the Procedure box to display the list of events. Events that already have procedures appear in bold. Clicking an event that is not bold creates the procedure header and End Sub statements for that event.

Step 7: **Complete the Testing**

➤ You should be back in Design view of the Completed Student Form. Pull down the **View menu** and change to the **Datasheet view** as shown in Figure 8.8g. (You can also click the **down arrow** next to the View button on the Form Design view and select Datasheet view.)

➤ Enter **222-22-2222** as a duplicate Social Security number for the first record. Press the **down arrow** (or click the appropriate **navigation button**) to attempt to move to the next record.

➤ You should see the error message in Figure 8.8g. The title bar displays the value of the application name entered earlier in the exercise.

➤ Click **OK** (or press **Esc**) to close the dialog box. Press **Esc** a second time to restore the original value of the Social Security number. Close the window.

➤ Exit Access if you do not want to continue with the next exercise at this time.

View button

Enter 222-22-2222 (duplicate Social Security number)

Title bar displays application name

Improved error message is displayed

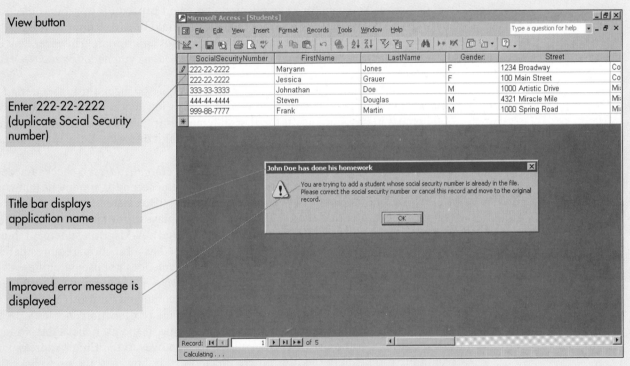

(g) Complete the Testing (step 7)

FIGURE 8.8 *Hands-on Exercise 3 (continued)*

LISTEN TO YOUR USER

One source of continual frustration to the end user is error messages steeped in technical jargon. What's obvious to you as a developer or student is often beyond the unsophisticated end user. Thus, anything that you can do to simplify a system will increase its chances for success. Listen to your users. Find out where they are having trouble and what they don't understand, then act accordingly.

Data validation is a crucial component of any system. The most basic type of validation is implemented automatically, without any additional effort on the part of the developer. A user cannot, for example, enter data that does not conform to the designated field type. The user cannot enter text into a numeric field, nor can one enter an invalid date—such as February 30—into a date field. Access also prevents you from entering a duplicate record (i.e., a record with the same primary key as another record).

Other validation checks are implemented by the developer, at either the field or record level. The former performs the validation as soon as you move from one field to the next within a table or form. The latter waits until all of the fields have been completed, then checks the entire record prior to updating the record. Both types of validation are essential to prevent invalid data from corrupting the system.

The developer can also use VBA to extend the data validation capabilities within Access. You can, for example, write an event procedure to remind the user that a field is empty and ask whether the record should be saved anyway. The field is not required and hence the Required property is not appropriate. However, you do not want to ignore the omitted field completely, and thus you need to create a VBA procedure.

The VBA code in Figure 8.9 implements this type of check through a *nested If statement* in which one If statement is contained inside another. The second (inner) If statement is executed only if the first statement is true. Thus, we first check to see whether the e-mail address has been omitted, and if it has, we ask the user whether he or she wants to save the record anyway.

The outer If statement in Figure 8.9, *If IsNull (EmailAddress),* checks to see if the e-mail address is blank, and if it is, it executes the second If statement that contains a MsgBox function, as opposed to a simple MsgBox statement. The difference between the two is that the MsgBox function displays a prompt to the user, then returns a value (such as which button a user clicked). A MsgBox statement, however, simply displays a message. MsgBox, when used as a function, requires parentheses around the arguments. MsgBox, as a statement, does not use parentheses.

Look carefully at the second argument, *vbYesNo + vbQuestion* within Figure 8.9. The intrinsic constant vbYesNo displays two command buttons (Yes and No) within the message box. The If in front of the message box function enables VBA to test the user's response and branch accordingly. Thus, if the user clicks the No button, the save operation is cancelled and the focus moves to the EmailAddress control in the form, where the user enters the address. If, however, the user clicks the Yes button, the If statement is false, and the record is saved without the e-mail address.

Nested If statement

Displays Yes and
No buttons with
message to user

```
Private Sub Form_BeforeUpdate(Cancel As Integer)
    If IsNull(EmailAddress) Then
        If MsgBox("You did not enter an e-mail address. Save anyway?", _
            vbYesNo + vbQuestion, ApplicationName) = vbNo Then
            Cancel = True
            EmailAddress.SetFocus
        End If
    End If
End Sub
```

FIGURE 8.9 *Procedure for Exercise 4*

DATA VALIDATION

Objective To use Field and Table properties to implement different types of data validation. Use Figure 8.10 as a guide in the exercise.

Step 1: **Set the Field Properties**

> ➤ Open the **Introduction to VBA database**. Click the **Tables button**, then open the **Students table** in Design view as shown in Figure 8.10a.
> ➤ Click the field selector column for the **Gender**. Click the **Validation Rule** box. Type **="M" or "F"** to accept only these values on data entry.
> ➤ Click the **Validation Text** box. Type **Please enter either M or F as the gender**.
> ➤ Click the **Required property** and change its value to **Yes**.

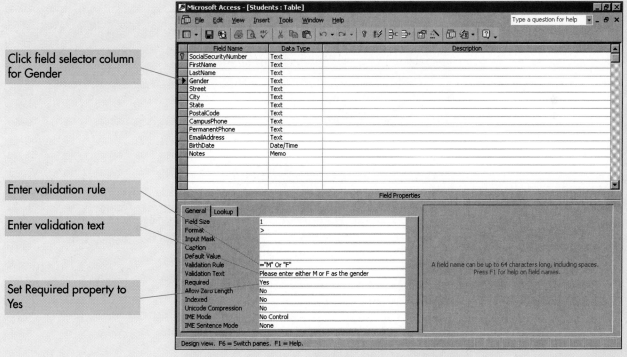

Click field selector column for Gender

Enter validation rule

Enter validation text

Set Required property to Yes

(a) Set the Field Properties (step 1)

FIGURE 8.10 *Hands-on Exercise 4*

OPTIMIZE DATA TYPES AND FIELD SIZES

The data type property determines the data that can be accepted into a field and the operations that can be performed on that data. Any field that is intended for use in a calculation should be given the numeric data type. You can, however, increase the efficiency of an Access database by specifying the appropriate value for the Field Size property of a numeric field. The Byte, Integer, and Long Integer field sizes hold values up to 256, 32,767, and 2,147,483,648, respectively.

Step 2:   **Set the Table Properties**

➤ Point to the **selector** box in the upper-left corner, then click the **right mouse button** and display the Table Properties dialog box as shown in Figure 8.10b.

➤ Click in the **Validation Rule** box and enter **[CampusPhone] Is Not Null Or [PermanentPhone] Is Not Null** to ensure that the user enters one phone number or the other. (The field names should not contain any spaces and are enclosed in square brackets.)

➤ Press **enter**, then type, **You must enter either a campus or permanent phone number** (which is the validation text that will be displayed in the event of an error).

➤ Click the **Save button** to save the table. Click **No** when you see the message asking whether existing data should be tested against the new rules.

➤ Close the Table Properties dialog box. Close the Students table.

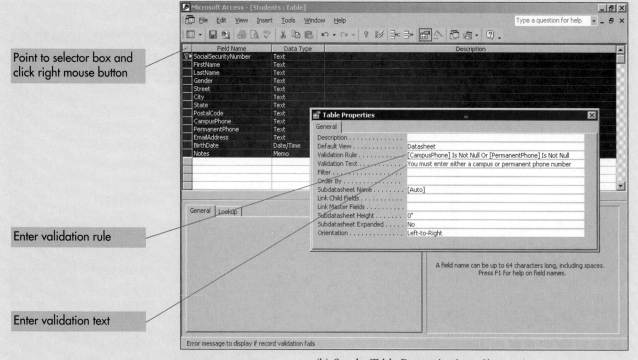

Point to selector box and click right mouse button

Enter validation rule

Enter validation text

(b) Set the Table Properties (step 2)

FIGURE 8.10   *Hands-on Exercise 4 (continued)*

DAY PHONE OR PERMANENT PHONE

You can set the required property of a field to force the user to enter data for that field. But what if you wanted the user to enter one of two fields and were indifferent to which field was chosen? Setting the Required property of either or both fields would not accomplish your goal. Thus, you need to implement this type of validation at the record (rather than the field) level by setting the properties of the table as a whole, rather than the properties of the individual fields.

Step 3: **Test the Validation Rules**

➤ Open the **Completed Student Form** in Form view. If necessary, move to Maryann Jones, the first record in the table.

➤ Click and drag to select the gender field, then type **X** to replace the gender. Press **enter**. You will see an error message pertaining to the gender field.

➤ Press **Esc** (or click **OK**) to close the dialog box. Press **Esc** a second time to restore the original value.

➤ Click and drag to select the existing CampusPhone number, then press the **Del key** to erase the phone number. Press the **Tab key** to move to the PermanentPhone field. Both phone numbers should be blank.

➤ Click the ▶ **button** to move to the next record. You should see the error message in Figure 8.10c pertaining to the table properties.

➤ Press **Esc** (or click **OK**) to close the dialog box. Press **Esc** a second time to restore the original value.

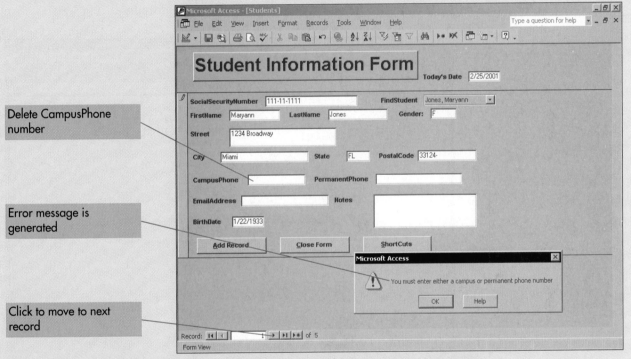

(c) Test the Validation Rules (step 3)

FIGURE 8.10 *Hands-on Exercise 4 (continued)*

VALIDATING AT THE FIELD VERSUS THE RECORD LEVEL

Data validation is performed at the field or record level. If it is done at the field level (e.g., by specifying the Required and Validation Rule properties for a specific field), Access checks the entry immediately as soon as you exit the field. If it is done at the record level, however (e.g., by checking that one of two fields has been entered), Access has to wait until it has processed every field in the record. Thus, it is only on attempting to move to the next record that Access informs you of the error.

Step 4: **Create the BeforeUpdate Event Procedure**

➤ Change to the Form Design view. Pull down the **View menu** and click **Code** (or click the **Code button**) on the Form Design toolbar. If necessary, click the **Procedure view button** to view one procedure at a time.

➤ Click the **down arrow** on the Objects list box and click **Form**. Click the **down arrow** on the Procedure list box to display the list of events for the form. Click **BeforeUpdate** to create a procedure for this event.

➤ Press the **Tab key** to indent, then enter the statements exactly as shown in Figure 8.10d. Note that as soon as you enter "EmailAddress," Access displays the methods and properties for the EmailAddress control.

➤ Type **set** (the first three letters in the SetFocus method), watching the screen as you enter each letter. Access moves through the displayed list automatically, until it arrives at the **SetFocus method**. Press **enter**.

➤ Add an **End If** statement to complete the If statement testing the MsgBox function. Press **enter**, then enter a second **End If** statement to complete the If statement testing the IsNull condition. Save the procedure.

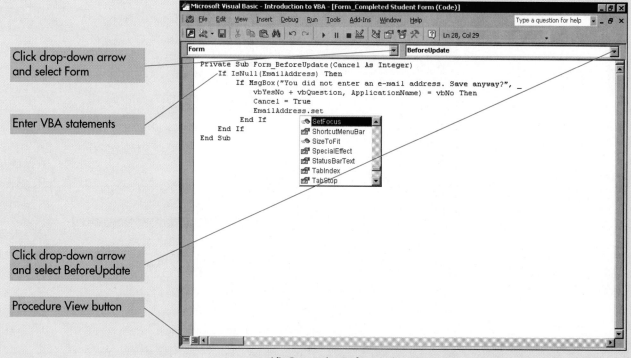

(d) Create the BeforeUpdate Event Procedure (step 4)

FIGURE 8.10 *Hands-on Exercise 4 (continued)*

AUTOLIST MEMBERS—HELP IN WRITING CODE

Access displays the methods and properties for a control as soon as you enter the period after the control name. Type the first several letters to select the method or property. Press the space bar to accept the selected item and remain on the same line, or press the enter key to accept the item and begin a new line.

Step 5: **Test the BeforeUpdate Event Procedure**

➤ Click the taskbar button for the Access form. Change to the **Form view**. Click in the **memo field** and enter the text shown in Figure 8.10e.

➤ Check the remaining fields, but be sure to leave the e-mail address blank. Click the navigation button to (attempt to) move to the next record.

➤ You should see the error message in Figure 8.10e. Note the entry in the title bar that corresponds to the value of the ApplicationName constant you entered earlier.

➤ Click **No** to cancel the operation, close the dialog box, and automatically position the insertion point within the text box for the e-mail address.

➤ Enter an e-mail address such as **mjones@anyschool.edu**, then move to the next record. This time Access does not display the error message and saves the record.

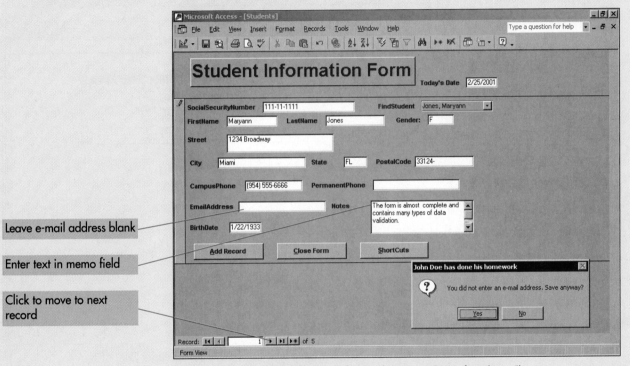

(e) Test the BeforeUpdate Event Procedure (step 5)

FIGURE 8.10 *Hands-on Exercise 4 (continued)*

MEMO FIELDS VERSUS TEXT FIELDS

A text field can store up to 255 characters. A memo field, however, can store up to 64,000 characters and is used to hold descriptive data that runs for several sentences, paragraphs, or even pages. A vertical scroll bar appears in the Form view when the memo field contains more data than is visible at one time. Note, too, that both text and memo fields store only the characters that have been entered; that is, there is no wasted space if the data does not extend to the maximum field size.

Step 6:   **Create the CloseForm Event Procedure**

> ➤ Change to the Form Design view, then click the **Code button** on the Form Design toolbar to display the Module window. If necessary, click the **Object** box to select Form, then click the **Procedure box** to select the **Close event**.
> ➤ You should see the partially completed event procedure in Figure 8.10f. Press **Tab** to indent the statement, then enter **MsgBox** followed by a blank space. The Quick Info feature displays the syntax of this statement.
> ➤ Complete the message, ending with the closing quotation mark and comma. The AutoList feature displays the list of appropriate arguments. Type **vbc**, at which point you can select the **vbCritical** parameter by typing a **comma**.
> ➤ Type a **space** followed by an **underscore** to continue the statement to the next line. Enter **ApplicationName** as the last parameter. Save the module.

Click drop-down arrow and select Form

Enter MsgBox statement

QuickInfo feature displays syntax

Enter vbc, the first letters in vbCritical

Click drop-down arrow and select Close

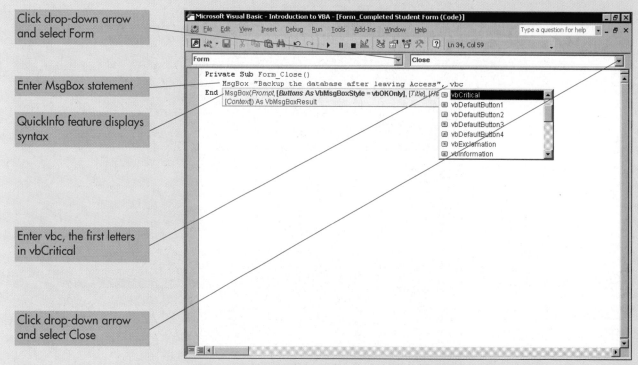

(f) Create the CloseForm Event Procedure (step 6)

FIGURE 8.10   *Hands-on Exercise 4 (continued)*

CHOOSE THE RIGHT EVENT

We associated the message prompting the user to back up the database with the Close event for the form. Would it work equally well if the message were associated with the Click event of the Close Form command button? The answer is no, because the user could bypass the command button and close the form by pulling down the File menu and choosing the Close command, and thus never see the message. Choosing the right object and associated event is one of the subtleties in VBA.

Step 7: **Close the Form**

➤ Click the **Access form button** on the taskbar. Return to Form view. The form looks very similar to the form with which we began, but it has been enhanced in subtle ways:

- The drop-down list box has been added to locate a specific student.
- Accelerator keys have been created for the command buttons (e.g., Alt+A to add a record).
- The SetFocus property was used to position the insertion point directly in the Social Security text box to add a new record.
- The Ctrl+1 and Ctrl+2 keyboard shortcuts have been created.
- The data validation has been enhanced through custom error messages.
- The application has been customized through the entry on the title bar.

➤ Click the **Close Form button** to display the dialog box in Figure 8.10g. Click **OK** to close the dialog box, which in turn closes the form.

➤ Close the database. Exit Access. Congratulations on a job well done.

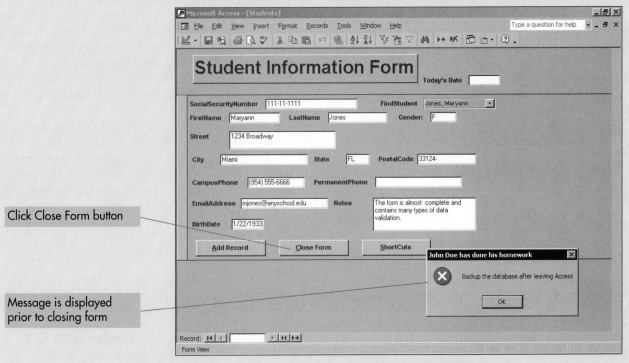

(g) Close the Form (step 7)

FIGURE 8.10   *Hands-on Exercise 4 (continued)*

BACK UP IMPORTANT FILES

It's not a question of if it will happen, but when—hard disks die, files are lost, or viruses may infect a system. It has happened to us and it will happen to you, but you can prepare for the inevitable by creating adequate backup before the problem occurs. Decide which files to back up, how often to do the backup, and where to keep the backup. Do it!

Visual Basic for Applications (VBA) is a subset of Visual Basic that is accessible from every application in Microsoft Office. VBA is different from traditional programming languages in that it is event driven. An event is any action that is recognized by Access. Visual Basic code is developed in units called event procedures that run automatically, in response to an event such as clicking a button or opening a form.

All VBA procedures are stored in modules. Every form in an Access database has its own module that contains the event procedures for that form. All procedures are either public or private. A private procedure is accessible only from within the module in which it is contained. A public procedure is accessible from anywhere. All procedures are displayed and edited in the Module window within Access. Additional procedures can be developed by expanding the existing code through inference and observation.

Several event procedures were created in this chapter to illustrate how VBA can be used to enhance an Access application. Hands-on exercise 1 focused on the Current event to synchronize the displayed record in a form with a combo box used to locate a record by last name. Exercise 2 developed a KeyDown event procedure to facilitate data entry. Exercise 3 developed the Error event to substitute application-specific error messages for the default messages provided by Access. Exercise 4 created a BeforeUpdate event procedure to enhance the data validation for the form. Additional procedures can be developed by expanding the existing code through inference and observation.

The MsgBox statement has three arguments—the prompt (or message to the user), a VBA intrinsic constant that specifies the icon to be displayed within the box, and the text that is to appear on the title bar of the box. MsgBox may be used as a statement or a function. The difference between the two is that the MsgBox function displays a prompt to the user, then returns a value (such as which button a user clicked). A MsgBox statement, however, simply displays a message. MsgBox, when used as a function, requires parentheses around the arguments. MsgBox, as a statement, does not use parentheses.

KEY TERMS

Argument (p. 372)
BeforeUpdate event (p. 404)
Case statement (p. 391)
Class module (p. 371)
Click event (p. 381)
Close Form Event (p. 372)
Complete Word tool (p. 385)
Concalenation (p. 376)
Continuation (p. 395)
Current event (p. 372)
Data validation (p. 400)
Default property (p. 381)
Error trapping (p. 391)

Event (p. 368)
Event procedure (p. 371)
Full Module view (p. 383)
General Declarations section
  (p. 391)
General procedure (p. 371)
If statement (p. 391)
Immediate window (p. 391)
Intrinsic constant (p. 372)
KeyDown event (p. 381)
Key Preview property (p. 386)
KeyCode argument (p. 382)
Module window (p. 371)

MsgBox statement (p. 372)
Nested If statement (p. 400)
Object box (p. 398)
Parameter (p. 372)
Private procedure (p. 371)
Procedure (p. 368)
Procedure box (p. 398)
Procedure header (p. 382)
Procedure view (p. 383)
Public procedure (p. 371)
SetFocus method (p. 382)
Visual Basic for Applications
  (VBA) (p. 368)

1. Which of the following applications can be enhanced through VBA?
   (a) Word and Excel
   (b) Access and PowerPoint
   (c) Outlook
   (d) All of the above

2. Which application enhancements are accomplished using VBA event procedures?
   (a) Improved data validation
   (b) Creation of keyboard shortcuts for data entry
   (c) Substitution of customized error messages for the standard messages provided by Access
   (d) All of the above

3. Which of the following is necessary in order to establish a keyboard shortcut to facilitate data entry on a form?
   (a) Create a procedure for the KeyUp event of the form and set the Key Preview property to No
   (b) Create a procedure for the KeyUp event of the form and set the Key Preview property to Yes
   (c) Create a procedure for the KeyDown event of the form and set the Key Preview property to No
   (d) Create a procedure for the KeyDown event of the form and set the Key Preview property to Yes

4. Which of the following characters continues a VBA statement?
   (a) A hyphen
   (b) An underscore
   (c) A hyphen and an ampersand
   (d) An underscore and an ampersand

5. Which of the following types of data validation requires an event procedure?
   (a) Checking that a required field has been entered
   (b) Checking that one of two fields has been entered
   (c) Prompting the user with a message indicating that an optional field has been omitted, and asking for further instruction
   (d) All of the above

6. Which of the following is *not* used to implement a validation check that requires the user to enter a value of Atlanta or Boston for the City field?
   (a) Set the Required property for the City field to Yes
   (b) Set the Validation Rule property for the City field to either "Atlanta" or "Boston"
   (c) Set the Default property for the City field to either "Atlanta" or "Boston"
   (d) Set the Validation Text property for the City field to display an appropriate error message if the user does not enter either Atlanta or Boston

7. Which of the following techniques would you use to require the user to enter either a home phone or a business phone?
   (a) Set the Required property of each field to Yes
   (b) Set the Validation Rule property for each field to true
   (c) Set the Validation Rule for the table to [HomePhone] or [BusinessPhone]
   (d) All of the above are equally acceptable

8. Which is a true statement about the Procedure box in the Module window?
   (a) Events that have procedures appear in bold
   (b) Clicking an event that appears in boldface displays the event procedure
   (c) Clicking an event that is not in bold creates a procedure for that event
   (d) All of the above

9. Which event procedure was created in conjunction with the combo box to locate a record on the form?
    (a) An On Current event procedure for the combo box control
    (b) An On Current event procedure for the form
    (c) A KeyDown event procedure for the combo box control
    (d) A KeyDown event procedure for the form

10. Which event procedure was created to warn the user that the e-mail address was omitted and asking whether the record is to be saved anyway?
    (a) An On Error event procedure for the combo box control
    (b) An On Error event procedure for the form
    (c) A BeforeUpdate event procedure for the e-mail control
    (d) A BeforeUpdate event procedure for the form

11. Which of the following does *not* create an event procedure for a form?
    (a) Display the Properties box for the form in Design View, click the Event tab, select the event, then click the Build button
    (b) Select the form in the Object box of the Module window, then click the event (displayed in regular as opposed to boldface) in the Procedure box
    (c) Pull down the View menu in the Database window and click the code command or click the Code button on the Database toolbar
    (d) All of the above create an event procedure

12. You want to display a message in conjunction with closing a form. Which of the following is the best way to accomplish this?
    (a) Write a VBA procedure for the Close Form event
    (b) Create a Close command button for the form, then write a VBA procedure for the On Click event of the command button to display the message
    (c) Either (a) or (b)
    (d) Neither (a) nor (b)

13. Which of the following is not an Access-intrinsic constant?
    (a) ApplicationName
    (b) vbCritical
    (c) acCtrlMask
    (d) vbKey1

14. What advantage, if any, is gained by using VBA to create a keyboard shortcut to enter the city, state, and zip code in an incoming record, as opposed to using the Default Value property in the table definition?
    (a) It's easier to use VBA than to specify the Default Value property
    (b) The Default Value property cannot be applied to multiple fields for the same record, and thus VBA is the only way to accomplish this task
    (c) VBA can be used to create different shortcuts for different sets of values, whereas the Default Value property is restricted to a single value
    (d) All of the above

15. Which of the following statements was used to display the Error Number associated with an error in data entry?
    (a) Debug.Print "Error Number = "
    (b) Debug.Print "Error Number = ", DataErr
    (c) Print "Error Number = "
    (d) Print "Error Number = ", DataErr

ANSWERS

1. d	**5.** c	**9.** b	**13.** a
2. d	**6.** c	**10.** d	**14.** c
3. d	**7.** c	**11.** c	**15.** b
4. b	**8.** d	**12.** a	

1. **MsgBox Examples:** VBA is different from Visual Basic in that its procedures must exist within an Office document. Hence, you need to start this exercise by creating a new database to hold the procedures in Figure 8.11. Click the Modules button from within the Database window and click the New button to create a general module (called Module1 by default). This opens the VBA editor as shown in Figure 8.11.

   a. Define a public constant to hold your name. The constant is included as the third parameter in all three MsgBox statements, so that your name will appear in the title bar of the associated dialog boxes.

   b. Create the first procedure, consisting of three simple MsgBox statements, with one, two, and three parameters, respectively. Click the procedure header, then click the Run button on the VBA toolbar to test the procedure. Do you see the effect of each procedure on the associated dialog boxes?

   c. Create the second procedure that uses the MsgBox function to test the value of the user's response by comparing it to the vbYes intrinsic constant. Change the second argument to vbYesNo+vbQuestion and note the effect in the resulting dialog box.

   d. Add the third procedure and test it as well. This procedure includes a statement to exit Access, so you will have to reopen the database to print the completed module.

   e. Pull down the File menu and click the Print command to print the entire module for your instructor.

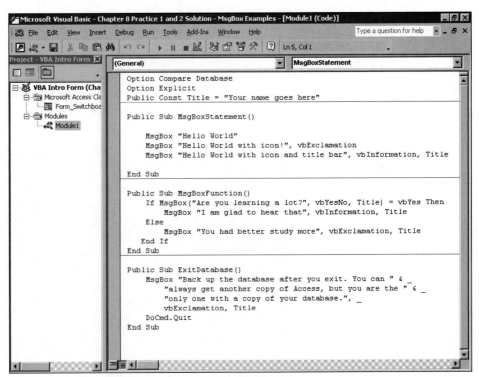

FIGURE 8.11 *MsgBox Examples (Exercise 1)*

BUILDS ON

PRACTICE
EXERCISE 1
PAGE 411

2. **MsgBox Example Switchboard:** Create a simple switchboard for the database in the previous exercise as shown in Figure 8.12. (The dialog box that you see in the figure appears when you click the MsgBox as a Function button.) Use the Startup property to display the switchboard automatically when the database is opened. Print the switchboard and table of switchboard items.

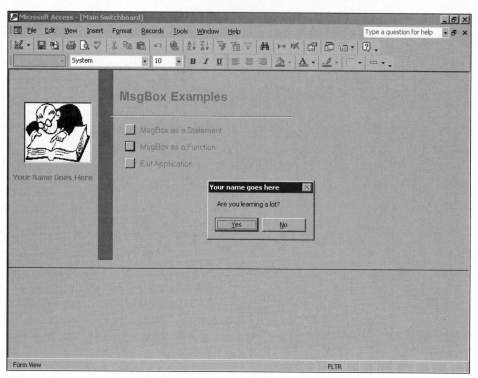

FIGURE 8.12 *MsgBox Example Switchboard (Exercise 2)*

BUILDS ON

HANDS-ON
EXERCISES
1, 2, 3, AND 4

3. Expanded Student Form: Do the four hands-on exercises in the chapter, then modify the completed form at the end of the fourth hands-on exercise to:
   a. Include a warning message that prompts the user if birth date is omitted as shown in Figure 8.13, and giving the user the option to save the record.
   b. Add a new keyboard shortcut, Ctrl+3, to enter data for New York, NY, 10010.
   c. Modify the VBA procedure associated with the Add Record button, so that the insertion point moves automatically to the Social Security control.

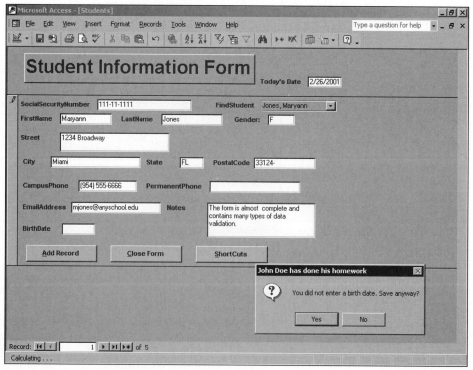

FIGURE 8.13 *Expanded Student Form (Exercise 3)*

BUILDS ON

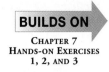

CHAPTER 7
HANDS-ON EXERCISES
1, 2, AND 3

4. Return to Soccer: Figure 8.14 contains a modified version of the Players form that has been enhanced with VBA procedures. Proceed as follows:

a. Add a combo box to the form to locate a player within the Players table. Create the necessary VBA procedure to update the contents of the combo box when the navigation buttons are used to move to a different record.

b. Add code to the Add Player button to position the user in the First Name text box after clicking the Add button.

c. Add a procedure to notify the user if the birth date is omitted, then ask the user if the record is to be saved anyway.

d. Add a procedure to display a message box asking the user to try out for an all-city team if a player rating of A (upper- or lowercase) is entered.

e. Create a Ctrl+1 keyboard shortcut to enter Miami, FL, and 33124 in the city, state, and zip code fields, respectively. Create a similar shortcut for Ctrl+2 to enter Coral Springs, FL, and 33071. Remember to set the KeyPreview property to "Yes." Add a shortcut button to display this information.

f. Print the completed VBA module for the Players form for your instructor.

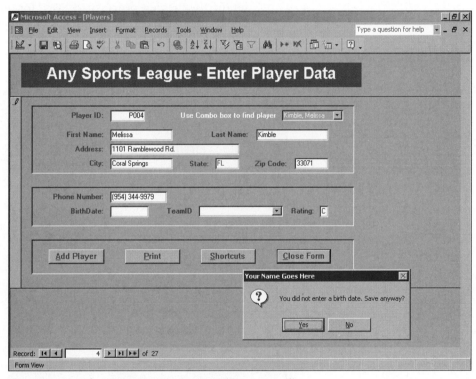

FIGURE 8.14 *Return to Soccer (Exercise 4)*

BUILDS ON

PRACTICE
EXERCISE 4
PAGE 413

5. The Coaches Form: Modify the Coaches form so that it parallels the Players form from the previous exercise. You may find it convenient to copy procedures, such as those that create and display keyboard shortcuts, from one form to another, as opposed to reentering the code. Proceed as follows:

a. Add a combo box to the form to locate a coach within the Coaches table.

b. Add code to the Add Coach button to position the user in the First Name text box after clicking the Add button.

c. Add a procedure to notify the user if the phone number is omitted, then ask the user if the record is to be saved anyway.

d. Create a Ctrl+1 keyboard shortcut to enter Miami, FL, and 33124 in the city, state, and zip code fields. Create a shortcut for Ctrl+2 to enter Coral Springs, FL, and 33071. Add a shortcut button to display this information.

e. Print the completed VBA module for the Coaches form for your instructor.

6. Acme Computers: The database in *Chapter 8 Practice 6* contains a partially completed version of the form in Figure 8.15. Your assignment is to modify that form to accommodate all of the following:
   a. Create a command button to add a new customer. The button should be created in such a way so that clicking the button takes the user directly to the FirstName field. (CustomerID is defined as an Autonumber field.)
   b. Change the table properties so that the user must enter either a home phone or a business phone.
   c. Create a BeforeUpdate event procedure that asks the user if the record should be saved if zip code is omitted.
   d. Add a combo box to find a customer record. Be sure to change the On Current event so that the value shown in the Find Customer control matches the customer information currently displayed on the form.
   e. Create a KeyDown procedure so that Ctrl+1 enters a credit rating of A and a credit limit of $10,000, Ctrl+2 enters a credit rating of B and a credit limit of $5,000, and Ctrl+3 enters a credit rating of C and a credit limit of $1,000. Create a command button to display the shortcuts for the user. Remember to set the KeyPreview property to "Yes" for the shortcuts to be operational.
   f. Use the completed form to add a record for yourself as a customer, then print that form for your instructor. Print the VBA module associated with the form as well.

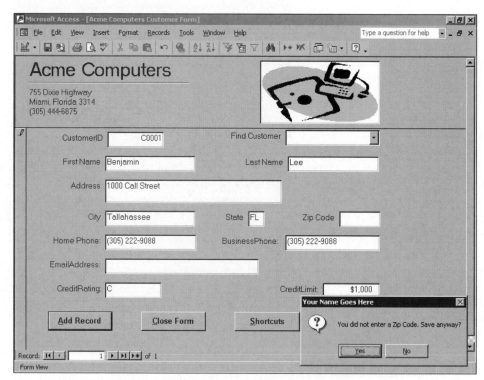

FIGURE 8.15   *Acme Computers Customer Form (Exercise 6)*

BUILDS ON

PRACTICE
EXERCISE 6
PAGE 414

7. String Processing: The procedure in Figure 8.16 consists of three simple If statements that validate the e-mail address within the Customers form of the previous problem. Use the VBA Help command to learn how the Len and InStr functions work, then create the procedure in Figure 8.16. Print the completed procedure for your instructor. Are there any other additional checks that you think should be included within this procedure?

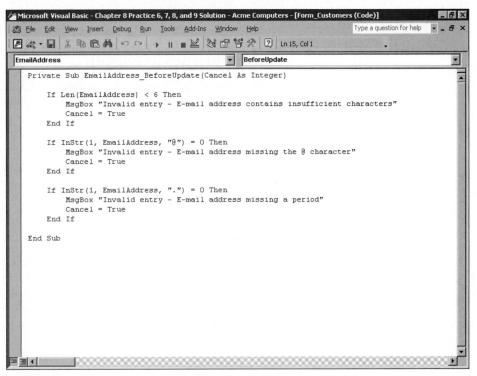

```
Private Sub EmailAddress_BeforeUpdate(Cancel As Integer)

    If Len(EmailAddress) < 6 Then
        MsgBox "Invalid entry - E-mail address contains insufficient characters"
        Cancel = True
    End If

    If InStr(1, EmailAddress, "@") = 0 Then
        MsgBox "Invalid entry - E-mail address missing the @ character"
        Cancel = True
    End If

    If InStr(1, EmailAddress, ".") = 0 Then
        MsgBox "Invalid entry - E-mail address missing a period"
        Cancel = True
    End If

End Sub
```

FIGURE 8.16   *String Processing (Exercise 7)*

BUILDS ON

PRACTICE
EXERCISE 7
PAGE 415

8. Acme Computers Switchboard: Create the switchboard shown in Figure 8.17 to provide access to the completed Customers form. The Exit Application button should display the message shown in the figure prior to closing the database. Use the Startup property to display the switchboard automatically when the database is opened.

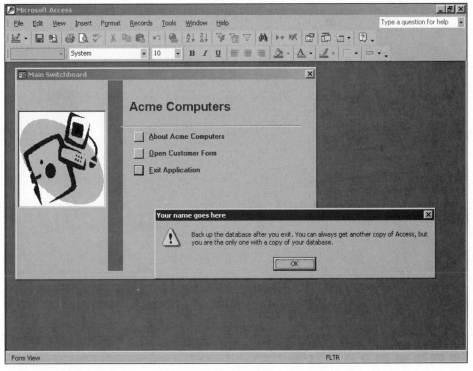

FIGURE 8.17   *Acme Computers Switchboard (Exercise 8)*

The Importance of Backup

Go to a real installation such as a doctor's or an attorney's office, the company where you work, or the computer lab at school. Determine the backup procedures that are in effect, then write a one-page report indicating whether the policy is adequate and, if necessary, offering suggestions for improvement. Your report should be addressed to the individual in charge of the business and it should cover all aspects of the backup strategy. Be sure to indicate which files are backed up, the responsible individual, how often the files are backed up, and where the backup copies are stored.

Debugging

The Debug toolbar contains several tools to help you debug a procedure if it does not work as intended. The Step Into command is especially useful as it executes the procedure one statement at a time. Choose any of the procedures you created in this chapter, then investigate the procedure in detail using the Debug toolbar. Summarize your results in a short note to your instructor.

Help for VBA

Review the hands-on exercises in the chapter to review the various ways to obtain help in VBA. In addition, you can click on any Visual Basic key word, then press the F1 key to display a context-sensitive help screen. Summarize this information in a short note to your instructor. It will be an invaluable reference as you continue to explore VBA in Access as well as other applications in Microsoft Office.

The Developer's Forum

Go to the Microsoft Developer's Forum at www.microsoft.com/office/developer to see what information is currently available. (The address of the page changes periodically, so you may have to search the site for developer resources.) In any event, locate at least one article of interest to you, then summarize your findings in a short note to your instructor.

APPENDIX A

Toolbars

Microsoft Access has 27 predefined toolbars that provide access to commonly used commands. The toolbars are displayed in Figure A.1 and are listed here for convenience: Alignment and Sizing, Database, Filter/Sort, Form Design, Form View, Formatting (Datasheet), Formatting (Form/Report), Formatting (Page), Formatting (PivotTable/PivotChart), Macro Design, Page Design, Page View, PivotChart, PivotTable, Print Preview, Query Datasheet, Query Design, Relationship, Report Design, Shortcut Menus, Source Code Control, Table Datasheet, Table Design, Toolbox, Utility 1, Utility 2, and Web.

The buttons on the toolbars are intended to indicate their functions. Clicking the Printer button (the fourth button from the left on the Database toolbar), for example, executes the Print command. If you are unsure of the purpose of any toolbar button, point to it, and a ScreenTip will appear that displays its name.

You can display multiple toolbars at one time, move them to new locations on the screen, customize their appearance, or suppress their display.

■ To display or hide a toolbar, pull down the View menu and click the Toolbars command. Select (deselect) the toolbar(s) that you want to display (hide). The selected toolbar(s) will be displayed in the same position as when last displayed. You may also point to any toolbar and click with the right mouse button to bring up a shortcut menu, after which you can select the toolbar to be displayed (hidden).

■ To change the size of the buttons, suppress the display of the ScreenTips, pull down the View menu, click Toolbars, and click Customize to display the Customize dialog box. If necessary, click the Options tab, then select (deselect) the appropriate check box. Alternatively, you can right click on any toolbar, click the Customize command from the context-sensitive menu, then select (deselect) the appropriate check box from within the Options tab in the Customize dialog box.

■ Toolbars are either docked (along the edge of the window) or floating (in their own window). A toolbar moved to the edge of the window will dock along that edge. A toolbar moved anywhere else in the window will float in its own window. Docked toolbars are one tool wide (high). Floating toolbars can be resized by clicking and dragging a border or corner as you would with any window.

- To move a docked toolbar, click anywhere in the gray background area and drag the toolbar to its new location. You can also click and drag the move handle (the vertical line) at the left of the toolbar.
- To move a floating toolbar, drag its title bar to its new location.

■ To customize a toolbar, display the toolbar on the screen, pull down the View menu, click Toolbars, and click Customize to display the Customize dialog box. Alternatively, you can click on any toolbar with the right mouse button and select Customize from the shortcut menu.

- To move a button, drag the button to its new location on that toolbar or any other displayed toolbar.
- To copy a button, press the Ctrl key as you drag the button to its new location on that toolbar or any other displayed toolbar.
- To delete a button, drag the button off the toolbar and release the mouse button.
- To add a button, click the Commands tab in the Customize dialog box, select the category from the Categories list box that contains the button you want to add, then drag the button to the desired location on the toolbar. (To see a description of a tool's function prior to adding it to a toolbar, select the tool, then click the Description command button.)
- To restore a predefined toolbar to its default appearance, click the Toolbars tab, select (highlight) the desired toolbar, and click the Reset command button.

■ Buttons can also be moved, copied, or deleted without displaying the Customize dialog box.

- To move a button, press the Alt key as you drag the button to the new location.
- To copy a button, press the Alt and Ctrl keys as you drag the button to the new location.
- To delete a button, press the Alt key as you drag the button off the toolbar.

■ To create your own toolbar, pull down the View menu, click Toolbars, click Customize, click the Toolbars tab, then click the New command button. Alternatively, you can click on any toolbar with the right mouse button, select Customize from the shortcut menu, click the Toolbars tab, and then click the New command button.

- Enter a name for the toolbar in the dialog box that follows. The name can be any length and can contain spaces. Click OK.
- The new toolbar will appear on the screen. Initially it will be big enough to hold only one button. Add, move, and delete buttons following the same procedures as outlined above. The toolbar will automatically size itself as new buttons are added and deleted.
- To delete a custom toolbar, pull down the View menu, click Toolbars, click Customize, and click the Toolbars tab. *Verify that the custom toolbar to be deleted is the only one selected (highlighted).* Click the Delete command button. Click OK to confirm the deletion. (Note that a predefined toolbar cannot be deleted.)

Alignment and Sizing

Align Left · Align Top · Size Height · Size Height/Width

Align Right · Align Bottom · Size Width

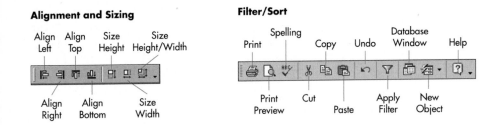

Filter/Sort

Print · Spelling · Copy · Undo · Database Window · Help

Print Preview · Cut · Paste · Apply Filter · New Object

Database

New · Save · Print · Spelling · Copy · Undo · Analyze · Microsoft Script Editor · Relationships · Help

Open · Search · Print Preview · Cut · Paste · Office Links · Code · Properties · New Object

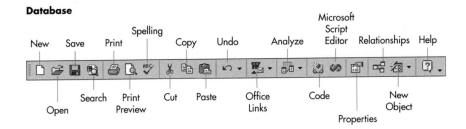

Form Design

View · Search · Print Preview · Copy · Format Painter · Redo · Field List · AutoFormat · Properties · Database Window

Save · Print · Cut · Paste · Undo · Insert Hyperlink · Toolbox · Code · Build · New Object · Help

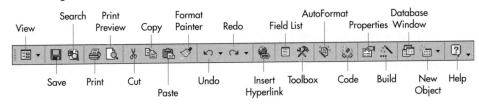

Form View

View · Search · Print Preview · Cut · Paste · Insert Hyperlink · Sort Descending · Filter by Form · Find · Delete Record · Database Window · Help

Save · Print · Spelling · Copy · Undo · Sort Ascending · Filter by Selection · Apply Filter · New Record · Properties · New Object

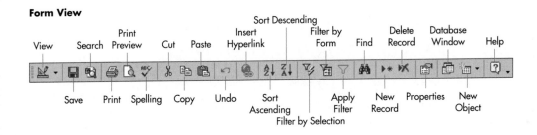

Formatting (Datasheet)

Go to Field · Font Size · Italic · Fill/Back Color · Line/Border Color · Special Effect

Font · Bold · Underline · Font/Fore Color · Gridlines

SSN · Arial · 10 · B I U

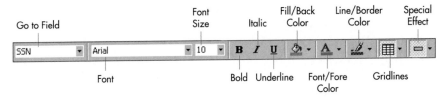

Formatting (Form/Report)

Object · Font Size · Italic · Align Left · Align Right · Font/Fore Color · Line/Border Width

Font · Bold · Underline · Center · Fill/Back Color · Line/Border Color · Special Effect

SSN · MS Sans Serif · 8 · B I U

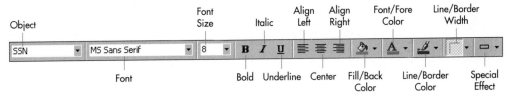

FIGURE A.1 *Access Toolbars*

Formatting (Page)

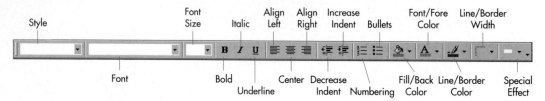

Formatting (PivotTable/Pivot Chart)

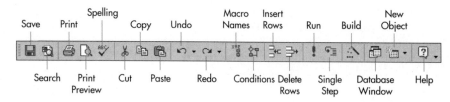

Macro Design

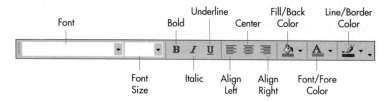

Page Design

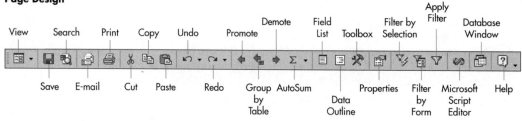

Page View

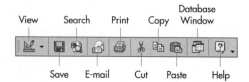

Pivot Chart

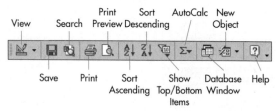

FIGURE A.1 *Access Toolbars (continued)*

Pivot Table

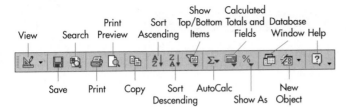

Print Preview

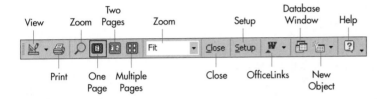

Query Datasheet

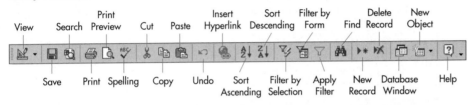

Query Design

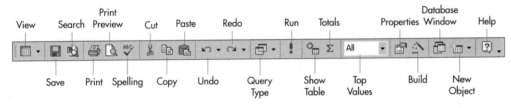

Relationship

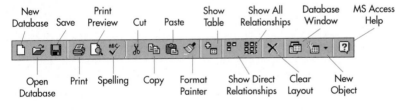

Report Design

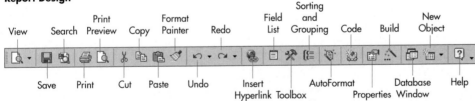

FIGURE A.1 *Access Toolbars (continued)*

Shortcut Menus

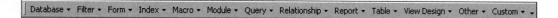

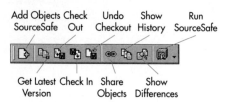

Source Code Control

Add Objects   Check   Undo   Show   Run
SourceSafe   Out   Checkout   History   SourceSafe

Get Latest   Check In   Share   Show
Version   Objects   Differences

Table Datasheet

View   Search   Print Preview   Cut   Paste   Insert Hyperlink   Sort Descending   Filter by Form   Find   Delete Record   New Object

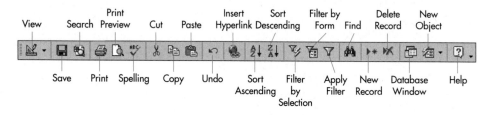

Save   Print   Spelling   Copy   Undo   Sort Ascending   Filter by Selection   Apply Filter   New Record   Database Window   Help

Table Design

View   Search   Print Preview   Cut   Paste   Redo   Indexes   Delete Rows   Build   New Object

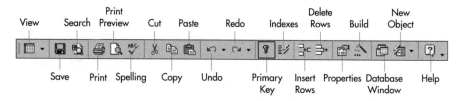

Save   Print   Spelling   Copy   Undo   Primary Key   Insert Rows   Properties   Database Window   Help

Toolbox

Select Objects   Label   Option Group   Option Button   Combo Box   Command Button   Unbound Object Frame   Page Break   Subform/ Subreport   Rectangle

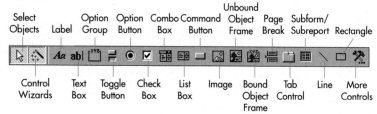

Control Wizards   Text Box   Toggle Button   Check Box   List Box   Image   Bound Object Frame   Tab Control   Line   More Controls

Utility 1   **Utility 2**

Add or Remove Buttons   Add or Remove Buttons

Web

Back   Stop Current Jump   Start Page   Favorites Menu   Show Only Web Toolbar

Forward   Refresh Current Page   Search the Web   Go Menu   Address

FIGURE A.1   *Access Toolbars (continued)*

APPENDIX *B*

Designing a Relational Database

OVERVIEW

An Access database consists of multiple tables, each of which stores data about a specific subject. To use Access effectively, you must relate the tables to one another. This in turn requires a knowledge of database design and an understanding of the principles of a relational database under which Access operates.

Our approach to teaching database design is to present two case studies, each of which covers a common application. The first case centers on franchises for fast food restaurants and incorporates the concept of a one-to-many relationship. One person can own many restaurants, but a given restaurant is owned by only one person. The second case is based on a system for student transcripts and incorporates a many-to-many relationship. One student takes many courses, and one course is taken by many students. The intent in both cases is to design a database capable of producing the desired information.

CASE STUDY: FAST FOOD FRANCHISES

The case you are about to read is set within the context of a national corporation offering franchises for fast food restaurants. The concept of a franchise operation is a familiar one and exists within many industries. The parent organization develops a model operation, then franchises that concept to qualified individuals (franchisees) seeking to operate their own businesses. The national company teaches the franchisee to run the business, aids the person in site selection and staffing, coordinates national advertising, and so on. The franchisee pays an initial fee to open the business followed by subsequent royalties and marketing fees to the parent corporation.

The essence of the case is how to relate the data for the various entities (the restaurants, franchisees, and contracts) to one another. One approach is to develop a single restaurant table, with each restaurant record containing data about the

423

owner and contract arrangement. As we shall see, that design leads to problems of redundancy whenever the same person owns more than one restaurant or when several restaurants have the same contract type. A better approach is to develop separate tables, one for each of the objects (restaurants, franchisees, and contracts).

The entities in the case have a definite relationship to one another, which must be reflected in the database design. The corporation encourages individuals to own multiple restaurants, creating a *one-to-many relationship* between franchisees and restaurants. One person can own many restaurants, but a given restaurant is owned by only one person. There is also a one-to-many relationship between contracts and restaurants because the corporation offers a choice of contracts to each restaurant.

The company wants a database that can retrieve all data for a given restaurant, such as the annual sales, type of contract in effect (contract types are described below), and/or detailed information about the restaurant owner. The company also needs reports that reflect the location of each restaurant, all restaurants in a given state, and all restaurants managed by a particular contract type. The various contract arrangements are described below:

Contract 1: 99-year term, requiring a one-time fee of $250,000 payable at the time the franchise is awarded. In addition, the franchisee must pay a royalty of 2 percent of the restaurant's gross sales to the parent corporation, and contribute an additional 2 percent of sales to the parent corporation for advertising.

Contract 2: 5-year term (renewable at franchisee's option), requiring an initial payment of $50,000. In addition, the franchisee must pay a royalty of 4 percent of the restaurant's gross sales to the parent corporation, and contribute an additional 3 percent of sales to the parent corporation for advertising.

Contract 3: 10-year term (renewable at franchisee's option), requiring an initial payment of $75,000. In addition, the franchisee must pay a royalty of 3 percent of the restaurant's gross sales to the parent corporation, and contribute an additional 3 percent of sales to the parent corporation for advertising.

Other contract types may be offered in the future. The company currently has 500 restaurants, of which 200 are company owned. Expansion plans call for opening an additional 200 restaurants each year for the next three years, all of which are to be franchised. There is no limit on the number of restaurants an individual may own.

Single-Table Solution

The initial concern in this, or any other, system is how best to structure the data so that the solution satisfies the information requirements of the client. We present two solutions. The first is based on a single restaurant table and will be shown to have several limitations. The second introduces the concept of a relational database and consists of three tables (for the restaurants, franchisees, and contracts).

The single-table solution is shown in Figure B.1a. Each record within the table contains data about a particular restaurant, its franchisee (owner), and contract type. There are five restaurants in our example, each with a *unique* restaurant number. At first glance, Figure B.1a appears satisfactory; yet there are three specific types of problems associated with this solution. These are:

1. Difficulties in the modification of data for an existing franchisee or contract type, in that the same change may be made in multiple places.
2. Difficulties in the addition of a new franchisee or contract type, in that these entities must first be associated with a particular restaurant.
3. Difficulties in the deletion of a restaurant, in that data for a particular franchisee or contract type may be deleted as well.

Restaurant Number	Restaurant Data (Address, annual sales . . .)	Franchisee Data (Name, telephone, address . . .)	Contract Data (Type, term, initial fee . . .)
R1	Restaurant data for Miami . . .	Franchisee data (Grauer . . .)	Contract data (Type 1 . . .)
R2	Restaurant data for Coral Gables . . .	Franchisee data (Moldof . . .)	Contract data (Type 1 . . .)
R3	Restaurant data for Fort Lauderdale. . .	Franchisee data (Grauer . . .)	Contract data (Type 2 . . .)
R4	Restaurant data for New York . . .	Franchisee data (Glassman . . .)	Contract data (Type 1 . . .)
R5	Restaurant data for Coral Springs . . .	Franchisee data (Coulter . . .)	Contract data (Type 3 . . .)

(a) Single-Table Solution

Restaurant Number	Restaurant Data	Franchisee Number	Contract Type
R1	Restaurant data for Miami . . .	F1	C1
R2	Restaurant data for Coral Gables . . .	F2	C1
R3	Restaurant data for Fort Lauderdale. . .	F1	C2
R4	Restaurant data for New York . . .	F3	C1
R5	Restaurant data for Coral Springs . . .	F4	C3

Contract Type	Contract Data
C1	Contract data. . .
C2	Contract data. . .
C3	Contract data. . .

Franchisee Number	Franchisee Data (Name, telephone, address, . . .)
F1	Grauer. . .
F2	Moldof. . .
F3	Glassman. . .
F4	Coulter. . .

(b) Multiple-Table Solution

FIGURE B.1   *Single- versus Multiple-Table Solution*

The first problem, modification of data about an existing franchisee or contract type, stems from **redundancy**, which in turn requires that any change to duplicated data be made in several places. In other words, any modification to a duplicated entry, such as a change in data for a franchisee with multiple restaurants (e.g., Grauer, who owns restaurants in Miami and Fort Lauderdale), requires a search through the entire table to find all instances of that data so that the identical modification can be made to each of the records. A similar procedure would have to be followed should data change about a duplicated contract (e.g., a change in the royalty percentage for contract Type 1, which applies to restaurants R1, R2, and R4). This is, to say the least, a time-consuming and error-prone procedure.

The addition of a new franchisee or contract type poses a different type of problem. It is quite logical, for example, that potential franchisees must apply to the corporation and qualify for ownership before having a restaurant assigned to them. It is also likely that the corporation would develop a new contract type prior to offering that contract to an existing restaurant. Neither of these events is easily accommodated in the table structure of Figure B.1a, which would require the creation of a dummy restaurant record to accommodate the new franchisee or contract type.

The deletion of a restaurant creates yet another type of difficulty. What happens, for example, if the company decides to close restaurant R5 because of insufficient sales? The record for this restaurant would disappear as expected, but so too would the data for the franchisee (Coulter) and the contract type (C3), which is not intended. The corporation might want to award Coulter another restaurant in the future and/or offer this contract type to other restaurants. Neither situation would be possible as the relevant data has been lost with the deletion of the restaurant record.

Multiple-Table Solution

A much better solution appears in Figure B.1b, which uses a different table for each of the entities (restaurants, franchisees, and contracts) that exist in the system. Every record in the restaurant table is assigned a unique restaurant number (e.g., R1 or R2), just as every record in the franchisee table is given a unique franchisee number (e.g., F1 or F2), and every contract record a unique contract number (e.g., C1 or C2).

The tables are linked to one another through the franchisee and/or contract numbers, which also appear in the restaurant table. Every record in the restaurant table is associated with its appropriate record in the franchisee table through the franchisee number common to both tables. In similar fashion, every restaurant is tied to its appropriate contract through the contract number, which appears in the restaurant record. This solution may seem complicated, but it is really quite simple and elegant.

Assume, for example, that we want the name of the franchisee for restaurant R5, and further, that we need the details of the contract type for this restaurant. We retrieve the appropriate restaurant record, which contains franchisee and contract numbers of F4 and C3, respectively. We then search through the franchisee table for franchisee F4 (obtaining all necessary information about Coulter) and search again through the contract table for contract C3 (obtaining the data for this contract type). The process is depicted graphically in Figure B.1b.

The multiple-table solution may require slightly more effort to retrieve information, but this is more than offset by the advantages of table maintenance. Consider, for example, a change in data for contract C1, which currently governs restaurants R1, R2, and R4. All that is necessary is to go into the contract table, find record C1, and make the changes. The records in the restaurant table are *not* affected because the restaurant records do not contain contract data per se, only the number of the corresponding contract record. In other words, the change in data for contract C1 is made in one place (the contract table), yet that change would be reflected for all affected restaurants. This is in contrast to the single-table solution of Figure B.1a, which would require the identical modification in three places.

The addition of new records for franchisees or contracts is done immediately in the appropriate tables of Figure B.1b. The corporation simply adds a franchisee or contract record as these events occur, without the necessity of a corresponding restaurant record. This is much easier than the approach of Figure B.1a, which required an existing restaurant in order to add one of the other entities.

The deletion of a restaurant is also easier than with the single-table organization. You could, for example, delete restaurant R5 without losing the associated franchisee and contract data as these records exist in different tables.

Queries to the Database

By now you should be convinced of the need for multiple tables within a database and that this type of design facilitates all types of table maintenance. However, the ultimate objective of any system is to produce information, and it is in this area that the design excels. Consider now Figure B.2, which expands upon the multiple table solution to include additional data for the respective tables.

As indicated, there are three tables—for restaurants, franchisees, and contracts, respectively. The tables are linked to one another through the franchisee and/or contract numbers that also appear in the restaurant table. These fields are color-coded so that you can see the relationships more clearly.

To be absolutely sure you understand the multiple-table solution of Figure B.2, use it to answer the questions at the top of the next page. Check your answers with those provided.

Restaurant Number	Street Address	City	State	Zip Code	Annual Sales	Franchisee Number	Contract Type
R1	1001 Ponce de Leon Blvd	Miami	FL	33361	$600,000	F1	C1
R2	31 West Rivo Alto Road	Coral Gables	FL	33139	$450,000	F2	C1
R3	333 Las Olas Blvd	Fort Lauderdale	FL	33033	$250,000	F1	C2
R4	1700 Broadway	New York	NY	10293	$1,750,000	F3	C1
R5	1300 Sample Road	Coral Springs	FL	33071	$50,000	F4	C3

(a) Restaurant Table

Franchisee Number	Franchisee Name	Telephone	Street Address	City	State	Zip Code
F1	Grauer	(305) 755-1000	2133 NW 102 Terrace	Coral Springs	FL	33071
F2	Moldof	(305) 753-4614	1400 Lejeune Blvd	Miami	FL	33365
F3	Glassman	(212) 458-5054	555 Fifth Avenue	New York	NY	10024
F4	Coulter	(305) 755-0910	1000 Federal Highway	Fort Lauderdale	FL	33033

(b) Franchisee Table

Contract Type	Term (years)	Initial Fee	Royalty Pct	Advertising Pct
C1	99	$250,000	2%	2%
C2	5	$50,000	4%	3%
C3	10	$75,000	3%	3%

(c) Contract Table

FIGURE B.2   *Fast Food Franchises (database queries)*

Questions

1. Who owns restaurant R2? What contract type is in effect for this restaurant?
2. What is the address of restaurant R4?
3. Which restaurant(s) are owned by Mr. Grauer?
4. List all restaurants with a contract type of C1.
5. Which restaurants in Florida have gross sales over $300,000?
6. List all contract types.
7. Which contract type has the lowest initial fee? How much is the initial fee? Which restaurant(s) are governed by this contract?
8. How many franchisees are there? What are their names?
9. What are the royalty and advertising percentages for restaurant R3?

Answers

1. Restaurant R2 is owned by Moldof and governed by contract C1.
2. Restaurant R4 is located at 1700 Broadway, New York, NY 10293.
3. Mr. Grauer owns restaurants R1 and R3.
4. R1, R2, and R4 are governed by contract C1.
5. The restaurants in Florida with gross sales over $300,000 are R1 ($600,000) and R2 ($450,000).
6. The existing contract types are C1, C2, and C3.
7. Contract C2 has the lowest initial fee ($50,000); restaurant R3 is governed by this contract type.
8. There are four franchisees: Grauer, Moldof, Glassman, and Coulter.
9. Restaurant R3 is governed by contract C2 with royalty and advertising percentages of four and three percent, respectively.

THE RELATIONAL MODEL

The restaurant case study illustrates a ***relational database***, which requires a separate table for every entity in the physical system (restaurants, franchisees, and contracts). Each occurrence of an ***entity*** (a specific restaurant, franchisee, or contract type) appears as a row within a table. The properties of an entity (a restaurant's address, owner, or sales) appear as columns within a table.

Every row in every table of a relational database must be distinct. This is accomplished by including a column (or combination of columns) to uniquely identify the row. The unique identifier is known as the ***primary key***. The restaurant number, for example, is different for every restaurant in the restaurant table. The franchisee number is unique in the franchisee table. The contract type is unique in the contract table.

The same column can, however, appear in multiple tables. The franchisee number, for example, appears in both the franchisee table, where its values are unique, and in the restaurant table, where they are not. The franchisee number is the primary key in the franchisee table, but it is a ***foreign key*** in the restaurant table. (A foreign key is simply the primary key of a related table.)

The inclusion of a foreign key in the restaurant table enables us to implement the one-to-many relationship between franchisees and restaurants. We enter the franchisee number (the primary key in the franchisee table) as a column in the restaurant table, where it (the franchisee number) is a foreign key. In similar fashion, contract type (the primary key in the contract table) appears as a foreign key in the restaurant table to implement the one-to-many relationship between contracts and restaurants.

It is helpful perhaps to restate these observations about a relational database in general terms:

1. Every entity in a physical system requires its own table in a database.
2. Each row in a table is different from every other row because of a unique column (or combination of columns) known as a primary key.
3. The primary key of one table can appear as a foreign key in another table.
4. The order of rows in a table is immaterial.
5. The order of columns in a table is immaterial, although the primary key is generally listed first.
6. The number of columns is the same in every row of the table.

THE KEY, THE WHOLE KEY, AND NOTHING BUT THE KEY

The theory of a relational database was developed by Dr. Edgar Codd, giving rise to the phrase, "*The key, the whole key, and nothing but the key . . . so help me Codd.*" The sentence effectively summarizes the concepts behind a relational database and helps to ensure the validity of a design. Simply stated, the value of every column other than the primary key depends on the key in that row, on the entire key, and on nothing but that key.

Referential Integrity

The concept of *referential integrity* requires that the tables in a database be consistent with one another. Consider once again the first row in the restaurant table of Figure B.2a, which indicates that the restaurant is owned by franchisee F1 and governed by contract type C1. Recall also how these values are used to obtain additional information about the franchisee or contract type from the appropriate tables in Figures B.2b and B.2c, respectively.

What if, however, the restaurant table referred to franchisee number F1000 or contract C9, neither of which exists in the database of Figure B.2? There would be a problem because the tables would be inconsistent with one another; that is, the restaurant table would refer to rows in the franchisee and contract tables that do not exist. It is important, therefore, that referential integrity be strictly enforced and that such inconsistencies be prevented from occurring. Suffice it to say that data validation is critical when establishing or maintaining a database, and that no system, relational or otherwise, can compensate for inaccurate or incomplete data.

CASE STUDY: STUDENT TRANSCRIPTS

Our second case is set within the context of student transcripts and expands the concept of a relational database to implement a *many-to-many relationship*. The system is intended to track students and the courses they take. The many-to-many relationship occurs because one student takes many courses, while at the same time, one course is taken by many students. The objective of this case is to relate the student and course tables to one another to produce the desired information.

The system should be able to display information about a particular student as well as information about a particular course. It should also display information about a student-course combination, such as *when* a student took the course and *what grade* he or she received.

Solution

The (intuitive and incorrect) solution of Figure B.3 consists of two tables, one for courses and one for students, corresponding to the two entities in the physical system. The student table contains the student's name, address, major, date of entry into the school, cumulative credits, and cumulative quality points. The course table contains the unique six-character course identifier, the course title, and the number of credits.

There are no problems of redundancy. The data for a particular course (its description and number of credits) appears only once in the course table, just as the data for a particular student appears only once in the student table. New courses will be added directly to the course table, just as new students will be added to the student table.

The design of the student table makes it easy to list all courses for one student. It is more difficult, however, to list all students in one course. Even if this were not the case, the solution is complicated by the irregular shape of the student table. The rows in the table are of variable length, according to the number of courses taken by each student. Not only is this design awkward, but how do we know in advance how much space to allocate for each student?

Course Number	Course Description	Credits
ACC101	Introduction to Accounting	3
CHM100	Survey of Chemistry	3
CHM101	Chemistry Lab	1
CIS120	Microcomputer Applications	3
ENG100	Freshman English	3
MTH100	Calculus with Analytic Geometry	4
MUS110	Music Appreciation	2
SPN100	Spanish I	3

(a) Course Table

Student Number	Student Data	Courses Taken with Grade and Semester											
S1	Student data (Adams. . .)	ACC101	SP01	A	CIS120	FA00	A	MU100	FA00	B			
S2	Student data (Fox. . .)	ENG100	SP01	B	MTH100	SP01	B	SPN100	SP01	B	CIS120	FA00	A
S3	Student data (Baker. . .)	ACC101	SP01	C	ENG100	SP01	B	MTH100	FA00	C	CIS120	FA00	B
S4	Student data (Jones. . .)	ENG100	SP01	A	MTH100	SP01	A						
S5	Student data (Smith. . .)	CIS120	SP01	C	ENG100	SP01	B	CIS120	FA00	F			

(b) Student Table

FIGURE B.3 *Student Transcripts (repeating groups)*

The problems inherent in Figure B.3 stem from the many-to-many relationship that exists between students and courses. The solution is to eliminate the ***repeating groups*** (course number, semester, and grade), which occur in each row of the student table in Figure B.3, in favor of the additional table shown in Figure B.4. Each row in the new table is unique because the *combination* of student number, course number, and semester is unique. Semester must be included since students are allowed to repeat a course. Smith (student number S5), for example, took CIS120 a second time after failing it initially.

The implementation of a many-to-many relationship requires an additional table, with a ***combined key*** consisting of (at least) the keys of the individual entities. The many-to-many table may also contain additional columns, which exist as a result of the combination (intersection) of the individual keys. The combination of student S5, course CIS120, and semester SP01 is unique and results in a grade of C.

Note, too, how the design in Figure B.4 facilitates table maintenance as discussed in the previous case. A change in student data is made in only one place (the student table), regardless of how many courses the student has taken. A new student may be added to the student table prior to taking any courses. In similar fashion, a new course can be added to the course table before any students have taken the course.

Review once more the properties of a relational database, then verify that the solution in Figure B.4 adheres to these requirements. To be absolutely sure that you understand the solution, and to illustrate once again the power of the relational model, use Figure B.4 to answer the following questions about the student database.

Course Number	Course Description	Credits
ACC101	Introduction to Accounting	3
CHM100	Survey of Chemistry	3
CHM101	Chemistry Lab	1
CIS120	Microcomputer Applications	3
ENG100	Freshman English	3
MTH100	Calculus with Analytic Geometry	4
MUS110	Music Appreciation	2
SPN100	Spanish I	3

(a) Course Table

Student Number	Student Data
S1	Student data (Adams. . .)
S2	Student data (Fox. . .)
S3	Student data (Baker. . .)
S4	Student data (Jones. . .)
S5	Student data (Smith. . .)

(b) Student Table

Student Number	Course Number	Semester	Grade
S1	ACC101	SP01	A
S1	CIS120	FA00	A
S1	MU100	SP00	B
S2	ENG100	SP01	B
S2	MTH100	SP01	B
S2	SPN100	SP01	B
S2	CIS120	FA00	A
S3	ACC101	SP01	C
S3	ENG100	SP01	B
S3	MTH100	FA00	C
S3	CIS120	FA00	B
S4	ENG100	SP01	A
S4	MTH100	SP01	A
S5	CIS120	SP01	C
S5	ENG100	SP01	B
S5	CIS120	FA00	F

(c) Student-Course Table

FIGURE B.4 *Student Transcripts (improved design)*

Questions

1. How many courses are currently offered?
2. List all three-credit courses.
3. Which courses has Smith taken during his stay at the university?
4. Which students have taken MTH100?
5. Which courses did Adams take during the Fall 2000 semester?
6. Which students took Microcomputer Applications in the Fall 2000 semester?
7. Which students received an A in Freshman English during the Spring 2001 semester?

Answers

1. Eight courses are offered.
2. The three-credit courses are ACC101, CHM100, CIS120, ENG100, and SPN100.
3. Smith has taken CIS120 (twice) and ENG100.
4. Fox, Baker, and Jones have taken MTH100.
5. Adams took CIS120 during the Fall 2000 semester.
6. Adams, Fox, Baker, and Smith took Microcomputer Applications in the Fall 2000 semester.
7. Jones was the only student to receive an A in Freshman English during the Spring 2001 semester.

SUMMARY

A relational database consists of multiple two-dimensional tables. Each entity in a physical system requires its own table in the database. Every row in a table is unique due to the existence of a primary key. The order of the rows and columns in a table is immaterial. Every row in a table contains the same columns in the same order as every other row.

A one-to-many relationship is implemented by including the primary key of one table as a foreign key in the other table. Implementation of a many-to-many relationship requires an additional table whose primary key combines (at a minimum) the primary keys of the individual tables. Referential integrity ensures that the information in a database is internally consistent.

KEY TERMS

APPENDIX C

Mail Merge: An Access Database and a Word Form Letter

OVERVIEW

One of the greatest benefits of using the Microsoft Office suite is the ability to combine data from one application with another. An excellent example is a *mail merge*, in which data from an Access table or query are input into a Word document to produce a set of individualized form letters. You create the *form letter* using Microsoft Word, then you merge the letter with the *records* in the Access table or query. The merge process creates the individual letters, changing the name, address, and other information as appropriate from letter to letter. The concept is illustrated in Figure C.1, in which John Smith uses a mail merge to seek a job upon graduation. John writes the letter describing his qualifications, then merges that letter with a set of names and addresses to produce the individual letters.

The mail merge process uses two input files (a main document and a data source) and produces a third file as output (the set of form letters). The *main document* (e.g., the cover letter in Figure C.1a) contains standardized text together with one or more *merge fields* that indicate where the variable information is to be inserted in the individual letters. The *data source* (the set of names and addresses in Figure C.1b) contains the data that varies from letter to letter and is a table (or query) within an Access database. (The data source may also be taken from an Excel list, or alternatively, it can be created as a table in Microsoft Word.)

The main document and the data source work in conjunction with one another, with the merge fields in the main document referencing the corresponding fields in the data source. The first line in the address of Figure C.1a, for example, contains three merge fields, each of which is enclosed in angle brackets, *<<Title>> <<FirstName>> <<LastName>>*. (These entries are not typed explicitly but are entered through special commands as described in the hands-on exercise that follows shortly.) The merge process examines each record in the data source and substitutes the appropriate field values for the corresponding merge fields as it creates

John H. Smith

426 Jenny Lake Drive •   **Coral Gables, FL 33146**   • **(305) 666-8888**

July 25, 2001

«Title» «FirstName» «LastName»
«JobTitle»
«Company»
«Address1»
«City», «State» «PostalCode»

Dear «Title» «LastName»:

I would like to inquire about a position with «Company» as an entry-level programmer. I have just graduated from the University of Miami with a Bachelor's Degree in Computer Information Systems (May 2001) and I am very interested in working for you. I am proficient in all applications in Microsoft Office and also have experience with Visual Basic, C++, and Java. I have had the opportunity to design and implement a few Web applications, both as a part of my educational program, and during my internship with Personalized Computer Designs, Inc.

I am eager to put my skills to work and would like to talk with you at your earliest convenience. I have enclosed a copy of my résumé and will be happy to furnish the names and addresses of my references. You may reach me at the above address and phone number. I look forward to hearing from you.

Sincerely,

John H. Smith

(a) The Form Letter (a Word document)

FIGURE **C.1** *The Mail Merge*

the individual form letters. For example, the first three fields in the first record will produce *Mr. Jason Frasher;* the same fields in the second record will produce, *Ms. Lauren Howard,* and so on.

The mail merge prepares the letters one at a time, with one letter created for every record in the data source until the file of names and addresses is exhausted. The individual form letters are shown in Figure C.1c. Each letter begins automatically on a new page.

A mail merge can be started from either **Microsoft Word** or **Microsoft Access**. Either way, two input files are required—the form letter (main document) and the data source. The order in which these files are created depends on how the merge is initiated. When starting in Microsoft Word, you begin with the form letter, then create the data source. The process is reversed in Access—you start with a table or query, then exit to Word to create the form letter. The merge itself, however, is always performed from within Microsoft Word.

	Title	First Name	Last Name	JobTitle	Company	Address1	City	State	Postal Code
▶	Mr.	Jason	Frasher	President	Frasher Systems	100 S. Miami Avenue	Miami	FL	33103-
	Ms.	Lauren	Howard	Director of Human Resources	Unique Systems	475 LeJeune Road	Coral Gables	FL	33146-
	Ms.	Elizabeth	Scherry	Director of Personnel	Custom Computing	8180 Kendall Drive	Miami	FL	33156-
*									

(b) The Data Source (an Access table or query)

John H. Smith

426 Jenny Lake Drive •   Coral Gables, FL 33146   • (305) 666-8888

July 25, 2001

Ms. Elizabeth Scherry
Director of Personnel
Custom Computing
8180 Kendall Drive
Miami, FL 33156

Dear Ms. Scherry:

I would like to inquire about a positi
programmer. I have just graduated from the
Computer Information Systems (May 2001)
proficient in all applications in Microsoft (
C++, and Java. I have had the opportunity to d
as a part of my educational program, and d
Designs, Inc.

I am eager to put my skills to work and
convenience. I have enclosed a copy of my ré
addresses of my references. You may reach
forward to hearing from you.

Sincerely,

John H. Smith

John H. Smith

426 Jenny Lake Drive •   Coral Gables, FL 33146   • (305) 666-8888

July 25, 2001

Ms. Lauren Howard
Director of Human Resources
Unique Systems
475 LeJeune Road
Coral Gables, FL 33146

Dear Ms. Howard:

I would like to inquire about a posit
programmer. I have just graduated from the
Computer Information Systems (May 2001
proficient in all applications in Microsoft
C++, and Java. I have had the opportunity to c
as a part of my educational program, and c
Designs, Inc.

I am eager to put my skills to work and
convenience. I have enclosed a copy of my ré
addresses of my references. You may reach
forward to hearing from you.

Sincerely,

John H. Smith

John H. Smith

426 Jenny Lake Drive •   Coral Gables, FL 33146   • (305) 666-8888

July 25, 2001

Mr. Jason Frasher
President
Frasher Systems
100 S. Miami Avenue
Miami, FL 33103

Dear Mr. Frasher:

I would like to inquire about a position with Frasher Systems as an entry-level
programmer. I have just graduated from the University of Miami with a Bachelor's Degree in
Computer Information Systems (May 2001) and I am very interested in working for you. I am
proficient in all applications in Microsoft Office and also have experience with Visual Basic,
C++, and Java. I have had the opportunity to design and implement a few Web applications, both
as a part of my educational program, and during my internship with Personalized Computer
Designs, Inc.

I am eager to put my skills to work and would like to talk with you at your earliest
convenience. I have enclosed a copy of my résumé and will be happy to furnish the names and
addresses of my references. You may reach me at the above address and phone number. I look
forward to hearing from you.

Sincerely,

John H. Smith

(c) The Printed Letters

FIGURE C.1   *The Mail Merge (continued)*

MAIL MERGE

Objective To merge data from an Access database with a Word document to create a set of individual form letters. Use Figure C.2 as a guide.

Step 1: **Open the Names and Addresses Database**

➤ Start Access. Open the **Names and Addresses database** in the Exploring Access folder. The Tables button is selected. The Contacts table is the only table in the database.

➤ Click the **down arrow** on the **Office Links button** on the Database toolbar, then click **Merge It with Microsoft Word** to display the dialog box in Figure C.2a.

➤ The form letter has already been created for you. Thus, you can select the option to **Link your data to an existing Word document**. Click **OK**.

Click drop-down arrow on Office Links button

Click option button to link data to an existing Word document

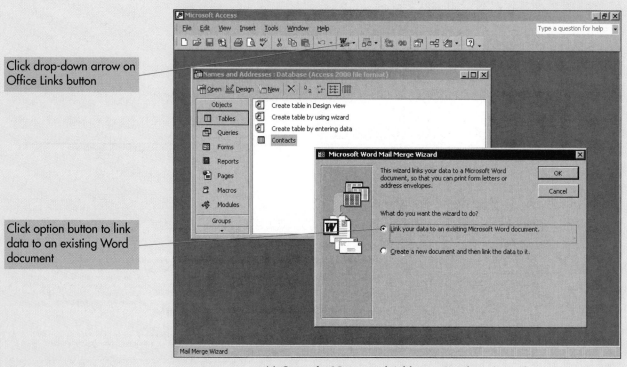

(a) Open the Names and Addresses Database (step 1)

FIGURE C.2   *Hands-on Exercise 1*

START ANYWHERE

A mail merge can be started from Microsoft Word or Microsoft Access. Either way, two input files are required, a form letter and a data source. The order in which these files are created is unimportant, and you can switch back and forth between the two. Eventually, however, the data source will be merged with the form letter to create the individual set of form letters.

Step 2: **Open the Form Letter**

➤ You should see the Select Microsoft Word Document dialog box as shown in Figure C.2b. Click the **down arrow** in the Look in box and select the **Exploring Access folder**.

➤ Select the **Form Letter** document and click the **Open button**. This starts Microsoft Word and opens the Form Letter document.

➤ Click anywhere within the date to select it, then press **Shift+F9** to toggle between the displayed value and the date code, which is set to always display today's date (see boxed tip below).

➤ The task pane also opens automatically. If necessary, maximize the application window for Word so that you have more room in which to work.

➤ Pull down the **File menu**, click the **Save As command** to display the Save As dialog box, and enter **Modified Form Letter** as the name of the document. Click **Save**.

➤ You are ready to begin the mail merge process.

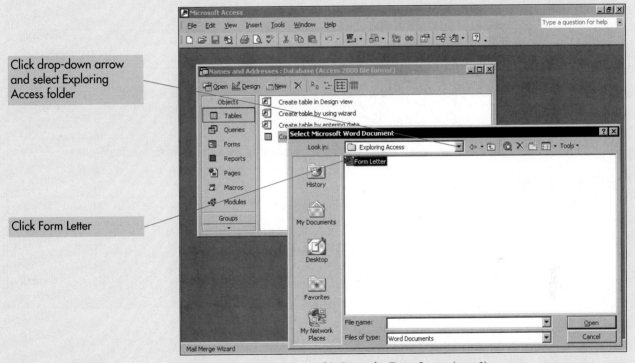

Click drop-down arrow and select Exploring Access folder

Click Form Letter

(b) Open the Form Letter (step 2)

FIGURE C.2 *Hands-on Exercise 1 (continued)*

THE INSERT DATE COMMAND

Pull down the Insert menu and click the Date and Time command to display the associated dialog box, where you choose the desired format for the date and/or time information. You can insert today's date as fixed date (by clearing the box to Update automatically). Alternatively, you can check the box, in which case the current date will appear whenever the document is opened.

Step 3: **Edit the Recipient List**

➤ Click the link to **Edit recipient list** to display the Mail Merge Recipients dialog box, as shown in Figure C.2c. Three names appear, corresponding to the records within the Names and Addresses database that you opened to begin the exercise.

➤ Clear the check box for Elizabeth Scherry. Click **OK**. The form letter will be sent to the two remaining recipients, Jason Frasher and Lauren Howard.

➤ Modify the letterhead to reflect your name and address. Select **"Your Name Goes Here"**, then type a new entry to replace the selected text. Enter your address on the second line.

➤ Save the document. Click the link to **Next: Write your letter** at the bottom of the task pane to continue with the mail merge.

Modify letterhead to reflect your name and address

Click link to Edit Recipient list

Clear check box for Elizabeth Scherry

Click link to Next: Write your letter

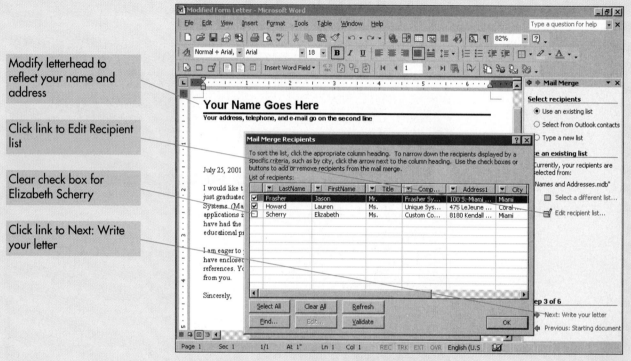

(c) Edit the Recipient List (step 3)

FIGURE C.2 *Hands-on Exercise 1 (continued)*

THE MAIL MERGE WIZARD

The Mail Merge Wizard simplifies the process of creating form letters and other types of merge documents through step-by-step directions that appear automatically in the task pane. The options for the current step appear in the top portion of the task pane and are self-explanatory. Click the link to the next step at the bottom of the pane to move forward in the process, or click the link to the previous step to return to a previous step to correct any mistakes you might have made.

Step 4:   **Insert the Fields**

➤ The task pane indicates that you are in step 4 of the merge process. Click immediately after the date. Press the **enter key** twice to insert a blank line. Click the link to the **Address block** in the task pane to display the dialog box in Figure C.2d.

➤ Verify that the three check boxes have been selected as shown in Figure C.2d. Click **OK** to insert the AddressBlock field into the document.

➤ Press the **enter key** twice to leave a blank line after the address block. Click the link to the **Greeting line** to display the Greeting Line dialog box. Choose the type of greeting you want.

➤ Change the comma that appears after the greeting to a colon since this is a business letter. Click **OK**. The GreetingLine field is inserted into the document and enclosed in angled brackets.

➤ Save the document. Click **Next: Preview your letters** to continue.

Click link to Address block

Check boxes should be checked

Click after date and press enter key twice

Task pane indicates step 4

Click Next: Preview your letters

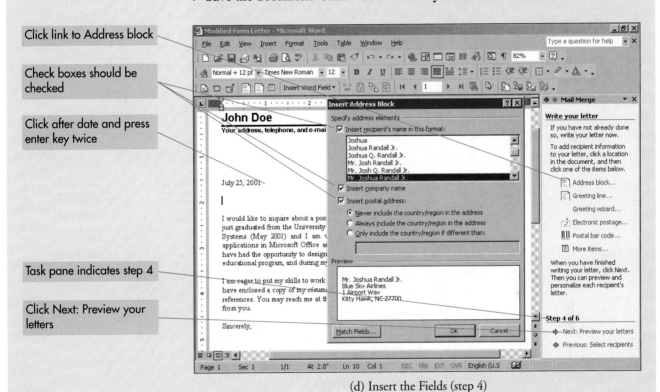

(d) Insert the Fields (step 4)

FIGURE C.2 *Hands-on Exercise 1 (continued)*

BLOCKS VERSUS INDIVIDUAL FIELDS

The Mail Merge Wizard simplifies the process of entering field names into a form letter by supplying two predefined entries, AddressBlock and GreetingLine, which contain multiple fields that are typical of the ways in which an address and salutation appear in a conventional letter. You can still insert individual fields, by clicking in the document where you want the field to go, then clicking the Insert Merge Fields button on the Mail Merge toolbar. The blocks are easier.

Step 5: **Preview the Letters**

➤ You should be in step 5 of the mail merge, where you see the first form letter, as shown in Figure C.2e. (If you see a date code, rather than an actual date, pull down the **Tools menu** and click the **Options command** to display the Options dialog box. Click the **View tab** and clear the check box next to Field Codes.)

➤ View the records individually to be sure that the form letter is correct and that the data has been entered correctly. Use the link to the previous step(s) at the bottom of the task pane to make corrections if necessary.

➤ Save the letter. Click the link to **Next: Complete the merge** to continue.

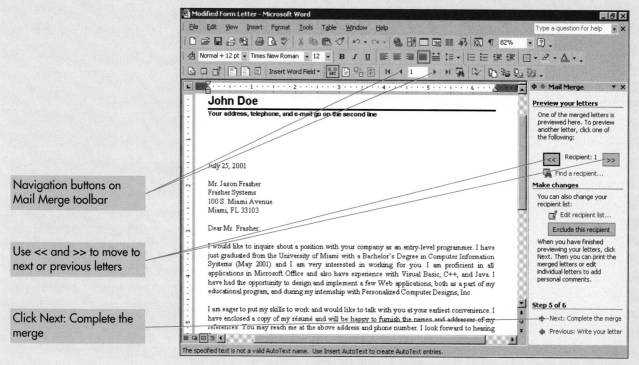

Navigation buttons on Mail Merge toolbar

Use << and >> to move to next or previous letters

Click Next: Complete the merge

(e) Preview the Letters (step 5)

FIGURE C.2 *Hands-on Exercise 1 (continued)*

THE MAIL MERGE TOOLBAR

The Mail Merge toolbar appears throughout the mail merge process and contains various buttons that apply to different steps within the process. Click the <<abc>> button to display field values rather than field codes. Click the button a second time, and you switch back to field codes from field values. Click the <<abc>> button to display the field values, then use the navigation buttons to view the different letters. Click the ▶ button, for example, and you move to the next letter. Click the ▶| button to display the form letter for the last record.

Step 6: **Edit and Print the Individual Letters**

➤ You should be in step 6 of the mail merge. Click the link to **Edit individual letters** in the task pane, which displays the Merge to New Document dialog box. The All option is selected. Click **OK** to create a third document (Letters1), consisting of the individual form letters as shown in Figure C.2f.

➤ Click the **Next (Previous) Page button** to move forward (backward) within the set of individual letters. (You have the option to personalize any of the individual letters.)

➤ Pull down the **File menu** and click the **Print command** to display the Print dialog box. Check the option to all of the letters. Click **OK**.

➤ Close the Letters1 document. Click **No** if prompted to save changes to this document because you can always re-create the individual letters from the form letter and Access database.

➤ Close the Modified Form Letter document. Click **Yes** when asked to save changes to this document.

➤ Exit Word. Exit Access.

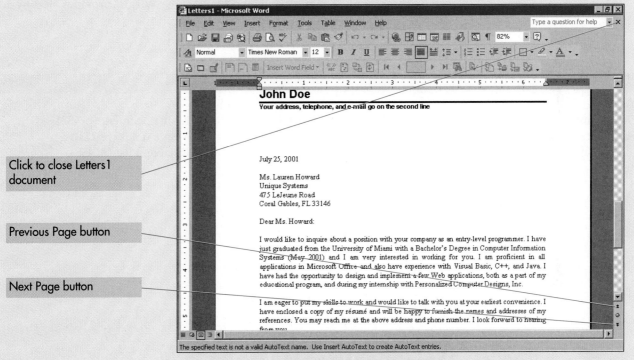

(f) Edit and Print the Individual Letters (step 6)

FIGURE C.2 *Hands-on Exercise 1 (continued)*

THREE DIFFERENT FILES

A mail merge works with a minimum of two files. The main document and data source are input to the mail merge, which creates a set of merged letters as output. The latter can be saved as a separate file, but typically that is not done. You can use the same data source (e.g., a set of names and addresses) with different main documents (a form letter and an envelope) and/or use the same main document with multiple data sources. You typically save, but do not print, the main document(s) and the data source(s). As indicated earlier, you print the set of merged letters, but typically do not save them.

One of the greatest benefits of the Microsoft Office suite is the ability to combine data from one application with that from another. A mail merge is an excellent example, as it combines data from an Access table or query with a Word document. The mail merge creates the same letter many times, changing only the variable data, such as the addressee's name and address, from letter to letter. The merge fields within the main document indicate where the variable information is to be inserted in the individual letters. The same data source can be used with different documents (e.g., to create form letters, envelopes, and/or mailing labels) for a single set of names and addresses. Conversely the same document (such as a form letter) can be used with different data sources as additional data is obtained.

A mail merge can be started from either Microsoft Word or Microsoft Access, but either way, two input files are required—the form letter and the data source. The order in which the files are created is not important. The main document and data source are saved but typically not printed. The merged file (e.g., the set of form letters) is usually printed, but not saved because you can always recreate the form letters by rerunning the mail merge. The Mail Merge Wizard provides step-by-step instructions.

KEY TERMS

Data source (p. 433)

Form letter (p. 433)

Insert Date command (p. 437)

Mail Merge toolbar (p. 440)

Mail Merge Wizard (p. 438)

Mail Merge (p. 433)

Main document (p. 433)

Merge fields (p. 433)

Recipient list (p. 438)

A Project for the Semester: Applying What You Have Learned

OVERVIEW

This appendix describes the student project we require in our course in Microsoft Access at the University of Miami. It is intended for both student and instructor, as it describes the various milestones in the administration of a class project. Our experience has been uniformly positive. Students work hard, but they are proud of the end result, and we are continually impressed at the diversity and quality of student projects. The project is what students remember most about our course, and it truly enhances the learning experience.

We begin our course with an overview of Access as it is presented in Chapter 1. We focus on the Bookstore and Employee databases, each of which contains a single table. We also touch on the concept of a relational database through the "Look Ahead" database at the end of the chapter. The initial emphasis in the course, however, is on databases with a single table, since students must develop proficiency with basic skills. This is accomplished through detailed coverage of Chapters 2 and 3, where students learn how to create tables, forms, queries, and reports.

We then move into a discussion of relational databases and database design. Students want to be proficient in Access, but it is equally important that they are comfortable with database design. Thus we present several different examples, starting in Chapter 4, followed by Appendix B, then reinforced through the opening sections in Chapters 5 and 6, and the associated case studies at the end of these chapters. It is at this point that we introduce the class project, which becomes the focal point of our course for the rest of the semester.

The Groups

The class is divided into groups of three or four students each, and students work together to submit a collective project. It is critical that the groups are balanced with respect to student abilities, and hence our groups are always formed after the first exam, when we have additional information with which to create the groups. We distribute a questionnaire in which we ask students whom they want to work with (and conversely, if there is anyone they would be uncomfortable working with). We try to honor the former requests, but will always honor the latter, so that the groups work as smoothly as possible.

Once the groups have been formed, we establish a series of milestones that are described in the remainder of the appendix. There is absolutely no requirement for you or your class to follow our milestones exactly. We have found, however, that providing detailed feedback through a series of continual assignments is the most effective way to move each group toward its final goal.

One other suggestion is to have the groups engage in a continuing presentation to the class as a whole. We allocate the beginning of each class period to group presentations of 10 to 15 minutes each on the current class assignment. The group presentations accomplish two goals—they enable students to learn from each other, and they provide valuable practice in presenting one's work to an audience.

Phase I—Preliminary Design

Describe, in a one- or two-page narrative, the relational database that your group will design and implement. You can select any of the case studies at the end of the chapters on one-to-many or many-to-many relationships, or alternatively you can choose an entirely different system. Regardless of which system you choose, the preliminary design is one of the most important aspects of the entire project since it is the foundation for the project. A good design will enable you to implement the project successfully, and hence you should give considerable thought to the document you prepare. Your project need not be unduly complex, but it must include at least three tables. The relationships between the tables can be one-to-many or many-to-many. The information can be contained in a written document to your instructor and/or a PowerPoint presentation for the class. Either way, it must do all of the following:

1. Describe the physical system for which you will create the database.
2. Develop a "wish list" describing in general terms the information the system is to produce.
3. Design a database capable of producing the required information. List the tables in the database, the fields in each table, and the relationships between the tables.
4. Describe in general terms how the database will be able to produce at least three of the reports on the wish list by describing the underlying queries, each of which references fields from multiple tables in the database.

Phase II—Detailed Design

Implement the refinements (if any) to the preliminary design from phase I, then expand that design to include all of the necessary fields in each table. You are also asked to develop the properties for each field at this time. Be sure to include adequate data validation and to use input masks as appropriate. One additional requirement is that the primary key of at least one table is an AutoNumber field.

After you have completed the design, create an Access database containing the necessary tables, with the All fields in each table, but no other objects. You do not have to enter any data at this time, but you are required to document your work. Use the Print Relationships command in the File menu to create a one-page document that gives you a visual overview of your database. Submit this document to your instructor.

You are also asked to provide detailed documentation for each table. Pull down the Tools menu, click Analyze, click Documentor. Select Tables in the Object Type drop-down list box, then select all of the tables. Click the Options button, then include for each table the Properties and Relationships but not the Permissions by User and Group. Include for each field Names, Data types, Sizes, and Properties. Do not include any information on indexes. Print the information for each table in the database and submit it to your instructor for review.

Phase III—The User Interface

Phase III focuses on the design of the switchboard and associated templates that will be replicated throughout the system. The switchboard, or user interface, is critical to the success of any system as a user spends his or her day in front of the screen. It should be functional and visually compelling. We have found that the best way to arrive at an attractive design is for each member to submit a design independently.

Thus, each member of the group creates a simple Help form for the group project, which is similar to the form that has appeared in the end-of-chapter exercises throughout the text. The form should include the names of all group members, a logo (clip art or other object), and an appropriate color scheme. All of the forms for each group are then imported into a single database (use the Get External Data command) that will be shown in class. The best design for each group can be picked by consensus, at which point the design is frozen, and development begins with the initial switchboard.

The switchboard should contain a logo for the project and establish a color scheme. The initial version need contain only two buttons—one to display the "Help About" form and one button to exit from the application. Use clip art as appropriate, but clip art for the sake of clip art is often juvenile. You may want to use different fonts and/or simple graphics (e.g., horizontal or vertical lines are often quite effective). A simple design is generally the best design.

Each group then creates a form template and a report template based on the design of the Help form and switchboard. The templates are created in Design view, without benefit of a Wizard, and neither object is based on a table or query. All subsequent forms and reports, however, are based on the templates, at which point the data source is specified. The result is a uniform look throughout the system that adds to its visual appeal. The switchboard is then expanded to include five items—the help form and exit buttons as before, new buttons to show the form and report templates, and a fifth button to print the relationships diagram from phase II. This switchboard is an essential milestone for the project because it contains the physical design (the relationships between the tables) as well as the visual design.

Phase IV—Create the Forms and Enter Test Data

Phase IV has you create the forms in which to enter test data, based on the template of Phase III. You need a form (or subform) for every table that will enable you to add, edit, and delete records in that table. You are also required to have at least one subform, and you must structure your forms to facilitate data entry in a logical way. All forms should have a consistent look (via a common template).

The forms should be user-friendly and display command buttons so that there is no requirement on the part of the end user to know Access. Each form is to include buttons to add, delete, find and print a record, and to close the form. A Help button is a nice touch. Include drop-down list boxes to facilitate data entry in at least two places. The forms should be designed so that they fit on one screen and do not require the user to scroll to access all of the fields and/or the command buttons. Decide on a common resolution, either 640×480 or 800×600, and follow that throughout.

Use the forms after they have been created to enter test data for each table. (Each table should contain 10 to 15 records.) Be sure that the data will adequately test all of the queries and reports that will be in your final system. Submit a printout of the data in each table to your instructor. (You can print the Datasheet view of each table.) In addition, submit a printed copy of each form to your instructor.

Phase V—Prototyping

Phase V has you develop a "complete" system using a switchboard and prototyping as described in Chapter 7. The main menu should be displayed automatically (via an AutoExec macro) when the database is opened, and the user should be able to step through the entire system. The final reports and queries need not be implemented at this time (a "not yet implemented" message is fine at this stage). The user should, however, be able to go from one form to the next without leaving Access or encountering an error message.

Phase VI—The Finishing Touches

The system should be "up and running" as you continue to build the various objects during the testing phase. (The reports should be based on the report template to promote a uniform look.) It is at this point that you can add the finishing touches through VBA as described in Chapter 8, if in fact you are able to cover that material during the semester. Another finishing touch to consider is the creation of a Web page for the group. The page can be simple and contain descriptive information about the project and the members in the group. Load the page onto your school server, then include a hyperlink on the main switchboard to display the page.

Phase VII—The Completed System

Submit the completed Access database that should contain all of the reports and/or queries needed to satisfy the initial wish list. To obtain a grade of A, you will need to satisfy the following requirements (many of which have been completed) in the earlier phases:

1. An approved design of sufficient complexity similar to the completed soccer database in Chapter 7.
2. Separation of the objects and tables into separate databases that are subsequently linked to one another.
3. Use of the Data Validation and Input Mask properties to validate and facilitate data entry. In addition, at least one table is to contain an AutoNumber field as its primary key.
4. Existing data in all tables with 10 to 15 records in each table.
5. An AutoExec macro to load the main menu and maximize the document window.
6. A Help button on one or more screens that displays the name of the group and an appropriate help message (e.g., a phone number). An "About" button on the opening switchboard that opens a form with introductory information about the project.

7. A working form (or subform) for each table in the database so that you can maintain each table. You must have at least one subform in your system. The forms should have a consistent look (via a common template). The system and especially the forms are to make sense; that is, just because you have all of the forms does not mean you satisfy the requirements of the project. Your forms should be designed to facilitate data entry in a logical way.

8. The forms should be user-friendly and display command buttons so that there is no requirement on the part of the end user to know Access. Each form is to include buttons to add, delete, find and print a record, and to close the form. Include drop-down list boxes to facilitate data entry in at least two places.

9. All forms should be designed for a common resolution, either 800×600 or 1024×768. The screens should be sufficiently compact so that no scrolling is required.

10. Three working reports, at least one of which is a group/total report.

11. Inclusion of a parameter query to drive a form or report.

12. At least one unmatched query. A top-value query is a nice touch, but depends on the system.

13. Various VBA modules on one or more forms that parallel the examples from Chapter 8. We suggest a combo box to locate a specific record, shortcuts for data entry (with a command button to display the shortcuts), and an error-trapping procedure for a duplicate record. Additional procedures can include a prompt to the user if a recommended field is omitted and a modified Add Record procedure to position the insertion point in the first control within the form.

14. The completed system should be as visually compelling as possible. Clip art for the sake of clip art tends to be juvenile without effect. In general, a consistent logo (one image) is much better from slide to slide than multiple images. No clip art is better than poor clip art or too much clip art.

15. You will be judged on whether your system actually works; that is, the instructor will enter and/or modify data at random. The effects of the new data should be manifest in the various reports and queries. In addition, the system cannot break; that is, the user must be able to go from one menu (form) to the next without difficulty.

The Written Document

In addition to demonstrating a working system, you are to submit a written document as described below. The submission of the written project will be an impressive (lengthy) document but easily generated, as much of the material is created directly from Access. The objective is for you to have a project of which you will be proud and something that you can demonstrate in the future. Include the following:

1. Title page plus table (list) of the contents; pages need not be numbered, but please include "loose-leaf" dividers for each section.

2. A one- or two-page description of the system taken from the earlier presentation to the class.

3. Technical documentation that includes the relationships diagram and table properties, as prepared in the detailed design phase.

4. Hard copy of each form (one per page).

5. Hard copy of each report (one per page).

6. A working disk.

Peer Evaluations

Sealed peer evaluations are to be submitted with each phase. Each member in the group is to evaluate every member in the group, including themselves, by awarding a total of 19 points; (e.g., 5, 5, 5, and 4 in a group with four people). The rationale for requesting evaluations at every milestone is to prevent problems before they occur. In assigning a final grade, I am not looking for small differences, but rather instances where one member is simply not doing his or her share. Should this occur, the instructor will meet privately with the group to correct the problem.

A Final Word

Throughout the project, you will be working with different versions of your database on different machines. You will also need to share your work with other members of your group. And, of course, you need to back up your work. The floppy disk is the medium of choice, but its capacity is only 1.4MB and an Access database can quickly exceed that. It becomes critical, therefore, that you understand the various ways of reducing the storage requirements.

In particular, you should learn how to *compact* an Access database, after which you can take advantage of a *file compression program* to reduce the size even further. You might also explore the use of *FTP* as an alternate means of transferring a file. You should also learn how to separate the data from the other objects in a database to further reduce storage requirements. And finally, you should realize that clip art and other bit map images are one of the primary reasons for a large database. Ask yourself whether you really need it.

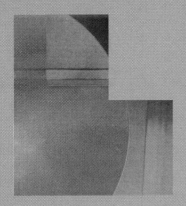

A VBA Primer: Extending Microsoft® Office XP

OBJECTIVES

AFTER READING THIS SUPPLEMENT YOU WILL BE ABLE TO:

1. Describe the relationship of VBA to Microsoft Office XP; explain how to open the VBA editor within an Office application.
2. Distinguish between key words, statements, procedures, and modules; use the Office Assistant to obtain detailed information about any VBA statement.
3. Explain how to create, edit, and run a VBA procedure; explain how the Quick Info and Complete Word tools facilitate VBA coding.
4. Explain how to continue a VBA statement from one line to the next; add and remove comments from a procedure.
5. Distinguish between the MsgBox and InputBox statements; describe at least two arguments for each statement.
6. Explain how to debug a procedure by stepping through its statements; describe the role of the Local and Immediate windows in debugging.
7. Use the If . . . Then . . . Else statement to implement a decision; explain the advantage of the Case statement over multiple ElseIf clauses.
8. Create a custom toolbar with buttons corresponding to the VBA procedures you have developed.
9. Describe several statements used to implement a loop; explain the difference between placing a condition at the beginning or end of a loop.
10. Distinguish between event-driven and traditional programming; create event procedures associated with opening and closing an Excel workbook and with an Access database.

OVERVIEW

Visual Basic for Applications (VBA) is a powerful programming language that is accessible from all major applications in Microsoft Office XP. You do not have to

1

know VBA in order to use Office effectively, but even a basic understanding will help you to create more powerful documents. Indeed, you may already have been exposed to VBA through the creation of simple macros in Word or Excel. A **macro** is a set of instructions (i.e., a program) that simplifies the execution of repetitive tasks. It is created through the **macro recorder** that captures commands as they are executed, then converts those commands to a VBA program. (The macro recorder is present in Word, Excel, and PowerPoint, but not in Access.) You can create and execute macros without ever looking at the underlying VBA, but you gain an appreciation for the language when you do.

The macro recorder is limited, however, in that it captures only commands, mouse clicks, and/or keystrokes. As you will see, VBA is much more than just recorded keystrokes. It is a language unto itself, and thus, it contains all of the statements you would expect to find in any programming language. This lets you enhance the functionality of any macro by adding extra statements as necessary—for example, an InputBox function to accept data from the user, followed by an If . . . Then . . . Else statement to take different actions based on the information supplied by the user.

This supplement presents the rudiments of VBA and is suitable for use with any Office application. We begin by describing the VBA Editor and how to create, edit, and run simple procedures. The examples are completely general and demonstrate the basic capabilities of VBA that are found in any programming language. We illustrate the MsgBox statement to display output to the user and the InputBox function to accept input from the user. We describe the For . . . Next statement to implement a loop and the If . . . Then . . . Else and Case statements for decision making. We also describe several debugging techniques to help you correct the errors that invariably occur. The last two exercises introduce the concept of event-driven programming, in which a procedure is executed in response to an action taken by the user. The material here is application-specific in conjunction with Excel and Access, but it can be easily extended to Word or PowerPoint.

One last point before we begin is that this supplement assumes no previous knowledge on the part of the reader. It is suitable for someone who has never been exposed to a programming language or written an Office macro. If, on the other hand, you have a background in programming or macros, you will readily appreciate the power inherent in VBA. VBA is an incredibly rich language that can be daunting to the novice. Stick with us, however, and we will show you that it is a flexible and powerful tool with consistent rules that can be easily understood and applied. You will be pleased at what you will be able to accomplish.

INTRODUCTION TO VBA

VBA is a programming language, and like any other programming language its programs (or procedures, as they are called) are made up of individual statements. Each **statement** accomplishes a specific task such as displaying a message to the user or accepting input from the user. Statements are grouped into **procedures**, and procedures, in turn, are grouped into **modules**. Every VBA procedure is classified as either public or private. A **private procedure** is accessible only from within the module in which it is contained. A **public procedure**, on the other hand, can be accessed from any module.

The statement, however, is the basic unit of the language. Our approach throughout this supplement will be to present individual statements, then to develop simple procedures using those statements in a hands-on exercise. As you read the discussion, you will see that every statement has a precise **syntax** that describes how the statement is to be used. The syntax also determines the **arguments** (or parameters) associated with that statement, and whether those arguments are required or optional.

The ***MsgBox statement*** displays information to the user. It is one of the most basic statements in VBA, but we use it to illustrate several concepts in VBA programming. Figure 1a contains a simple procedure called MsgBoxExamples, consisting of four individual MsgBox statements. All procedures begin with a ***procedure header*** and end with the ***End Sub statement***.

The MsgBox statement has one required argument, which is the message (or prompt) that is displayed to the user. All other arguments are optional, but if they are used, they must be entered in a specified sequence. The simplest form of the MsgBox statement is shown in example 1, which specifies a single argument that contains the text (or prompt) to be displayed. The resulting message box is shown in Figure 1b. The message is displayed to the user, who responds accordingly, in this case by clicking the OK button.

Example 2 extends the MsgBox statement to include a second parameter that displays an icon within the resulting dialog box as shown in Figure 1c. The type of icon is determined by a VBA ***intrinsic*** (or predefined) ***constant*** such as vbExclamation, which displays an exclamation point in a yellow triangle. VBA has many such constants that enable you to simplify your code, while at the same time achieving some impressive results.

Example 3 uses a different intrinsic constant, vbInformation, to display a different icon. It also extends the MsgBox statement to include a third parameter that is displayed on the title bar of the resulting dialog box. Look closely, for example, at Figures 1c and 1d, whose title bars contain "Microsoft Excel" and "Grauer/Barber", respectively. The first is the default entry (given that we are executing the procedure from within Microsoft Excel). You can, however, give your procedures a customized look by displaying your own text in the title bar.

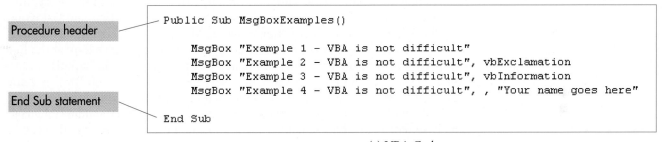

```
Public Sub MsgBoxExamples()

    MsgBox "Example 1 - VBA is not difficult"
    MsgBox "Example 2 - VBA is not difficult", vbExclamation
    MsgBox "Example 3 - VBA is not difficult", vbInformation
    MsgBox "Example 4 - VBA is not difficult", , "Your name goes here"

End Sub
```

Procedure header

End Sub statement

(a) VBA Code

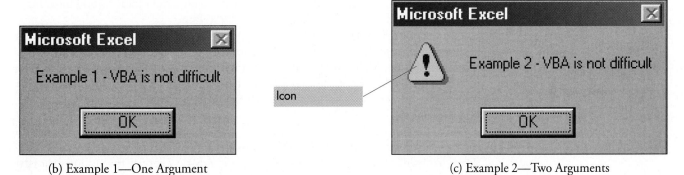

Icon

(b) Example 1—One Argument

(c) Example 2—Two Arguments

FIGURE 1 *The MsgBox Statement*

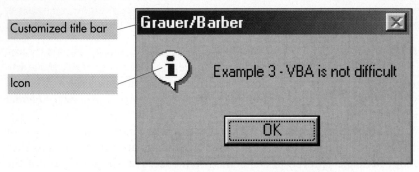

Customized title bar

Icon

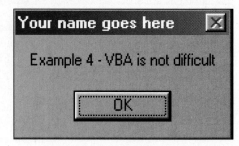

(d) Example 3—Three Arguments   (e) Example 4—Omitted Parameter

FIGURE 1   *The MsgBox Statement (continued)*

Example 4 omits the second parameter (the icon), but includes the third parameter (the entry for the title bar). The parameters are positional, however, and thus the MsgBox statement contains two commas after the message to indicate that the second parameter has been omitted.

THE INPUTBOX FUNCTION

The MsgBox statement displays a prompt to the user, but what if you want the user to respond to the prompt by entering a value such as his or her name? This is accomplished using the ***InputBox function***. Note the subtle change in terminology in that we refer to the InputBox *function*, but the MsgBox *statement*. That is because a function returns a value, in this case the user's name, which is subsequently used in the procedure. In other words, the InputBox function asks the user for information, then it stores that information (the value returned by the user) for use in the procedure.

Figure 2 displays a procedure that prompts the user for a first and last name, after which it displays the information using the MsgBox statement. (The Dim statement at the beginning of the procedure is explained shortly.) Let's look at the first InputBox function, and the associated dialog box in Figure 2b. The InputBox function displays a prompt on the screen, the user enters a value ("Bob" in this example), and that value is stored in the variable that appears to the left of the equal sign (strFirstName). The concept of a variable is critical to every programming language. Simply stated, a ***variable*** is a named storage location that contains data that can be modified during program execution.

The MsgBox statement then uses the value of strFirstName to greet the user by name as shown in Figure 2c. This statement also introduces the ampersand to ***concatenate*** (join together) two different character strings, the literal "Good morning", followed by the value within the variable strFirstName.

The second InputBox function prompts the user for his or her last name. In addition, it uses a second argument to customize the contents of the title bar (VBA Primer in this example) as can be seen in Figure 2d. Finally, the MsgBox statement in Figure 2e displays both the first and last name through concatenation of multiple strings. This statement also uses the ***underscore*** to continue a statement from one line to the next.

VBA is not difficult, and you can use the MsgBox statement and InputBox function in conjunction with one another as the basis for several meaningful procedures. You will get a chance to practice in the hands-on exercise that follows shortly.

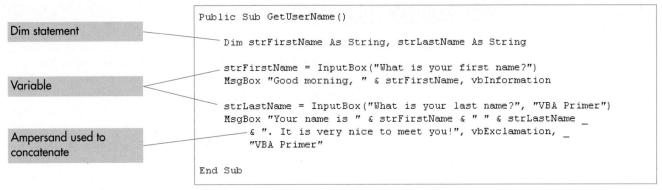

Dim statement

Variable

Ampersand used to concatenate

```
Public Sub GetUserName()

    Dim strFirstName As String, strLastName As String

    strFirstName = InputBox("What is your first name?")
    MsgBox "Good morning, " & strFirstName, vbInformation

    strLastName = InputBox("What is your last name?", "VBA Primer")
    MsgBox "Your name is " & strFirstName & " " & strLastName _
        & ". It is very nice to meet you!", vbExclamation, _
        "VBA Primer"

End Sub
```

(a) VBA Code

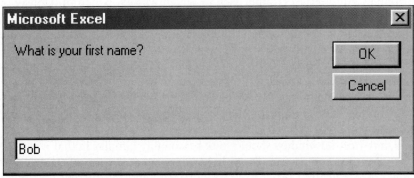

(b) InputBox

(c) Concatenation

(d) InputBox includes Argument for Title Bar

(e) Concatenation and Continuation

FIGURE 2   *The InputBox Statement*

Declaring Variables

Every variable must be declared (defined) before it can be used. This is accomplished through the ***Dim*** (short for Dimension) ***statement*** that appears at the beginning of a procedure. The Dim statement indicates the name of the variable and its type (for example, whether it will hold characters or numbers), which in turn reserves the appropriate amount of memory for that variable.

A variable name must begin with a letter and cannot exceed 255 characters. It can contain letters, numbers, and various special characters such as an underscore, but it cannot contain a space or the special symbols !, @, &, $, or #. Variable names typically begin with a prefix to indicate the type of data that is stored within the variable such as "str" for a character string or "int" for integers. The use of a prefix is optional with respect to the rules of VBA, but it is followed almost universally.

All VBA procedures are created using the **Visual Basic Editor** as shown in Figure 3. You may already be familiar with the editor, perhaps in conjunction with creating and/or editing macros in Word or Excel, or event procedures in Microsoft Access. Let's take a moment, however, to review its essential components.

The left side of the editor displays the **Project Explorer**, which is similar in concept and appearance to the Windows Explorer, except that it displays the objects associated with the open document. If, for example, you are working in Excel, you will see the various sheets in a workbook, whereas in an Access database you will see forms and reports.

The VBA statements for the selected module (Module1 in Figure 3) appear in the code window in the right pane. The module, in turn, contains declarations and procedures that are separated by horizontal lines. There are two procedures, MsgBoxExamples and GetUserName, each of which was explained previously. A **comment** (nonexecutable) statement has been added to each procedure and appears in green. It is the apostrophe at the beginning of the line, rather than the color, that denotes a comment.

The **Declarations section** appears at the beginning of the module and contains a single statement, **Option Explicit**. This option requires every variable in a procedure to be explicitly defined (e.g., in a Dim statement) before it can be used elsewhere in the module. It is an important option and should appear in every module you write (see exercise 5 at the end of the chapter).

The remainder of the window should look reasonably familiar in that it is similar to any other Office application. The title bar appears at the top of the window and identifies the application (Microsoft Visual Basic) and the current document (VBA Examples.xls). The right side of the title bar contains the Minimize, Restore, and Close buttons. A menu bar appears under the title bar. Toolbars are displayed under the menu bar. Commands are executed by pulling down the appropriate menu, via buttons on the toolbar, or by keyboard shortcuts.

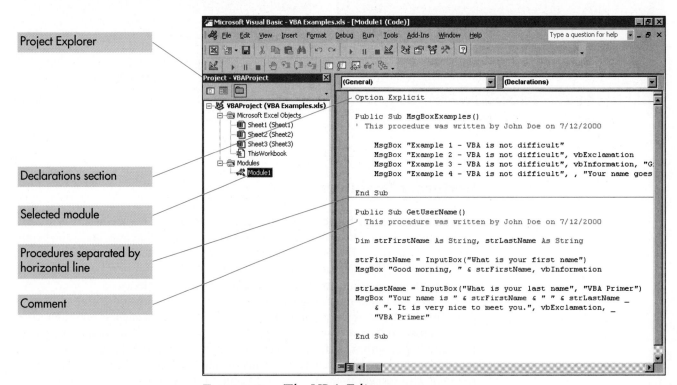

FIGURE 3 *The VBA Editor*

INTRODUCTION TO VBA

Objective   To create and test VBA procedures using the MsgBox and InputBox statements. Use Figure 4 as a guide in the exercise. You can do the exercise in any Office application.

Step 1a: **Start Microsoft Excel**

➤ We suggest you do the exercise in either Excel or Access (although you could use Word or PowerPoint just as easily). Go to step 1b for Access.

➤ Start **Microsoft Excel** and open a new workbook. Pull down the **File menu** and click the **Save command** (or click the **Save button** on the Standard toolbar) to display the Save As dialog box. Choose an appropriate drive and folder, then save the workbook as **VBA Examples**.

➤ Pull down the **Tools menu**, click the **Macro command**, then click the **Visual Basic Editor command** as shown in Figure 4a. Go to step 2.

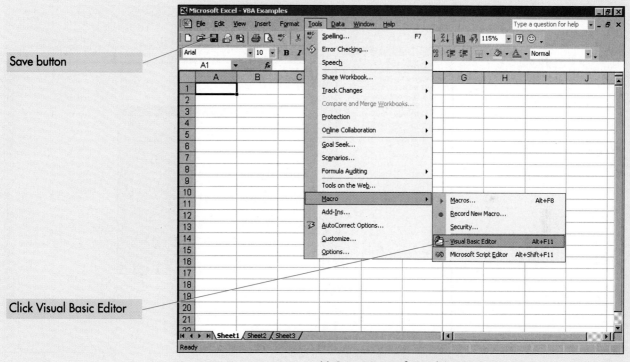

(a) Start Microsoft Excel (step 1a)

FIGURE 4   *Hands-on Exercise 1*

Step 1b: **Start Microsoft Access**

➤ Start **Microsoft Access** and choose the option to create a **Blank Access database**. Save the database as **VBA Examples**.

➤ Pull down the **Tools menu**, click the **Macro command**, then click the **Visual Basic Editor command**. (You can also use the **Alt+F11** keyboard shortcut to open the VBA editor without going through the Tools menu.)

Step 2:   **Insert a Module**

➤ You should see a window similar to Figure 4b, but Module1 is not yet visible. Close the Properties window if it appears.

➤ If necessary, pull down the **View menu** and click **Project Explorer** to display the Project Explorer pane at the left of the window. Our figure shows Excel objects, but you will see the "same" window in Microsoft Access.

➤ Pull down the **Insert menu** and click **Module** to insert Module1 into the current project. The name of the module, Module1 in this example, appears in the Project Explorer pane.

➤ The Option Explicit statement may be entered automatically, but if not, click in the code window and type the statement **Option Explicit**.

➤ Pull down the **Insert menu** a second time, but this time select **Procedure** to display the Add Procedure dialog box in Figure 4b. Click in the **Name** text box and enter **MsgBoxExamples** as the name of the procedure. (Spaces are not allowed in a procedure name.)

➤ Click the option buttons for a **Sub procedure** and for **Public scope**. Click **OK**. The sub procedure should appear within the module and consist of the Sub and End Sub statements.

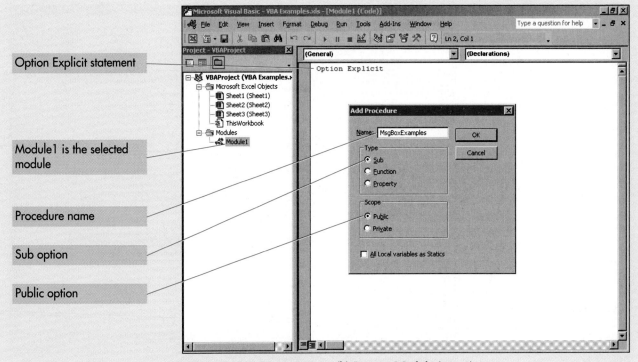

(b) Insert a Module (step 2)

FIGURE 4   *Hands-on Exercise 1 (continued)*

OPTION EXPLICIT

We say more about this important statement later on, but for now be sure that it appears in every module. See exercise 5 at the end of the chapter.

Step 3:   **The MsgBox Statement**

> ➤ The insertion point (the flashing cursor) appears below the first statement. Press the **Tab key** to indent, type the key word **MsgBox**, then press the **space bar**. VBA responds with Quick Info that displays the syntax of the statement as shown in Figure 4c.
> ➤ Type a **quotation mark** to begin the literal, enter the text of your message, **This is my first VBA procedure**, then type the closing **quotation mark**.
> ➤ Click the **Run Sub button** on the Standard toolbar (or pull down the **Run menu** and click the **Run Sub command**) to execute the procedure. You should see a dialog box, containing the text you entered, within the Excel workbook (or other Office document) on which you are working.
> ➤ After you have read the message, click **OK** to return to the VBA Editor.

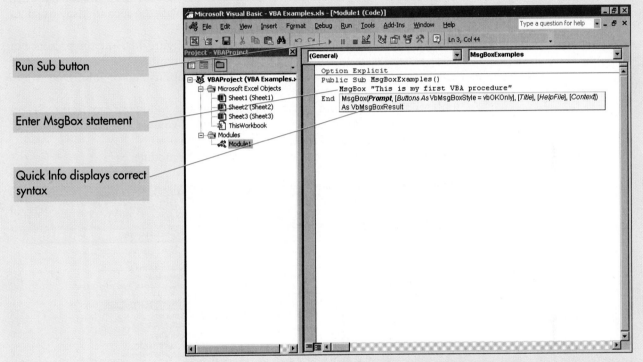

Run Sub button

Enter MsgBox statement

Quick Info displays correct syntax

(c) The MsgBox Statement (step 3)

FIGURE 4   *Hands-on Exercise 1 (continued)*

QUICK INFO—HELP WITH VBA SYNTAX

Press the space bar after entering the name of a statement (e.g., MsgBox), and VBA responds with a Quick Info box that displays the syntax of the statement. You see the arguments in the statement and the order in which those arguments appear. Any argument in brackets is optional. If you do not see this information, pull down the Tools menu, click the Options command, then click the Editor tab. Check the box for Auto Quick Info and click OK.

Step 4:   **Complete the Procedure**

➤ You should be back within the MsgBoxExamples procedure. If necessary, click at the end of the MsgBox statement, then press **enter** to begin a new line. Type **MsgBox** and press the **space bar** to begin entering the statement.

➤ The syntax of the MsgBox statement will appear on the screen. Type a **quotation mark** to begin the message, type **Add an icon** as the text of this message, then type the closing **quotation mark**. Type a **comma**, then press the **space bar** to enter the next parameter.

➤ VBA automatically displays a list of appropriate parameters, in this case a series of intrinsic constants that define the icon or command button that is to appear in the statement.

➤ You can type the first several letters (e.g., **vbi**, for vbInformation), then press the **space bar**, or you can use the **down arrow** to select **vbInformation** and then press the **space bar**. Either way you should complete the second MsgBox statement as shown in Figure 4d. Press **enter**.

➤ Enter the third MsgBox statement as shown in Figure 4d. Note the presence of the two consecutive commas to indicate that we omitted the second parameter within the MsgBox statement. Enter your name instead of John Doe where appropriate. Press **enter**.

➤ Enter the fourth (and last) MsgBox statement following our figure. Select **vbExclamation** as the second parameter, type a **comma**, then enter the text of the title bar, as you did for the previous statement.

➤ Click the **Save button** to save the changes to the module.

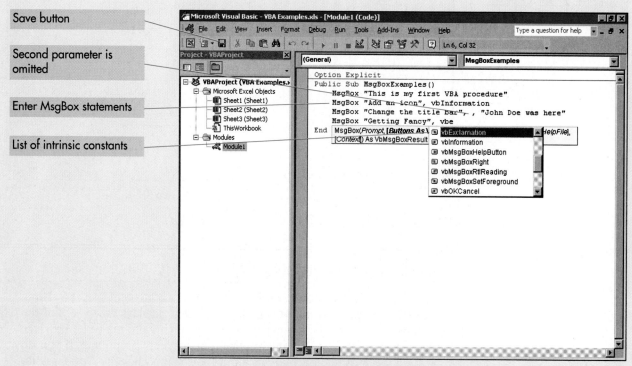

Save button

Second parameter is omitted

Enter MsgBox statements

List of intrinsic constants

(d) Complete the Procedure (step 4)

FIGURE 4   *Hands-on Exercise 1 (continued)*

Step 5: **Test the Procedure**

➤ It's convenient if you can see the statements in the VBA procedure at the same time you see the output of those statements. Thus we suggest that you tile the VBA Editor and the associated Office application.

• Minimize all applications except the VBA Editor and the Office application (e.g., Excel).

• Right click the taskbar and click **Tile Windows Horizontally** to tile the windows as shown in Figure 4e. (It does not matter which window is on top. (If you see more than these two windows, minimize the other open window, then right click the taskbar and retile the windows.)

• Click anywhere in the VBA procedure, then click the **Run Sub button** on the Standard toolbar.

• The four messages will be displayed one after the other. Click **OK** after each message.

➤ Maximize the VBA window to continue working.

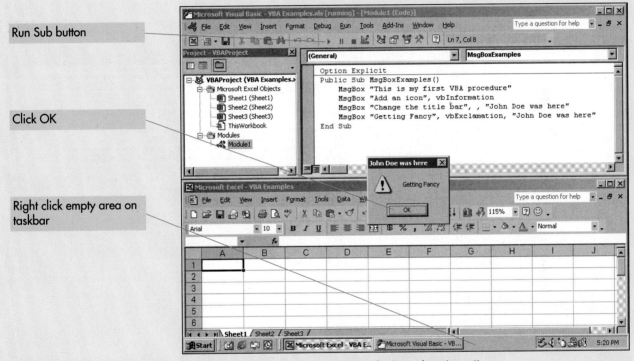

(e) Test the Procedure (step 5)

FIGURE 4 *Hands-on Exercise 1 (continued)*

HIDE THE WINDOWS TASKBAR

You can hide the Windows taskbar to gain additional space on the desktop. Right click any empty area of the taskbar to display a context-sensitive menu, click Properties to display the Taskbar properties dialog box, and if necessary click the Taskbar Options tab. Check the box to Auto Hide the taskbar, then click OK. The taskbar disappears from the screen but will reappear as you point to the bottom edge of the desktop.

Step 6: **Comments and Corrections**

➤ All VBA procedures should be documented with the author's name, date, and other comments as necessary to explain the procedure. Click after the procedure header. Press the **enter key** to leave a blank line.

➤ Press **enter** a second time. Type an **apostrophe** to begin the comment, then enter a descriptive statement similar to Figure 4f. Press **enter** when you have completed the comment. The line turns green to indicate it is a comment.

➤ The best time to experiment with debugging is when you know your procedure is correct. Go to the last MsgBox statement and delete the quotation mark in front of your name. Move to the end of the line and press **enter**.

➤ You should see the error message in Figure 4f. Unfortunately, the message is not as explicit as it could be; VBA cannot tell that you left out a quotation mark, but it does detect an error in syntax.

➤ Click **OK** in response to the error. Click the **Undo button** twice, to restore the quotation mark, which in turn corrects the statement.

➤ Click the **Save button** to save the changes to the module.

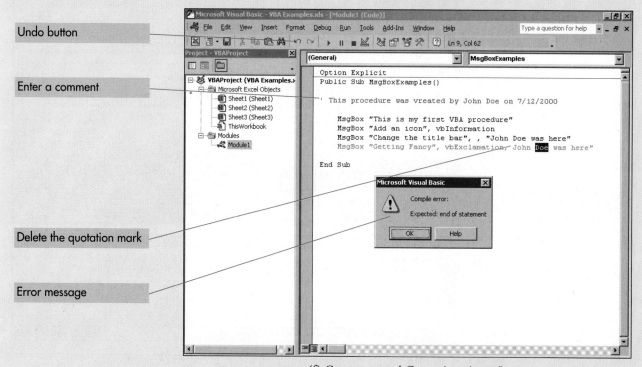

Undo button

Enter a comment

Delete the quotation mark

Error message

(f) Comments and Corrections (step 6)

FIGURE 4 *Hands-on Exercise 1 (continued)*

RED, GREEN, AND BLUE

Visual Basic for Applications uses different colors for different types of statements (or a portion of those statements). Any statement containing a syntax error appears in red. Comments appear in green. Key words, such as Sub and End Sub, appear in blue.

Step 7: **Create a Second Procedure**

➤ Pull down the **Insert menu** and click **Procedure** to display the Add Procedure dialog box. Enter **InputBoxExamples** as the name of the procedure. (Spaces are not allowed in a procedure name.)

➤ Click the option buttons for a **Sub procedure** and for **Public scope**. Click **OK**. The new sub procedure will appear within the existing module below the existing MsgBoxExamples procedure.

➤ Enter the statements in the procedure as they appear in Figure 4g. Be sure to type a space between the ampersand and the underscore in the second MsgBox statement. Click the **Save button** to save the procedure before testing it.

➤ You can display the output of the procedure directly in the VBA window if you minimize the Excel window. Thus, **right click** the Excel button on the taskbar to display a context-sensitive menu, then click the **Minimize command**. There is no visible change on your monitor.

➤ Click the **Run Sub button** to test the procedure. This time you see the Input box displayed on top of the VBA window because the Excel window has been minimized.

➤ Enter your first name in response to the initial prompt, then click **OK**. Click **OK** when you see the message box that says "Hello".

➤ Enter your last name in response to the second prompt and click **OK**. You should see a message box similar to the one in Figure 4g. Click **OK**.

➤ Return to the VBA procedure to correct any mistakes that might occur. Save the module.

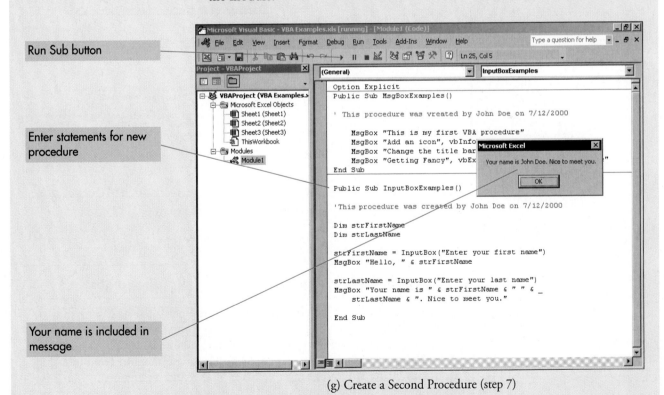

(g) Create a Second Procedure (step 7)

FIGURE 4   *Hands-on Exercise 1 (continued)*

Step 8: Create a Public Constant

➤ Click after the Options Explicit statement and press **enter** to move to a new line. Type the statement to define the constant, **ApplicationTitle**, as shown in Figure 4h, and press **enter**.

➤ Click anywhere in the MsgBoxExamples procedure, then change the third argument in the last MsgBox statement to ApplicationTitle. Make the four modifications in the InputBoxExamples procedure as shown in Figure 4h.

➤ Click anywhere in the InputBoxExamples procedure, then click the **Run Sub button** to test the procedure. The title bar of each dialog box will contain a descriptive title corresponding to the value of the ApplicationTitle constant.

➤ Change the value of the ApplicationTitle constant in the General Declarations section, then rerun the InputBoxExamples procedure. The title of every dialog box changes to reflect the new value. Save the procedure.

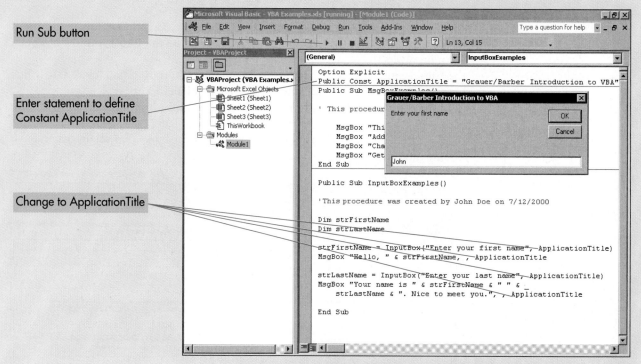

(h) Create a Public Constant (step 8)

FIGURE 4 *Hands-on Exercise 1 (continued)*

CONTINUING A VBA STATEMENT—THE & AND THE UNDERSCORE

A VBA statement can be continued from one line to the next by typing a space at the end of the line to be continued, typing the underscore character, then continuing on the next line. You may not, however, break a line in the middle of a literal (character string). Thus, you need to complete the character string with a closing quotation mark, add an ampersand (as the concatenation operator to display this string with the character string on the next line), then leave a space followed by the underscore to indicate continuation.

Step 9: **Help with VBA**

➤ You should be in the VBA editor. If necessary, pull down the **Help menu** and click **Microsoft Visual Basic Help** (or press the **F1 key**) to display the Office Assistant.

➤ Click the **Assistant**, type **InputBox**, then click the **Search button** in the Assistant's balloon for a list of topics pertaining to this entry. Click the first entry, **InputBox function,** to display the Help window.

➤ Click the **down arrow** on the Options button in the Help window, then click **Show tabs** to expand the Help window to include the Contents, Answer Wizard, and Index tabs as shown in Figure 4i.

➤ Take a minute to explore the information that is available. The Office Assistant functions identically in VBA as it does in all other Office applications. Close the Help window.

➤ Pull down the **File menu** and click the **Close command** (or click the **Close button** on the VBA title bar) to close the VBA window and return to the application. Click **Yes** if asked whether to save the changes to Module1.

➤ You should be back in the Excel (or Access) application window. Close the Office application if you do not want to continue with the next hands-on exercise at this time.

➤ Congratulations! You have just completed your first VBA procedure. Remember to use Help anytime you have a question.

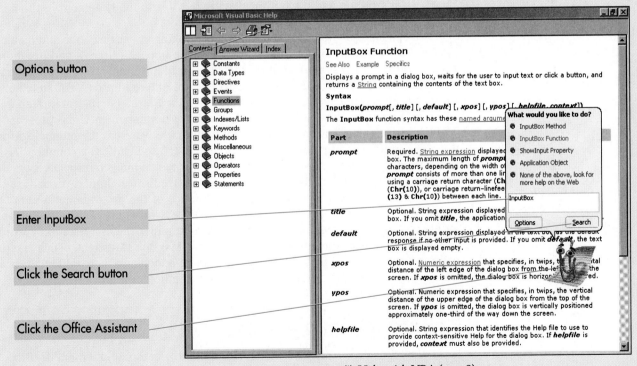

(i) Help with VBA (step 9)

FIGURE 4   *Hands-on Exercise 1 (continued)*

The ability to make decisions within a program, and then execute alternative sets of statements based on the results of those decisions, is crucial to any programming language. This is typically accomplished through an **If statement**, which evaluates a condition as either true or false, then branches accordingly. The If statement is not used in isolation, however, but is incorporated into a procedure to accomplish a specific task as shown in Figure 5a. This procedure contains two separate If statements, and the results are displayed in the message boxes shown in the remainder of the figure.

The InputBox statement associated with Figure 5b prompts the user for the name of his or her instructor, then it stores the answer in the variable strInstructorName. The subsequent If statement then compares the user's answer to the literal "Grauer". If the condition is true (i.e., Grauer was entered into the input box), then the message in Figure 5c is displayed. If, however, the user entered any other value, then the condition is evaluated as false, the MsgBox is not displayed, and processing continues with the next statement in the procedure.

The second If statement includes an optional **Else clause**. Again, the user is asked for a value, and the response is compared to the number 50. If the condition is true (i.e., the value of intUserStates equals 50), the message in Figure 5d is displayed to indicate that the response is correct. If, however, the condition is false (i.e., the user entered a number other than 50), the user sees the message in Figure 5e. Either way, true or false, processing continues with the next statement in the procedure. That's it—it's simple and it's powerful, and we will use the statement in the next hands-on exercise.

You can learn a good deal about VBA by looking at existing code and making inferences. Consider, for example, the difference between literals and numbers. **Literals** (also known as **character strings**) are stored differently from numbers, and this is manifested in the way that comparisons are entered into a VBA statement. Look closely at the condition that references a literal (strInstructorName = "Grauer") compared to the condition that includes a number (intUserStates = 50). The literal ("Grauer") is enclosed in quotation marks, whereas the number (50) is not. (The prefix used in front of each variable, "str" and "int", is a common VBA convention to indicate the variable type—a string and an integer, respectively.)

Note, too, that indentation and spacing are used throughout a procedure to make it easier to read. This is for the convenience of the programmer and not a requirement for VBA. The If, Else, and End If key words are aligned under one another, with the subsequent statements indented under the associated key word. We also indent a continued statement, such as a MsgBox statement, which is typically coded over multiple lines. Blank lines can be added anywhere within a procedure to separate blocks of statements from one another.

THE MSGBOX FUNCTION—YES OR NO

A simple MsgBox statement merely displays information to the user. MsgBox can also be used as a function, however, to accept information from the user such as clicking a Yes or No button, then combined with an If statement to take different actions based on the user's input. In essence, you enclose the arguments of the MsgBox function in parentheses (similar to what is done with the InputBox function), then test for the user response using the intrinsic constants vbYes and vbNo. See exercise 10 at the end of the chapter.

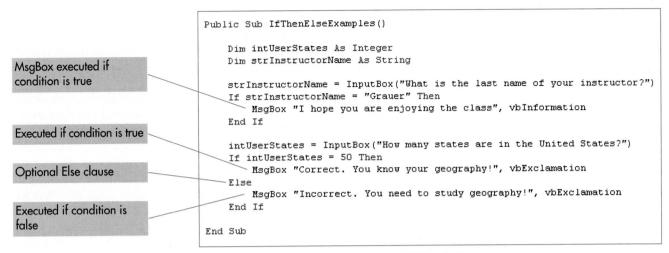

```
Public Sub IfThenElseExamples()

    Dim intUserStates As Integer
    Dim strInstructorName As String

    strInstructorName = InputBox("What is the last name of your instructor?")
    If strInstructorName = "Grauer" Then
        MsgBox "I hope you are enjoying the class", vbInformation
    End If

    intUserStates = InputBox("How many states are in the United States?")
    If intUserStates = 50 Then
        MsgBox "Correct. You know your geography!", vbExclamation
    Else
        MsgBox "Incorrect. You need to study geography!", vbExclamation
    End If

End Sub
```

MsgBox executed if condition is true

Executed if condition is true

Optional Else clause

Executed if condition is false

(a) VBA Code

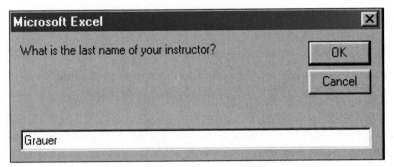

(b) Input Box Prompts for User Response

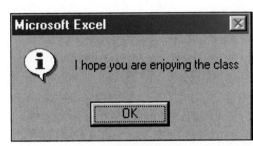

(c) Condition Is True

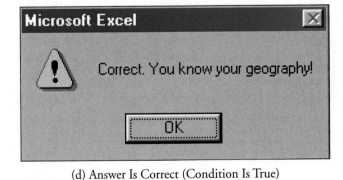

(d) Answer Is Correct (Condition Is True)

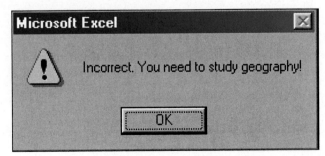

(e) Answer Is Wrong (Condition Is False)

FIGURE 5 *The If Statement*

The If statement is ideal for testing simple conditions and taking one of two actions. Although it can be extended to include additional actions by including one or more ElseIf clauses (If . . . Then . . . ElseIf . . . ElseIf . . .), this type of construction is often difficult to follow. Hence, the **Case statement** is used when multiple branches are possible.

The procedure in Figure 6a accepts a student's GPA, then displays one of several messages, depending on the value of the GPA. The individual cases are evaluated in sequence. Thus, we check first to see if the GPA is greater than or equal to 3.9, then 3.75, then 3.5, and so on. If none of the cases is true, the statement following the Else clause is executed.

Note, too, the format of the comparison in that numbers (such as 3.9 or 3.75) are not enclosed in quotation marks because the associated variable (sngUserGPA) was declared as numeric. If, however, we had been evaluating a string variable (such as, strUserMajor), quotation marks would have been required around the literal values (e.g., Case Is = "Business", Case Is = "Liberal Arts", and so on.) The distinction between numeric and character (string) variables is important.

```
Public Sub CaseExample()

    Dim sngUserGPA As Single

    sngUserGPA = InputBox("What is your GPA?")
    Select Case sngUserGPA
        Case Is >= 3.9
            MsgBox "Congratulations! You are graduating Summa Cum Laude!"
        Case Is >= 3.75
            MsgBox "Well Done! You are graduating Magna Cum Laude!"
        Case Is >= 3.5
            MsgBox "Congratulations! You are graduating Cum Laude!"
        Case Is >= 1.8
            MsgBox "You made it"
        Case Else
            MsgBox "Check the schedule for Summer School"
    End Select

End Sub
```

Numbers are not enclosed in quotes

Executed if none of the cases is true

(a) VBA Code

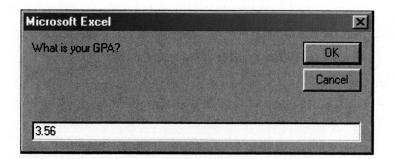

(b) Enter the GPA

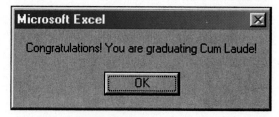

(c) Third Option Is Selected

FIGURE 6   *The Case Statement*

A VBA procedure can be executed in several different ways. It can be run from the Visual Basic Editor, by pulling down the Run menu, clicking the Run Sub button on the Standard toolbar, or using the F5 function key. It can also be run from within the Office application (Word, Excel, or PowerPoint, but not Access), by pulling down the Tools menu, clicking the Macro command, then choosing the name of the macro that corresponds to the name of the procedure.

Perhaps the best way, however, is to create a *custom toolbar* that is displayed within the application as shown in Figure 7. The toolbar has its own name (Bob's Toolbar), yet it functions identically to any other Office toolbar. You have your choice of displaying buttons only, text only, or both buttons and text. Our toolbar provides access to four commands, each corresponding to a procedure that was discussed earlier. Click the Case Example button, for example, and the associated procedure is executed, starting with the InputBox statement asking for the user's GPA.

A custom toolbar is created via the Toolbars command within the View menu. The new toolbar is initially big enough to hold only a single button, but you can add, move, and delete buttons following the same procedure as for any other Office toolbar. You can add any command at all to the toolbar; that is, you can add existing commands from within the Office application, or you can add commands that correspond to VBA procedures that you have created. Remember, too, that you can add more buttons to existing office toolbars.

Once the toolbar has been created, it is displayed or hidden just like any other Office toolbar. It can also be docked along any edge of the application window or left floating as shown in Figure 7. It's fun, it's easy, and as you may have guessed, it's time for the next hands-on exercise.

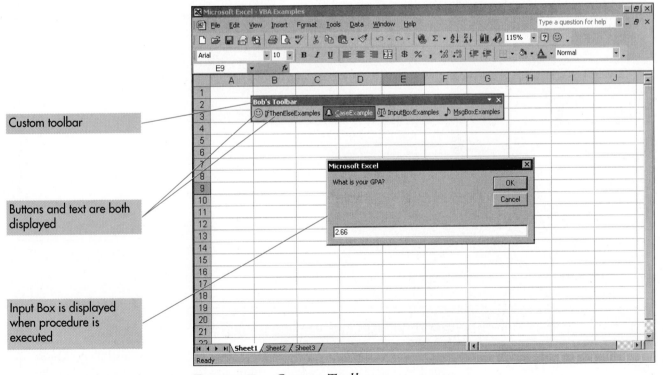

Custom toolbar

Buttons and text are both displayed

Input Box is displayed when procedure is executed

FIGURE 7 *Custom Toolbars*

Objective   To create procedures with If . . . Then . . . Else and Case statements, then create a custom toolbar to execute those procedures. Use Figure 8 as a guide in the exercise.

Step 1:   **Open the Office Document**

> ➤ Open the **VBA Examples workbook** or Access database from the previous exercise. The procedure differs slightly, depending on whether you are using Access or Excel. In Access, you simply open the database. In Excel, however, you will be warned that the workbook contains a macro as shown in Figure 8a. Click the button to **Enable Macros**.
> ➤ Pull down the **Tools menu**, click the **Macro command**, then click the **Visual Basic Editor command**. You can also use the **Alt+F11** keyboard shortcut to open the VBA Editor without going through the Tools menu.

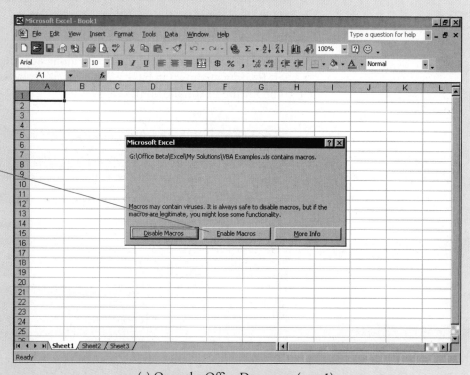

Click Enable Macros

(a) Open the Office Document (step 1)

FIGURE 8   *Hands-on Exercise 2*

MACRO VIRUSES AND VBA PROCEDURES

An Excel macro is always associated with a VBA procedure. Thus, whenever Excel detects a procedure within a workbook, it warns you that the workbook contains a macro, which in turn may carry a macro virus. If you are confident the workbook is safe, click the button to Enable macros; otherwise open the workbook with the macros disabled.

Step 2: **Insert a New Procedure**

➤ You should be in the Visual Basic Editor as shown in Figure 8b. If necessary, double click **Module1** in the Explorer Window to open this module. Pull down the **Insert menu** and click the **Procedure command** to display the Add Procedure dialog box.

➤ Click in the **Name** text box and enter **IfThenElseExamples** as the name of the procedure. Click the option buttons for a **Sub procedure** and for **Public scope**. Click **OK**. The sub procedure should appear within the module and consist of the Sub and End Sub statements.

➤ Click within the newly created procedure, then click the **Procedure View button** at the bottom of the window. The display changes to show just the current procedure.

➤ Click the **Save button** to save the module with the new procedure.

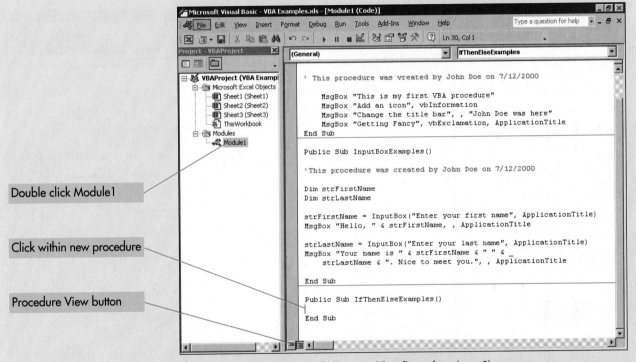

Double click Module1

Click within new procedure

Procedure View button

(b) Insert a New Procedure (step 2)

FIGURE 8 *Hands-on Exercise 2 (continued)*

PROCEDURE VIEW VERSUS FULL MODULE VIEW

The procedures within a module can be displayed individually, or alternatively, multiple procedures can be viewed simultaneously. To go from one view to the other, click the Procedure View button at the bottom of the window to display just the procedure you are working on, or click the Full Module View button to display multiple procedures. You can press Ctrl+PgDn and Ctrl+PgUp to move between procedures in either view.

Step 3: **Create the If . . . Then . . . Else Procedure**

➤ Enter the IfThenElseExamples procedure as it appears in Figure 8c, but use your instructor's name instead of Bob's. Note the following:
- The Dim statements at the beginning of the procedure are required to define the two variables that are used elsewhere in the procedure.
- The syntax of the comparison is different for string variables versus numeric variables. String variables require quotation marks around the comparison value (e.g., strInstructorName = "Grauer"). Numeric variables (e.g., intUserStates = 50) do not.
- Indentation and blank lines are used within a procedure to make the code easier to read, as distinct from a VBA requirement. Press the **Tab key** to indent one level to the right.

➤ Save the procedure.

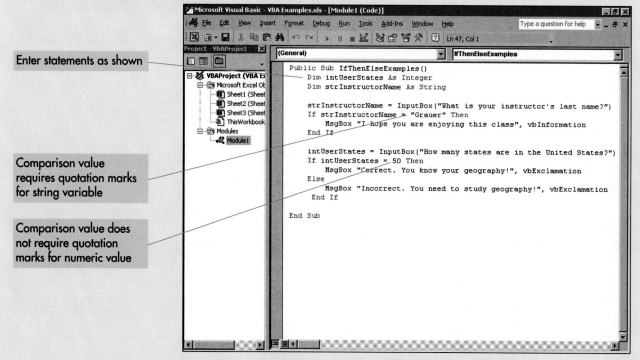

Enter statements as shown

Comparison value requires quotation marks for string variable

Comparison value does not require quotation marks for numeric value

```
Public Sub IfThenElseExamples()
    Dim intUserStates As Integer
    Dim strInstructorName As String

    strInstructorName = InputBox("What is your instructor's last name?")
    If strInstructorName = "Grauer" Then
        MsgBox "I hope you are enjoying this class", vbInformation
    End If

    intUserStates = InputBox("How many states are in the United States?")
    If intUserStates = 50 Then
        MsgBox "Correct. You know your geography!", vbExclamation
    Else
        MsgBox "Incorrect. You need to study geography!", vbExclamation
    End If

End Sub
```

(c) Create the If . . . Then . . . Else Procedure (step 3)

FIGURE 8   *Hands-on Exercise 2 (continued)*

THE COMPLETE WORD TOOL

It's easy to misspell a variable name within a procedure, which is why the Complete Word tool is so useful. Type the first several characters in a variable name (e.g., "intU" or "strI" in the current procedure), then press Ctrl+Space. VBA will complete the variable for you, if you have already entered a sufficient number of letters for a unique reference. Alternatively, it will display all of the elements that begin with the letters you have entered. Use the down arrow to scroll through the list until you find the item, then press the space bar to complete the entry.

Step 4: **Test the Procedure**

➤ The best way to test a procedure is to display its output directly in the VBA window (without having to switch back and forth between that and the application window). Thus, right click the Excel button on the taskbar to display a context-sensitive menu, then click the **Minimize command**.

➤ There is no visible change on your monitor. Click anywhere within the procedure, then click the **Run Sub button**. You should see the dialog box in Figure 8d.

➤ Enter your instructor's name, exactly as it was spelled within the VBA procedure. Click **OK**. You should see a second message box that hopes you are enjoying the class. This box will be displayed only if you spell the instructor's name correctly. Click **OK**.

➤ You should see a second input box that asks how many states are in the United States. Enter **50** and click **OK**. You should see a message indicating that you know your geography. Click **OK** to close the dialog box.

➤ Click the **Run Sub button** a second time, but enter a different set of values in response to the prompts. Misspell your instructor's name, and you will not see the associated message box.

➤ Enter any number other than 50, and you will be told to study geography. Continue to test the procedure until you are satisfied it works under all conditions.

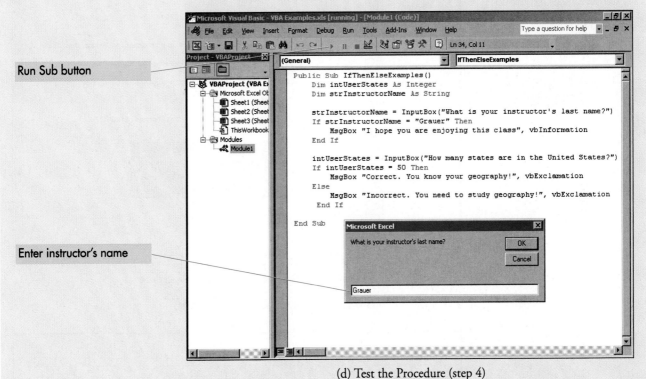

(d) Test the Procedure (step 4)

FIGURE 8 *Hands-on Exercise 2 (continued)*

Step 5: **Create and Test the CaseExample Procedure**

➤ Pull down the **Insert menu** and create a new procedure called **CaseExample**, then enter the statements exactly as they appear in Figure 8e. Note:

- The variable sngUserGPA is declared to be a single-precision floating-point number (as distinct from the integer type that was used previously). A floating-point number is required in order to maintain a decimal point.
- You may use any editing technique with which you are comfortable. You could, for example, enter the first case, copy it four times in the procedure, then modify the copied text as necessary.
- The use of indentation and blank lines is for the convenience of the programmer and not a requirement of VBA.

➤ Click the **Run Sub button**, then test the procedure. Be sure to test it under all conditions; that is, you need to run it several times and enter a different GPA each time to be sure that all of the cases are working correctly.

➤ Save the procedure.

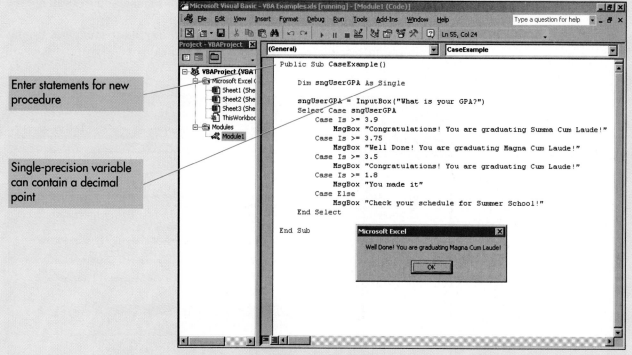

Enter statements for new procedure

Single-precision variable can contain a decimal point

(e) Create and Test the CaseExample Procedure (step 5)

FIGURE 8   *Hands-on Exercise 2 (continued)*

RELATIONAL OPERATORS

The condition portion of an If or Case statement uses one of several relational operators. These include =, <, and > for equal to, less than, or greater than, respectively. You can also use >=, <=, or <> for greater than or equal to, less than or equal to, or not equal. This is basic, but very important, information if you are to code these statements correctly.

Step 6: **Create a Custom Toolbar**

➤ Click the **Excel** (or **Access**) **button** to display the associated application window. Pull down the **View menu**, click (or point to) the **Toolbars command**, then click **Customize** to display the Customize dialog box in Figure 8f. (Bob's toolbar is not yet visible.) Click the **Toolbars tab**.

➤ Click the **New button** to display the New Toolbar dialog box. Enter the name of your toolbar—e.g., **Bob's toolbar**—then click **OK** to create the toolbar and close the dialog box.

➤ Your toolbar should appear on the screen, but it does not yet contain any buttons. If necessary, click and drag the title bar of your toolbar to move the toolbar within the application window.

➤ Toggle the check box that appears next to your toolbar within the Customize dialog box on and off to display or hide your toolbar. Leave the box checked to display the toolbar and continue with this exercise.

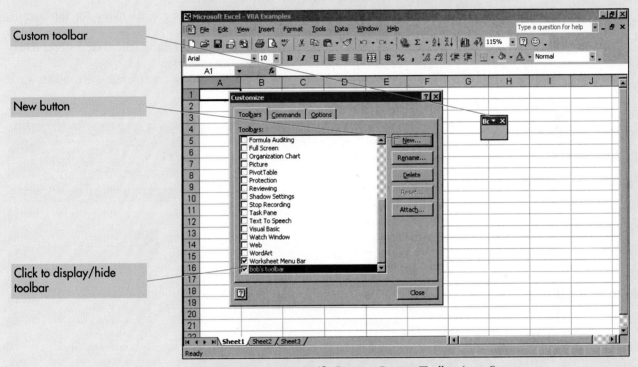

Custom toolbar

New button

Click to display/hide toolbar

(f) Create a Custom Toolbar (step 6)

FIGURE 8 *Hands-on Exercise 2 (continued)*

FIXED VERSUS FLOATING TOOLBARS

A toolbar may be docked (fixed) along the edge of the application window, or it can be displayed as a floating toolbar anywhere within the window. You can switch back and forth by dragging the move handle of a docked toolbar to move the toolbar away from the edge. Conversely, you can drag the title bar of a floating toolbar to the edge of the window to dock the toolbar. You can also click and drag the border of a floating toolbar to change its size.

Step 7: **Add Buttons to the Toolbar**

➤ Click the **Commands tab** in the Customize dialog box, click the **down arrow** in the Categories list box, then scroll until you can select the **Macros category**. (If you are using Access and not Excel, you need to select the **File category**, then follow the steps as described in the boxed tip on the next page.)

➤ Click and drag the **Custom button** to your toolbar and release the mouse. A "happy face" button appears on the toolbar you just created. (You can remove a button from a toolbar by simply dragging the button from the toolbar.)

➤ Select the newly created button, then click the **Modify Selection command button** (or right click the button to display the context-sensitive menu) in Figure 8g. Change the button's properties as follows:

  • Click the **Assign Macro command** at the bottom of the menu to display the Assign Macro dialog box, then select the **IfThenElseExamples** macro (procedure) to assign it to the button. Click **OK**.

  • Click the **Modify Selection button** a second time.

  • Click in the **Name Textbox** and enter an appropriate name for the button, such as **IfThenElseExamples**.

  • Click the **Modify Selection button** a third time, then click **Text Only (Always)** to display text rather than an image.

➤ Close the Customize dialog box when you have completed the toolbar. Save the workbook.

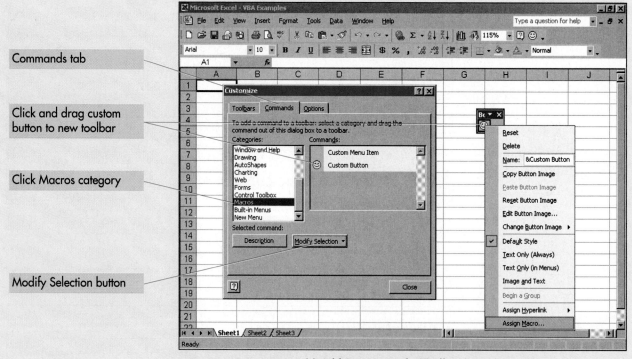

Commands tab

Click and drag custom button to new toolbar

Click Macros category

Modify Selection button

(g) Add Buttons to the Toolbar (step 7)

FIGURE 8   *Hands-on Exercise 2 (continued)*

Step 8:   **Test the Custom Toolbar**

➤ Click any command on your toolbar as shown in Figure 8h. We clicked the **InputBoxExamples button**, which in turn executed the InputBoxExamples procedure that was created in the first exercise.

➤ Enter the appropriate information in any input boxes that are displayed. Click **OK**. Close your toolbar when you have completed testing it.

➤ If this is not your own machine, you should delete your toolbar as a courtesy to the next student. Pull down the **View menu**, click the **Toolbars command**, click **Customize** to display the Customize dialog box, then click the **Toolbars tab**. Select (highlight) the toolbar, then click the **Delete button** in the Customize dialog box. Click **OK** to delete the button. Close the dialog box.

➤ Exit Office if you do not want to continue with the next exercise.

Click button to run
associated macro

Enter requested
information

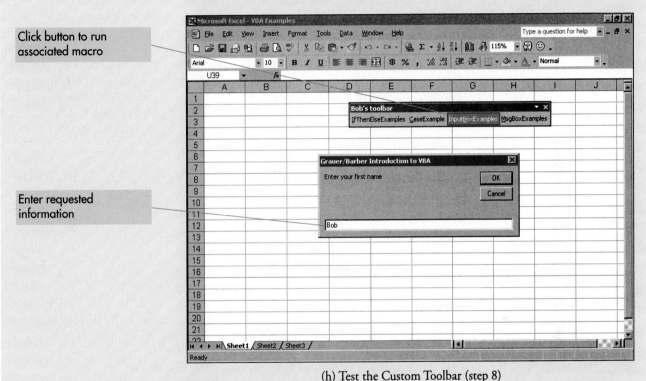

(h) Test the Custom Toolbar (step 8)

FIGURE 8   *Hands-on Exercise 2 (continued)*

ACCESS IS DIFFERENT

The procedure to create a custom toolbar in Access is different from the procedure in Excel. Select the File category within the Customize dialog box, then click and drag the Custom command to the newly created toolbar. Select the command on the toolbar, then click the Modify Selection command button in the dialog box. Click Properties, click the On Action text box, then type the name of the procedure you want to run in the format, =procedurename(). Close the dialog boxes, then press Alt+F11 to return to the VBA Editor. Change the key word "Sub" that identifies the procedure to "Function". Return to the database window, then test the newly created toolbar.

The *For . . . Next statement* executes all statements between the words For and Next a specified number of times, using a counter to keep track of the number of times the statements are executed. The simplest form of the statement, For intCounter = 1 To N, executes the statements within the loop N times.

The procedure in Figure 9 contains two For . . . Next statements that sum the numbers from 1 to 10, counting by one and two, respectively. The Dim statements at the beginning of the procedure declare two variables, intSumofNumbers to hold the sum and intCounter to hold the value of the counter. The sum is initialized to zero immediately before the first loop. The statements in the loop are then executed 10 times, each time incrementing the sum by the value of the counter. The result (the sum of the numbers from 1 to 10) is displayed after the loop in Figure 9b.

The second For . . . Next statement increments the counter by two rather than by one. (The increment or step is assumed to be one unless a different value is specified.) The sum of the numbers is reset to zero prior to entering the second loop, the loop is entered, and the counter is initialized to the starting value of one. Each subsequent time through the loop, however, the counter is incremented by two. Each time the value of the counter is compared to the ending value, until it (the counter) exceeds the ending value, at which point the For . . . Next statement is complete. Thus the second loop will be executed for values of 1, 3, 5, 7, and 9. After the fifth time through the loop, the counter is incremented to 11, which is greater than the ending value of 10, and the loop is terminated.

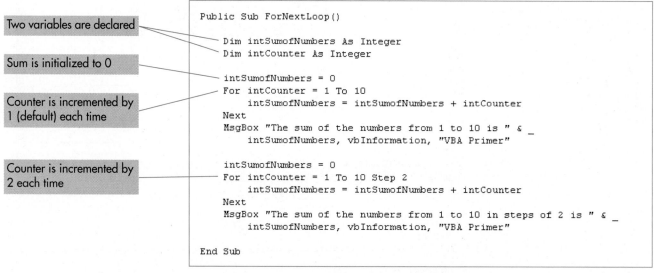

Two variables are declared

Sum is initialized to 0

Counter is incremented by 1 (default) each time

Counter is incremented by 2 each time

```
Public Sub ForNextLoop()

    Dim intSumofNumbers As Integer
    Dim intCounter As Integer

    intSumofNumbers = 0
    For intCounter = 1 To 10
        intSumofNumbers = intSumofNumbers + intCounter
    Next
    MsgBox "The sum of the numbers from 1 to 10 is " & _
        intSumofNumbers, vbInformation, "VBA Primer"

    intSumofNumbers = 0
    For intCounter = 1 To 10 Step 2
        intSumofNumbers = intSumofNumbers + intCounter
    Next
    MsgBox "The sum of the numbers from 1 to 10 in steps of 2 is " & _
        intSumofNumbers, vbInformation, "VBA Primer"

End Sub
```

(a) VBA Code

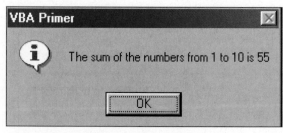

(b) In Increments of 1

(c) In Increments of 2

FIGURE 9 *For . . . Next Loops*

The For ... Next statement is ideal when you know in advance how many times you want to go through a loop. There are many instances, however, when the number of times through the loop is indeterminate. You could, for example, give a user multiple chances to enter a password or answer a question. This type of logic is implemented through a Do loop. You can repeat the loop as long as a condition is true (Do While), or until a condition becomes true (Do Until). The choice depends on how you want to state the condition.

Regardless of which key word you choose, Do While or Do Until, two formats are available. The difference is subtle and depends on whether the key word (While or Until) appears at the beginning or end of the loop. Our discussion will use the Do Until statement, but the Do While statement works in similar fashion.

Look closely at the procedure in Figure 10a, which contains two different loops. In the first example, the Until condition appears at the end of the loop, which means the statements in the loop are executed, and then the condition is tested. This ensures that the statements in the loop will be executed at least once. The second loop, however, places the Until condition at the beginning of the loop, so that it (the condition) is tested prior to the loop being executed. Thus, if the condition is satisfied initially, the second loop will never be executed. In other words, there are two distinct statements **Do ... Loop Until** and **Do Until ... Loop**. The first statement executes the loop, then tests the condition. The second statement tests the condition, then enters the loop.

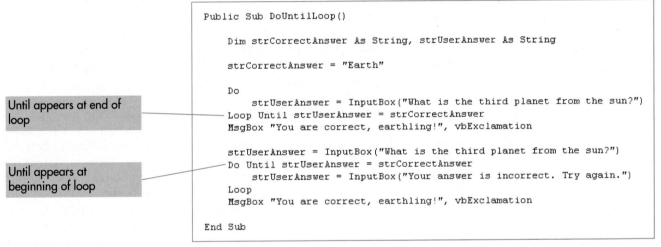

```
Public Sub DoUntilLoop()

    Dim strCorrectAnswer As String, strUserAnswer As String

    strCorrectAnswer = "Earth"

    Do
        strUserAnswer = InputBox("What is the third planet from the sun?")
    Loop Until strUserAnswer = strCorrectAnswer
    MsgBox "You are correct, earthling!", vbExclamation

    strUserAnswer = InputBox("What is the third planet from the sun?")
    Do Until strUserAnswer = strCorrectAnswer
        strUserAnswer = InputBox("Your answer is incorrect. Try again.")
    Loop
    MsgBox "You are correct, earthling!", vbExclamation

End Sub
```

Until appears at end of loop

Until appears at beginning of loop

(a) VBA Code

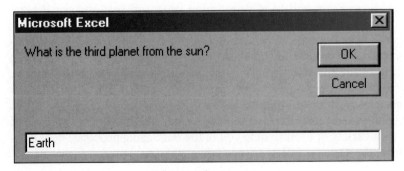

(b) Input the Answer

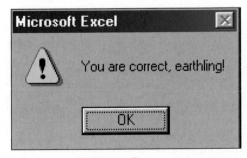

(c) Correct Response

FIGURE 10   *Do Until Loops*

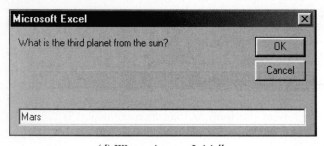

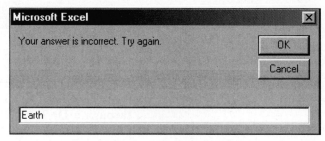

| (d) Wrong Answer Initially | (e) Second Chance |

FIGURE 10   *Do Until Loops (continued)*

It's tricky, but stay with us. In the first example, the user is asked the question within the loop, and the loop is executed repeatedly until the user gives the correct answer. In the second example, the user is asked the question outside of the loop, and the loop is bypassed if the user answers it correctly. The latter is the preferred logic because it enables us to phrase the question differently, before and during the loop. Look carefully at the difference between the InputBox statements and see how the question changes within the second loop.

DEBUGGING

As you learn more about VBA and develop more powerful procedures, you are more likely to make mistakes. The process of finding and correcting errors within a procedure is known as *debugging* and it is an integral part of programming. Do not be discouraged if you make mistakes. Everyone does. The important thing is how quickly you are able to find and correct the errors that invariably occur. We begin our discussion of debugging by describing two types of errors, *compilation errors* and *execution* (or *run-time*) *errors*.

A compilation error is simply an error in VBA syntax. (Compilation is the process of translating a VBA procedure to machine language, and thus a compilation error occurs when the VBA Editor is unable to convert a statement to machine language.) Compilation errors occur for many reasons, such as misspelling a key word, omitting a comma, and so on. VBA recognizes the error before the procedure is run and displays the invalid statement in red together with an associated error message. The programmer corrects the error and then reruns the procedure.

Execution errors are caused by errors in logic and are more difficult to detect because they occur without any error message. VBA, or for that matter any other programming language, does what you tell it to do, which is not necessarily what you want it to do. If, for example, you were to compute the sales tax of an item by multiplying the price by 60% rather than 6%, VBA will perform the calculation and simply display the wrong answer. It is up to you to realize that the results of the procedure are incorrect, and you will need to examine its statements and correct the mistake.

So how do you detect an execution error? In essence, you must decide what the expected output of your procedure should be, then you compare the actual results of the procedure to the intended result. If the results are different, an error has occurred, and you have to examine the logic in the procedure to find the error. You may see the mistake immediately (e.g., using 60% rather than 6% in the previous example), or you may have to examine the code more closely. And as you might expect, VBA has a variety of tools to help you in the debugging process. These tools are accessed from the *Debug toolbar* or the *Debug menu* as shown in Figure 11.

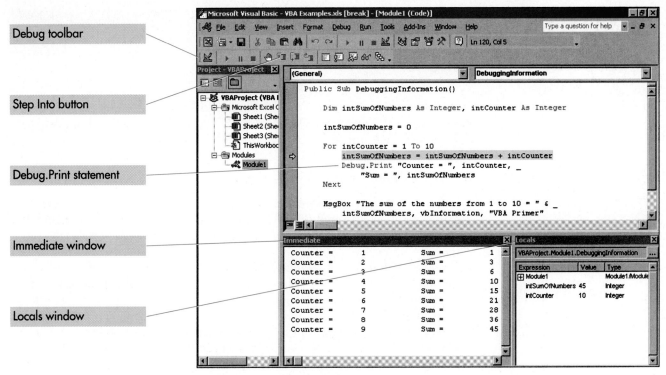

Labels for the figure (left side):
- Debug toolbar
- Step Into button
- Debug.Print statement
- Immediate window
- Locals window

FIGURE 11   *Debugging*

The procedure in Figure 11 is a simple For . . . Next loop to sum the integers from 1 to 10. The procedure is correct as written, but we have introduced several debugging techniques into the figure. The most basic technique is to step through the statements in the procedure one at a time to see the sequence in which the statements are executed. Click the **Step Into button** on the Debug toolbar to enter (step into) the procedure, then continue to click the button to move through the procedure. Each time you click the button, the statement that is about to be executed is highlighted.

Another useful technique is to display the values of selected variables as they change during execution. This is accomplished through the **Debug.Print statement** that displays the values in the **Immediate window**. The Debug.Print statement is placed within the For . . . Next loop so that you can see how the counter and the associated sum change during execution.

As the figure now stands, we have gone through the loop nine times, and the sum of the numbers from 1 to 9 is 45. The Step Into button is in effect so that the statement to be executed next is highlighted. You can see that we are back at the top of the loop, where the counter has been incremented to 10, and further, that we are about to increment the sum.

The **Locals window** is similar in concept except that it displays only the current values of all the variables within the procedure. Unlike the Immediate window, which requires the insertion of Debug.Print statements into a procedure to have meaning, the Locals window displays its values automatically, without any effort on the part of the programmer, other than opening the window. All three techniques can be used individually, or in conjunction with one another, as the situation demands.

We believe that the best time to practice debugging is when you know there are no errors in your procedure. As you may have guessed, it's time for the next hands-on exercise.

LOOPS AND DEBUGGING

Objective To create a loop using the For . . . Next and Do Until statements; to open the Locals and Immediate windows and illustrate different techniques for debugging. Use Figure 12 as a guide in the exercise.

Step 1: **Insert a New Procedure**

➤ Open the **VBA Examples workbook** or the Access database from the previous exercise. Either way, pull down the **Tools menu**, click the **Macro command**, then click **Visual Basic Editor** (or use the **Alt+F11** keyboard shortcut) to start the VBA editor.

➤ If necessary, double click **Module1** within the Project Explorer window to open this module. Pull down the **Insert menu** and click the **Procedure command** to display the Add Procedure dialog box.

➤ Click in the **Name** text box and enter **ForNextLoop** as the name of the procedure. Click the option buttons for a **Sub procedure** and for **Public scope**. Click **OK**. The sub procedure should appear within the module and consist of the Sub and End Sub statements.

➤ Click the **Procedure View button** at the bottom of the window as shown in Figure 12a. The display changes to show just the current procedure, giving you more room in which to work.

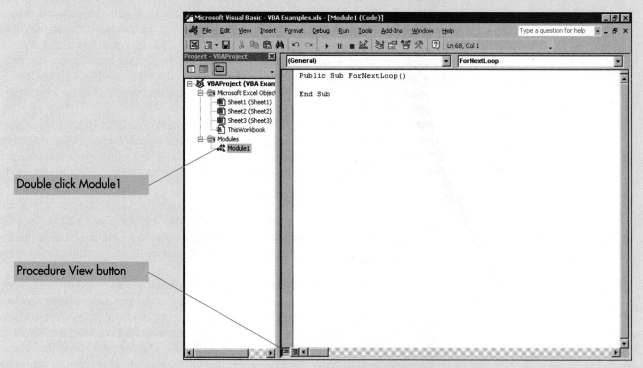

(a) Insert a New Procedure (step 1)

FIGURE 12 *Hands-on Exercise 3*

Step 2:   **Test the For . . . Next Procedure**

➤ Enter the procedure exactly as it appears in Figure 12b. Note the following:
  - A comment is added at the beginning of the procedure to identify the author and the date.
  - Two variables are declared at the beginning of the procedure, one to hold the sum of the numbers and the other to serve as a counter.
  - The sum of the numbers is initialized to zero. The For . . . Next loop varies the counter from 1 to 10.
  - The statement within the For . . . Next loop increments the sum of the numbers by the current value of the counter. The equal sign is really a replacement operator; that is, replace the variable on the left (the sum of the numbers) by the expression on the right (the sum of the numbers plus the value of the counter.
  - Indentation and spacing within a procedure are for the convenience of the programmer and not a requirement of VBA. We align the For and Next statements at the beginning and end of a loop, then indent all statements within a loop.
  - The MsgBox statement displays the result and is continued over two lines.
➤ Click the **Save button** to save the module. Right click the **Excel button** on the Windows taskbar to display a context-sensitive menu, then click the **Minimize command**.
➤ Click the **Run Sub button** to test the procedure, which should display the MsgBox statement in Figure 12b. Correct any errors that may occur.

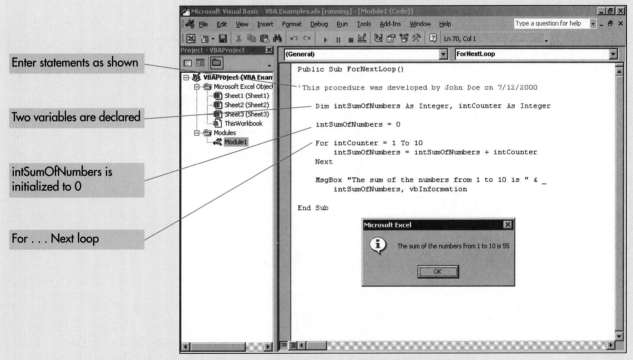

(b) Test the For . . . Next Procedure (step 2)

FIGURE 12   *Hands-on Exercise 3 (continued)*

Step 3: **Compilation Errors**

➤ The best time to practice debugging is when you know that the procedure is working properly. Accordingly, we will make some deliberate errors in our procedure to illustrate different debugging techniques.

➤ Pull down the **View menu**, click the **Toolbars command**, and (if necessary) toggle the Debug toolbar on, then dock it under the Standard toolbar.

➤ Click on the statement that initializes intSumOfNumbers to zero and delete the "s" at the end of the variable name. Click the **Run Sub button**.

➤ You will see the message in Figure 12c. Click **OK** to acknowledge the error, then click the **Undo button** to correct the error.

➤ The procedure header is highlighted, indicating that execution is temporarily suspended and that additional action is required from you to continue testing. Click the **Run Sub button** to retest the procedure.

➤ This time the procedure executes correctly and you see the MsgBox statement indicating that the sum of the numbers from 1 to 10 is 55. Click **OK**.

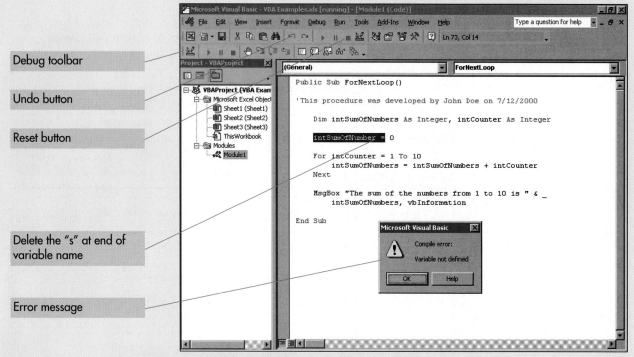

Debug toolbar

Undo button

Reset button

Delete the "s" at end of variable name

Error message

(c) Compilation Errors (step 3)

FIGURE 12   *Hands-on Exercise 3 (continued)*

USE HELP AS NECESSARY

Pull down the Help menu at any time (or press the F1 key) to access the VBA Help facility to explore at your leisure. You can also obtain context-sensitive help by clicking the Help button when it appears within a dialog box. Click the Help button in Figure 12c, for example, and you will be advised to correct the spelling of the variable.

Step 4: **Step Through a Procedure**

➤ Pull down the **View menu** a second time and click the **Locals Window command** (or click the **Locals Window button** on the Debug toolbar).

➤ If necessary, click and drag the top border of the Locals window to size the window appropriately as shown in Figure 12d.

➤ Click anywhere within the procedure. Pull down the **Debug menu** and click the **Step Into command** (or click the **Step Into button** on the Debug toolbar). The first statement (the procedure header) is highlighted, indicating that you are about to enter the procedure.

➤ Click the **Step Into button** (or use the **F8** keyboard shortcut) to step into the procedure and advance to the next executable statement. The statement that initializes intSumOfNumbers to zero is highlighted, indicating that this statement is about to be executed.

➤ Continue to press the **F8 key** to step through the procedure. Each time you execute a statement, you can see the values of intSumOfNumbers and intCounter change within the Locals window. (You can click the **Step Out button** at any time to end the procedure.)

➤ Correct errors as they occur. Click the **Reset button** on the Standard or Debug toolbars at any time to begin executing the procedure from the beginning.

➤ Eventually you exit from the loop, and the sum of the numbers (from 1 to 10) is displayed within a message box.

➤ Click **OK** to close the message box. Press the **F8 key** a final time, then close the Locals window.

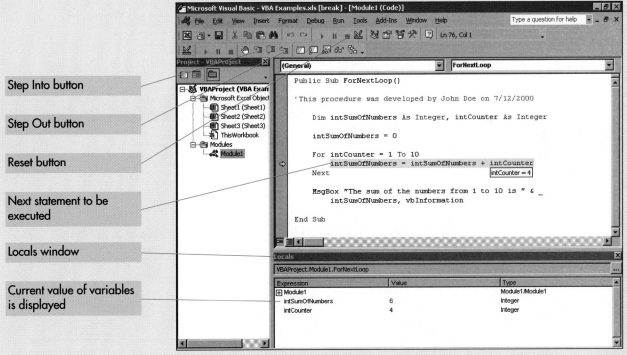

Step Into button

Step Out button

Reset button

Next statement to be executed

Locals window

Current value of variables is displayed

(d) Step Through a Procedure (step 4)

FIGURE 12 *Hands-on Exercise 3 (continued)*

Step 5: **The Immediate Window**

➤ You should be back in the VBA window. Click immediately to the left of the Next statement and press **enter** to insert a blank line. Type the **Debug.Print** statement exactly as shown in Figure 12e. (Click **OK** if you see a message indicating that the procedure will be reset.)

➤ Pull down the **View menu** and click the **Immediate Window command** (or click the **Immediate Window button** on the Debug toolbar). The Immediate window should be empty, but if not, you can click and drag to select the contents, then press the Del key to clear the window.

➤ Click anywhere within the For ... Next procedure, then click the **Run Sub button** on the Debug toolbar to execute the procedure. You will see the familiar message box indicating that the sum of the numbers is 55. Click **OK**.

➤ You should see 10 lines within the Immediate window as shown in Figure 12e, corresponding to the values displayed by the Debug.Print statement as it was executed within the loop.

➤ Close the Immediate window.

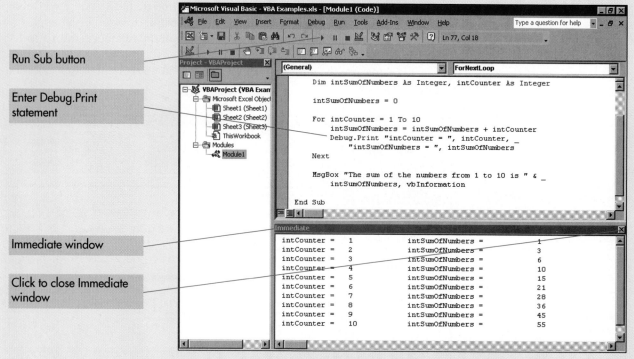

(e) The Immediate Window (step 5)

FIGURE 12   *Hands-on Exercise 3 (continued)*

INSTANT CALCULATOR

Use the Print method (action) in the Immediate window to use VBA as a calculator. Press Ctrl+G at any time to display the Immediate window. Click in the window, then type the statement Debug.Print, followed by your calculation, for example, Debug.Print 2+2, and press enter. The answer is displayed on the next line in the Immediate window.

Step 6: **A More General Procedure**

➤ Modify the existing procedure to make it more general; for example, to sum the values from any starting value to any ending value:

- Click at the end of the existing Dim statement to position the insertion point, press **enter** to create a new line, then add the second Dim statement as shown in Figure 12f.
- Click before the For statement, press **enter** to create a blank line, press **enter** a second time, then enter the two InputBox statements to ask the user for the beginning and ending value.
- Modify the For statement to execute from **intStart** to **intEnd** rather than from 1 to 10.
- Change the MsgBox statement to reflect the values of intStart and intEnd, and a customized title bar. Note the use of the ampersand and the underscore, to indicate concatenation and continuation, respectively.

➤ Click the **Save button** to save the module.

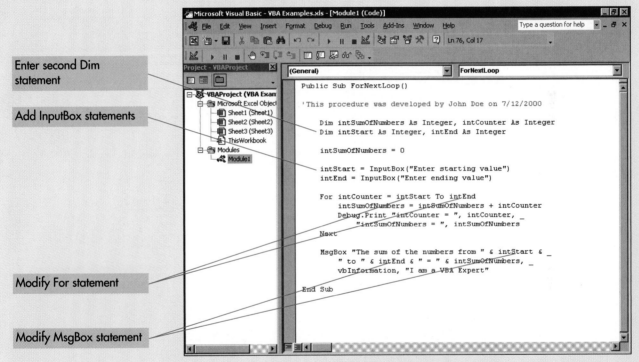

(f) A More General Procedure (step 6)

FIGURE 12 *Hands-on Exercise 3 (continued)*

USE WHAT YOU KNOW

Use the techniques acquired from other applications such as Microsoft Word to facilitate editing within the VBA window. Press the Ins key to toggle between the insert and overtype modes as you modify the statements within a VBA procedure. You can also cut, copy, and paste statements (or parts of statements) within a procedure and from one procedure to another. The Find and Replace commands are also useful.

Step 7: **Test the Procedure**

➤ Click the **Run Sub button** to test the procedure. You should be prompted for a beginning and an ending value. Enter any numbers you like, such as 10 and 20, respectively, to match the result in Figure 12g.

➤ The value displayed in the MsgBox statement should reflect the numbers you entered. For example, you will see a sum of 165 if you entered 10 and 20 as the starting and ending values.

➤ Look carefully at the message box that is displayed in Figure 12g. Its title bar displays the literal "I am a VBA expert", corresponding to the last argument in the MsgBox statement.

➤ Note, too, the spacing that appears within the message box, which includes spaces before and after each number. Look at your results and, if necessary, modify the MsgBox statement so that you have the same output. Click **OK**.

➤ Save the procedure.

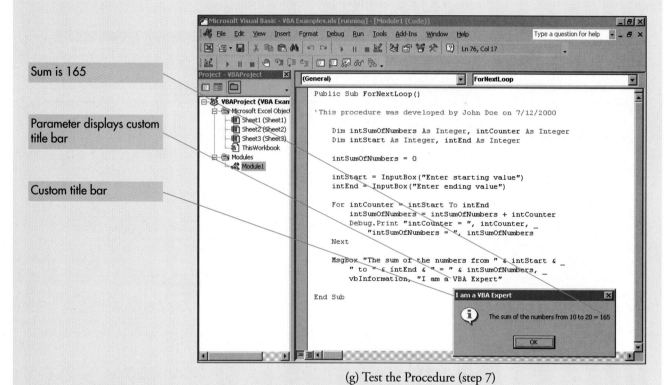

(g) Test the Procedure (step 7)

FIGURE 12 *Hands-on Exercise 3 (continued)*

CHANGE THE INCREMENT

The For ... Next statement can be made more general by supplying an increment within the For statement. Try For intCount = 1 To 10 Step 2, or more generally, For intCount = intStart to intEnd Step intStepValue. "Step" is a Visual Basic key word and must be entered that way. intCount, intEnd, and intStepValue are user-defined variables. The variables must be defined at the beginning of a procedure and can be initialized by requesting values from the user through the InputBox statement.

Step 8:   **Create a Do Until Loop**

➤ Pull down the **Insert menu** and click the **Procedure command** to insert a new procedure called **DoUntilLoop**. Enter the procedure as it appears in Figure 12h. Note the following:

- Two string variables are declared to hold the correct answer and the user's response, respectively.
- The variable strCorrectAnswer is set to "Earth", the correct answer for our question.
- The initial InputBox function prompts the user to enter his/her response to the question. A second InputBox function appears in the loop that is executed if and only if the user enters the wrong answer.
- The Until condition appears at the beginning of the loop, so that the loop is entered only if the user answers incorrectly. The loop executes repeatedly until the correct answer is supplied.
- A message to the user is displayed at the end of the procedure after the correct answer has been entered.

➤ Click the **Run Sub button** to test the procedure. Enter the correct answer on your first attempt, and you will see that the loop is never entered.

➤ Rerun the procedure, answer incorrectly, then note that a second input box appears, telling you that your answer was incorrect.

➤ Save the procedure.

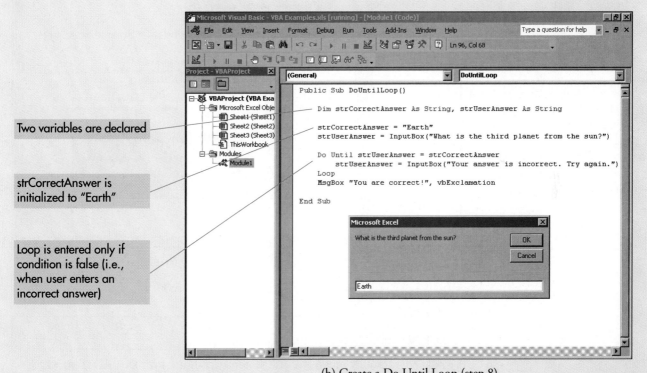

(h) Create a Do Until Loop (step 8)

FIGURE 12   *Hands-on Exercise 3 (continued)*

Step 9: **A More Powerful Procedure**

➤ Modify the procedure as shown in Figure 12i to include the statements to count and print the number of times the user takes to get the correct answer.
  • The variable intNumberOfAttempts is declared as an integer and is initialized to 1 after the user inputs his/her initial answer.
  • The Do loop is expanded to increment intNumberOfAttempts by 1 each time the loop is executed.
  • The MsgBox statement after the loop is expanded prints the number of attempts the user took to answer the question.
➤ Save the module, then click the **Run Sub button** to test the module. You should see a dialog box similar to the one in Figure 12i. Click **OK**.
➤ Pull down the **File menu** and click the **Print command** to display the Print dialog box. Click the option button to print the current module. Click **OK**.
➤ Exit Office if you do not want to continue at this time.

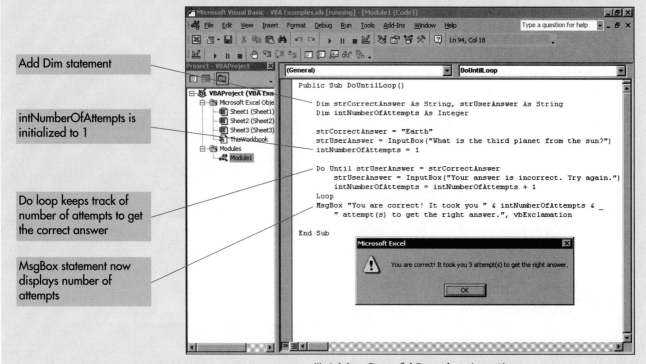

(i) A More Powerful Procedure (step 9)

FIGURE 12 *Hands-on Exercise 3 (continued)*

IT'S NOT EQUAL, BUT REPLACE

All programming languages use statements of the form $N = N + 1$, in which the equal sign does not mean equal in the literal sense; that is, N cannot equal $N + 1$. The equal sign is really a replacement operator. Thus, the expression on the right of the equal sign is evaluated, and that result replaces the value of the variable on the left. In other words, the statement $N = N + 1$ increments the value of N by one.

Our approach thus far has focused on VBA as an independent entity that can be run without specific reference to the applications in Microsoft Office. We have covered several individual statements, explained how to use the VBA editor to create and run procedures, and how to debug those procedures, if necessary. We hope you have found the material to be interesting, but you may be asking yourself, "What does this have to do with Microsoft Office?" In other words, how can you use your knowledge of VBA to enhance your ability in Microsoft Excel or Access? The answer is to create *event procedures* that run automatically in response to events within an Office application.

VBA is different from traditional programming languages in that it is event-driven. An *event* is defined as any action that is recognized by an application such as Excel or Access. Opening or closing an Excel workbook or an Access database is an event. Selecting a worksheet within a workbook is also an event, as is clicking on a command button on an Access form. To use VBA within Microsoft Office, you decide which events are significant, and what is to happen when those events occur. Then you develop the appropriate event procedures.

Consider, for example, Figure 13, which displays the results of two event procedures in conjunction with opening and closing an Excel workbook. (If you are using Microsoft Access instead of Excel, you can skip this discussion and the associated exercise, and move to the parallel material for Access that appears after the next hands-on exercise.) The procedure associated with Figure 13a displays a message that appears automatically after the user executes the command to close the associated workbook. The procedure is almost trivial to write, and consists of a single MsgBox statement. The effect of the procedure is quite significant, however, as it reminds the user to back up his or her work after closing the workbook. Nor does it matter how the user closes the workbook—whether by pulling down the menu or using a keyboard shortcut—because the procedure runs automatically in response to the Close Workbook event, regardless of how that event occurs.

The dialog box in Figure 13b prompts the user for a password and appears automatically when the user opens the workbook. The logic here is more sophisticated in that the underlying procedure contains an InputBox statement to request the password, a Do Until loop that is executed until the user enters the correct password or exceeds the allotted number of attempts, then additional logic to display the worksheet or terminate the application if the user fails to enter the proper password. The procedure is not difficult, however, and it builds on the VBA statements that were covered earlier.

The next hands-on exercise has you create the two event procedures that are associated with Figure 13. As you do the exercise, you will gain additional experience with VBA and an appreciation for the potential event procedures within Microsoft Office.

HIDING AND UNHIDING A WORKSHEET

Look carefully at the workbooks in Figures 13a and 13b. Both figures reference the identical workbook, Financial Consultant, as can be seen from the title bar. Look at the worksheet tabs, however, and note that two worksheets are visible in Figure 13a, whereas the Calculations worksheet is hidden in Figure 13b. This was accomplished in the Open workbook procedure and was implemented to hide the calculations from the user until the correct password was entered. See exercise 7 at the end of the chapter.

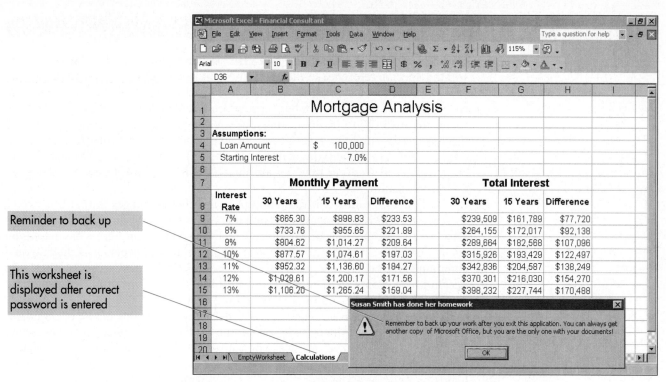

Reminder to back up

This worksheet is displayed after correct password is entered

(a) Message to the User (Close Workbook event)

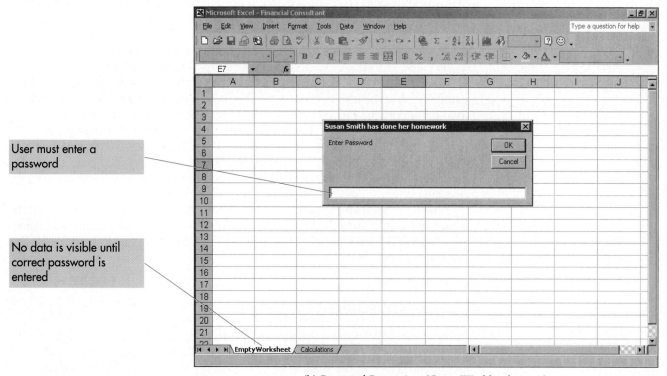

User must enter a password

No data is visible until correct password is entered

(b) Password Protection (Open Workbook event)

FIGURE 13   *Event-Driven Programming*

EVENT-DRIVEN PROGRAMMING (MICROSOFT EXCEL)

Objective To create an event procedure to implement password protection that is associated with opening an Excel workbook; to create a second event procedure that displays a message to the user upon closing the workbook. Use Figure 14 as a guide in the exercise.

Step 1: **Create the Close Workbook Procedure**

➤ Open the **VBA Examples workbook** you have used for the previous exercises and enable the macros. If you have been using Access rather than Excel, start Excel, open a new workbook, then save the workbook as **VBA Examples**.

➤ Pull down the **Tools menu**, click the **Macro command**, then click the **Visual Basic Editor command** (or use the **Alt+F11** keyboard shortcut).

➤ You should see the Project Explorer pane as shown in Figure 14a, but if not, pull down the **View menu** and click the **Project Explorer**. Double click **ThisWorkbook** to create a module for the workbook as a whole.

➤ Enter the **Option Explicit statement** if it is not there already, then press **enter** to create a new line. Type the statement to declare the variable, **Application-Title**, using your name instead of Susan Smith.

➤ Click the **down arrow** in the Object list box and select **Workbook**, then click the **down arrow** in the Procedure list box and select the **BeforeClose event** to create the associated procedure. (If you choose a different event by mistake, click and drag to select the associated statements, then press the **Del key** to delete the procedure.)

➤ Enter the MsgBox statement as it appears in Figure 14a. Save the procedure.

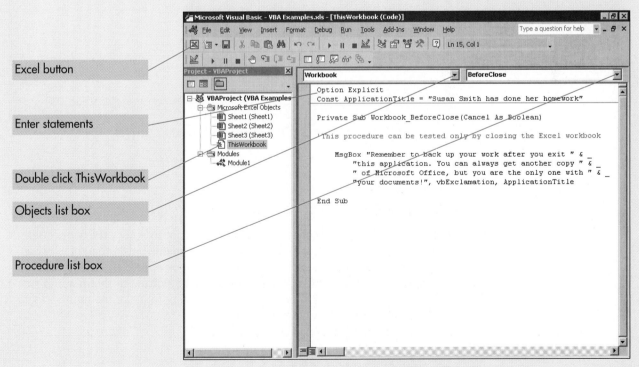

(a) Create the Close Workbook Procedure (step 1)

FIGURE 14   *Hands-on Exercise 4*

Step 2:   **Test the Close Workbook Procedure**

➤ Click the **Excel button** on the Standard toolbar or on the Windows taskbar to view the Excel workbook. The workbook is not empty; that is, it does not contain any cell entries, but it does contain multiple VBA procedures.

➤ Pull down the **File menu** and click the **Close command**, which runs the procedure you just created and displays the dialog box in Figure 14b. Click **OK** after you have read the message, then click **Yes** if asked to save the workbook.

➤ Pull down the **File menu** and reopen the **VBA Examples workbook**, enabling the macros. Press **Alt+F11** to return to the VBA window to create an additional procedure.

➤ Double click **ThisWorkbook** from within the Projects Explorer pane to return to the BeforeClose procedure and make the necessary corrections, if any.

➤ Save the procedure.

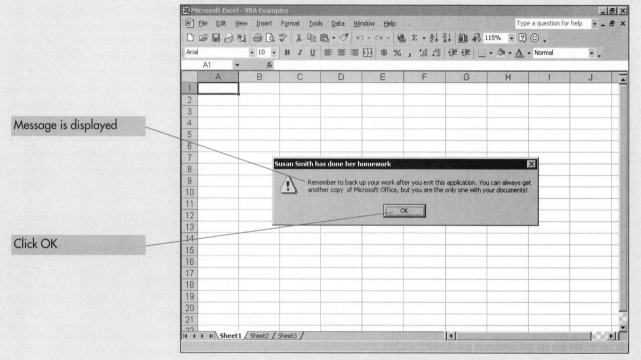

Message is displayed

Click OK

(b) Test the Close Workbook Procedure (step 2)

FIGURE 14   *Hands-on Exercise 4 (continued)*

THE MOST RECENTLY OPENED FILE LIST

One way to open a recently used workbook is to select the workbook directly from the File menu. Pull down the File menu, but instead of clicking the Open command, check to see if the workbook appears on the list of the most recently opened workbooks located at the bottom of the menu. If so, just click the workbook name, rather than having to make the appropriate selections through the Open dialog box.

Step 3: **Start the Open Workbook Event Procedure**

➤ Click the **Procedure View button** at the bottom of the Code window. Click the **down arrow** in the Procedure list box and select the **Open event** to create an event procedure.

➤ Enter the VBA statements as shown in Figure 14c. Note the following:
  • Three variables are required for this procedure—the correct password, the password entered by the user, and the number of attempts.
  • The user is prompted for the password, and the number of attempts is set to one. The user is given two additional attempts, if necessary, to get the password correct. The loop is bypassed, however, if the user supplies the correct password on the first attempt.

➤ Minimize Excel. Save the procedure, then click the **Run Sub button** to test it. Try different combinations in your testing; that is, enter the correct password on the first, second, and third attempts. The password is **case-sensitive**.

➤ Correct errors as they occur. Click the **Reset button** at any time to begin executing the procedure from the beginning. Save the procedure.

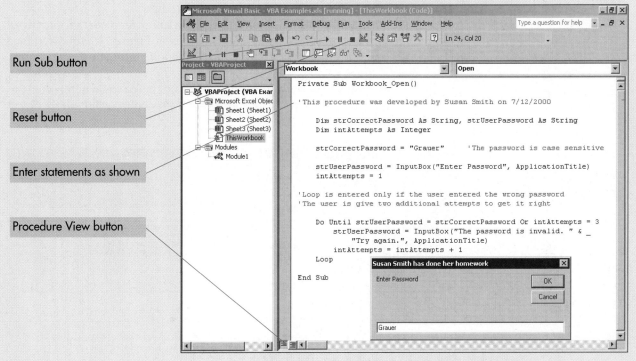

(c) Start the Open Workbook Event Procedure (step 3)

FIGURE 14 *Hands-on Exercise 4 (continued)*

THE OBJECT AND PROCEDURE BOXES

The Object box at the top of the code window displays the selected object such as an Excel workbook, whereas the Procedure box displays the name of the events appropriate to that object. Events that already have procedures appear in bold. Clicking an event that is not bold creates the procedure header and End Sub statements for that event.

Complete the Open Workbook Event Procedure

➤ Enter the remaining statements in the procedure as shown in Figure 14d. Note the following:
- The If statement determines whether the user has entered the correct password and, if so, displays the appropriate message.
- If, however, the user fails to supply the correct password, a different message is displayed, and the workbook will close due to the **Workbooks.Close statement** within the procedure.
- As a precaution, put an apostrophe in front of the Workbooks.Close statement so that it is a comment, and thus it is not executed. Once you are sure that you can enter the correct password, you can remove the apostrophe and implement the password protection.

➤ Save the procedure, then click the **Run Sub button** to test it. Be sure that you can enter the correct password (**Grauer**), and that you realize the password is case-sensitive.

➤ Delete the apostrophe in front of the Workbooks.Close statement. The text of the statement changes from green to black to indicate that it is an executable statement rather than a comment. Save the procedure.

➤ Click the **Run Sub button** a second time, then enter an incorrect password three times in a row. You will see the dialog box in Figure 14d, followed by a message reminding you to back up your workbook, and then the workbook will close.

➤ The first message makes sense, the second does not make sense in this context. Thus, we need to modify the Close Workbook procedure when an incorrect password is entered.

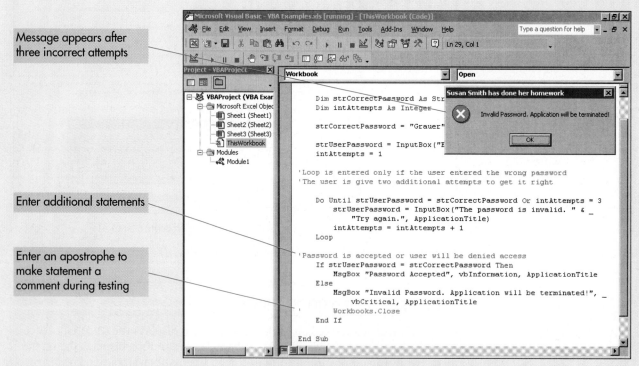

(d) Complete the Open Workbook Event Procedure (step 4)

FIGURE 14 *Hands-on Exercise 4 (continued)*

Step 5: **Modify the Before Close Event Procedure**

➤ Reopen the **VBA Examples workbook**. Click the button to **Enable Macros**.
➤ Enter the password, **Grauer** (the password is case-sensitive), press **enter**, then click **OK** when the password has been accepted.
➤ Press **Alt+F11** to reopen the VBA Editor, and (if necessary) double click **ThisWorkbook** within the list of Microsoft Excel objects.
➤ Click at the end of the line defining the ApplicationTitle constant, press **enter**, then enter the statement to define the **binNormalExit** variable as shown in Figure 14e. (The statement appears initially below the line ending the General Declarations section, but moves above the line when you press enter.)
➤ Modify the BeforeClose event procedure to include an If statement that tests the value of the binNormalExit variable as shown in Figure 14e. You must, however, set the value of this variable in the Open Workbook event procedure as described in step 6. Save the procedure.

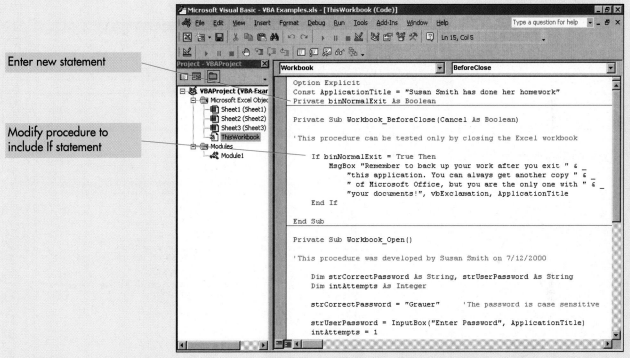

(e) Modify the Before Close Event Procedure (step 5)

FIGURE 14   *Hands-on Exercise 4 (continued)*

SETTING A SWITCH

The use of a switch (binNormalExit, in this example) to control an action within a procedure is a common programming technique. The switch is set to one of two values according to events that occur within the system, then the switch is subsequently tested and the appropriate action is taken. Here, the switch is set when the workbook is opened to indicate either a valid or invalid user. The switch is then tested prior to closing the workbook to determine whether to print the closing message.

Step 6: **Modify the Open Workbook Event Procedure**

➤ Scroll down to the Open Workbook event procedure, then modify the If statement to set the value of binNormExit as shown in Figure 14f:
- Take advantage of the Complete Word tool to enter the variable name. Type the first few letters, "binN", then press Ctrl+Space, and VBA will complete the variable name.
- The indentation within the statement is not a requirement of VBA per se, but is used to make the code easier to read. Blank lines are also added for this purpose.
- Comments appear throughout the procedure to explain its logic.
- Save the modified procedure.

➤ Click the **Run Sub button**, then enter an incorrect password three times in a row. Once again, you will see the dialog box indicating an invalid password, but this time you will not see the message reminding you to back up your workbook. The workbook closes as before.

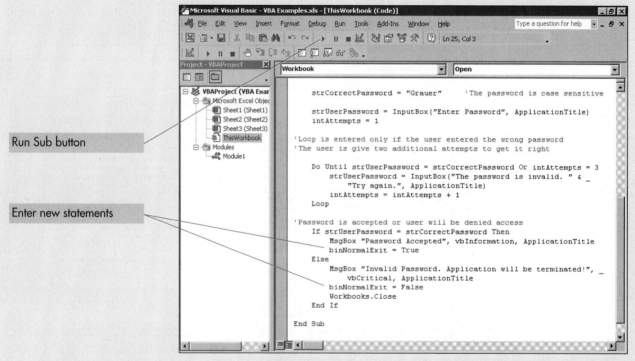

(f) Modify the Open Workbook Event Procedure (step 6)

FIGURE 14 *Hands-on Exercise 4 (continued)*

TEST UNDER ALL CONDITIONS

We cannot overemphasize the importance of thoroughly testing a procedure, and further, testing it under all conditions. VBA statements are powerful, but they are also complex, and a misplaced or omitted character can have dramatic consequences. Test every procedure completely at the time it is created, so that the logic of the procedure is fresh in your mind.

Step 7: **Open a Second Workbook**

> ➤ Reopen the **VBA Examples workbook**. Click the button to **Enable Macros**.
> ➤ Enter the password, **Grauer**, then press **enter**. Click **OK** when you see the second dialog box telling you that the password has been accepted.
> ➤ Pull down the **File menu** and click the **Open command** (or click the **Open button** on the Standard toolbar) and open a second workbook. We opened a workbook called **Financial Consultant**, but it does not matter which workbook you open.
> ➤ Pull down the **Window menu**, click the **Arrange command**, click the **Horizontal option button**, and click **OK** to tile the workbooks as shown in Figure 14g. The title bars show the names of the open workbooks.
> ➤ Pull down the **Tools menu**, click **Macro**, then click **Visual Basic Editor**.

Financial Consultant workbook

VBA Examples workbook

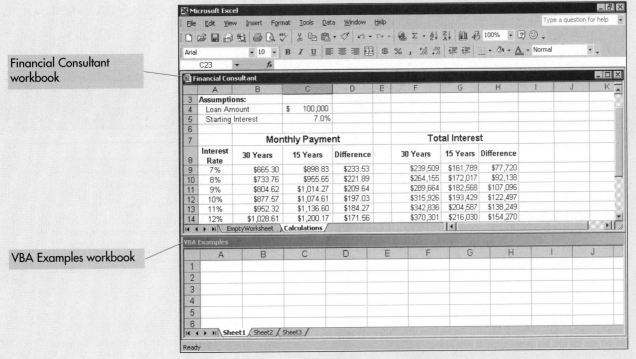

(g) Open a Second Workbook (step 7)

FIGURE 14 *Hands-on Exercise 4 (continued)*

THE COMPARISON IS CASE-SENSITIVE

Any literal comparison (e.g., strInstructorName = "Grauer") is case-sensitive, so that the user has to enter the correct name and case in order for the condition to be true. A response of "GRAUER" or "grauer", while containing the correct name, will be evaluated as false because the case does not match. You can, however, use the UCase (uppercase) function to convert the user's response to uppercase, and test accordingly. In other words, UCase(strInstructorName) = "GRAUER" will be evaluated as true if the user enters "Grauer" in any combination of upper or lowercase letters.

Step 8: **Copy the Procedure**

➤ You should be back in the Visual Basic Editor as shown in Figure 14h. Copy the procedures associated with the Open and Close Workbook events from the VBA Examples workbook to the other workbook, Financial Consultant.

  • Double click **ThisWorkbook** within the list of Microsoft Excel objects under the VBA Examples workbook.

  • Click and drag to select the definition of the ApplicationTitle constant in the General Declarations section plus the two procedures (to open and close the workbook) in their entirety.

  • Click the **Copy button** on the Standard toolbar.

  • If necessary, expand the Financial Consultant VBA Project, then double click **ThisWorkbook** with the list of Excel objects under the Financial Consultant workbook. Click underneath the **Option Explicit command**.

  • Click the **Paste button** on the Standard toolbar. The VBA code should be copied into this module as shown in Figure 14h.

➤ Click the **Save button** to save the module.

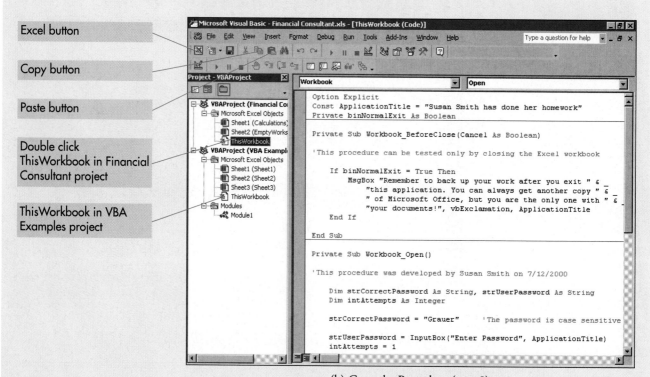

Excel button

Copy button

Paste button

Double click
ThisWorkbook in Financial
Consultant project

ThisWorkbook in VBA
Examples project

(h) Copy the Procedure (step 8)

FIGURE 14   *Hands-on Exercise 4 (continued)*

KEYBOARD SHORTCUTS—CUT, COPY, AND PASTE

Ctrl+X, Ctrl+C, and Ctrl+V are shortcuts to cut, copy, and paste, respectively, and apply to all applications in the Office suite as well as to Windows applications in general. (The shortcuts are easier to remember when you realize that the operative letters X, C, and V are next to each other at the bottom left side of the keyboard.)

Step 9: **Test the Procedure**

➤ Click the **Excel button** on the Standard toolbar within the VBA window (or click the **Excel button** on the Windows taskbar) to view the Excel workbook. Click in the window containing the Financial Consultant workbook (or whichever workbook you are using), then click the **Maximize button**.

➤ Pull down the **File menu** and click the **Close command**. (The dialog box in Figure 14i does not appear initially because the value of binNormalExit is not yet set; you have to open the workbook to set the switch.) Click **Yes** if asked whether to save the changes to the workbook.

➤ Pull down the **File menu** and reopen the workbook. Click the button to **Enable Macros**, then enter **Grauer** when prompted for the password. Click **OK** when the password has been accepted.

➤ Close this workbook, close the **VBA Examples workbook**, then pull down the **File menu** and click the **Exit command** to quit Excel.

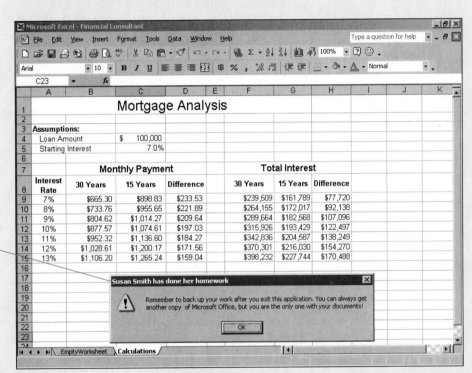

Title bar has been customized

(i) Test the Procedure (step 9)

FIGURE 14 *Hands-on Exercise 4 (continued)*

SCREEN CAPTURE

Prove to your instructor that you have completed the hands-on exercise correctly by capturing a screen, then pasting the screen into a Word document. Do the exercise until you come to the screen that you want to capture, then press the PrintScreen key at the top of the keyboard. Click the Start button to start Word and open a Word document, then pull down the Edit menu and click the Paste command to bring the captured screen into the Word document. See exercise 1 at the end of the chapter.

The same VBA procedure can be run from multiple applications in Microsoft Office, despite the fact that the applications are very different. The real power of VBA, however, is its ability to detect events that are unique to a specific application and to respond accordingly. An event is defined as any action that is recognized by an application. Opening or closing an Excel workbook or an Access database is an event. Selecting a worksheet within a workbook is also an event, as is clicking on a command button on an Access form. To use VBA within Microsoft Office, you decide which events are significant, and what is to happen when those events occur. Then you develop the appropriate *event procedures* that execute automatically when the event occurs.

Consider, for example, Figure 15, which displays the results of two event procedures in conjunction with opening and closing an Access database. (These are procedures similar to those we created in the preceding pages in conjunction with opening and closing an Excel workbook.) The procedure associated with Figure 15a displays a message that appears automatically after the user clicks the Switchboard button to exit the database. The procedure is almost trivial to write, and consists of a single MsgBox statement. The effect of the procedure is quite significant, however, as it reminds the user to back up his or her work. Indeed, you can never overemphasize the importance of adequate backup.

The dialog box in Figure 15b prompts the user for a password and appears automatically when the user opens the database. The logic here is more sophisticated in that the underlying procedure contains an InputBox statement to request the password, a Do Until loop that is executed until the user enters the correct password or exceeds the allotted number of attempts, then additional logic to display the switchboard or terminate the application if the user fails to enter the proper password. The procedure is not difficult, however, and it builds on the VBA statements that were covered earlier.

The next hands-on exercise has you create the event procedures that are associated with the database in Figure 15. The exercise references a switchboard, or user interface, that is created as a form within the database. The switchboard displays a menu that enables a nontechnical person to move easily from one object in the database (e.g., a form or report) to another.

The switchboard is created through a utility called the Switchboard Manager that prompts you for each item you want to add to the switchboard, and which action you want to be taken in conjunction with that menu item. You could do the exercise with any database, but we suggest you use the database we provide to access the switchboard that we created for you. The exercise begins, therefore, by having you download a data disk from our Web site.

EVENT-DRIVEN VERSUS TRADITIONAL PROGRAMMING

A traditional program is executed sequentially, beginning with the first line of code and continuing in order through the remainder of the program. It is the program, not the user, that determines the order in which the statements are executed. VBA, on the other hand, is event-driven, meaning that the order in which the procedures are executed depends on the events that occur. It is the user, rather than the program, that determines which events occur, and consequently which procedures are executed. Each application in Microsoft Office has a different set of objects and associated events that comprise the application's object model.

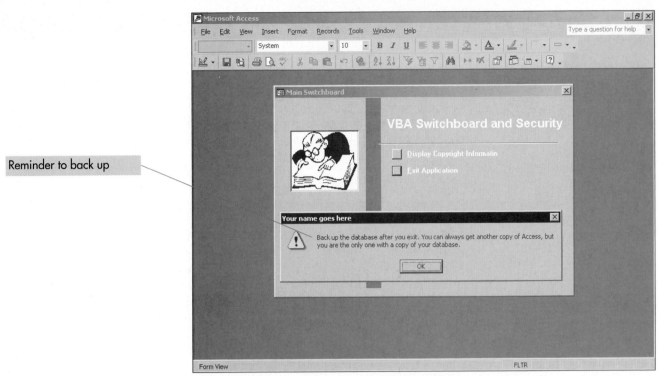

Reminder to back up

(a) Reminder to the User (Exit Application event)

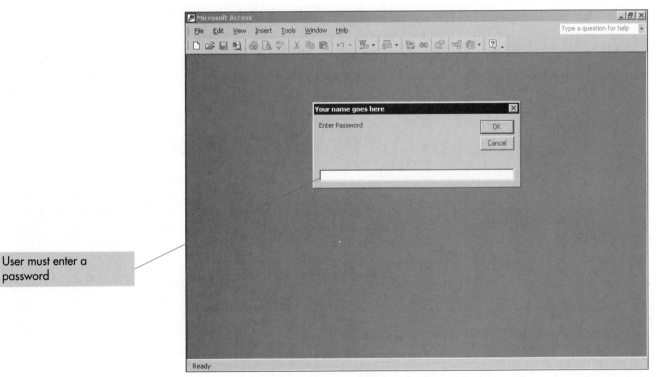

User must enter a password

(b) Password Protection (Open Form event)

FIGURE 15 *Event-Driven Programming (Microsoft Access)*

EVENT-DRIVEN PROGRAMMING (MICROSOFT ACCESS)

Objective   To implement password protection for an Access database; to create a second event procedure that displays a message to the user upon closing the database. Use Figure 16 as a guide in the exercise.

Step 1:   **Open the Access Database**

➤ You can do this exercise with any database, but we suggest you use the database we have provided. Go to **www.prenhall.com/grauer**, click the **Office 2000 book**, click the **Student Resources tab**, then click the link to download the data disk.

➤ Scroll until you can select the disk for the **VBA Primer**. Download the file to the Windows desktop, then double click the file once it has been downloaded to your PC.

➤ Double click the file and follow the onscreen instructions to expand the self-extracting file that contains the database.

➤ Go to the newly created **Exploring VBA folder** and open the **VBA Switchboard and Security database** as shown in Figure 16a.

➤ Pull down the **Tools menu**, click the **Macro command**, then click the **Visual Basic Editor command**. Maximize the VBA Editor window.

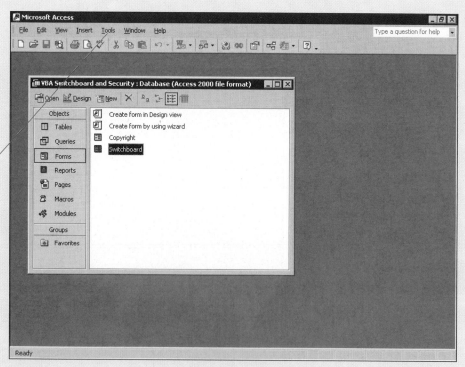

Pull down Tools menu

(a) Open the Access Database (step 1)

FIGURE 16   *Hands-on Exercise 5*

Step 2: **Create the ExitDatabase Procedure**

> ➤ Pull down the **Insert menu** and click **Module** to insert Module1. Complete the **General Declarations section** by adding your name to the definition of the ApplicationTitle constant as shown in Figure 16b.
> ➤ Pull down the **Insert menu** and click **Procedure** to insert a new procedure called **ExitDatabase**. Click the option buttons for a **Sub procedure** and for **Public scope**. Click **OK**.
> ➤ Complete the ExitDatabase procedure by entering the **MsgBox** and **DoCmd.Quit** statements. The DoCmd.Quit statement will close Access, but it is entered initially as a comment by beginning the line with an apostrophe.
> ➤ Click anywhere in the procedure, then click the **Run Sub button** to test the procedure. Correct any errors that occur, then when the MsgBox displays correctly, **delete the apostrophe** in front of the DoCmd.Quit statement.
> ➤ Save the module. The next time you execute the procedure, you should see the message box you just created, and then Access will be terminated.

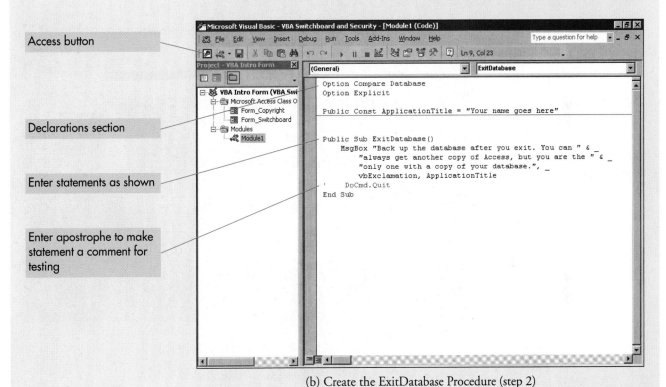

(b) Create the ExitDatabase Procedure (step 2)

FIGURE 16 *Hands-on Exercise 5 (continued)*

CREATE A PUBLIC CONSTANT

Give your application a customized look by adding your name or other identifying message to the title bar of the message and/or input boxes that you use. You can add the information individually to each statement, but it is easier to declare a public constant from within a general module. That way, you can change the value of the constant in one place and have the change reflected automatically throughout your application.

Step 3:   **Modify the Switchboard**

➤ Click the **Access button** on the Standard toolbar within the VBA window to switch to the Database window (or use the **F11** keyboard shortcut).
➤ Pull down the **Tools menu**, click the **Database Utilities command**, then choose **Switchboard Manager** to display the Switchboard Manager dialog box in Figure 16c.
➤ Click the **Edit button** to edit the Main Switchboard and display the Edit Switchboard Page dialog box. Select the **&Exit Application command** and click its **Edit button** to display the Edit Switchboard Item dialog box.
➤ Change the command to **Run Code**. Enter **ExitDatabase** in the Function Name text box. Click **OK**, then close the two other dialog boxes. The switchboard has been modified so that clicking the Exit button will run the VBA procedure you just created.

Edit button

Edit button

Select &Exit Application

Click drop-down arrow and select Run Code

Enter ExitDatabase

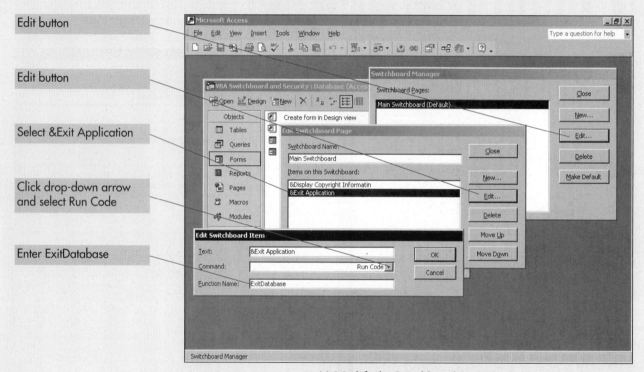

(c) Modify the Switchboard (step 3)

FIGURE 16   *Hands-on Exercise 5 (continued)*

CREATE A KEYBOARD SHORTCUT

The & has special significance when used within the name of an Access object because it creates a keyboard shortcut to that object. Enter "&Exit Application", for example, and the letter E (the letter immediately after the ampersand) will be underlined and appear as "Exit Application" on the switchboard. From there, you can execute the item by clicking its button, or you can use the Alt+E keyboard shortcut (where "E" is the underlined letter in the menu option).

Step 4:   **Test the Switchboard**

➤ If necessary, click the **Forms tab** in the Database window. Double click the **Switchboard form** to open the switchboard as shown in Figure 16d. The switchboard contains two commands.

➤ Click the **Display Copyright Information command** to display a form that we use with all our databases. (You can open this form in Design view and modify the text to include your name, rather than ours. If you do, be sure to save the modified form, then close it.)

➤ Click the **Exit Application command** (or use the **Alt+E** keyboard shortcut). You should see the dialog box in Figure 16d, corresponding to the MsgBox statement you created earlier. Click **OK** to close the dialog box.

➤ Access itself will terminate because of the DoCmd.Quit statement within the ExitDatabase procedure. (If this does not happen, return to the VBA Editor and remove the apostrophe in front of the DoCmd statement.)

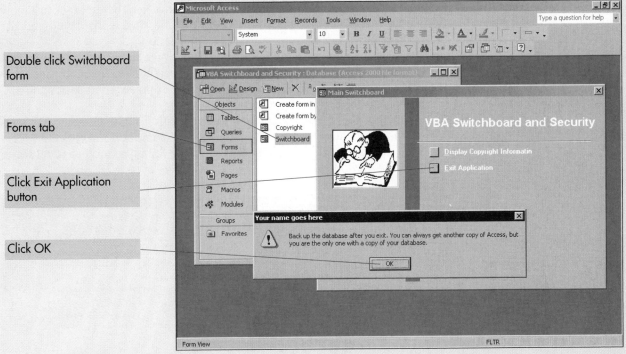

Double click Switchboard form

Forms tab

Click Exit Application button

Click OK

(d) Test the Switchboard (step 4)

FIGURE 16   *Hands-on Exercise 5 (continued)*

BACK UP IMPORTANT FILES

It's not a question of if it will happen, but when—hard disks die, files are lost, or viruses may infect a system. It has happened to us and it will happen to you, but you can prepare for the inevitable by creating adequate backup before the problem occurs. The essence of a backup strategy is to decide which files to back up, how often to do the backup, and where to keep the backup. Do it!

Step 5:   **Complete the Open Form Event Procedure**

➤ Start Access and reopen the **VBA Switchboard and Security database**. Press **Alt+F11** to start the VBA Editor. Click the **plus sign** next to Microsoft Access Class objects, double click the module called **Form_Switchboard**, then look for the **Form_Open procedure** as shown in Figure 16e.

➤ The procedure was created automatically by the Switchboard Manager. You must, however, expand this procedure to include password protection. Note the following:

• Three variables are required—the correct password, the password entered by the user, and the number of attempts.

• The user is prompted for the password, and the number of attempts is set to one. The user is given two additional attempts, if necessary, to get the correct password.

• The If statement at the end of the loop determines whether the user has entered the correct password, and if so, it executes the original commands that are associated with the switchboard. If, however, the user fails to supply the correct password, an invalid password message is displayed and the **DoCmd.Quit** statement terminates the application.

• We suggest you place an **apostrophe** in front of the statement initially so that it becomes a comment, and thus it is not executed. Once you are sure that you can enter the correct password, you can remove the apostrophe and implement the password protection.

➤ Save the procedure. You cannot test this procedure from within the VBA window; you must cause the event to happen (i.e., open the form) for the procedure to execute. Click the **Access button** on the Standard toolbar to return to the Database window.

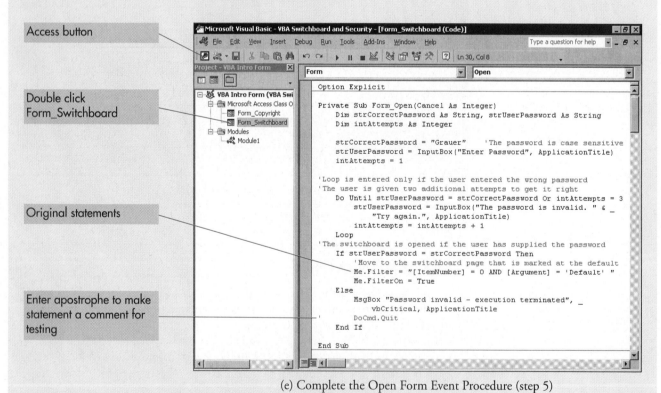

(e) Complete the Open Form Event Procedure (step 5)

FIGURE 16   *Hands-on Exercise 5 (continued)*

Step 6: **Test the Procedure**

➤ Close all open windows within the Access database except for the Database window. Click the **Forms tab**, then double click the **Switchboard Form**.

➤ You should be prompted for the password as shown in Figure 16f. The password (in our procedure) is **Grauer**.

➤ Test the procedure repeatedly to include all possibilities. Enter the correct password on the first, second, and third attempts to be sure that the procedure works as intended. Each time you enter the correct password, you will have to close the switchboard, then reopen it.

➤ Test the procedure one final time, by failing to enter the correct password. You will see a message box indicating that the password is invalid and that execution will be terminated. Termination will not take place, however, because the DoCmd.Quit statement is currently entered as a comment.

➤ Press **Alt+F11** to reopen the VBA Editor. Delete the apostrophe in front of the DoCmd.Quit statement. The text of the statement changes from green to black to indicate that it is an executable statement. Save the procedure.

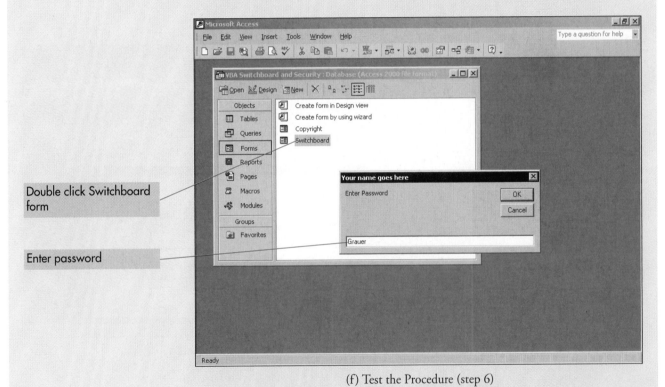

Double click Switchboard form

Enter password

(f) Test the Procedure (step 6)

FIGURE 16 *Hands-on Exercise 5 (continued)*

TOGGLE COMMENTS ON AND OFF

Comments are used primarily to explain the purpose of VBA statements, but they can also be used to "comment out" code as distinct from deleting the statement altogether. Thus you can add or remove the apostrophe in front of the statement, to toggle the comment on or off.

Step 7:   **Change the Startup Properties**

➤ Click the **Access button** on the VBA Standard toolbar to return to the Database window. Pull down the **Tools menu** and click **Startup** to display the Startup dialog box as shown in Figure 16g.

➤ Click in the **Application Title** text box and enter the title of the application, **VBA Switchboard and Security** in this example.

➤ Click the **drop-down arrow** in the Display Form/Page list box and select the **Switchboard form** as the form that will open automatically in conjunction with opening the database.

➤ Clear the check box to display the Database window. Click **OK** to accept the settings and close the dialog box. The next time you open the database, the switchboard should open automatically, which in turn triggers the Open Form event procedure that will prompt the user to enter a password.

➤ Close the Switchboard form.

Click drop-down arrow and select Switchboard

Clear check box

Enter Application Title

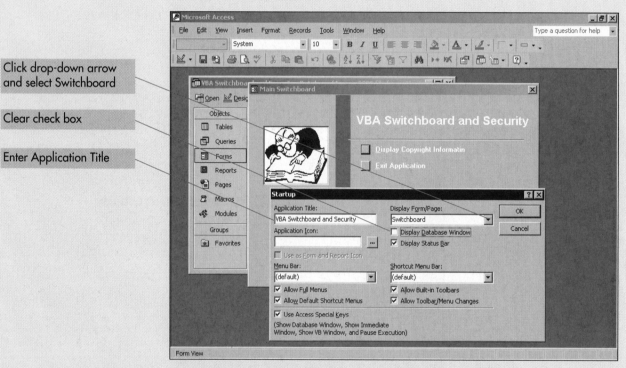

(g) Change the Startup Properties (step 7)

FIGURE 16   *Hands-on Exercise 5 (continued)*

HIDE THE DATABASE WINDOW

Use the Startup property to hide the Database window from the novice user. You avoid confusion and you may prevent the novice from accidentally deleting objects in the database. Of course, anyone with some knowledge of Access can restore the Database window by pulling down the Window menu, clicking the Unhide command, then selecting the Database window from the associated dialog box. Nevertheless, hiding the Database window is a good beginning.

Step 8: **Test the Database**

➤ Close the database, then reopen the database to test the procedures we have created in this exercise. The sequence of events is as follows:
  • The database is loaded and the switchboard is opened but is not yet visible. The Open Form procedure for the switchboard is executed, and you are prompted for the password as shown in Figure 16h.
  • The password is entered correctly and the switchboard is displayed. The Database window is hidden, however, because the Startup Properties have been modified.
➤ Click the **Exit Application command** (or use the **Alt+E** keyboard shortcut). You will see the message box reminding you to back up the system, after which the database is closed and Access is terminated.
➤ Testing is complete and you can go on to add the other objects to your Access database. Congratulations on a job well done.

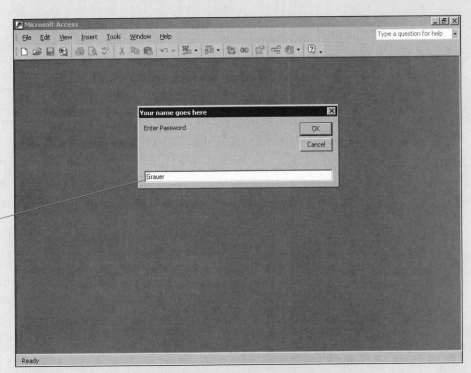

Enter password

(h) Test the Database (step 8)

FIGURE 16 *Hands-on Exercise 5 (continued)*

HIDE MENUS AND TOOLBARS

You can use the Startup property to hide menus and/or toolbars from the user by clearing the respective check boxes. A word of caution, however— once the menus are hidden, it is difficult to get them back. Start Access, pull down the File menu, and click Open to display the Open dialog box, select the database to open, then press and hold the Shift key when you click the Open button. This powerful technique is not widely known.

Visual Basic for Applications (VBA) is a powerful programming language that is accessible from all major applications in Microsoft Office XP. A VBA statement accomplishes a specific task such as displaying a message to the user or accepting input from the user. Statements are grouped into procedures, and procedures in turn are grouped into modules. Every procedure is classified as either private or public.

The MsgBox statement displays information to the user. It has one required argument, which is the message (or prompt) that is displayed to the user. The other two arguments, the icon that is to be displayed in the dialog box and the text of the title bar, are optional. The InputBox function displays a prompt to the user requesting information, then it stores that information (the value returned by the user) for use later in the procedure.

Every variable must be declared (defined) before it can be used. This is accomplished through the Dim (short for Dimension) statement that appears at the beginning of a procedure. The Dim statement indicates the name of the variable and its type (for example, whether it will hold a character string or an integer number), which in turn reserves the appropriate amount of memory for that variable.

The ability to make decisions within a procedure, then branch to alternative sets of statements is implemented through the If . . . Then . . . Else or Case statements. The Else clause is optional, but may be repeated multiple times within an If statement. The Case statement is preferable to an If statement with multiple Else clauses.

The For . . . Next statement (or For . . . Next loop as it is also called) executes all statements between the words For and Next a specified number of times, using a counter to keep track of the number of times the loop is executed. The Do . . . Loop Until and/or Do Until . . . Loop statements are used when the number of times through the loop is not known in advance.

VBA is different from traditional programming languages in that it is event-driven. An event is defined as any action that is recognized by an application, such as Excel or Access. Opening or closing an Excel workbook or an Access database is an event. Selecting a worksheet within a workbook is also an event, as is clicking on a command button on an Access form. To use VBA within Microsoft Office, you decide which events are significant, and what is to happen when those events occur. Then you develop the appropriate event procedures.

KEY TERMS

Argument (p. 2)
Case statement (p. 18)
Character string (p. 16)
Comment (p. 6)
Compilation error (p. 30)
Complete Word tool (p. 22)
Concatenate (p. 4)
Custom toolbar (p. 19)
Debug menu (p. 30)
Debug toolbar (p. 30)
Debug.Print statement (p. 31)
Debugging (p. 30)
Declarations section (p. 6)
Dim statement (p. 5)
Do Loops (p. 29)
Else clause (p. 16)
End Sub statement (p. 3)
Event (p. 41)

Event procedure (Access) (p. 52)
Event procedure (Excel) (p. 41)
Execution error (p. 30)
For . . . Next Statement (p. 28)
Full Module view (p. 21)
Help (p. 15)
If statement (p. 16)
Immediate window (p. 31)
InputBox function (p. 4)
Intrinsic constant (p. 3)
Literal (p. 16)
Locals window (p. 31)
Macro (p. 2)
Macro recorder (p. 2)
Module (p. 2)
MsgBox statement (p. 3)
Object box (p. 45)
Option Explicit (p. 6)

Private procedure (p. 2)
Procedure (p. 2)
Procedure box (p. 45)
Procedure header (p. 3)
Procedure view (p. 21)
Project Explorer (p. 6)
Public procedure (p. 2)
Quick Info (p. 9)
Run-time error (p. 30)
Statement (p. 2)
Step Into button (p. 31)
Syntax (p. 2)
Underscore (p. 4)
Variable (p. 4)
VBA (p. 1)
Visual Basic Editor (p. 6)
Visual Basic for Applications (p. 2)

1. Which of the following applications in Office XP has access to VBA?
   (a) Word
   (b) Excel
   (c) Access
   (d) All of the above

2. Which of the following is a valid name for a VBA variable?
   (a) Public
   (b) Private
   (c) strUserFirstName
   (d) int Count Of Attempts

3. Which of the following is true about an If statement?
   (a) It evaluates a condition as either true or false, then executes the statement(s) following the keyword "Then" if the condition is true
   (b) It must contain the keyword Else
   (c) It must contain one or more ElseIf statements
   (d) All of the above

4. Which of the following lists the items from smallest to largest?
   (a) Module, procedure, statement
   (b) Statement, module, procedure
   (c) Statement, procedure, module
   (d) Procedure, module, statement

5. Given the statement, MsgBox "Welcome to VBA" , , "Bob was here", which of the following is true?
   (a) "Welcome to VBA" will be displayed within the resulting message box
   (b) "Welcome to VBA" will appear on the title bar of the displayed dialog box
   (c) The two adjacent commas will cause a compilation error
   (d) An informational icon will be displayed with the message

6. Where are the VBA procedures associated with an Office document stored?
   (a) In the same folder, but in a separate file
   (b) In the Office document itself
   (c) In a special VBA folder on drive C
   (d) In a special VBA folder on the local area network

7. The Debug.Print statement is associated with the:
   (a) Locals window
   (b) Immediate window
   (c) Project Explorer
   (d) Debug toolbar

8. Which of the following is the proper sequence of arguments for the MsgBox statement?
   (a) Text for the title bar, prompt, button
   (b) Prompt, button, text for the title bar
   (c) Prompt, text for the title bar, button
   (d) Button, prompt, text for the title bar

9. Which of the following is a true statement about Do loops?
   (a) Placing the Until clause at the beginning of the loop tests the condition prior to executing any statements in the loop
   (b) Placing the Until clause at the end of the loop executes the statements in the loop, then it tests the condition
   (c) Both (a) and (b)
   (d) Neither (a) nor (b)

10. Given the statement, For intCount = 1 to 10 Step 3, how many times will the statements in the loop be executed (assuming that there are no statements in the loop to terminate the execution)?
(a) 10
(b) 4
(c) 3
(d) Impossible to determine

11. Which of the following is a *false* statement?
(a) A dash at the end of a line indicates continuation
(b) An ampersand indicates concatenation
(c) An apostrophe at the beginning of a line signifies a comment
(d) A pair of quotation marks denotes a character string

12. What is the effect of deleting the apostrophe that appears at the beginning of a VBA statement?
(a) A compilation error will occur
(b) The statement is converted to a comment
(c) The color of the statement will change from black to green
(d) The statement is made executable

13. Which of the following If statements will display the indicated message if the user enters a response other than "Grauer" (assuming that "Grauer" is the correct password)?
(a) If strUserResponse <> "Grauer" Then MsgBox "Wrong password"
(b) If strUserResponse = "Grauer" Then MsgBox "Wrong password"
(c) If strUserResponse > "Grauer" Then MsgBox "Wrong password"
(d) If strUserResponse < "Grauer" Then MsgBox "Wrong password"

14. Which of the following will execute the statements in the loop at least once?
(a) Do ... Loop Until
(b) Do Until ..... Loop
(c) Both (a) and (b)
(d) Neither (a) nor (b)

15. The copy and paste commands can be used to:
(a) Copy statements within a procedure
(b) Copy statements from a procedure in one module to a procedure in another module within the same document
(c) Copy statements from a module in an Excel workbook to a module in an Access database
(d) All of the above

ANSWERS

1. d	**6.** b	**11.** a
2. c	**7.** b	**12.** d
3. a	**8.** b	**13.** a
4. c	**9.** c	**14.** a
5. a	**10.** b	**15.** a

1. **Screen Capture:** The ability to capture a screen, then print the captured screen as part of a document, is very useful. The Word document in Figure 17, for example, captures the Excel screen as a workbook is opened, with the dialog box in place.

   Open the completed workbook from the fourth hands-on exercise. Press the PrintScreen key when prompted for the password to copy the screen to the Windows clipboard, an area of memory that is accessible to any Windows application. Next, start (or switch to) a Word document, and then execute the Paste command in the Edit menu to paste the contents of the clipboard into the current document. That's all there is to it. The screen is now part of the Word document, where it can be moved and sized like any other Windows object. Print the Word document for your instructor.

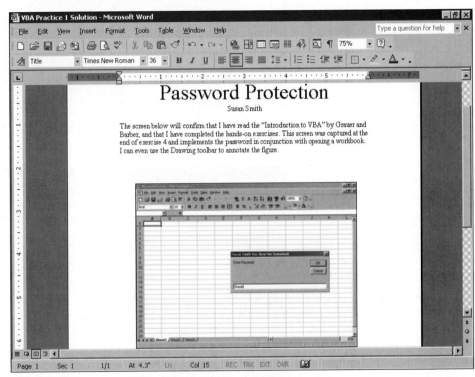

FIGURE 17 *Screen Capture (Exercise 1)*

2. **VBA in a Word Document:** Everything that you have learned with respect to creating VBA event procedures in Excel or Access is also applicable to Microsoft Word. Accordingly, start Microsoft Word and create the document in Figure 18. Read the document carefully, then create the Document_Close event procedure to display the indicated message box, adding your name to the title bar. Prove to your professor that you have completed this assignment by capturing the screen in Figure 18, as described in the previous exercise.

3. **The Before Print Event:** Open the Excel workbook that you used in the fourth hands-on exercise to create an event procedure associated with the Before_Print event. The procedure is to contain a MsgBox statement to remind the user to print a workbook with both displayed values and cell contents as shown in Figure 19.

   The easiest way to switch between the two views is to press Ctrl+~. (The tilde is located at the upper-left of the keyboard.) Prove to your professor that you have completed this assignment by capturing the screen in Figure 19.

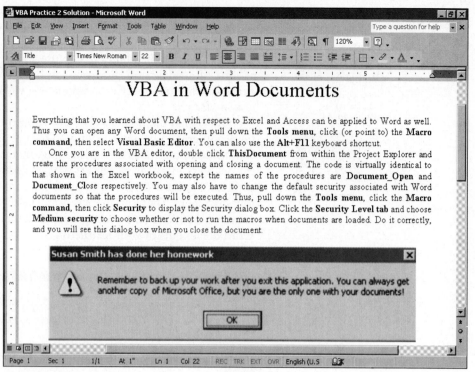

FIGURE 18   *VBA in a Word Document (Exercise 2)*

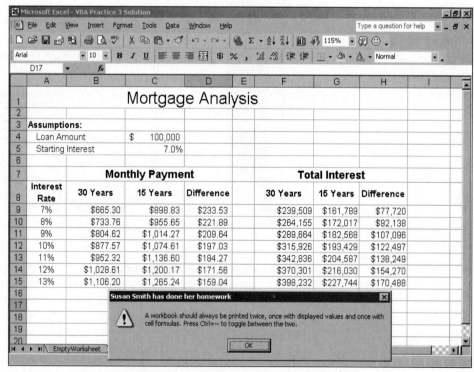

FIGURE 19   *The Before Print Event (Exercise 3)*

BUILDS ON

HANDS-ON
EXERCISE 5
PAGES 54–61

4. **The On Click Event:** Open the Access database that you used in the fifth hands-on exercise to create an event procedure associated with the On Click event for the indicated command button.

a. Open the Copyright form from the switchboard, then change to the Design view. Modify the form so that it contains your name rather than ours.

b. Right click the Technical Support button to display a context-sensitive menu, click Properties, click the Event tab, then select the On Click event. Click the Build button, select Code Builder as shown in Figure 20, and click OK.

c. The VBA Editor will position you within the On Click event procedure for the command button. All you need to do is add a single MsgBox statement to identify yourself as "Tech Support". Be sure to include the parameter to display your name on the title bar of the message box.

d. Save the form, then go to form view and click the button to view the message box you just created. Prove to your professor that you have completed this assignment by capturing the associated screen, as described in exercise 1.

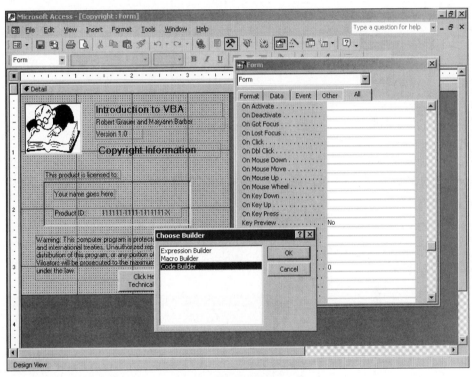

FIGURE 20 *The On Click Event (Exercise 4)*

5. **The Option Explicit Statement:** The Option Explicit statement should appear at the beginning of every module, but this is not a VBA requirement, only a suggestion from the authors. Omitting the statement can have serious consequences in that the results of a procedure are incorrect, a point that is illustrated in Figure 21.

a. What is the answer that is displayed in the message box of Figure 21? What is the answer that should be displayed?

b. Look at the statements within the For ... Next loop to see if you can detect the reason for the error. (*Hint:* Look closely at the variable names.)

c. What does the Option Explicit statement do? How would including the statement in the procedure of Figure 21 help to ensure the correct result?

d. Summarize your answers in a note to your instructor.

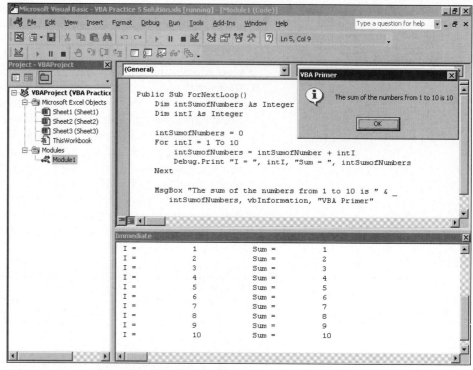

FIGURE 21 *The Option Explicit Statement (Exercise 5)*

6. String Processing: The procedure in Figure 22 illustrates various string processing functions to validate a user's e-mail address. Answer the following:
   a. What are the specific checks that are implemented to check the user's e-mail address? Are these checks reasonable?
   b. What does the VBA Len function do? What does the InStr function do? (Use the VBA Help menu to learn more about these functions.)
   c. What is the purpose of the variable binValidEmail within the procedure?

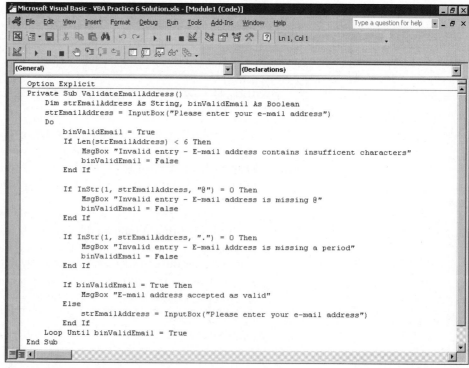

FIGURE 22 *String Processing (Exercise 6)*

BUILDS ON

HANDS-ON
EXERCISE 4
PAGES 43–51

7. Hiding a Worksheet: Figure 23 expands on the procedure to implement password protection in an Excel workbook by hiding the worksheet until the correct password has been entered.
   a. What additional statements have been added to the procedure in Figure 23 that were not present in Hands-on Exercise 4? What is the purpose of each statement?
   b. What statement could you add to the procedure to hide the empty worksheet after the correct password has been entered?
   c. Summarize your answers in a note to your instructor.

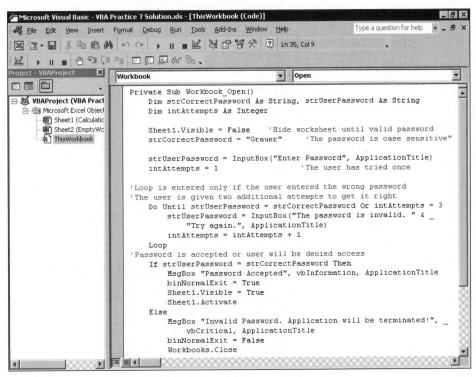

FIGURE 23   *Hiding a Worksheet (Exercise 7)*

8. Help with VBA: Help is just a mouse click away and it is invaluable. Use the Help facility to look up detailed information that expands a topic that was discussed in the chapter. The screen in Figure 24, for example, explains the integer data type and its use within a Dim statement. The information is quite detailed, but if you read carefully, you will generally find the answer. Print three different Help-screens for your instructor.

9. Invoking a Procedure: The same statement (or set of statements) is often executed from many places within a single procedure or from multiple procedures within an application. You can duplicate the code as necessary, but it is far more efficient to create a single procedure that contains the repeated statements, and then invoke that procedure. The advantage to this approach is that you have to write (or modify) the procedure only once.

   The module in Figure 25 illustrates how this is accomplished. The History-Quiz procedure asks the user multiple questions, then displays one of two messages, depending on whether the response is correct. These messages are contained in two separate procedures, then the appropriate procedure (CorrectAnswer or IncorrectAnswer) is called from within the HistoryQuiz procedure, depending on whether the user's answer is right or wrong. Create and test the module in Figure 25 to be sure you understand this technique.

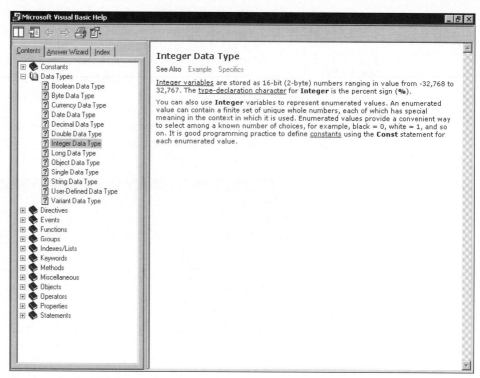

FIGURE 24 *Help with VBA (Exercise 8)*

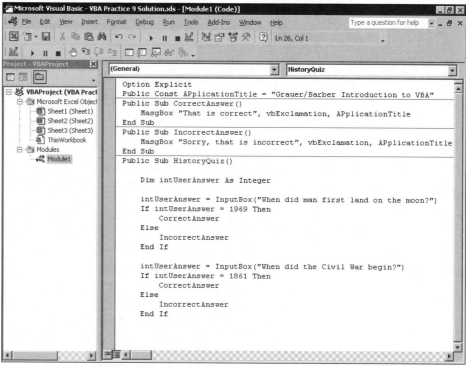

FIGURE 25 *Invoking a Procedure (Exercise 9)*

10. The MsgBox Function: The procedure in Figure 26 shows how the MsgBox statement can accept information from the user and branch accordingly. A simple MsgBox statement merely displays a message. If, however, you enclose the parameters of the MsgBox statement in parentheses, it becomes a function and returns a value (in this example, a mouse click indicating whether the user clicked yes or no). The use of parentheses requires that you include a second parameter such as vbYesNo to display the Yes and No command buttons. You then embed the MsgBox function within an If statement that tests for the intrinsic contstants, vbYes and vbNo, respectively.

You can concatenate the vbYesNo intrinsic constant with another constant such as vbQuestion to display an icon next to the buttons as shown in Figure 26. You can also use other intrinsic constants such as vbOKCancel to display different sets of command buttons.

Add the procedure in Figure 26 to the VBA Examples workbook (or Access database) that you created in the chapter. Print the procedure for your instructor.

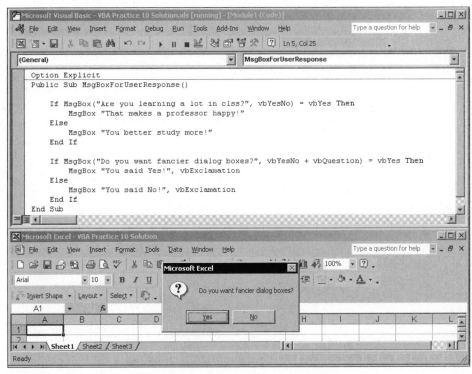

FIGURE 26   *The MsgBox Function (Exercise 10)*

INDEX